CIMA

STUDY TEXT

Intermediate level Paper 6

Financial Accounting

BPP's STUDY TEXT FOR CIMA's 2003 SYLLABUS

- Targetted to the **syllabus** and **learning outcomes**
- **Quizzes** and **questions** to check your understanding
- Incorporates CIMA's **Official Terminology**
- Clear layout and style designed to save you time
- Plenty of exam-style questions
- **Chapter Roundups** and summaries to help revision
- **Diagrams** to clarify key points

NEW IN JULY 2003 EDITION

- May 2003 syllabus changes
- Exam focus points showing question requirements from past papers
- Fresh material on regulatory framework
- Enhanced material on tangible fixed assets
- Additional material on share capital transactions

BPP Professional Education
July 2003

First edition July 2000
Fourth edition July 2003

ISBN 0 7517 1190 X (previously 0 7517 3758 5)

British Library Cataloguing-in-Publication Data
A catalogue record for this book
is available from the British Library

Published by

BPP Professional Education
Aldine House, Aldine Place
London W12 8AW

www.bpp.com

Printed in Great Britain by Ashford Colour Press

We are grateful to the Chartered Institute of Management Accountants for permission to reproduce past examination questions. The suggested solutions to the illustrative questions have been prepared by BPP Professional Education.

	Page

MULTIPLE CHOICE QUESTION CARDS

Multiple choice questions form a large part of the exam. To give you further practice in this style of question, we have produced a bank of **150 multiple choice question cards**, covering the syllabus. This bank contains exam style questions in a format to help you **revise on the move**.

COMPUTER-BASED LEARNING PRODUCTS FROM BPP

If you want to reinforce your studies by **interactive** learning, try BPP's **i-Learn** product, covering major syllabus areas in an interactive format. For **self-testing**, try **i-Pass,** which offers a large number of **objective test questions**, particularly useful where objective test questions form part of the exam.

See the order form at the back of this text for details of these innovative learning tools.

VIRTUAL CAMPUS

The Virtual Campus uses BPP's wealth of teaching experience to produce a fully **interactive** e-learning resource **delivered via the Internet**. The site offers comprehensive **tutor support** and features areas such as **study**, **practice**, **email service**, **revision** and **useful resources**.

Visit our website www.bpp.com/virtualcampus/cima to sample aspects of the campus free of charge.

LEARNING TO LEARN ACCOUNTANCY

BPP's ground-breaking **Learning to learn accountancy** book is designed to be used both at the outset of your CIMA studies and throughout the process of learning accountancy. It challenges you to consider how you study and gives you helpful hints about how to approach the various types of paper which you will encounter. It can help you **get your studies both subject and exam focused**, enabling you to **acquire knowledge, practice and revise efficiently and effectively**.

THE BPP STUDY TEXT

Aims of this Study Text

To provide you with the knowledge and understanding, skills and application techniques that you need if you are to be successful in your exams

This Study Text has been written around the **Financial Accounting** syllabus.

- It is **comprehensive**. It covers the syllabus content. No more, no less.
- It is written at the **right level**. Each chapter is written with CIMA's precise learning outcomes in mind.
- It is targeted to the **exam**. We have taken account of the pilot paper and the papers set to date, questions put to the examiner and the assessment methodology.

To allow you to study in the way that best suits your learning style and the time you have available, by following your personal Study Plan

You may be studying at home on your own until the date of the exam, or you may be attending a full-time course. You may like to (and have time to) read every word, or you may prefer to (or only have time to) skim-read and devote the remainder of your time to question practice. Wherever you fall in the spectrum, you will find the BPP Study Text meets your needs in designing and following your personal Study Plan.

To tie in with the other components of the BPP Effective Study Package to ensure you have the best possible chance of passing the exam

Recommended period of use	Elements of the BPP Effective Study Package
From the outset and throughout	**Learning to learn accountancy** Read this invaluable book as you begin your studies and refer to it as you work through the various elements of the BPP Effective Study Package. It will help you to acquire knowledge, practice and revise, efficiently and effectively.
Three to twelve months before the exam	**Study Text and i-Learn** Use the Study Text to acquire knowledge, understanding, skills and the ability to apply techniques. Use BPP's **i-Learn** product to reinforce your learning.
Throughout	**Virtual Campus** Study, practice, revise and take advantage of other useful resources with BPP's fully interactive e-learning site with comprehensive tutor support.
Throughout	**MCQ cards and i-Pass** Revise your knowledge and ability to apply techniques, as well as practising this key exam question format, with 150 multiple choice questions. **i-Pass**, our computer-based testing package, provides objective test questions in a variety of formats and is ideal for self-assessment.
One to six months before the exam	**Practice & Revision Kit** Try the numerous examination-format questions, for which there are realistic suggested solutions prepared by BPP's own authors. Then attempt the two mock exams.
From three months before the exam until the last minute	**Passcards** Work through these short, memorable notes which are focused on what is most likely to come up in the exam you will be sitting.
One to six months before the exam	**Success Tapes** These audio tapes cover the vital elements of your syllabus in less than 90 minutes per subject. Each tape also contains exam hints to help you fine tune your strategy.

HELP YOURSELF STUDY FOR YOUR CIMA EXAMS

Exams for professional bodies such as CIMA are very different from those you have taken at college or university. You will be under **greater time pressure before** the exam - as you may be combining your study with work. There are many different ways of learning and so the BPP Study Text offers you a number of different tools to help you through. Here are some hints and tips: they are not plucked out of the air, but **based on research and experience**. (You don't need to know that long-term memory is in the same part of the brain as emotions and feelings - but it's a fact anyway.)

The right approach

1 **The right attitude**

Believe in yourself	Yes, there is a lot to learn. Yes, it is a challenge. But thousands have succeeded before and you can too.
Remember why you're doing it	Studying might seem a grind at times, but you are doing it for a reason: to advance your career.

2 **The right focus**

Read through the Syllabus and learning outcomes	These tell you what you are expected to know and are supplemented by exam focus points in the text.
Study the Exam Paper section	Past papers are a reasonable guide of what you should expect in the exam.

3 **The right method**

The big picture	You need to grasp the detail - but keeping in mind how everything fits into the big picture will help you understand better. • The **Introduction** of each chapter puts the material in context. • The **Syllabus content, learning outcomes** and **Exam focus points** show you what you need to **grasp.**
In your own words	To absorb the information (and to practise your written communication skills), it helps to **put it into your own words.** • **Take notes.** • Answer the **questions** in each chapter. You will practise the assessment formats used in the exam and your written communication skills, which become increasingly important as you progress through your CIMA exams. • Draw **mind maps**. We have an example for the whole syllabus. • Try 'teaching' a subject to a colleague or friend.

Give yourself cues to jog your memory	The BPP Study Text uses **bold text** to **highlight key points** and **icons** to identify key features, such as **Exam focus points** and **Key terms.** • Try **colour coding** with a highlighter pen. • Write **key points** on cards.

4 **The right review**

Review, review, review	It is a **fact** that regularly reviewing a topic in summary form can **fix it in your memory**. Because **review** is so important, the BPP Study Text helps you to do so in many ways. • **Chapter roundups** summarise the key points in each chapter. Use them to recap each study session. • The **Quick quiz** is another review tool to ensure that you have grasped the essentials. • Go through the **Examples** in each chapter a second or third time.

Developing your personal Study Plan

The BPP *Learning to Learn Accountancy* book emphasises (see page (iv)) the need to prepare (and use) a study plan. Planning and sticking to the plan are key elements of learning success.

There are four steps you should work through.

Step 1. How do you learn?

First you need to be aware of your style of learning. The BPP *Learning to Learn Accountancy* book commits a chapter to this **self-discovery**. What types of intelligence do you display when learning? You might be advised to brush up on certain study skills before launching into this Study Text.

> BPP's **Learning to learn accountancy** book helps you to identify what intelligences you show more strongly and then details how you can tailor your study process through your preferences. It also includes handy hints on how to develop intelligences you exhibit less strongly, but which might be needed as you study accountancy.

Are you a **theorist** or are you more **practical**? If you would rather get to grips with a theory before trying to apply it in practice, you should follow the study sequence on the next page. If the reverse is true (you need to know why you are learning theory before you do so), you might be advised to flick through Study Text chapters and look at questions, case studies and examples (Steps 7, 8 and 9 in the **suggested study sequence**) before reading through the detailed theory.

Step 2. How much time do you have?

Work out the time you have available per week, given the following.

- The standard you have set yourself
- The time you need to set aside later for work on the Practice & Revision Kit and Passcards
- The other exam(s) you are sitting
- Very importantly, practical matters such as work, travel, exercise, sleep and social life

		Hours
Note your time available in box A.	A	

Step 3. Allocate your time

- Take the time you have available per week for this Study Text shown in box A, multiply it by the number of weeks available and insert the result in box B. — B
- Divide the figure in Box B by the number of chapters in this text and insert the result in box C. — C

Remember that this is only a rough guide. Some of the chapters in this book are longer and more complicated than others, and you will find some subjects easier to understand than others.

Step 4. Implement

Set about studying each chapter in the time shown in box C, following the key study steps in the order suggested by your particular learning style.

This is your personal **Study Plan**. You should try and combine it with the study sequence outlined below. You may want to modify the sequence a little (as has been suggested above) to adapt it to your **personal style**.

Suggested study sequence

It is likely that the best way to approach this Study Text is to tackle the chapters in the order in which you find them. Taking into account your individual learning style, you could follow this sequence.

Key study steps	Activity
Step 1 **Topic list**	Each numbered topic is a numbered section in the chapter.
Step 2 **Introduction**	This gives you the **big picture** in terms of the **context** of the chapter, the **content** you will cover, and the **learning outcomes** the chapter assesses - in other words, it sets your **objectives for study.**
Step 3 **Knowledge brought forward boxes**	In these we highlight information and techniques that it is assumed you have 'brought forward' with you from your earlier studies. If there are topics which have changed recently due to legislation for example, these topics are explained in more detail.
Step 4 **Explanations**	Proceed methodically through the chapter, reading each section thoroughly and making sure you understand.

Key study steps	Activity
Step 5 **Key terms and Exam focus points**	• **Key terms** can often earn you *easy marks* if you state them clearly and correctly in an appropriate exam answer (and they are highlighted in the index at the back of the text). • **Exam focus points** give you a good idea of how we think the examiner intends to examine certain topics.
Step 6 **Note taking**	Take brief notes, if you wish. Avoid the temptation to copy out too much. Remember that being able to put something into your own words is a sign of being able to understand it. If you find you cannot explain something you have read, read it again before you make the notes.
Step 7 **Examples**	Follow each through to its solution very carefully.
Step 8 **Case examples**	Study each one, and try to add flesh to them from your own experience – they are designed to show how the topics you are studying come alive (and often come unstuck) in the real world.
Step 9 **Questions**	Make a very good attempt at each one.
Step 10 **Answers**	Check yours against ours, and make sure you understand any discrepancies.
Step 11 **Chapter roundup**	Work through it very carefully, to make sure you have grasped the major points it is highlighting.
Step 12 **Quick quiz**	When you are happy that you have covered the chapter, use the **Quick quiz** to check how much you have remembered of the topics covered and to practise questions in a variety of formats.
Step 13 **Question(s) in the Exam Question bank**	Either at this point, or later when you are thinking about revising, make a full attempt at the **Question(s)** suggested at the very end of the chapter. You can find these at the end of the Study Text, along with the **Answers** so you can see how you did. We highlight those that are introductory, and those which are of the standard you would expect to find in an exam. If you have purchased the **MCQ cards** or **i-Pass**, use these too.
Step 14 **Multiple choice questions**	Use the bank of MCQs at the back of this Study Text to practise this important assessment format and to determine how much of the Study Text you have absorbed. If you have bought the **MCQ cards** or **i-Pass**, use these too.

Short of time: Skim study technique?

You may find you simply do not have the time available to follow all the key study steps for each chapter, however you adapt them for your particular learning style. If this is the case, follow the **skim study** technique below (the icons in the Study Text will help you to do this).

- Study the chapters in the order you find them in the Study Text.
- For each chapter
    - Follow the key study steps 1-3, and then skim-read through step 4. Jump to step 11, and then go back to step 5.
    - Follow through steps 7 and 8, and prepare outline answers to questions (steps 9/10).
    - Try the Quick quiz (step 12), following up any items you can't answer, then do a plan for the Question (step 13), comparing it against our answers.
    - You should probably still follow step 6 (note-taking), although you may decide simply to rely on the BPP Passcards for this.

Moving on...

However you study, when you are ready to embark on the practice and revision phase of the BPP Effective Study Package, you should still refer back to this Study Text, both as a source of **reference** (you should find the index particularly helpful for this) and as a way to **review** (the Chapter roundups and Quick quizzes help you here).

And remember to keep careful hold of this Study Text – you will find it invaluable in your work.

SYLLABUS AND LEARNING OUTCOMES

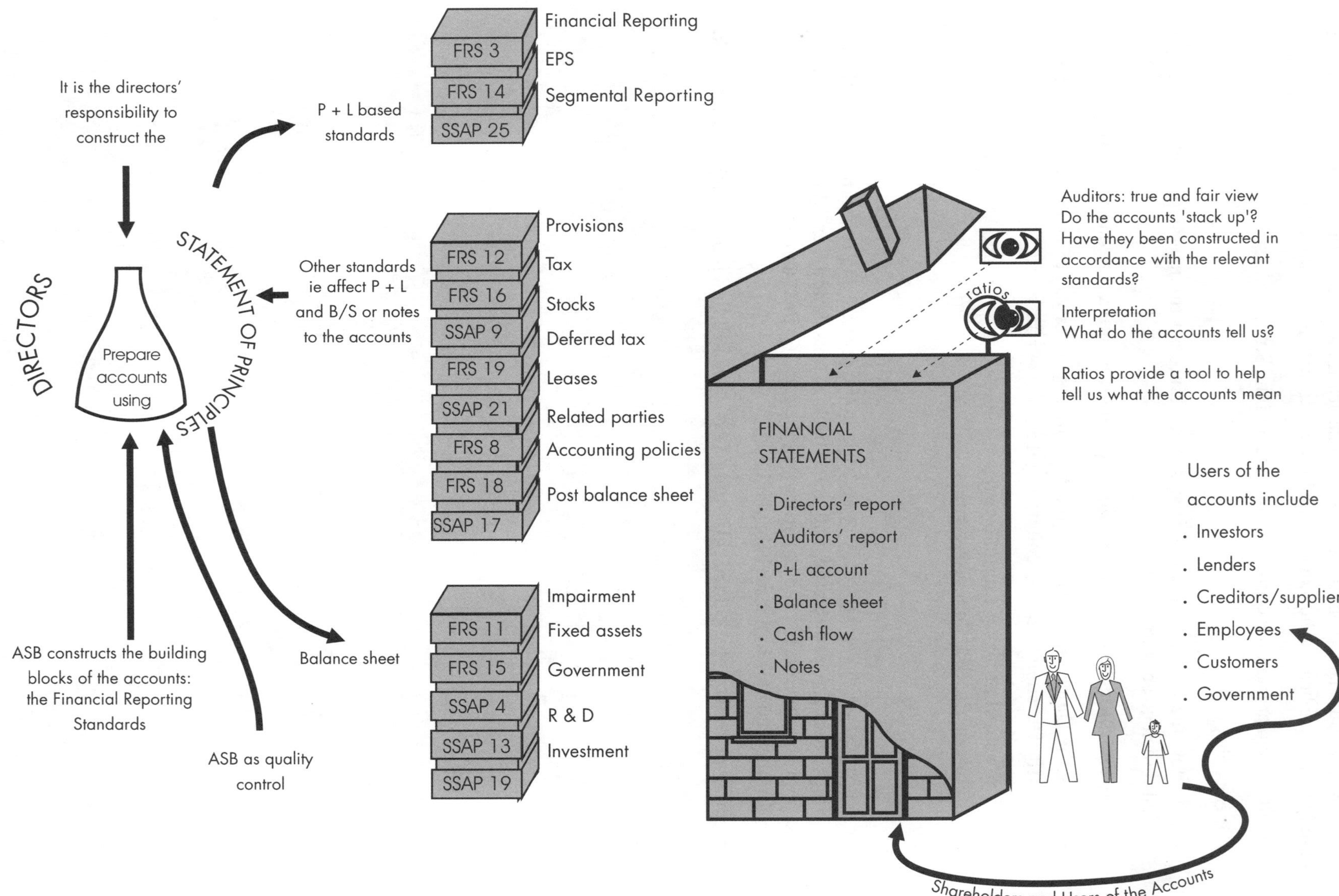

Syllabus overview

The syllabus deals with the financial statements of a non-group organisation and aims to build upon Financial Accounting Fundamentals and Business Law at the Foundation Level. Although the emphasis in this syllabus is on accounting techniques, students will be expected to understand the basic principles of accounting theory including the Accounting Standards Board's (ASB) Statement of Principles. Students will be required to answer in terms of Financial Reporting Standards (FRSs) and Statements of Standard Accounting Practice (SSAPs) in so far as they affect topics in the syllabus. It should also be noted that certain concepts draw upon terms seen in the wider accounting literature and not just those found in FRSs and SSAPs.

Aims

This syllabus aims to test the student's ability to:

- Explain and evaluate the regulatory framework governing the preparation of financial statements and corporate reports
- Prepare financial statements for non-group organisations
- Identify and apply the correct treatment for transactions in accordance with UK Generally Accepted Accounting Practice (GAAP)
- Analyse the position and performance disclosed by the financial statements of a non-group organisation

Assessment

There will be a written paper of 3 hours. There will be three sections: Section A will be compulsory, comprising 10 multiple choice questions for 20% of the marks; Section B will be a compulsory question for 30% of the marks; and Section C will offer a choice of two from four questions for 50% of the marks.

Learning outcomes and syllabus content

(i) Regulation - 10%

Learning outcomes	*Covered in chapter*
On completion of their studies students should be able to:	
(a) Explain the elements of the regulatory framework within which published accounts are produced	1
(b) Explain the role and structure of the Financial Reporting Council (FRC), ASB, Urgent Issues Task Force (UITF) and Financial Reporting Review Panel (FRRP) and their relationship to the International Accounting Standards Committee (IASC) and the International Organisation of Securities Commissions (IOSCO) and to company law.	1
(c) Explain the process leading to the promulgation of a standard practice	1
(d) Evaluate the relationship of the Statement of Principles to the standard setting process	1
(e) Explain the role of the external auditor	13
(f) Explain the elements of the audit report and the 'qualification' of that report	13

Syllabus and learning outcomes

Syllabus content		*Covered in chapter*
(1)	The Regulatory Framework within which published accounts are produced	1
(2)	The role and structure of the FRC, ASB, UITF, FRRP and their relationship to company law, IASB and IOSCO	1
(3)	The process leading to the promulgation of a standard practice	1
(4)	The powers and duties of the external auditors; the audit report and its qualification for accounting statements not in accordance with best practice	13

(ii) Accounting Statements - 40%

Learning outcomes		*Covered in chapter*
On completion of their studies students should be able to:		
(a)	Explain the regulatory requirements	1
(b)	Prepare financial statements in a form suitable for publication, with appropriate notes	2
(c)	Prepare a cash flow statement in a form suitable for publication	4
(d)	Explain and apply the rules for reporting performance	3
(e)	Explain and apply the rules for the disclosure of related parties to a business	10
(f)	Explain and apply the rules governing share capital transactions	11

Syllabus content		*Covered in chapter*
(1)	The ASB Statement of Principles	1
(2)	Preparation of the accounts of non group limited companies; the regulatory requirements for published accounts (Companies Act 1985 plus FRS 18)	2
(3)	The preparation of cash flow statements (FRS 1)	4
(4)	Reporting Performance (FRS 3); the measurement of income, the 'layered effect', exceptional and extraordinary items, prior year adjustments and the Statement of Total Recognised Gains and Losses (STGL) and the Reconciliation of Movements in Shareholders Funds. Segmental reporting (SSAP 25)	3
(5)	The treatment in company accounts of shares, debentures, dividends and interest; the recognition of revenue, the distribution of profit and the maintenance of capital	11
(6)	The disclosure of related parties to a business (FRS 8)	10
(7)	Definitions and treatment of share issues and redemption costs (FRS 4). The issue and redemption of shares, the share premium account, the capital redemption reserve and the purchase by a company of its own shares	11

(iii) Accounting treatment of significant transactions - 30%

Learning outcomes		*Covered in chapters*
On completion of their studies students should be able to:		
(a)	Explain the accounting rules contained in Financial Reporting Standards which provide guidance as to the appropriate treatment of certain transactions	3, 5-10
(b)	Identify, apply and evaluate the accounting treatment of significant transactions	3, 5-10

Syllabus content		*Covered in chapter*
(1)	Tangible Fixed Assets (FRS 15 plus FRS 11) – the calculation of depreciation and the effect of revaluation, changes to economic useful life, impairment in value, repairs, improvements and disposals (Note: for FRS 11 no value in use calculations are required, only a knowledge of basic principles)	5
(2)	Goodwill (excluding goodwill arising on consolidation) and intangible fixed assets (FRS 10 and FRS 11), recognition, valuation, amortisation and impairment (Note: for FRS 11, no 'value in use' calculations are required, only a basic knowledge of basic principles)	6
(3)	Investment properties (SSAP 19)	5
(4)	Research and development (SSAP 13) – arguments for and against capitalisation and the criteria to be met before development expenditure should be capitalised	6
(5)	Stock and long term contracts (SSAP 9) to cover methods of determining cost, NRV, the inclusion of overheads, and the measurement of profit on uncompleted contracts	7
(6)	Tax in financial accounts and government grants (SSAP 4 and FRS 16), and deferred taxation (FRS 19)	8
(7)	Post balance sheet events (SSAP 17), Provisions, contingent liabilities and contingent assets (FRS 12)	10
(8)	The principle of substance over form (FRS 5) and its application to transactions for sale and repurchase agreements and consignment stock	9
(9)	Leases and hire purchase contracts (SSAP 21) – operating leases and finance leases in the books of the lessor and lessee	9
(10)	Earnings per share (FRS 14 plus FRS 3) to include the effect of bonus issues, rights issues and convertible stock	3

(iv) Interpretation - 20%

Learning outcomes		*Covered in chapter*
On completion of their studies students should be able to:		
(a)	Calculate a full range of accounting ratios	12
(b)	Analyse financial statements to comment on the performance and position	12
(c)	Explain the limitations of accounting ratio analysis	12

Syllabus content		*Covered in chapter*
(1)	The analysis of financial statements to interpret the position and performance of a business	12
(2)	The application of ratio analysis to financial statements and its limitations	12

THE EXAM PAPER

Format of the paper

		Number of marks
Section A:	Ten multiple choice questions	20
Section B:	One compulsory question	30
Section C:	Two questions from four	50
		100

Time allowed: 3 hours

Analysis of past papers

May 2003

Section A

1 10 Multiple choice questions

Section B

2 Preparation of financial statements in a form suitable for publication and in accordance with current regulations

Section B

3 Finance leases, revision of useful economic life and initial recognition of tangible fixed assets
4 P/E ratio calculation. Accounting ratios and interpretation of accounts. Non-financial factors relating to a take-over target
5 *Statement of Principles*, characteristics of useful information, application of SOP to FRS 18, true and fair override
6 Post balance sheet events. Decommissioning costs.

November 2002

Section A

1 (a) Preparation of financial statements in a form suitable for publications with notes
  (b) Accounting treatment of sales
  (c) Considerations of the external auditor in assessing accounting policies
  (d) Disagreement in the auditor's report
2 Ratio analysis; substance over form; earnings per share

Section B (2 out of 4 questions)

3 Fixed assets, depreciation and FRS 15
4 Long term contracts
5 Accounting for the issue of shares; bonus issues; different types of share
6 FRS 12

May 2002

Section A

1 (a) Preparation of published balance sheet and profit and loss account. Reconciliation of movements in shareholders funds. Statement of total recognised gains and losses

(b) Interpretation of profitability ratios. Information provided by financial statements on wealth creation

2 Preparation of cash flow statement

Section B (2 out of 4 questions)

3 Use of accounting ratios to identify differences in business practice between companies. Limitations of ratio analysis

4 Accounting treatment of claims against a company. FRS 12.

5 Role of FRRP. FRRP and the external auditor

6 Deferred taxation. FRS 19. Deferred tax asset in respect of company pension scheme

November 2001

Section A

1 (a) Preparation of financial statement in a form suitable for publication, with appropriate notes

(b) Statement of principles. Regulatory systems. Review of accounting policies. Relevance and reliability

2 Revaluation of fixed assets. Disclosures. Impact on accounting ratios and company position

Section B (2 out of 4 questions)

3 Accounting ratios. Assessment of management teams

4 Closing stocks and SSAP 9

5 Cash flow statements. Assessment of cash management efficiency

6 SSAP 13. Research costs. Development expenditure. True and fair override

May 2001

Section A

1 Preparation of profit and loss account and balance sheet. EPS and FRS 14

2 Deferred tax. The auditor's report and their duties

Section B (2 out of 4 questions)

3 Working capital cycle

4 Related party disclosures

5 Purchase of own shares by a company

6 Leases, ratios and gearing

Pilot paper

Section A

1 Preparation of a published profit and loss account, balance sheet and notes to the accounts

2 Revaluation of fixed assets. Depreciation. Investment properties

Section B (2 out of 4 questions)

3 Calculation of ratios and explanation of a company's performance

4 Calculation and discussion of the disclosure of long-term contracts

5 Explanation of SSAP 21 and the Statement of Principles

6 Explanation and preparation of the pensions note as per SSAP 24

WHAT THE EXAMINER MEANS

The table below has been prepared by CIMA to help you interpret exam questions.

Learning objective	Verbs used	Definition
1 Knowledge What you are expected to know	• List • State • Define	• Make a list of • Express, fully or clearly, the details of/facts of • Give the exact meaning of
2 Comprehension What you are expected to understand	• Describe • Distinguish • Explain • Identify • Illustrate	• Communicate the key features of • Highlight the differences between • Make clear or intelligible/state the meaning of • Recognise, establish or select after consideration • Use an example to describe or explain something
3 Application Can you apply your knowledge?	• Apply • Calculate/compute • Demonstrate • Prepare • Reconcile • Solve • Tabulate	• To put to practical use • To ascertain or reckon mathematically • To prove with certainty or to exhibit by practical means • To make or get ready for use • To make or prove consistent/compatible • Find an answer to • Arrange in a table
4 Analysis Can you analyse the detail of what you have learned?	• Analyse • Categorise • Compare and contrast • Construct • Discuss • Interpret • Produce	• Examine in detail the structure of • Place into a defined class or division • Show the similarities and/or differences between • To build up or compile • To examine in detail by argument • To translate into intelligible or familiar terms • To create or bring into existence
5 Evaluation Can you use your learning to evaluate, make decisions or recommendations?	• Advise • Evaluate • Recommend	• To counsel, inform or notify • To appraise or assess the value of • To advise on a course of action

TACKLING OBJECTIVE TEST QUESTIONS

What is an objective test question?

An objective test (**OT**) question is made up of some form of **stimulus**, usually a question, and a **requirement** to do something.

(a) **Filling in a blank or blanks in a sentence**

(b) **Listing items in rank order**

(c) **Stating a definition**

(d) **Identifying a key issue, term or figure**

(e) **Calculating a specific figure**

(f) **Completing gaps in a set of data where the relevant numbers can be calculated from the information given**

(g) **Identifying points/zones/ranges/areas on graphs or diagrams**

(h) **Matching items or statements**

(i) **Stating whether statements are true or false**

(j) **Writing brief (in a specified number of words) explanations to the data given**

Multiple choice questions (MCQs) – selecting the most appropriate option from a number of options provided – are the most common form of OT questions.

CIMA has offered the following **guidance** about OT questions in the exam.

- **Only your answers will be marked,** not workings or any justifications.
- If you **exceed a specified limit on the number of words** you can use in an answer, you will **not be awarded any marks.**
- If you make **more than one attempt** at a question, clearly **cross through** any answers that you do not want to submit. If you don't do this, only your first answer will be marked.

We strongly suggest therefore, that you **take note of the guidance given above when answering OT questions in the exams from May 2003 onwards.**

TACKLING MULTIPLE CHOICE QUESTIONS

Of the total marks available for this paper, objective test questions comprise:

A 10%
B 20%
C 30%
D 40%
E 50%

The correct answer is B.

The multiple choice questions (MCQs) in your exam contain four possible answers. You have to **choose the option that best answers the question**. The three incorrect options are called distracters. There is a skill in answering MCQs quickly and correctly. By practising MCQs you can develop this skill, giving you a better chance of passing the exam.

You may wish to follow the approach outlined below, or you may prefer to adapt it.

Step 1. **Skim read** all the MCQs and **identify** what appear to be the easier questions.

Step 2. Attempt each question – **starting with the easier questions** identified in Step 1. Read the question thoroughly. You may prefer to work out the answer before looking at the options, or you may prefer to look at the options at the beginning. Adopt the method that works best for you.

Step 3. Read the four options and see if one matches your own answer. **Be careful with numerical questions**, as the distracters are designed to match answers that incorporate common errors. Check that your calculation is correct. Have you followed the requirement exactly? Have you included every stage of the calculation?

Step 4. You may **find that none of the options matches your answer**.

- Re-read the question to ensure that you understand it and are answering the requirement.
- Eliminate any obviously wrong answers.
- Consider which of the remaining answers is the most likely to be correct and select the option.

Step 5. If you are still **unsure** make a note **and continue to the next question**.

Step 6. **Revisit unanswered** questions. When you come back to a question after a break you often find you are able to answer it correctly straight away. If you are still unsure have a guess. You are not penalised for incorrect answers, so **never leave a question unanswered!**

Exam focus. After extensive practice and revision of MCQs, you may find that you recognise a question when you sit the exam. Be aware that the detail and/or requirement may be different. If the question seems familiar read the requirement and options carefully – do not assume that it is identical.

BPP's **MCQ cards** and **i-Pass** for this paper provide you with plenty of opportunity for further practice of MCQs.

Part A
Regulation

Chapter 1

THE REGULATORY FRAMEWORK

	Topic list	Syllabus reference	Ability required
1	**The regulatory framework**	(i)	Comprehension
2	**ASB *Statement of Principles***	(i)	Evaluation
3	**Current Financial Reporting Standards**	(i)	Comprehension

Introduction

This is an important chapter. In it, the current financial reporting environment is examined, including the process leading to the creation of Financial Reporting Exposure Drafts (FREDs) and Financial Reporting Standards (FRSs). The role and structure of the major bodies involved in the financial reporting regime are discussed, particularly the Accounting Standards Board (ASB).

Refer back to this chapter as you work through Part C of this Study Text. The FRSs and SSAPs described in Part C, and particularly the process leading to their publication, are relevant to the 'regulation' section of the syllabus.

We begin by looking at the important elements in financial reports. From your studies at Foundation you will know that the financial or annual report of a company consists of:

(a) A balance sheet.
(b) A profit and loss account.
(c) A statement of recognised gains and losses.
(d) A cash flow statement.
(e) Notes to these statements.
(f) A directors' report.
(g) An auditors' report.
(h) A chairman's report.

You should read relevant articles in *Management Accounting* and other professional journals. Background reading can provide insights which may prove helpful in the exam.

Learning outcomes covered in this chapter

- **Explain** the elements of the regulatory framework within which published accounts are produced
- **Explain** the role and structure of the Financial Reporting Council (FRC), ASB, Urgent Issues Task Force (UITF) and Financial Reporting Review Panel (FRRP) and their relationship to the International Accounting Standards Committee (IASC) (now the international Accounting Standards Board) and the International Organisation of Securities Commissions (IOSCO) and to company law
- **Explain** the process leading to the promulgation of a standard practice
- **Evaluate** the relationship of the Statement of Principles to the standard setting process

Syllabus content covered in this chapter

- The Regulatory Framework within which published accounts are produced
- The role and structure of the FRC, ASB, UITF, FRRP and their relationship to company law, IASC and IOSCO
- The process leading to the promulgation of a standard practice

1 THE REGULATORY FRAMEWORK

Exam focus point

There are several developments in this area of regulation going on in practice so something might come up in the exam.

Some of the material lends itself to a direct question, but you may need to create your answer from different sections.

Unincorporated businesses

1.1 In the UK these can usually prepare their financial statements in **any form** they choose (subject to the constraints of specific legislation, such as the Financial Services Act 1986 for investment businesses, for example).

Companies

1.2 **All companies** must comply with the provisions of the **Companies Act 1985** in preparing their financial statements and also with the provisions of *Statements of Standard Accounting Practice* (SSAPs) and *Financial Reporting Standards* (FRSs) which are issued by a body called the **Accounting Standards Board**.

1.3 In its *Foreword to Accounting Standards* the Accounting Standards Board states that accounting standards are applicable to all financial statements whose purpose is to give a **true and fair view** (explained in Chapter 2). This necessarily includes the financial statements of every company incorporated in the UK.

1.4 The regulatory framework over company accounts is therefore based on several sources.

- **Company law**
- **Accounting** or **financial reporting standards** and other related pronouncements
- **International accounting standards** (and the influence of other national standard setting bodies)
- The requirements of the **Stock Exchange**

Role of company law

1.5 The Companies Act 1985 (CA 1985) consolidated the bulk of previous company legislation which is relevant to your syllabus. This was substantially amended by the **Companies Act 1989** (CA 1989), and all references in this text are to CA 1985 as amended by CA 1989.

1.6 The CA 1985 has various key impacts on financial reporting requirements.

(a) Every UK registered company is required to prepare a balance sheet and profit and loss account for each financial year which gives a true and fair view.

(b) The financial statements must comply with Schedule 4 to CA 1985 as regards format and additional information provided by way of note.

(c) Accounting standards are accorded legal status as statements of standard accounting practice by such body or bodies as may be prescribed by regulation ie the Accounting Standards Board.

Company law review

1.7 Currently the DTI is carrying out a comprehensive review of UK company law, following the initial consultation paper *Modern Company Law for a Competitive Economy* published in 1998.

1.8 The review project has now reached the Government white paper stage. The topics covered by the white paper, *Modernising Company Law*, issued on 16 July, 2002 include the following matters.

- Small and private companies
- Corporate governance
- Capital maintenance
- Groups of companies
- Reconstructions and mergers

Influence of EU directives

1.9 Since the United Kingdom became a member of the **European Union** (EU) it has been obliged to comply with legal requirements decided on by the EU. It does this by enacting UK laws to implement EU directives.

1.10 There are various key areas where EC directives have influence on the UK financial reporting regime.

(a) Implementation of prescribed formats and detailed disclosure requirements for financial statements.

(b) Definition of a subsidiary and permission of various exemptions from Companies Act requirements.

(c) Introduction of various exemptions from Companies Act requirements in respect of small and medium sized companies.

1.11 Remember that **EU directives** are only **mandatory** when actually **enacted** into **legislation** by **Parliament.** Other EU directives only hold advisory status.

Exam focus point

Although your syllabus does not require you to be an expert on EU procedure, you should be aware that the form and content of company accounts can be influenced by international developments.

Accounting standards

KEY TERM

An **accounting standard** is a rule or set of rules which prescribes the method (or methods) by which accounts should be prepared and presented.

1.12 These 'working regulations' are issued by a national or international body of the accountancy profession.

1.13 In the UK, such standards were called *Statements of Standard Accounting Practice* (SSAPs) and were until 31 July 1990 formulated by the Accounting Standards Committee (ASC). SSAPs are gradually being replaced by *Financial Reporting Standards* (FRSs) produced by the successor to the ASC, the Accounting Standards Board (ASB).

1.14 Accounting standards **interact** with company law in several ways.

(a) '**Realised**' profits and losses are determined by reference to generally accepted accounting practice, ie SSAPs and FRSs (s 262 (3)).

(b) The accounts must state whether the provisions of accounting standards have been followed or give reasons for, and disclosures of any **material departures** (see below): para 36A, Sch 4.

Regulatory organisations

1.15 The Financial Reporting Council (FRC) with its subsidiaries, the Accounting Standard Board (ASB) and Financial Reporting Review Panel (FRRP) together make up an organisation whose purpose it to promote and secure good financial reporting. Although the FRC is the parent of the ASB and the FRRP, they are **independent of the FRC, and of each other**, in the performance of their functions.

1.16 The ASB has various committees including:

(a) Urgent Issues Task Force (UITF)
(b) Committee on Accounting for Smaller Entities (CASE)

1.17 The structure can be depicted in the following diagram.

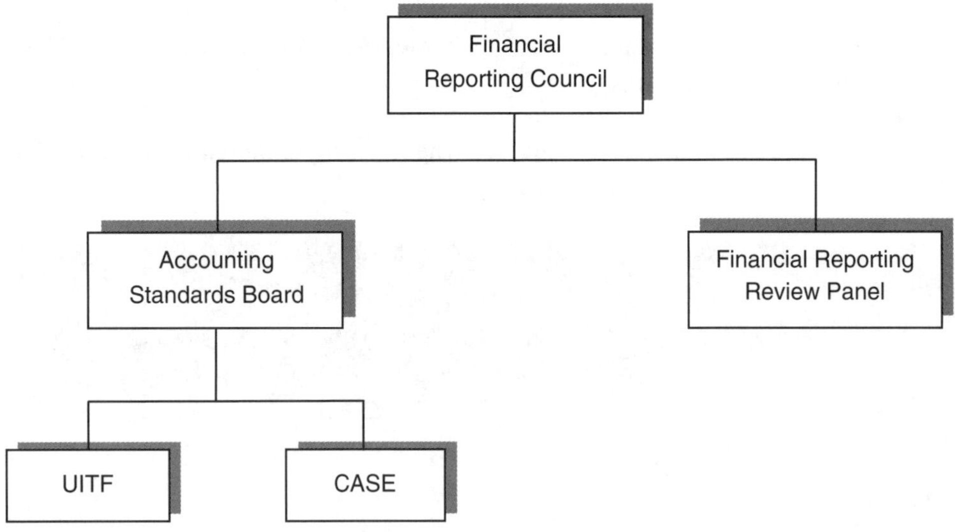

Exam focus point

It is worth logging on to the websites of the various regulatory bodies to keep up-to-date with any changes. Moreover, a first hand feel of the organisations may help the learning process.

1.18 The FRC, ASB and FRRP enjoy strong governmental support but are **not government controlled**. They are a part of the **private sector** process of **self-regulation**.

Financial Reporting Council

1.19 The remit of the FRC is to provide support to the ASB and FRPP and to encourage good financial reporting generally. In meeting its remit, the FRC caries out various functions.

(a) From time to time, making **representations** to **Government** on the **current working** of **legislation** and any **desirable developments**.

(b) Providing guidance to the **ASB** on **work programmes** and on **broad policy issues**.

(c) Verifying new arrangement are conducted with efficiency and cost effectiveness, as well as being adequately funded.

1.20 Other items of useful information about the FRC are:

- It meets twice a year
- It comprises a Chairman, three Deputy Chairmen and up to thirty members.
- Each year it publishes:
  - An annual review describing the activities during the year of the ASB and the FRRP
  - Report and financial statements, as required by the Companies Act
  - Press releases
  - Other relevant information

1.21 Projects in which the FRC was involved in 2002 included:

(a) Participation in a group set up by the government, post Enron, to **co-ordinate** the work of **UK regulators** in the **audit** and **accountancy** sector.

(b) Submitting a **report** to the Treasury Select Committee, which, in the wake of Enron is enquiring into the **financial regulation of public limited companies**.

(c) advising the *Department of Trade and Industry* on ways in which the *Company Law Review* might be implemented.

1.22 In 2003, the FRP was involved in preparing a revised text for the *Higgs model code of corporate governance*. Derek Higgs, the deputy chairman of a listed company was asked by the government to conduct an independent review into the role and effectiveness of non-executive directors. The Higgs Report was issued in February 2003 and the FRC is taking feedback before providing a revised model text.

The Accounting Standards Board

Role

1.23 The role of the ASB, as recognised by the Companies Act, is to issue accounting standards. It took over this role from its predecessor, the Accounting Standards Committee (ASC) in 1990.

1.24 Unlike the ASC, the ASB can issue accounting standards on its own authority, without the approval of any other body.

1.25 ASB accounting standards are developed having regard to the ASB's *Statement of Principles.*

Membership

1.26 The ASB has a maximum membership of ten which may be depicted as follows.

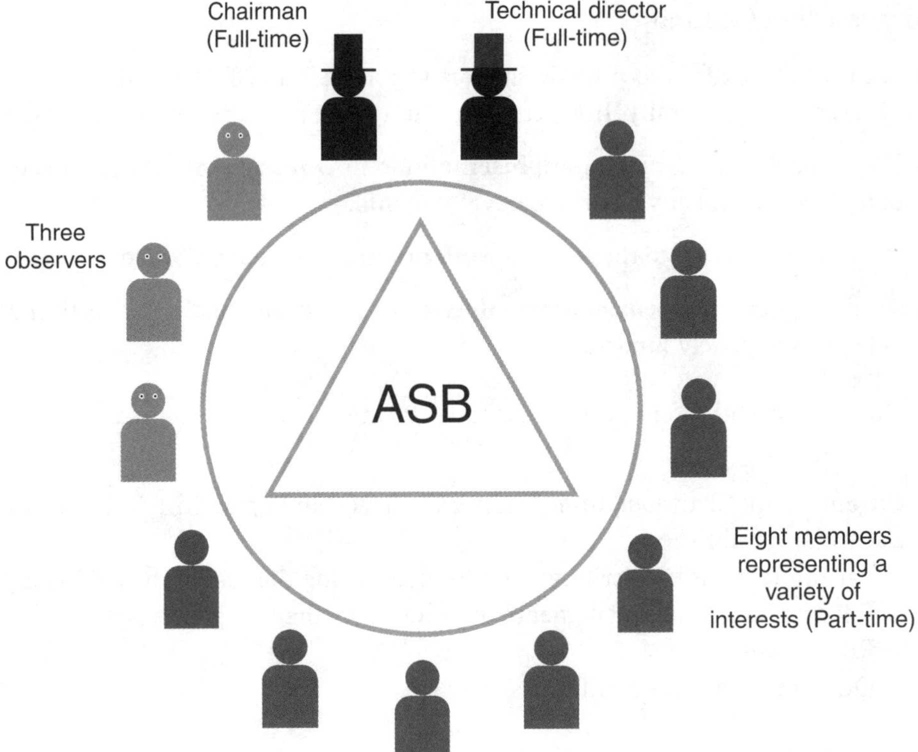

Voting criteria

1.27 Any decision to **adopt**, **revise** or **withdraw** an accounting standard usually requires the vote of **seven** members (**six** when there are fewer than ten members).

Objectives of the ASB

1.28 The objectives of the ASB as set out in its *Statement of aims* are to establish and improve standards of financial accounting and reporting, for the **benefit** of:

- **Users**
- **Prepares**
- **Auditors**

1.29 The ASB states that it intends to achieve its objectives by:

(a) **Developing principles** to guide it in establishing standards and to provide a **framework** within which others can **exercise judgement** in **resolving accounting issues**.

(b) Issuing new accounting standards, or amending existing ones, in **response** to evolving **business practices**, new **economic developments** and deficiencies being identified in **current practice**.

(c) **Addressing urgent issues promptly**.

ASB Standards setting process

1.30 The ASB standards setting process can be best viewed in the following diagram, which is based on information shown in the ASB's own website.

STEP 1
Identify topic based on own research or input from outside

↓

STEP 2
Set up project management structure and identify project resources and expertise

↓

STEP 3
Publish a *Discussion Paper.* The objective here is to canvas the views of the interested public on the possible approaches

↓

STEP 4
Analyse and publish feedback received

↓

STEP 5
Conduct any necessary further research or field-test possible procedures

↓

STEP 6
Publish *Financial reporting exposure draft* (FRED) for further public comment. Sometimes comments on alternative approaches might be invited

↓

STEP 7
Analyse and consider further feedback received from interested parties

↓

STEP 8
Issue final pronouncement in the form of a *Financial Reporting Standard* (FRS) or other publication, which specifies the date on which it becomes effective

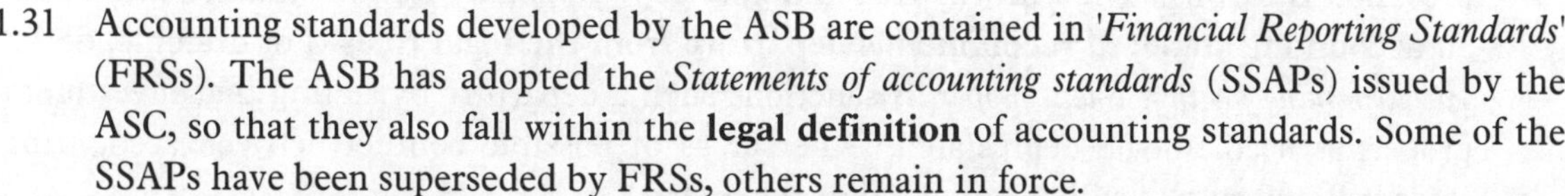

Exam focus point

The above seems an obvious area for an exam question. You would of course answer it in narrative or point form rather than use a chart, which we have provided to help the learning process!

1.31 Accounting standards developed by the ASB are contained in '*Financial Reporting Standards*' (FRSs). The ASB has adopted the *Statements of accounting standards* (SSAPs) issued by the ASC, so that they also fall within the **legal definition** of accounting standards. Some of the SSAPs have been superseded by FRSs, others remain in force.

1.32 Accounting standards apply to **all companies**, and other kinds of entities that **prepare accounts** that are intended to provide a **true and fair view**.

KEY TERMS

The foreword to Accounting Standards explains the authority, scope and application of accounting standards.

(a) It will normally be necessary to **comply** with the **standards** to show a **true and fair view**.

(b) In applying the standards, the **user** should be **guided by** their **spirit** and **reasoning**.

(c) In *rare* **cases** it may be necessary to **depart** from a standard to show a true and fair view.

(d) **Departures** should be dealt with **objectively** according to the '**economic and commercial characteristics** of the circumstances'; the departure and its financial effect should be **disclosed.**

(e) The **Review Panel** and the **DTI** have powers and procedures to **investigate departures** and to require a **restatement** through the **court**.

(f) Accounting standards **need not** be **applied** to **immaterial items.**

1.33 The **ASB collaborates** with accounting **standard-setters** from other countries and the International Accounting Standards Board (IASB) in order to ensure that its standards are developed with due regard to international developments.

1.34 The ASB publicises its activities through press releases and its **quarterly newsletter** 'Inside Track' which provides a broad, non-technical report on the ASB's activities. The ASB also runs a **website** at www.asb.org.uk.

Authority of accounting standards

1.35 Accounting standards are intended to apply to **all financial accounts** which were 'intended to give **a true and fair view** of the financial position and profit and loss'. This includes overseas companies included in UK group account. A standard can, however, specify (ie restrict) the 'scope' of its application. For example, FRS14 on earnings per share applies only to the audited accounts of companies (companies whose shares are listed on the Stock Exchange).

1.36 Although there are some areas where the contents of accounting standards overlap with provisions of company law, standards are **detailed working regulations** within the framework of government legislation, and they **cover areas** in which the **law is silent**. In addition, standards are not intended to override exemptions from disclosure which are allowed to special cases of companies by law.

1.37 The Companies Act 1985 states that a departure from its provisions is permissible if that provision is inconsistent with the true and fair view. This may lead to situations in which an **accounting standard recommends departure from the legal rules**. For example, SSAP 19 *Accounting for investment properties* sanctions such a departure by stating that investment properties need not be depreciated. Other areas of possible conflict between accounting standards and statute will be noted in later chapters.

1.38 Members of the **Consultative Committee of Accounting Bodies** (CCAB), of which the CIMA is a member, are expected to **observe accounting standards** in their roles either as preparers or auditors of financial information.

Urgent Issues, Task Force (UITF)

1.39 The main role of the UITF is to **assist the ASB** in areas where an accounting standard or Companies Act provision exists, but where **unsatisfactory** or **conflicting interpretations** have developed or seem likely to develop.

1.40 Its **consensus pronouncements** are issued as UITF Abstracts, which the ASB expects be regarded as **accepted practice** in the area in question, and part of the corpus of practices forming the basis for what determines a true and fair view.

1.41 A UITF Abstract may be taken into **consideration** by the **FRRP** in deciding whether a company's financial statements **call for review**.

Financial Reporting Review Panel

1.42 The role of the Review Panel is to **examine material departures** from the **accounting requirements** of the Companies Act 1985, including **applicable accounting** standard, and if necessary to seek **an order from the court** to remedy them. It has about 15 members from which smaller panels are formed to tackle cases as they arise.

1.43 By agreement with the Department of Trade and Industry the normal ambit of the Panel is **pubic and large private companies**, the Department dealing with all other cases.

1.44 The Panel is concerned with an examination of **material departures** from accounting standards with a view to considering whether the accounts in question nevertheless meet the statutory requirement to give a **true and fair view**. While such a departure does not necessarily mean that a company's account fail the true and fair test it will raise the question. Remember that the Companies Act 1985 requires large companies to disclose in their accounts any such departures together with the reasons for them thus enabling them to be readily identified and considered.

1.45 The Panel does **not scrutinise on a routine basis all company accounts** falling within its ambit. Instead it **acts on matters drawn to its attention, either directly or indirectly**.

1.46 The Panel normally aims to discharge its tasks by **seeking voluntary agreement** with the directors of a company on any **necessary revisions** to the accounts in question. But if that **approach fails** and the Panel believes that revision to the accounts are necessary it will seek :

(a) A **declaration from the court** that the **annual accounts** of the company concerned **do not** comply with the requirements of the Companies Act 1985,

(b) An **order requiring** the **directors** of the company to **prepare revised accounts**. If the court grants such an order it may also require the directors to meet the **costs** of the proceedings and of revising the accounts.

STEP 1. Voluntary agreement to revise

STEP 2. Court order to revise

1.47 Where accounts are revised at the instance of the Panel, either voluntarily or by order of the court, but the company's **auditor** had **not qualified his audit report** on the **defective accounts** the Panel will draw this fact to the **attention** of the **auditor's professional body**.

Exam focus point

The May 2002 exam included a 20 mark question on the role and operation of the FRRP

Question 1

Discuss the function of:

(a) The Accounting Standards Board
(b) The Review Panel
(c) The Financial Reporting Council
(d) The Urgent Issues Task Force

Answer

See Paragraphs 1.23 –1.47.

International Accounting Standards

1.48 **International Accounting Standards** (IASs) were originally produced by the **International Accounting Standards Committee** (IASC), now the **International Accounting Standards Board** (IASB). The IASB **develops financial reporting standards through an international process that involves the world-wide accountancy profession, the preparers and users of financial statements, and national standard setting bodies.**

1.49 The **objectives** of the IASB are:

(a) **Develop**, in the public interest, a **single set** of high quality, understandable and **enforceable global accounting standards** that require high quality, transparent and comparable information in financial statements and other financial reporting to help participants in the various **capital markets** of the world and other users of the **information** to make **economic decisions.**

(b) **Promote** the use and **rigorous application** of those standards.

(c) Work actively with national standard-setters to bring about **convergence** of national accounting standards and **International Financial Reporting Standards (IFRSs).**

1.50 A substantial number of **multinational companies** now prepare financial statements in accordance with IASs. IASs are also endorsed by many countries as their own standards, whether unchanged or with minor amendments.

1.51 A great many **stock exchanges** now **accept IASs** for **cross-border listing purposes** (ie when a company in one country wishes to list its shares on another country's stock exchange), but Canada, Japan and the United States were exceptions.

1.52 In May 2000, the Presidents Committee of the International Organisation of Securities Commissions (IOSCO) recommended the IOSCO members permit **incoming multinational issuers** to use the **IASC core standards** to prepare their financial statements for **cross-border offerings and listings**. The core standards include all IASs except for IAS 15, IAS 26 and the recently issued IASs 40 and 41.

1.53 On 25 May 2000, the US Securities and Exchange Commission recommended that IASs should now be accepted for use in **cross-border listings** in the United States, without reconciliation to results under US GAAP.

1.54 As the use of IASs grew, the role of the IASC expanded and as a result, the member bodies approved the restructuring of the IASC. As a result, on 1 April 2001, the new IASB assumed the IASC's standard-setting responsibilities. Future standards issued by the IASB will be known as International Financial Reporting Standards (IFRSs). Existing IASs and SICs were adopted by the IASB.

The use and application of IASs

1.55 IASs have helped to both **improve** and **harmonise** financial reporting around the world. The standards are used:

- As national requirements, often after a national process
- As the basis for all or some national requirements
- As an international benchmark for those countries which develop their own requirements
- By regulatory authorities for domestic and foreign companies
- By companies themselves

Effects of IASs on UK regulation

1.56 **Before the ASB** came into existence, the effect of IASs and other IASC publications on UK standard setting was limited and haphazard. Many SSAPs and IASs were in agreement, but some were not, and some covered completely different topics.

1.57 In its FRSs, the ASB identifies the **compliance** of the standards with IASs or IAS exposure drafts. The ASB sees itself as closely aligned with the IASC, now the IASB. However, it seems that the ASB will only follow the relevant IAS if it fits in with the desired UK practice. The IASB is revising and improving its current IASs and one of the reasons is the elimination or reduction of alternative accounting treatments.

Harmonisation in Europe

1.58 In June 2000, the European Commission proposed that all publicly listed EU companies should be required to implement IASs for their consolidation financial statements by 2005.

1.59 The objective of the European Commission is to build a fully integrated, globally competitive capital market. A key element of this is the establishment of a level playing field for the EU financial reporting, supported by an effective enforcement regime.

1.60 Harmonised financial reporting standards are intended to provide a platform for wider investment choice, a more efficient capital market, lower cost of capital and enhanced business development.

1.61 In March 2002, the European Parliament voted to endorse the use of international standards for publicly limited companies in the EU.

1.62 Member states were expected to approve the regulation in June 2002, requiring the implementation of the IAS and IFRS regime by 1 January 2005.

The ASB's convergence policy

1.63 The following statement is taken from the ASB Convergence Handbook.

> The ASB is working with the IASB and other national standard setters in order to seek improvements in IFRS and convergence of national and international standards. The ASB is one of several national standard setters that have a formal liaison relationship with the IASB. This relationship involves regular meetings and other consultations as well as several joint standard setting projects, including the ASB's joint project with the IASB on reporting financial performance. One member of the IASB (Professor Geoffrey Whittington) is directly responsible for liaison with the ASB.
>
> The ASB intends to align UK accounting standards with IFRS whenever practicable. It proposes to do this, in the main, by a phased replacement of existing UK standards with new UK standards based on the equivalent IFRS.

Exam focus point

Consider the likelihood of small general discursive questions on how the work of the ASB, IASB, EU etc link into the process of globalisation. Consider how harmonisation might be helpful to both the multi-national company as well as global investors.

The Stock Exchange

1.64 In the UK there are two different markets on which it is possible for a company to have its securities quoted:

- The **Stock Exchange**
- The **Alternative Investment Market** (AIM)

1.65 Shares quoted on the main market, the Stock Exchange, are said to be '**listed**' or to have obtained a 'listing'. In order to receive a listing for its securities, a company must conform with Stock Exchange regulations contained in the **Listing Rules** or **Yellow Book** issued by the Council of The Stock Exchange. The company commits itself to certain procedures and standards, including matters concerning the disclosure of accounting information, which are more extensive than the disclosure requirements of the Companies Acts. The requirements of the AIM are **less stringent** than the main Stock Exchange. It is aimed at new, higher risk or smaller companies.

1.66 Many requirements of the Yellow Book do not have the backing of law, but the ultimate sanction which can be imposed on a listed company which fails to abide by them is the **withdrawal** of its securities from the Stock Exchange List: the company's shares would no longer be traded on the market.

2 ASB STATEMENT OF PRINCIPLES **Pilot paper**

Exam focus point

The pilot paper contained a question concerning *The Statement of Principles*. This is a key area as it is the framework upon which all accounting standards are (and will be) based.

The November 2001 exam included a question on the role of the *Statement of Principles* within the system of regulation.

The May 2003 paper asked candidates to explain the role of the *Statement of Principles* in the consistent and logical formulation of FRSs.

There will nearly always be small parts of questions or references in questions regarding the *Statements of Principles.*

What is a conceptual framework?

2.1 A **conceptual framework**, in the field we are concerned with, is a statement of generally accepted theoretical principles which form the frame of reference for financial reporting. These theoretical principles provide the basis for the **development of new reporting standards** and the **evaluation of those already in existence**. A conceptual framework will form the theoretical basis for determining which events should be **accounted for,** how they should be **measured** and how they should be **communicated** to the user. Although it is theoretical in nature, a conceptual framework for financial reporting has highly **practical final aims.**

Why is a conceptual framework needed?

2.2 There are a number of reasons.

(a) UK standards have developed in a the haphazard way over recent years. Had an agreed framework existed, the old ASC could have acted as an **architect or designer**, rather than a **fire-fighter**.

(b) Fundamental principles were tackled **more than once** in different standards, thereby producing contradictions and **inconsistencies** and leading to ambiguity. This affected the true and fair concept of financial reporting.

(c) A financial reporting environment governed by specific rules rather than general principles would be avoided if a **cohesive set of principles** were in place.

(d) A conceptual framework would also **support standard setters** in the face of political pressure from various 'lobby groups' and interested parties.

2.3 The Accounting Standards Board (ASB) published (in November 1995) an exposure draft of its *Statement of Principles for Financial Reporting.* In March 1999, the text was substantially revised with particular attention being given to the clarity of expression. This draft was finalised as a Statement in December 1999.

2.4 The Statement consists of eight chapters.

(1) The objective of financial statements
(2) The reporting entity
(3) The qualitative characteristics of financial information
(4) The elements of financial statements
(5) Recognition in financial statements
(6) Measurement in financial statements
(7) Presentation of financial information
(8) Accounting for interests in other entities

Chapter 1 The objective of financial statements

2.5 The main points raised here are as follows.

(a) 'The objective of financial statements is to provide information about the reporting entity's **performance and financial position** that is useful to a wide range of users for assessing the stewardship of management and for making economic decisions.'

(b) It is acknowledged that while not all the information needs of users can be met by financial statements, there are needs that are common to all users. Financial statements that meet the needs of providers of risk capital to the enterprise will also meet most of the needs of other users that financial statements can satisfy.

Users of financial statements other than investors include the following.

(i) Lenders
(ii) Suppliers and other creditors
(iii) Employees
(iv) Customers
(v) Government and their agencies
(vi) The public

(c) The limitations of financial statements are emphasised as well as the strengths.

(d) Investors are the defining choice of user because they focus on the entity's cash-generation ability or financial adaptability.

(e) The information required by investors relates to:

(i) Financial performance
(ii) Financial position
(iii) Generation and use of cash
(iv) Financial adaptability

The *Statement of Principles* discusses the importance of each of these elements and why they are disclosed in the financial statements.

Question 2

Consider the information needs of the users of financial information listed above, including shareholders.

Answer

(a) Shareholders

(i) Information is required to help make a decision about buying or selling shares, taking up a rights issue and voting at the Annual General Meeting (AGM).

(ii) The shareholder must have information about the level of dividend, past, present and future and any changes in share price.

(iii) The shareholders will also need to know whether the management has been running the company efficiently.

(iv) As well as the position indicated by the profit and loss account, balance sheet and earnings per share (EPS), the shareholders will want to know about the liquidity position of the company, the company's future prospects, and how the company's shares compare with those of its competitors.

(b) *Employees* need information about the security of employment and future prospects for jobs in the company, and to help with collective pay bargaining.

(c) *Lenders* need information to help them decide whether to lend to a company. They will also need to check that the value of any security remains adequate, that the interest repayments are secure, that the cash is available for redemption at the appropriate time and that any financial restrictions (such as maximum debt/equity ratios) have not been breached. Investors will need information about loans which are traded on the stock market to decide whether to buy or sell them.

(d) *Suppliers* need to know whether the company will be a good customer and pay its debts.

(e) *Customers* need to know whether the company will be able to continue producing and supplying goods.

(f) *Government's* interest in a company may be one of creditor or customer, as well as being specifically concerned with compliance with tax and company law, ability to pay tax and the general contribution of the company to the economy.

(g) The *public* at large would wish to have information for all the reasons mentioned above, but it could be suggested that it would be impossible to provide general purpose accounting information which was specifically designed for the needs of the public.

Chapter 2 The reporting entity

2.6 This chapter makes the point that it is important that entities that ought to prepare financial statements, in fact do so. The entity must be a cohesive economic unit. It has a determinable boundary and is held to account for all the things it can control. For this purpose, first direct control and secondly direct plus indirect control are taken into account.

KEY TERM

Control means two things:

(a) The ability to deploy the economic resources involved
(b) the ability to benefit (or to suffer) from their deployment.

An entity will have control of a second entity if it has the ability to direct that entity's operating and financial policies with a view to gaining economic benefit from its activities.

Control must be distinguished from **management**, where the entity is not exposed to the benefits arising from or risks inherent in the activities of the second entity.

Chapter 3 Qualitative characteristics of financial information

2.7 The Statement gives a diagrammatic representation of the discussion, shown below.

(a) Qualitative characteristics that relate to **content** are **relevance** and **reliability**.

(b) Qualitative characteristics that relate to **presentation** are **comparability** and **understandability**.

KEY TERM

Materiality is the significance or importance of a particularly matter (or item) in the context of financial statements as a whole. A matter is material if its omission or misstatement would influence the decision of a user of the accounts. Materiality may be considered in the context of any individual primary statement within the financial statements or of individual items included in them. Materiality is not capable of general mathematical definition as it has both qualitative and quantitative aspects.

The diagram shown here is reasonably self-explanatory.

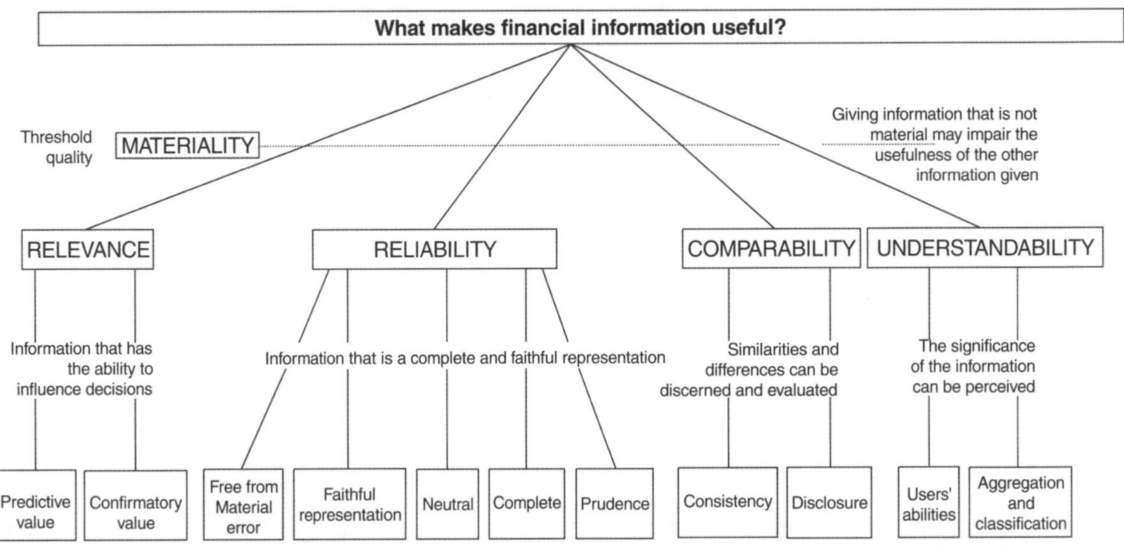

Exam focus point

The November 2001 exam asked candidates to apply relevance and reliability to the provision of future warranty costs.

The November 2002 paper required candidates to discuss the relevance and reliability of cost and valuation figures.

The May 2003 exams ask for a discussion of the four key characteristics that make financial information useful.

Chapter 4 Elements of financial statements

2.8 Any item that does not fall within one of the definitions of elements should not be included in financial statements. The definitions are as follows.

(a) **Assets** are rights or other access to **future economic benefits** controlled by an entity as a result of past transactions or events.

(b) **Liabilities** are obligations of an entity to **transfer economic benefits** as a result of past transactions or events.

(c) **Ownership interest** is the residual amount found by deducting all of the entity's liabilities from all of the entity's assets.

(d) **Gains** are **increases** in **ownership interest,** other than those relating to contributions from owners.

(e) **Losses** are **decreases** in **ownership interest**, other than those relating to distributions to owners.

(f) **Contributions from owners** are increases in ownership interest resulting from investments made by owners in their capacity as owners.

(g) **Distributions to owners** are decreases in ownership interest resulting from **transfers** made to owners in their capacity as owners.

Exam focus point

The November 2002 exam asked candidates to apply the definitions of assets and liabilities to explain how profits and losses arise.

The definitions of assets and liabilities are vital and well worth fully understanding and learning.

Chapter 5 Recognition in financial statements

2.9 The following diagram summarises the principles for recognition in financial statements. :

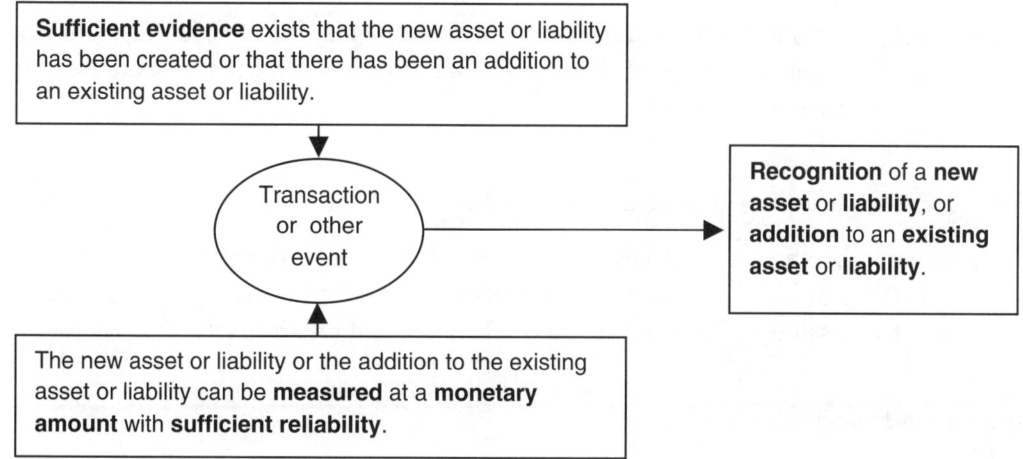

2.10 In a transaction involving the provision of services or goods for a net gain, the recognition criteria described above will be met on the occurrence of the **critical event** in the **operating cycle** involved.

2.11 An asset or liability will be wholly or partly derecognised if:

(a) Sufficient evidence exists that a transaction or other past event has eliminated a previously recognised asset or liability.

(b) Or although the item continues to be an asset or a liability the criteria for recognition are no longer met.

2.12 The objective of financial statements is achieved to a large extent through the recognition of elements in the primary financial statements – in other words, the depiction of elements both in words and by monetary amounts, and the inclusion of those amounts in the primary financial statement totals. **Recognition is a process that has the following stages.**

(a) **Initial recognition,** which is where an item is depicted in the primary financial statements for the first time.

(b) **Subsequent remeasurement,** which involves changing the amount at which an already recognised asset or liability is stated in the primary financial statements.

(c) **Derecognition**, which is where an item that was until then recognised ceases to be recognised.

2.13 Even though **matching** is **not used by the *Statement*** to drive the recognition process, it still plays an important role in the approach described in the draft in **allocating the cost of assets across reporting periods** and in telling preparers where they may find assets and liabilities.

Chapter 6 Measurement in financial statements

2.14 A monetary carrying amount needs to be assigned so an asset or liability can be recognised. There are two measurements that can be used: **historical cost** or **current value**.

(a) Initially, when an asset is purchased or a liability incurred, the asset/liability is recorded at the **transaction cost**, that is **historical cost**, which **at that time is equal to current replacement cost**.

(b) An asset/liability may subsequently be '**remeasured**'. In a historical cost system, this can involve writing down an asset to its **recoverable amount**. For a liability, the corresponding treatment would be amendment of the monetary amount to the amount ultimately expected to be paid.

(c) Such re-measurements will, however, only be recognised if there is **sufficient evidence** that the **monetary amount of the asset/liability has changed** and the **new amount can be reliably measured**.

Chapter 7 Presentation of financial information

2.15 Aspects of this chapter have also given rise to some controversy. The chapter begins by making the general point that financial statements need to be as **simple, straightforward** and **brief** as possible while retaining their **relevance and reliability**.

Components of financial statements

2.16 The primary financial statements are as follows.

Statement	Measure of
Profit and loss account	Financial performance
Statement of total recognised gains and losses	Financial performance
Balance sheet	Financial position
Cash flow statement	Cash inflows and outflows

2.17 The notes to the financial statements '**amplify and explore**' the primary statements; together they form an '**integrated whole**'. Disclosure in the notes does not correct or justify non-disclosure or misrepresentation in the primary financial statements.

2.18 '**Supplementary information**' embraces **voluntary disclosures** and information which is **too subjective for disclosure in the primary financial statement and the notes.**

Chapter 8 Accounting for interests in other entities

2.19 Financial statements need to reflect the effect on the reporting entity's financial performance and financial position of its interests in other entities. This involves various measurement, presentation and consolidation issues which are dealt with in this chapter of the *Statement.* (This is however, outside the scope of the syllabus.)

Summary

2.20 The *Statement of Principles* does not have a direct effect on financial reporting. It is **not an accounting standard** with which companies have to comply. Having said that, **it is influential**, especially where there is no specific standard dealing with an issue. There is still some controversy surrounding this document.

2.21 The ASB published a *question and answer booklet* on the *Statement of Principles*. The booklet aims to clear up 'misunderstandings' by stating that the Statement is not intended to be a mandatory standard, **bedrock notions (eg true and fair)** will remain and a system of current cost accounting is not envisaged.

3 CURRENT ACCOUNTING STANDARDS

3.1 The following standards are extant at the date of writing. The SSAPs which were in force at the date the ASB was formed have been adopted by the Board. They are gradually being superseded by the new Financial Reporting Standards.

UK accounting standards

Title			*Issue date*
		Foreword to accounting standards	Jun 93
FRS 1	#	Cash flow statements (revised Oct 96)	Sep 91
FRS 2		Accounting for subsidiary undertakings	July 92
FRS 3	#	Reporting financial performance	Oct 92
FRS 4	#	Capital instruments	Dec 93
FRS 5	#	Reporting the substance of transactions	Apr 94
FRS 6		Acquisitions and mergers	Sep 94
FRS 7		Fair values in acquisition accounting	Sep 94
FRS 8	#	Related party disclosures	Oct 95
FRS 9		Associates and joint ventures	Nov 97
FRS 10	#	Goodwill and intangible assets	Dec 98
FRS 11	#	Impairment of fixed assets and goodwill	Jul 98
FRS 12	#	Provisions, contingent liabilities and contingent assets	Sep 98
FRS 13		Derivatives and other financial instruments: disclosures	Sep 98
FRS 14	#	Earnings per share	Oct 98
FRS 15	#	Tangible fixed assets	Feb 99
FRS 16	#	Current tax	Dec 99
FRS 17		Retirement benefits	Nov 00
FRS 18	#	Accounting policies	Dec 00
FRS 19	#	Deferred tax	Dec 00
FRSSE		Financial Reporting Standard for Smaller Entities	Nov 97
SSAP 4	#	Accounting for government grants	Jul 90
SSAP 5		Accounting for value added tax	Apr 74
SSAP 9	#	Stocks and long-term contracts	Sep 88
SSAP 13	#	Accounting for research and development	Jan 89
SSAP 17	#	Accounting for post balance sheet events	Aug 80
SSAP 19	#	Accounting for investment properties	Nov 81
SSAP 20		Foreign currency translation	Apr 83
SSAP 21	#	Accounting for leases and hire purchase contracts	Aug 84
SSAP 25	#	Segmental reporting	Jun 90

On the Paper 6 syllabus (ie the rest are *not* on the syllabus).

Exam focus point

You are not expected to know anything about exposure drafts or discussion papers from the ASB. You should, however, be familiar with the ASB document on the *Operating and Financial Review* (see Chapter 12) and, of course, the *Statement of Principles*.

In the case of newer accounting standards, you may be asked to discuss why such a standard was needed and how the standard was developed. You *must* therefore follow current developments in the field to be able to understand the impact of standards – it is not sufficient to learn their content.

Think not only about what is going on in the UK but how global issues and problems might affect UK standards and how they might be dealt with in the UK framework.

Question 3

In between now and your examination, make sure you set aside time *every* week or month to read *Management Accounting* and either the *Financial Times, The Economist* or any other equivalent publication. Look for news about the actions of the Accounting Standards Board and the other bodies we have discussed in this chapter and read about the accounts of individual companies as they are discussed in the press.

Chapter roundup

- At this stage in your studies, you should be confident in your knowledge of:
  - Double entry bookkeeping
  - Basic accounting definitions
  - A simple balance sheet
  - A simple profit and loss account
- If you still feel a little rusty, go back to your Foundation study material (which you should still have!) and practise a few questions.
- This is a very important chapter. You must understand all aspects of the *regulatory environment* and the arguments behind current thinking.
- You should be able to discuss the **role** and **impact** of the following bodies.
  - Accounting Standards Board
  - Financial Reporting Council
  - Review Panel
  - Urgent Issues Task Force
  - European Union
  - The Stock Exchange
  - Company Law
  - International Accounting Standards Committee (now defunct)
  - International Accounting Standards Board
  - Accounting Standards Committee (now defunct)
- While this text gives you a thorough explanation of the function of each of these bodies, you will find the material much easier to remember if you keep **up to date** with developments in the accountancy or financial press; these bodies and their actions are discussed constantly. You should also log on regularly onto their website to keep track of current developments.
- The ASB's *Statement of Principles,* provides the backbone of the conceptual framework in the UK.
- *Key elements* in the statement are as follows.
  - Financial statements should give financial information useful for assessing stewardship of management and for making economic decisions.
  - Financial information should be relevant, reliable, comparable and understandable.
  - The *Statement* is **not** an accounting standard.
  - The balance sheet and P&L are **equally important**.
  - Current cost account is **not** on the agenda.
  - It will affect accounting practice by **influencing** the standard setting process.
- You must develop an excellent understanding and knowledge of the *Statement of Principles,* because it is likely to appear on your paper in many guises though direct and indirect questions.

Quick quiz

1 The UK regulatory framework is derived from:

- ....
- .... and other related pronouncements
- .... (and the influence of other national standard setting bodies)
- The requirements of the ....

2 Outline the role of the Review Panel.

3 One objective of the IASB is to promote the preparation of financial statements using the Euro.

True ☐

False ☐

4 A conceptual framework is:

A A theoretical expression of accounting standards
B A list of key terms used by the ASB
C A statement of theoretical principles which form the frame of reference for financial reporting
D The proforma financial statements

5 Which of the following are chapters in the *Statement of Principles*?

A Subsidiaries, associates and joint ventures
B Profit measurement in financial statements
C The objective of financial statements
D Accounting for interest in other entities
E Recognition in financial statements
F Presentation of financial information
G Substance of transactions in financial statements
H The qualitative characteristics of financial information
I The quantitative characteristics of financial information
J Measurement in financial statements
K The reporting entity
L The elements of financial statements.

6 Name **five** of the **six** user groups identified in the *Statement of Principles*.

7 A **gain** as defined by the *Statement of Principles* is an increase in the net assets of the entity.

True ☐

False ☐

8 Financial statements need to be as ...., ... and .... as possible while retaining their .... and ....

9 Describe the process involved in developing Financial Reporting Standards.

10 Can financial statements not follow an accounting standard?

Answers to quick quiz

1 See paragraph 1.4.

2 Your answer should centre on **material departures.** (see paras 1.40 – 1.45)

3 False. (1.49)

4 C (2.1)

5 C, D, E, F, H, J, K and L. (2.4)

6 See paragraph 2.5(b)

7 False. (2.8)

8 See para 2.15.

9 The ASB produce Discussion Papers, then FREDs and finally FRSs. (1.28)

10 Yes. To show a true and fair view. (Key terms (c) on pg 10.)

Now try the question below from the Exam Question Bank

Number	Level	Marks	Time
1	Introductory	n/a	30 mins

Part B
Accounting statements

Chapter 2

COMPANIES ACT REQUIREMENTS AND THE FORMAT OF ACCOUNTS

	Topic list	Syllabus reference	Ability required
1	**FRS 18 *Accounting policies***	**(ii)**	**Comprehension**
2	**True and fair view**	**(ii)**	**Comprehension**
3	**Published accounts**	**(ii)**	**Application**
4	**The format of the accounts**	**(ii)**	**Application**
5	**Notes to the accounts**	**(ii)**	**Application**
6	**The directors' report**	**(ii)**	**Comprehension**
7	**Other items in the annual report**	**(ii)**	**Comprehension**

Introduction

This chapter may look daunting. It lays out the Companies Act formats for the balance sheet and profit and loss account and the disclosures required in the notes to the accounts. These are fundamental to the study of financial accounting.

Published accounts questions require knowledge of Companies Act formats and disclosure requirements. Do **not** attempt to learn these formats and requirements by rote. Become familiar with this material by practising on as many practical questions as you can. Refer to actual examples of annual reports of limited companies to appreciate how the accounts are laid out.

This chapter is predominantly concerned with Companies Act requirements, but you should refer back to this chapter when you have finished Chapter 3, because of the way **FRS 3** has affected the format of published accounts and the notes required.

We will mention the Companies Act requirements for each of the individual items mentioned in the rest of the chapters in this part of the Study Text. You should refer back to this chapter frequently to remind yourself of the position of each item in the accounts.

An Appendix to this Study Text lays out guidance for the preparation of 'published accounts' questions, but you should only refer to this at the end of Part C.

Learning outcomes covered in this chapter

- **Explain** the regulatory requirements
- **Prepare** financial statements in a form suitable for publication with appropriate notes

Syllabus content covered in this chapter

- Preparation of the accounts of non-group limited companies; the regulatory requirements for published accounts (Companies Act 1985 and FRS 18).

1 FRS 18 ACCOUNTING POLICIES

1.1 The following is a brief summary of SSAP 2 *Disclosures of Accounting policies*, from your earlier studies to help you position the new FRS 18.

Knowledge brought forward from earlier studies

SSAP 2 Disclosure of accounting policies

SSAP 2 defines three important terms.

- **Fundamental accounting concepts** are the broad basic assumptions which underlie the periodic financial accounts of business enterprises.
- **Accounting bases** are the methods developed for applying fundamental accounting concepts to financial transactions and items, for the purpose of financial accounts; and in particular:
  - For determining the accounting periods in which revenue and costs should be recognised in the P & L a/c.
  - For determining the amounts at which material items should be stated in the B/S.
- **Accounting policies:** a business entity's accounting policies are simply the accounting bases which they have chosen to follow in a situation where there is a choice of accounting bases: eg depreciation of fixed assets.

Fundamental concepts

SSAP 2 dealt with the four fundamental concepts.

- The '**going concern**' **concept:** the enterprise will continue in operational existence for the foreseeable future.
- The '**accruals**' **concept:** revenue and costs are accrued (that is, recognised as they are earned or incurred, not as money is received or paid).
- The '**consistency**' **concept:** there is consistency of accounting treatment of like items within each accounting period and from one period to the next.
- The **concept of** '**prudence**': revenue and profits are not anticipated, but are recognised by inclusion in the P&L a/c only when realised in the form either of cash or of assets, the ultimate cash realisation of which can be assessed with reasonable certainty

1.2 CA 1985 and SSAP 2 share the following requirements.

(a) **Accounting policies should be applied consistently** from one financial year to the next.

(b) If accounts are prepared on the basis of assumptions which differ in material respects from any of the generally accepted fundamental accounting concepts (principles) the details, **reasons for and the effect of, the departure from the fundamental concepts must be given in a note to the accounts.**

(c) The **accounting policies** adopted by a company in determining the (material) amounts to be included in the balance sheet and in determining the profit or loss for the year **must be stated by a note to the accounts.**

Exam focus point

For examination purposes, it is useful to give the accounting policy note as the first note to the accounts, making sure that the explanations are clear, fair and as brief as possible.

FRS 18 Accounting policies

Exam focus point

Some aspects of FRS 18 may look like the old SSAP 2 but you need to understand the differences, so that when you use the terminology in your answers it reflects the new flavours of FRS 18 rather than serving up the old SSAP 2 terminology and interpretation we have become accustomed to in the past. FRS 18 is an important standard as it impacts extensively on financial reporting work.
The *Student Accountant* of 17 October 2001 includes an excellent article on FRS 18 written by Mr Paul Robins. The section below draws on his work.

1.3 FRS 18 *Accounting policies* replaces SSAP 2 *Disclosure of accounting policies.* It builds on the concepts outlined in SSAP 2 (issued almost 30 years ago) and attempts to align them with the ASB *Statement of Principles*.

Desirable features

1.4 The most obvious change is the **relegation** of two fundamental accounting concepts

- **Prudence**
- **Consistency**

These concepts are now **desirable features** of financial statements.

Pervasive concepts

1.5 The **bedrocks** of accounting are

- **Accruals basis of accounting**
- **Going concern assumption**

1.6 FRS 18 places great **importance** upon these concepts. Although these are on the face of it, similar to the previously matching and going concern concepts, there are subtle but important differences.

Accruals basis

1.7 Within FRS 18, the accruals basis goes to the heart of the definition of assets and liabilities, and plays an important role in the way these items are recognised.

Basic requirement

The accruals basis of accounting requires the **non-cash impact** of transactions to be reflected in the financial statements for the **period in which they occur**, and not, for example, in the period any cash involved is received or paid.

1.8 From the above, it can be seen that FRS 18 adopts a slightly different approach to SSAP 2 on the accruals concept. Together with the definitions of assets and liabilities set out in FRS 5, *Reporting the Substance of Transactions*, FRS 18 in effect provides a discipline within which the old SSAP 2 matching process can operate.

> **KEY TERMS**
>
> - **Asset**: right to **future economic benefits** controlled by an entity as result of past events.
> - **Liability**: entity's **obligation** to **transfer economic benefits** as result of past events.

1.9 FRS 18, like CA 1985, does not refer to matching.

1.10 EXAMPLE

How would you assess whether expenditure such as unexpired advertising or unused stationery should be carried forward to the next year?

1.11 SOLUTION

Under the old SSAP 2 regime, the decision on whether to carry expenditure forward into next year would involve the matching concept and whether there is a reasonable expectation of future revenue.

Under the new FRS 18 regime, the **decision to carry forward** depends on whether the item being considered meets the **definition of an asset**.

FRS 18 effectively updates SSAP 2 within the ambit of the **Statement of Principles** and FRS 5.

Realisation

1.12 The article written by Mr Paul Robins, in the *Student Accountant* of October 2001 suggests that the concept of accruals is also closely related to the concept of **realisation**. CA 1985 only allows realised profits to be recognised in the **profit and loss account**. However, CA 1985 does not adequately define the expression 'realised'. Neither does FRS 18 define 'realised'. What FRS 18 does do is to link realisation with the **creation of new assets and liabilities** and hence with the **concept of accruals**.

Going concern assumption

Criteria

1.13 FRS 18 requires financial statements to be prepared on a going concern basis, except where:

(a) An entity is being liquidated and has ceased trading

(b) The directors have no realistic alternative but to cease trading or liquidate the business.

In these circumstances, the **directors have an option** to prepare its financial statements on a **basis other than that of a going concern**. Remember, where the criteria are met, the **decision is discretionary** rather than mandatory, to prepare the financial statements on a non-going concern basis.

Disclosures

1.14 The following information should be disclosed in the financial statements in relation to the going concern assessment required by FRS 18.

(a) Any material uncertainties, of which the directors are aware in making their assessment, related to events or conditions that may cast significant doubt upon the entity's ability to continue as a going concern.

(b) Where the foreseeable future considered by the directors has been limited to a period of less than one year from the date of approval of the financial statements, that fact.

(c) When the financial statements are not prepared on a going concern basis, that fact, together with the basis on which the financial statements are prepared and the reason why the entity is not regarded as a going concern.

Statement of Principles

1.15 FRS 18 is designed to sit alongside the *Statement of Principles* framework. This helps explain the downplaying of the previously important prudence and consistency concepts.

1.16 The preparers of financial statements must now consider the following accounting policy objectives.

- Relevance
- Reliability
- Comparability
- Understandability

Exam focus point

The May 2003 exam required candidates to use FRS 18 to demonstrate the use of the *Statement of Principles* in developing financial reporting standards.

Prudence and neutrality

1.17 In terms of FRS 18, **prudence** relates to the **uncertainty** that may be associated with the **recognition** and **measurement** of **assets** and **liabilities**.

1.18 FRS 18 suggest different levels of confirmatory evidence regarding the recognition of assets and liabilities, where uncertainty exists. In such circumstances, the existence of an **asset or gain** requires **stronger confirmatory evidence** than that required to acknowledge the existence of a liability or loss.

1.19 FRS 18 emphasises that prudence may only be called upon to justify setting up a provision if uncertainty exists. **Prudence** should **not** be **invoked** to **justify setting up hidden reserves, excessive provisions** or **understating assets**. Prudence should not be seen as a tool for smoothing profits in financial statements. (Avoid using the out-of-date notion that where there are alternative treatments, prudence dictates that the most cautious or conservative alternative should be selected.)

1.20 FRS 18 emphasises that **if financial statements are not neutral they cannot be reliable.** Tension often exists between neutrality and prudence. This should be reconciled by finding a balance that ensures that the deliberate and systematic understatement of assets and gains, and overstatement of liabilities and losses, does not occur.

1.21 Several recent FRSs, especially FRS 12, have adopted a more '**even-handed**' approach to the challenge of **measuring** and **recognising** income, expenses, assets and liabilities in financial statements.

Comparability

1.22 FRS 18 suggest that this is achieved through:

(a) Consistency
(b) Disclosure

Hence, consistency, **no longer a fundamental accounting concept it its own right**, is subsumed under the objective of comparability. Under the old SSAP 2 regime, **consistency implied** a *status quo* approach to financial reporting.

1.23 In practice, **comparability** will often be achieved through **consistency**. However, there may be circumstances where a change in the method of presenting financial information increases the usefulness of the financial report for users.

1.24 The relationship between pervasive concepts, desirable features and accounting policy objectives may be summarised briefly in the following diagram.

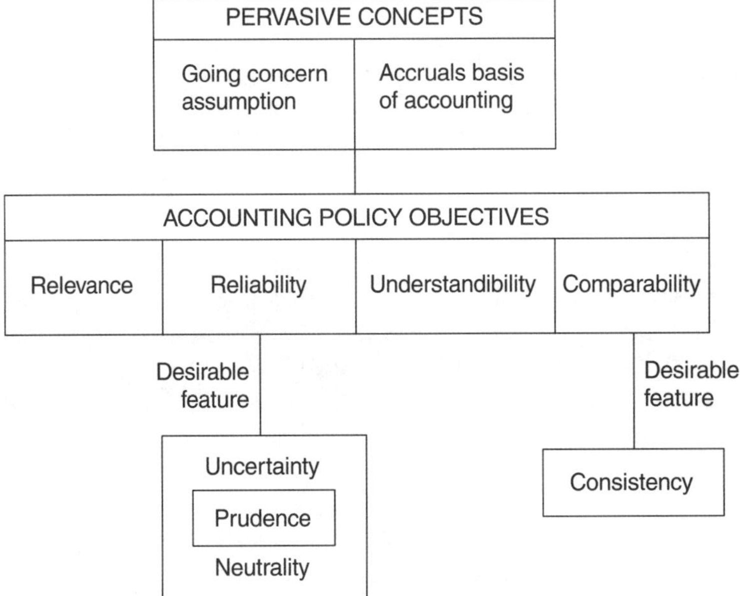

Accounting policies

> **Exam focus point**
> The November 2002 exam asked candidates to identify the main considerations used in assessing whether an accounting policy is acceptable.

Relevance

1.25 FRS 18 specifies key criteria for assessing the relevance of financial information.

- Helpful in **making economic decisions.**
- Useful for **assessing** the **stewardship** of management.
- Is provided in **good time** for the above.
- Possesses either **predictive** or **confirmatory value**, or both.

Reliability

1.26 FRS 18 explains that financial information is reliable for a variety of reasons.

- It **faithfully represents** what it is supposed to.
- It **represents** the **substance of transactions** or events that have occurred.
- It is **neutral** ie free from **deliberate** or **systematic** bias.
- It is **free from material error**.
- Where there is **uncertainty**, prudence has been applied.

Exam focus point

Relevance and reliability where tested in November 2001, November 2002 and May 2003. Sensibly you must get a good grip of them.

Balancing relevance and reliability

1.27 There may be situations where there is tension between relevance and reliability. These may be resolved by applying a two step approach.

(a) Identify the various **reliable alternative treatments**.
(b) Select the **most relevant treatment** from the above.

1.28 FRS 18 prescribes the **regular consideration of the entity's accounting policies**. The **best** accounting **policy** should be adopted at **all times.** This is the major reason for downplaying consistency (and to a lesser extent prudence). An entity **cannot retain** an **accounting policy** merely **because** it was **used last** year **or** because it **gives a prudent view**.

1.29 However, the entity should consider how a **change** in accounting policy may affect **comparability**. Essentially a **balance** must be struck between selecting the **most appropriate policies** and presenting **coherent and useful** financial statements. The **overriding guidance** is that the financial statements should give a **true and fair view** of the entity's business. Chopping and changing accounting policies year on year is likely to jeopardise the true and fair view but so too is retaining accounting policies which do not present the **most useful information** to the **users** of the accounts.

1.30 FRS 18 suggests that the need to balance the cost of providing information should be balanced with the likely benefit of such information to the users of the entity's financial statements. However, FRS 18 also cautions against the use of cost and benefit considerations to justify the adoption of an accounting policy that is inconsistent with the requirements of accounting standards, UITF Abstracts and CA 1985.

Disclosure

1.31 FRS 18 requires the disclosure of

- A **description of each accounting policy** which is material to the entity's financial statements
- A description of any significant estimation technique
- **Changes** to accounting policies
- The effects of any material change to an estimation technique

Estimation techniques

1.32 An estimation technique is material **only where a large range** of monetary values may be arrived at. The entity should vary the assumptions it uses, to assess how sensitive monetary values are under that technique. In most cases the range of values will be relatively narrow (consider the useful life of motor vehicles for example).

Changes to accounting policies

1.33 The disclosure of new accounting policies also requires

- An explanation of the **reason for change**
- The **effects of a prior period adjustment** on the previous years results (in accordance with FRS 3)
- The **effects of the change in policy** on the previous year's results

If it is **not possible** to disclose the last two points then the **reason** for this should be disclosed instead.

Exam focus point

You need to be confident about the application of FRS 18. Make sure that you can **identify** a change in accounting policy and the **reason** that it is a change in accounting policy as opposed to a change in estimation technique. You will have to **discuss** the decision you have reached **and justify** your conclusions.

1.34 The most complex aspect to FRS 18 is the **application of the terms and definitions** within the standard. SSAP 2 defined accounting policies and accounting bases. There was some confusion as to what an accounting base was. FRS 18 has dispensed with the term accounting base. However, the term which seems to replace it**, estimation technique**, may also prove difficult to apply in practice.

1.35 It is essential that you **learn the following definitions**. However, once you have read them you should **apply them** to the questions later in this section to make sure that you understand them.

KEY TERM

Accounting policies. The principles, conventions, rules and practices applied by an entity that prescribe how transactions and other events are to be reflected in its financial statements.

1.36 Accounting policies are **not** estimation techniques.

1.37 An accounting policy includes the

- Recognition
- Presentation
- And measurement basis

Of assets, liabilities, gains, losses and changes to shareholders funds.

KEY TERM

Estimation technique. The methods used by an entity to establish the estimated monetary amounts associated with the measurement bases selected for assets, liabilities, gains, losses and changes to shareholder's funds.

1.38 Estimation techniques are used to **implement the measurement basis** of an accounting policy. The accounting policy specifies the measurement basis and the estimation technique is used when there is an uncertainty over this amount.

1.39 The method of **depreciation is an estimation technique**. The accounting policy is to spread the cost of the asset over its useful economic life. Depreciation is the measurement basis. The estimation technique would be, say, straight line depreciation as opposed to reducing balance.

1.40 A change of estimation technique should **not** be accounted for as a prior period adjustment unless the following apply.

- It is the correction of a fundamental error
- The Companies Act, an accounting standard or a UITF Abstract **requires the change to be accounted** for as a prior period adjustment.

Application of FRS 18

1.41 FRS 18 gives a number of examples of its application in an appendix to the standard. When a change is required to an accounting policy then **three criteria** must be **considered** to ensure that the change is affecting the accounting policy and not an estimation technique.

1 Recognition
2 Presentation
3 Measurement basis

1.42 If **any one of the criteria apply** then a change has been made to the accounting policy. If they do **not** apply then a change to an estimation technique has taken place.

1.43 You should note that where an **accounting standard gives a choice** of treatments (i.e. SSAP 9 states that stock can be recognised on a FIFO or weighted average cost basis) then adopting the alternative treatment is a **change of accounting policy.** Also note that FRS 15 states that a **change in depreciation method is not** a change in accounting policy.

Example		Recognition	Change to Presentation	Measurement basis?	Change of Accounting Policy
1	Changing from capitalisation of finance costs associated with the construction of fixed assets to charging them through the profit and loss	Yes	Yes	No	Yes
2	A reassessment of an entity's cost centres means that all three will have production overheads allocated to them instead of just two	No	No	No	No
3	Overheads are reclassified from distribution to cost of sales	No	Yes	No	Yes
4	Change from straight-line depreciation to machine hours	No	No	No	No
5	Reallocate depreciation from administration to cost of sales	No	Yes	No	Yes
6	A provision is revised upwards and the estimates of future cash flows are now discounted in accordance with FRS 12. They were not discounted previously as the amounts involved were not material	No	No	No	No
7	Deferred tax is now reported on a discounted basis. It was previously undiscounted	No	No	Yes	Yes
8	A foreign subsidiary's profit and loss account is now to be translated at the closing rate. It was previously translated at the average rate	No	No	Yes	Yes
9	Fungible stocks are to be measured on the weighted average cost basis instead of the previously used FIFO basis	No	No	Yes	Yes

Fungible assets

KEY TERM

Fungible assets are similar assets which are grouped together as there is no reason to view them separately in economic terms. Shares and items of stock are examples of fungible assets.

1.44 The last example (example 9) is based on a **change to fungible assets**. The standard states that when fungible assets are considered in **aggregate** a change from weighted average cost to FIFO (or vice versa), is a change to the **measurement base**. The standard also recommends that fungible assets should **always be considered in aggregate** in order to enhance **comparability** of financial statements.

Question 1

The board of Nice Produx plc decide to change the depreciation method they use on their plant and machinery from 30% reducing balance to 20% straight line to better reflect the way the assets are used within the business. Is this a change of accounting policy ?

Answer

No. This is a change to the **estimation technique**. The same measurement basis is used. The historic cost is allocated over the asset's estimated useful life.

Question 2

The board of Nice Produx plc also decide to change their stock valuation. They replace their FIFO valuation method for an AVCO method to better reflect the way that stock is used within the business. Is this a change in accounting policy?

Answer

Yes. This is a change to the **measurement basis**. The paragraphs on fungible assets discuss this further.

Question 3

The board of Nice Produx plc decide in the following year that the development costs the business incurs should not be capitalised and presented on the balance sheet. Instead they agree that all development expenditure should be expended in the profit and loss account. Is this an accounting policy change?

Answer

Yes. The choice to capitalise or not is given in SSAP 13. The criteria affected by this decision are **recognition and presentation.**

Question 4

Nice Produx plc's board are also considering reallocating the depreciation charges made on its large fleet of company cars to administration expenses, they were previously shown in cost of sales. Is this an accounting policy change?

Answer

Yes. Nice Produx would be changing the way they **presented** the depreciation figure.

Summary

1.45 FRS 18 requires an entity to conduct a review on an annual basis in order to ensure that it is using the most appropriate accounting policies.

1.46 The three criteria:

- Recognition
- Presentation
- Measurement basis

are considered in order to establish whether there has been a change of accounting policy or merely a change of estimation technique.

1.47 The accounting policy objectives are:

- Reliability
- Relevance
- Comparability
- Understandability

1.48 The above must be fulfilled by the accounting policies adopted. This requirement helps prevent entities from changing accounting policies too often.

1.49 FRS 18 introduces subtle changes into the meaning of accruals and going concern. Whereas matching was driven by the need to ensure completeness in the profit and loss account, the accruals basis approaches recognition from the need to ensure the validity of assets and liabilities, ie more of a balance sheet driven approach.

1.50 Prudence and consistency have a lesser role in the accounting policy framework. There may be tension between prudence and neutrality. Prudence should not be used as an excuse for setting up excessive provisions or understating assets. The use of prudence must be linked to uncertainty.

1.51 FRS 18 provides a bridge between the standards setting process and the *Statement of Principles*.

2 TRUE AND FAIR VIEW

Interpretation of true and fair

2.1 Section 226 of CA 1985 states that:

> 'the balance sheet shall give a true and fair view of the state of affairs of the company as at the end of the financial year, and the profit and loss account shall give a true and fair view of the profit or loss of the company for the financial year.'

The balance sheet and profit and loss account should also comply with the requirements of the Fourth Schedule (s 226(3) CA 1985).

KEY TERM

'**True and fair view**' has no set definition. Broadly speaking it means 'reasonably accurate and not misleading'.

2.2 The term 'true and fair view' is **not defined** in the **Companies Acts**, nor in **SSAPs** or **FRSs**, which also claim to be authoritative statements on what is a true and fair view. Moreover, the **courts** have **never tried to define it**.

2.3 In view of the ASB's policy of **reviewing** and, if necessary, **altering** or **replacing existing accounting standards**, a question **arises** as to whether the concept defined by '**true and fair view**' is constant or is **evolving** over a period of years.

2.4 The ASC sought Counsel's opinion on this question. Very briefly, Counsel's opinion included various key points.

- **Accuracy** and **completeness** are two key ingredients that contribute to a true and fair view.
- There might **not** be **consensus** amongst reasonable businessman and accountants as to the degree of accuracy and completeness required.
- The concept of **true and fair is dynamic**.
- **Judges** will look for **guidance** to the **ordinary practices** of **professional accountants.**

2.5 A later opinion obtained by the ASB, confirms the above views. This opinion also provides further clues on how to interpret the expression true and fair. The opinion suggests that the courts are **unlikely** to **look for synonyms** for the words '**true**' and '**fair**'. **Instead,** the courts will take an approach of trying to **apply** the **concepts implied** by the expression '**true and fair**'.

2.6 The **Statement of Principles** echos the above, but carefully avoids providing a formal definition of **true and fair.**

- The true and fair view is a **dynamic concept** and evolves in **response** to changes in **accounting** and **business practice.**
- **Relevance** and **reliability** are **prime indicators** of the **quality** of **financial information.**

True and fair override

IMPORTANT!

S 226 (5) CA 1985 makes an important statement about the need to give a true and fair view. It states that if, in **special circumstances**, compliance with any of the Act's provisions would be inconsistent with the requirement to give a true and fair view, then the directors should depart from that provision to the extent necessary to give a true and fair view. This is the **true and fair override.**

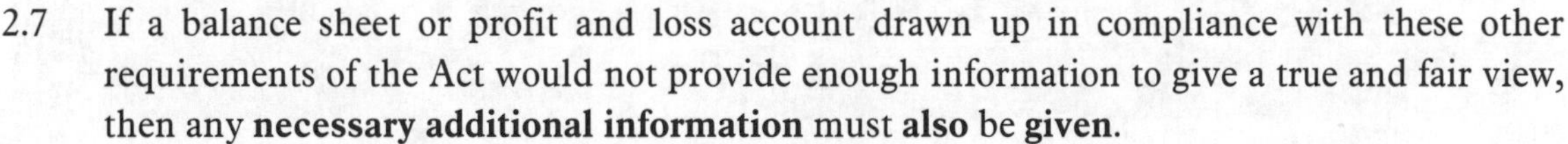

2.7 If a balance sheet or profit and loss account drawn up in compliance with these other requirements of the Act would not provide enough information to give a true and fair view, then any **necessary additional information** must **also** be **given.**

2.8 The overriding priority to give a true and fair view **has in the past been treated as an important 'loophole' in the law,** and is the subject of debate within the accounting profession. For example, the CA 1985 permits only realised profits to be recognised in the profit and loss account, whereas SSAP 9 requires unrealised profits on long-term contracts to be credited to profit and loss. This is justified by **invoking** the **overriding requirement** to show a true and fair view.

2.9 If companies do depart from the other requirements of the Act in order to give a true and fair view, they **must explain the particulars of and reasons for the departure, and its effects on the accounts,** in a note to the accounts. As already stated, the **Fourth Schedule** also requires a statement in a **note to the accounts** that the accounts have been prepared in accordance with **applicable accounting standards** and **particulars of any material departure from** those **standards and the reasons** (s 36A Sch 4).

True and fair override disclosures

2.10 As we saw above, where the **directors depart** from provisions of CA 1985 to the extent **necessary** to **give a true and fair view**, the Act required that '**particulars** of any such departure, the **reasons** for it and its **effect** shall be given in a note to the accounts'. **FRS 18** ***Accounting Policies*** seeks to clarify the meaning of that sentence. Any **material departure** from the Companies Act, an accounting standard or a UITF abstract should lead to the following information being disclosed. This is also clarified by UITF Abstract 7.

(a) **A statement that there has been a departure** from the requirements of companies legislation, an accounting standard or a UITF abstract, and that the departure is **necessary to give a true and fair view.**

(b) **A description of the treatment normally required** and also a description of the **treatment actually used.**

(c) An explanation of why the **prescribed treatment would not give a true and fair view.**

(d) **Its effect:** a description of how the position shown in the accounts is different as a result of the departure, with quantification if possible, or an explanation of the circumstances.

2.11 The disclosures required should either be **included in or cross referenced** to the note required about **compliance with accounting standards**, particulars of any material departure from those standards and the reasons for it (Paragraph 36A Sch 4).

2.12 If the departure occurs in **subsequent accounting periods**, the above disclosures should be made in subsequent financial statements including the **corresponding amounts** for previous years. If the departure only affects the corresponding amounts then the disclosure should relate to the corresponding amounts.

Exam focus point

The November 2001 paper asked for a description of the advantages and disadvantages of offering companies the facility to use the true and fair override.

The November 2002 exam asked candidates to explain the true and fair override and the consequential disclosure requirements.

3 PUBLISHED ACCOUNTS

3.1 **Statutory accounts** are part of the price to be paid for the benefits of **limited liability. Limited companies must produce such accounts annually and they must appoint an independent person to audit and report on them.** Once prepared, a copy of the accounts **must be sent to the Registrar of Companies**, who maintains a separate file for every company. The Registrar's files may be inspected for a nominal fee by any member of the public. This is why the statutory accounts are often referred to as **published accounts**.

3.2 It is the responsibility of the company's directors to produce accounts which show a **true and fair view** of the company's results for the period and its financial position at the end of the period (see Section 3 of this chapter). The board evidence their approval of the accounts by the signature of one director on the balance sheet. Once this has been done, and the auditors have completed their report, the accounts are laid before the members of the company in general meeting. When the members have adopted the accounts they are sent to the Registrar for filing.

3.3 The documents which must be included by law in the accounts laid before a general meeting of the members are:

(a) A **profit and loss account** (or an income and expenditure account in the case of a non-trading company).

(b) A **balance sheet** as at the date to which the profit and loss account is made up.

(c) A **directors' report**.

(d) An **auditors' report** addressed to the members (not to the directors) of the company.

3.4 In addition, **FRS 1** requires a **cash flow** statement to be given. This statement is discussed in Chapter 4. FRS 3 has also introduced a new statement and notes, covered in Chapter 3. Here we will look at the **legally required** accounting statements, the profit and loss account and balance sheet.

Exam Focus Point

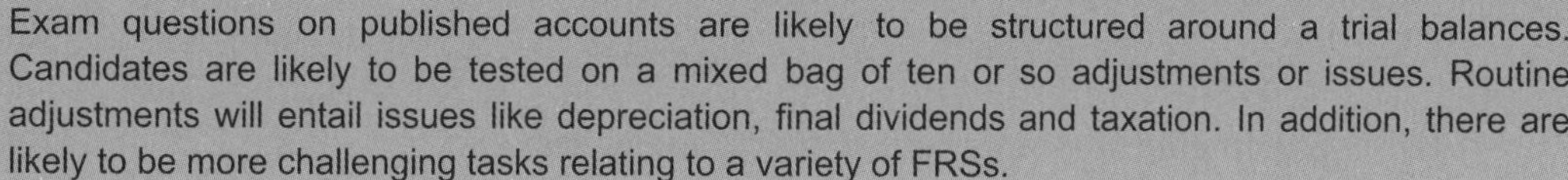

Exam questions on published accounts are likely to be structured around a trial balances. Candidates are likely to be tested on a mixed bag of ten or so adjustments or issues. Routine adjustments will entail issues like depreciation, final dividends and taxation. In addition, there are likely to be more challenging tasks relating to a variety of FRSs.

The accounting reference period

3.5 The Companies Act 1985 contains the following rules (ss 223 to 225).

(a) Accounts must be prepared for an **accounting reference period** (ARP), known as the '**financial year**' of the company (whether it is a calendar year or not).

(b) The profit and loss account should cover the **ARP** or a period ending not more than **seven days before or after the accounting reference date.** Subsequent accounts should cover the period beginning on the day following the last day covered by the previous profit and loss account, and ending as specified above.

(c) A company can decide its accounting reference period by giving **notice to the Registrar** of the date on which the accounting period will end each year. This date will be the **accounting reference date**. S 225 makes provisions for the alteration of the accounting reference date.

The laying and delivery of accounts

3.6 S 241 CA 1985 specifies that the directors shall lay before the company in general meeting and also deliver to the Registrar, in respect of each accounting reference period, a copy of every document comprising the accounts for that period. However, the CA 1989 has amended the CA 1985 to allow the members of private companies to elect unanimously to dispense with general meetings. This does **not**, however, exempt the company from providing accounts to members.

3.7 Unlimited companies (with some exceptions) are exempt from the duty to deliver copies of their accounts to the Registrar.

3.8 The period allowed for laying and delivering accounts varies (s 244).

(a) For **private** companies, it is ten months after the end of the accounting reference period.

(b) For **other** (public etc) companies, it is seven months.

Accounting records

3.9 S 221 requires that every company's **accounting records** must:

(a) Be **sufficient** to show and explain the company's transactions.

(b) Disclose with **reasonable accuracy** at any time the financial position of the company at that time.

(c) Enable the directors to ensure that any profit and loss account or balance sheet gives a **true and fair view** of the company's financial position.

3.10 S 221 also specifies that accounting records should contain:

(a) Day-to-day entries for money received and paid, with an explanation of why the **receipts and payments occurred** (ie the nature of the transactions).

(b) A record of the company's **assets and liabilities.**

(c) Where the company deals in goods.

(i) Statements of **stocks** held at the financial year end.

(ii) Statements of stocktakings on which the figures in (c)(i) are based.

(iii) With the exception of goods sold on retail, statements of all goods bought and sold identifying for each item the suppliers or customers.

3.11 S 222 specifies that the accounting records are to be kept at the registered office of the company or at such other place as the directors think fit, and they should be open to inspection at all times by **officers** of the company.

3.12 Also in s 222 is a requirement for companies to preserve their accounting records:

(a) Private companies, for 3 years.
(b) Other companies, for 6 years.

The classification of companies

3.13 A company is considered to be **private** unless it is registered as a **public** company. A major advantage for a public company is that it can raise new funds from the general public by issuing shares or loan stock; s 81 CA 1985 prohibits a private company from offering shares or debentures to the public.

Related party transactions

3.14 It is generally agreed that separate disclosure of transactions between a company and **related parties** may be needed if the user of the accounts is to be able to gain a full understanding of the results for the accounting period. FRS 8 was developed on this basis.

3.15 Two parties are considered to be **related** when either:

(a) One party is able to **exercise control** or **significant influence** over the other party.

(b) Both parties are subject to **common control** or **significant influence** from the same source.

For example, companies within the same group will be related parties, or a company and its directors will be related parties (see Chapter 10).

3.16 The CA 1985 concentrates on requiring disclosure of related party transactions between a company and its directors (or persons 'connected' to directors), including loans and credit transactions.

4 THE FORMAT OF THE ACCOUNTS Pilot paper, 5/01

Exam focus point

In the pilot paper, the compulsory section of the paper included the preparation of accounts plus notes as the first question. The May 2001 exam also required preparation of published accounts in the first question. It is probably safe to assume that this trend will continue. It is therefore vital that you familiarise yourself fully with these formats.

The November 2001, May 2002, November 2002 and May 2003, exams all included questions on published accounts.

The form and content of the balance sheet

4.1 The Companies Act 1985 sets out **two formats** for the **balance sheet**, one **horizontal** and the other **vertical**. Once a company has chosen a format it must adhere to it for subsequent financial years unless, in the opinion of the directors, there are special reasons for a change. Details of any **change** and the **reason** for it must be disclosed by **note to the accounts**.

4.2 Each item on the balance sheet format is referenced by letters and roman and Arabic numbers. These reference labels do not have to be shown in a company's published accounts but are given in the Act for the guidance of companies and are relevant in identifying the:

(a) Extent to which **information** may be **combined** or disclosed by **note** (rather than on the face of the accounts).

(b) **Headings** and **sub-headings** which may be **adapted** or re-arranged to suit the special **nature of the company**.

(c) Items which do not need to be disclosed in modified accounts for small and medium-sized companies.

4.3 The following points should be borne in mind.

(a) Any item preceded by letters or roman numbers **must** be shown on the face of the balance sheet, unless it has a nil value for both the current and the previous year.

(b) Items preceded by arabic numbers **may** be amalgamated:

- If their individual amounts are not material
- If amalgamation facilitates the assessment of the company's state of affairs (but then the individual items must be disclosed by note)

(c) Items preceded by arabic numbers **may** be:

- Adapted (eg title altered)
- Re-arranged (in position)

in any case where the special nature of the company's business requires such an alteration.

(d) Any item required to be shown **may** be shown in greater detail than required by the prescribed format.

(e) A company's balance sheet (or profit and loss account) **may** include an item not otherwise covered by any of the items listed, except that the **following must not be treated as assets in any company's balance sheet:**

(i) Preliminary expenses.
(ii) Expenses of and commission on any issue of shares or debentures.
(iii) Costs of research.

4.4 Schedule 4 includes the following notes about the balance sheet format.

(a) **Concessions, patents, licences, trademarks,** etc (Item B I 2) may only be shown if:

(i) They were acquired at a purchase cost, and do not consist of goodwill
(ii) They are assets created by the company itself

(b) **Goodwill** (Item B I 3) should be included only to the extent that it is purchased goodwill.

(c) **Own shares** (Item B III 7). CA 1985 allows a company to purchase or acquire its own shares.

(d) **Debtors** (Items C II 1 – 6). Any amounts not falling due until after more than one year should be disclosed separately.

(e) **Debenture loans** (Items El and H1). Convertible loans should be shown separately from other debenture loans.

(f) **Payments received (in advance) on account** (Items E3 and H3). These should be shown unless they are accounted for as deductions from the value of stocks (as in the case of progress payments for work in progress on long-term contracts).

The form and content of the profit and loss account

4.5 The Companies Act 1985 sets out **two horizontal** and **two vertical formats** for the profit and loss account. The rules applying to the balance sheet formats described above also apply to the profit and loss account.

4.6 The two different formats are **distinguished** by the **way** in which **expenditure is analysed**. Format 1 analyses costs by type of operation or function, whereas Format 2 analyses costs by items of expense.

4.7 In all the examples given below, you can ignore items marked † as those are to do with group accounts or other complex matters and so are beyond the scope of your syllabus.

PROFORMA BALANCE SHEET (VERTICAL FORMAT)

		£	£	£
A	CALLED UP SHARE CAPITAL NOT PAID*			X
B	FIXED ASSETS			
I	Intangible assets			
1	Development costs	X		
2	Concessions, patents, licences, trade marks and similar rights and assets	X		
3	Goodwill	X		
4	Payments on account	X		
			X	
II	Tangible assets			
1	Land and buildings	X		
2	Plant and machinery	X		
3	Fixtures, fittings, tools and equipment	X		
4	Payments on account and assets in course of construction	X		
			X	
III	Investments			
1	Shares in group undertakings †	X		
2	Loans to group undertakings †	X		
3	Participating interest †	X		
4	Loans to undertakings in which the company has a participating interest †	X		
5	Other investments other than loans	X		
6	Other loans	X		
7	Own shares	X		
			X	
C	CURRENT ASSETS			
I	Stocks			
1	Raw materials	X		
2	Work in progress	X		
3	Finished goods and goods for resale	X		
4	Payments on account	X		
			X	
II	Debtors			
1	Trade debtors	X		
2	Amounts owed by group undertakings †	X		
3	Amounts owed by undertakings in which the company has a participating interest †	X		
4	Other debtors	X		
5	Called up share capital not paid*	X		
6	Prepayments and accrued income**	X		
			X	
III	Investments			
1	Shares in group undertakings †	X		
2	Own shares	X		
3	Other investments	X		
IV	Cash at bank and in hand		X	
			X	

	£	£	£
D PREPAYMENTS AND ACCRUED INCOME**		X	
E CREDITORS: AMOUNTS FALLING DUE WITHIN ONE YEAR			
1 Debenture loans	X		
2 Bank loans and overdrafts	X		
3 Payments received on account	X		
4 Trade creditors	X		
5 Bills of exchange payable	X		
6 Amounts owed to group undertakings †	X		
7 Amounts owed to undertakings in which the company has a participating interest †	X		
8 Other creditors including taxation and social security	X		
9 Accruals and deferred income ***	X		
		(X)	
F NET CURRENT ASSETS (LIABILITIES)			X
G TOTAL ASSETS LESS CURRENT LIABILITIES			X
H CREDITORS: AMOUNTS FALLING DUE AFTER MORE THAN ONE YEAR			
1 Debenture loans	X		
2 Bank loans and overdrafts	X		
3 Payments received on account	X		
4 Trade creditors	X		
5 Bills of exchange payable	X		
6 Amounts owed to group undertakings †	X		
7 Amounts owed to undertakings in which the company has a participating interest †	X		
8 Other creditors including taxation and social security	X		
9 Accruals and deferred income***	X		
		(X)	
I PROVISIONS FOR LIABILITIES AND CHARGES			
1 Pensions and similar obligations †	X		
2 Taxation, including deferred taxation	X		
3 Other provisions	X		
		(X)	
J ACCRUALS AND DEFERRED INCOME ***		(X)	
			(X)
			X
K CAPITAL AND RESERVES			
I Called up share capital			X
II Share premium account			X
III Revaluation reserve			X
IV Other reserves			
1 Capital redemption reserve		X	
2 Reserve for own shares		X	
3 Reserves provided for by the articles of association		X	
4 Other reserves		X	
			X
V Profit and loss account			X
			X

(*), (**), (***). These items may be shown in either of the positions indicated.

4.8 Both vertical formats of the profit and loss account are reproduced below.

PROFORMA PROFIT AND LOSS ACCOUNT: FORMAT 1

		£	£
1	Turnover		X
2	Cost of sales *		(X)
3	Gross profit or loss *		X
4	Distribution costs *	(X)	
5	Administrative expenses *	(X)	
			(X)
			X
6	Other operating income		X
			X
7	Income from shares in group undertakings †	X	
8	Income from shares in undertakings in which the company has a participating interest †	X	
9	Income from other fixed asset investments	X	
10	Other interest receivable and similar income	X	
			X
			X
11	Amounts written off investments	(X)	
12	Interest payable and similar charges	(X)	
			(X)
	Profit or loss on ordinary activities before taxation		X
13	Tax on profit or loss on ordinary activities		(X)
14	Profit or loss on ordinary activities after taxation		X
15	Extraordinary income	X	
16	Extraordinary charges	(X)	
17	Extraordinary profit or loss	X	
18	Tax on extraordinary profit or loss	(X)	
			X
			X
19	Other taxes not shown under the above items		(X)
20	Profit or loss for the financial year		X

* These figures will all include depreciation.

PROFORMA PROFIT AND LOSS ACCOUNT: FORMAT 2

		£	£	£
1	Turnover			X
2	Change in stocks of finished goods and work in progress		(X)	or X
3	Own work capitalised			X
4	Other operating income			X
				X
5	(a) Raw materials and consumables	(X)		
	(b) Other external charges	(X)		
			(X)	
6	Staff costs:			
	(a) wages and salaries	(X)		
	(b) social security costs	(X)		
	(c) other pension costs	(X)		
			(X)	
			(X)	
7	(a) Depreciation and other amounts written off tangible and intangible fixed assets **	(X)		
	(b) Exceptional amounts written off current assets	(X)		
			(X)	
8	Other operating charges		(X)	
				(X)
9	Income from shares in group undertakings †		X	
10	Income from shares in undertakings in which the company has a participating interest †		X	
11	Income from other fixed asset investments		X	
12	Other interest receivable and similar income		X	
				X
				X
13	Amounts written off investments		(X)	
14	Interest payable and similar charges		(X)	
				(X)
	Profit or loss on ordinary activities before taxation			X
15	Tax on profit or loss on ordinary activities			(X)
16	Profit or loss on ordinary activities after taxation			X
17	Extraordinary income		X	
18	Extraordinary charges		(X)	
19	Extraordinary profit or loss		X	
20	Tax on extraordinary profit or loss		(X)	
				X
				X
21	Other taxes not shown under the above items			(X)
22	Profit or loss for the financial year			X

** This figure will be disclosed by way of a note in Format 1.

Note that because the captions have arabic number references, they do not have to be shown on the face of the profit and loss account but may instead be shown in the notes.

Corresponding amounts for the previous financial year

4.9 Corresponding amounts for the previous financial year must be given for every item shown in a company's balance sheet or profit and loss account. Where a **corresponding amount** for the previous year is **not properly comparable** with an amount disclosed for the current year, the **previous year's amount should be adjusted** (and **details** of the adjustment given in a **note** to the **accounts**).

Some items in more detail

4.10 In the balance sheet, item A and item CII5 are 'called up share capital not paid'. This item is more relevant to other countries in the EU than to Britain (remember that the Fourth Directive applies to all EU countries). However, if at the balance sheet date a company has called up some share capital and not all the called up amounts have been paid, these will be a short-term debt (see Chapter 11 on the issue of shares). This would probably be shown (if material) as item CII5. Item A should not be expected in the accounts of British companies.

4.11 Item BIII7 in the balance sheet, investments in 'own shares', refers to shares which have been bought back by the company, but which have not yet been cancelled.

4.12 'Turnover' is defined by the 1985 Act as 'the amounts derived from the provision of goods and services, falling within the company's ordinary activities, after deduction of:

(a) Trade discounts.
(b) Value added tax.
(c) Any other taxes based on the amounts so derived'.

4.13 'Cost of sales' (format 1) is not defined, nor are 'distribution costs', nor are 'administrative expenses'. The division of costs between these three categories is based on accepted practice.

4.14 Format 1, unlike Format 2, does not itemise depreciation and wages costs, but:

- Provisions for depreciation charged in the year
- Wages and salaries, social security costs and other pension costs

must be disclosed separately in notes to the accounts.

4.15 The Act extends the requirements of FRS 3 about extraordinary profits or losses (see later chapters). The extraordinary profit or loss must be shown as the gross amount, with taxation on it separately disclosed. Extraordinary items are now **very** rare.

4.16 The profit and loss account must show profit or loss on ordinary activities before taxation, as well as dividends paid and proposed and transfers to reserves. This means inevitably, that retained profit or loss for the financial year will also be disclosed. There is no requirement, however, to show on the face of the profit and loss account:

	£
Retained profit for the financial year	X
Profit and loss account brought forward	X
Profit and loss account carried forward	X

However, this well-established practice 'ties together' the information in the profit and loss account with the notes to the balance sheet about movements on reserves and so is often used.

4.17 In itemising staff costs, wages and salaries consist of gross amounts (net pay plus deductions) and social security costs comprise employer's National Insurance contributions.

5 NOTES TO THE ACCOUNTS — Pilot paper

5.1 Part III of the Fourth Schedule deals with notes to the balance sheet and profit and loss account. These are sub-divided into:

(a) Disclosure of accounting policies.
(b) Notes to the balance sheet.
(c) Notes to the profit and loss account.

5.2 A note to the accounts must disclose the accounting policies adopted by the company (including the policy used to account for depreciation or the fall in value of assets). This gives statutory backing to the disclosure requirement in SSAP 2. Companies must also now state that all relevant accounting standards have been complied with and if not, what the departures are and the reasons for the departure.

Exam focus point

It is impossible for the Examiner to test every disclosure note in any one exam. Do not waste time producing notes that are irrelevant to the question because of lack of information (eg an analysis of turnover by class of business). This will earn you no marks and will leave the examiner with the impression that you have merely memorised a template and do not understand the question.

5.3 The following example shows a **pro forma** profit and loss account and balance sheet with the required notes covering your syllabus. These notes are expanded in the subsequent chapters on different accounting standards and disclosures.

STANDARD PLC
PROFIT AND LOSS ACCOUNT FOR THE YEAR ENDED
31 DECEMBER 20X5

	Notes	£'000	£'000
Turnover	2		X
Cost of sales			X
Gross profit			X
Distribution costs			X
Administrative expenses			X
Operating profit	3		X
Income from fixed asset investments			X
			X
Interest payable and similar charges	6		X
Profit on ordinary activities before taxation			X
Tax on profit on ordinary activities	7		X
Profit on ordinary activities after taxation			X
Dividend paid and proposed	8	X	
Transfer to general reserve	19	X	
			X
Retained profit for the financial year			X

STANDARD PLC
BALANCE SHEET AS AT 31 DECEMBER 20X5

	Notes	£'000	£'000
Fixed assets			
Intangible assets	9		X
Tangible assets	10		X
Fixed asset investments	11		X
			X
Current assets			
Stocks	12	X	
Debtors	13	X	
Cash at bank and in hand		X	
		X	
Creditors: amounts falling due within one year	14	X	
Net current assets			X
Total assets less current liabilities			X
Creditors: amounts falling due after more than one year	16		X
Accruals and deferred income	17		X
			X

Capital and reserves		
Called up share capital	18	X
Share premium account	19	X
Revaluation reserve	19	X
General reserve	19	X
Profit and loss account	19	X
		X

Approved by the board on ....

.... Director

The notes on pages XX to XX form part of these accounts.

NOTES TO THE ACCOUNTS

1 *Accounting policies*

(a) These accounts have been prepared under the historical cost convention of accounting and in accordance with applicable accounting standards.

(b) Depreciation has been provided on a straight line basis in order to write off the cost of depreciable fixed assets over their estimated useful lives. The rates used are:

Buildings	X%
Plant and machinery	X%
Fixtures and fittings	X%

(c) Stocks have been valued at the lower of cost and net realisable value.

(d) Development expenditure relating to specific projects intended for commercial exploitation is carried forward and amortised over the period expected to benefit commencing with the period in which related sales are first made. Expenditure on pure and applied research is written off as incurred.

Notes

(a) Accounting policies are those followed by the company and used in arriving at the figures shown in the profit and loss accounts and balance sheet.

(b) CA 1985 requires policies in respect of depreciation and foreign currency translation to be included. Others are required by accounting standards insofar as they apply to the company.

2 *Turnover*

Turnover represents amounts derived from the provision of goods and services falling within the company's ordinary activities, after deduction of trade discounts, value added tax and any other tax based on the amounts so derived.

	Turnover	*Profit before tax*
Principal activities	£'000	£'000
Electrical components	X	X
Domestic appliances	X	X
	X	X
Geographical analysis		
UK	X	
America	X	
Europe	X	
	X	

Notes

(a) Directors are to decide on classification and then apply them consistently.

(b) Geographical analysis must be by destination of sale.

(c) If the directors believe this disclosure to be seriously prejudicial to the business the information need not be disclosed.

(d) The profit after tax figures are only required by SSAP 25 (see Chapter 3) for larger companies.

3 *Operating profit*

Operating profit is stated after charging:

	£'000
Depreciation	X
Amortisation	X
Hire of plant and machinery (SSAP 21: see Chapter 9)	X
Auditors' remuneration	X
Exceptional items	X
Directors' emoluments (see note 4)	X
Staff costs (see note 5)	X
Research and development	X

Notes

Separate totals are required to be disclosed for:

- Audit fees and expenses
- Fees paid to auditors for non-audit work

This disclosure is not required for small or medium-sized companies.

Question 5

Amity Ltd receives an invoice in respect of the current year from its auditors made up as follows.

	£
Audit of accounts	10,000
Taxation computation and advice	1,500
Travelling expenses: audit	1,100
Consultancy fees charged by another firm of accountants	1,600
	14,200

What figure should be disclosed as auditors' remuneration in the notes to the profit and loss account?

Answer

	£
Audit of accounts	10,000
Expenses	1,100
Taxation computation and advice	1,500
	12,600

The consultancy fees are not received by the auditors.

4 *Directors' emoluments*

Requirements for the disclosure of directors' remuneration were revised by *The Company Accounts (Disclosure of Directors' Emoluments) Regulations 1997* (SI 1997/570). A distinction is made between listed/AIM companies and unlisted companies.

	£'000
Directors	
Aggregate emoluments	X
Gains made on exercise of share options (listed/AIM company only)	X
Amounts receivable (unlisted company: excludes shares) under long-term incentive schemes	X
Company pension contributions	X
Compensation for loss of office	X
Sums paid to third parties for directors' services	X
	X
Highest paid director	
Aggregate emoluments, gains on share options exercised and benefits under long-term incentive schemes (listed/AIM company only)	X
Company pension contributions	X
Accrued pension	X
	X

Notes

(a) All companies must disclose aggregate emoluments paid to/receivable by a director in respect of 'qualifying services'.

(b) Unlisted companies do **not** need to disclose:

(i) The amount of gains made when directors exercise options, only the number of directors who exercised options.

(ii) The net value of any assets that comprise shares, which would otherwise be disclosed in respect of assets received under long-term incentive schemes, but **only** the number of directors in respect of whose qualifying service shares were receivable under long-term incentive schemes.

(c) For listed companies, the disclosure requirements for share options do not refer to qualifying services, so gains made on the exercise of shares **before appointment** must therefore be included.

(d) Information about the highest paid director only needs to be given if the aggregate of emoluments, gains on exercise of share options, and amounts receivable by the directors under long-term incentive schemes is > £200,000. For unlisted companies, state whether the highest paid director exercised any share options and/or received any shares in respect of qualifying services under a long-term incentive scheme.

(e) The details relating to pensions are beyond the scope of your syllabus.

(f) **Definitions**

(i) **Emoluments**. Salary, fees, bonuses, expense allowances, money value of other benefits, except share options granted, pension amounts and amounts paid under a long-term incentive scheme. Includes 'golden hellos'.

(ii) **Qualifying services**. Services as a director of a company and services in connection with the management of the company's affairs.

(iii) **Listed company**. A company whose securities have been admitted to the Official List of the Stock Exchange (or AIM).

(iv) **Long-term incentive schemes**. Any agreement or arrangement under which money or other assets become receivable by a director and where one or more of the qualifying conditions relating to service cannot be fulfilled in a single financial year. Bonuses relating to an individual year, termination payments and retirement benefits are excluded.

5 *Employee information*

(a) The *average number of persons* employed during the year was:

By product	
Electrical components	X
Domestic appliances	X
	X
By activity	
Production	X
Selling	X
Administration	X
	X

(b) *Employment costs*

	£'000
Aggregate wages and salaries	X
Social security costs	X
Other pension costs	X
	X

Notes

(a) Classification to be decided by the directors and applied consistently year on year. Must state whether executive directors are included or excluded.

(b) Social security costs are employer's NI.

(c) Other pension costs are contributions by the company to a pension scheme.

(d) **Definitions**

(i) **Staff costs**. Costs incurred in respect of persons employed under contract of service. They include part time employees under contract.

(ii) **Average number**

(1) Ascertain number employed under contracts each week.
(2) Aggregate these numbers.
(3) Divide by the number of months in the period.

Include those persons working wholly or mainly overseas.

Question 6

During a 12 month accounting period, the administration department of Relaks Ltd had the following employees.

(a) 12 worked overseas, of whom 1 returned to work in the UK and 2 resigned after 6 months.

(b) 30 UK employees (including 1 executive director).

(c) 20 part-timers who only worked over the three months' summer season and of whom only 8 were employed under a service contract.

Determine the average number of employees (assuming executive directors are included) to be disclosed for the administration department.

Note. The employee information note may include or exclude executive directors and the company must state which option they have chosen.

Answer

Average number

	No
Overseas (12 – (2 × ½))	11
UK employees	30
Contract part-timers	2
(8 for 3 months, which averages out at 2 per year)	
	43

6 *Interest payable and similar charges*

	£'000
Interest payable on:	
Bank overdrafts and loans	X
Other loans	X
Lease and HP finance charges allocated for the year	X
	X

Note

Similar charges might include arrangement fees for loans.

7 *Tax on profits on ordinary activities*

	£'000
UK corporation tax (at x% on taxable profit for the year)	X
Transfer to/from deferred taxation	X
Under/over provision in prior years	X
Unrelieved overseas taxation	X
	X

Note

The rate of tax must be disclosed (FRS 16: see Chapter 8).

8 *Dividends*

			£'000
Preference:	8% paid		X
Ordinary:	interim	3.5p paid	X
	final	7.0p proposed	X
			X

Note

Show for each class of share distinguishing between amounts paid and proposed. Only advisable (and not required) to show amount per share. If the aggregate **proposed** dividend is not shown in the note to the accounts, it must be shown on the face of the P&L a/c.

9 *Intangible fixed assets*

	Development expenditure £'000
Cost	
At 1 January 20X5	X
Expenditure	X
At 31 December 20X5	X
Amortisation	
At 1 January 20X5	X
Charge for year	X
At 31 December 20X5	X
Net book value at 31 December 20X5	X
Net book value 31 December 20X4	X

Note

The above disclosure should be given for each intangible asset.

10 *Tangible fixed assets*

	Freehold land and buildings	*Leasehold land and buildings*		*Plant and machinery*	*Fixtures and fittings*	*Total*
		Long leases	*Short leases*			
	£'000	£'000	£'000	£'000	£'000	£'000
Cost (or valuation)						
At 1 Jan 20X5	X	X	X	X	X	X
Additions	X	-	X	-	X	X
Revaluation	X	-	-	-	-	X
Disposals	(X)	-	-	(X)	(X)	(X)
At 31 Dec 20X5	X	X	X	X	X	X
Depreciation						
At 1 Jan 20X5	X	X	X	X	X	X
Charge for year	X	X	X	X	X	X
Revaluation	(X)	-	-	-	-	(X)
Disposals	(X)	-	-	(X)	(X)	(X)
At 31 Dec 20X5	X	X	X	X	X	X
Net book value						
At 31 Dec 20X5	X	X	X	X	X	X
At 31 Dec 20X4	X	X	X	X	X	X

Notes

(a) Long leases are ≥ 50 years unexpired at balance sheet date.

(b) Classification by asset type represents arabic numbers from formats.

(c) Motor vehicles (unless material) are usually included within plant and machinery.

(d) Revaluations in the year: state for each asset revalued:

- Method of valuation
- Date of valuation
- The historical cost equivalent of the above information as if the asset had not been revalued

11 *Fixed asset investments*

	£'000
Shares at cost	
At 1 January 20X5	X
Additions	X
Disposals	(X)
At 31 December 20X5	X

The market value (in aggregate) of the listed investments is £X.

Note

An AIM investment is **not** a listed investment. All stock exchanges of repute allowed. Aggregate market value (ie profits less losses) to be disclosed if material.

12 *Stocks*

	£'000
Raw materials and consumables	X
Work in progress	X
Finished goods	X
	X

The replacement cost of stock is £X higher than its book value.

13 *Debtors*

	£'000
Trade debtors	X
Other debtors	X
Prepayments and accrued income	X
	X

14 *Creditors: amounts falling due within one year*

	£'000
Debenture loans: 8% stock 20X9	X
Bank loans and overdrafts	X
Trade creditors	X
Other creditors including taxation and social security (see note 15)	X
Accruals and deferred income	X
	X

The bank loans and overdraft are secured by a floating charge over the company's assets.

Notes

(a) Give details of security given for all secured creditors.

(b) Include the current portion of instalment creditors here.

15 *Other creditors including taxation and social security*

	£'000
UK corporation tax	X
Social security	X
Proposed dividend	X
	X

Notes

(a) Liabilities for taxation and social security must be shown separately from other creditors.

(b) Dividend liabilities to be disclosed separately.

16 *Creditors: amounts falling due after more than one year*

	£'000
8½% unsecured loan stock 20Y9	X

Notes

(a) Very long-term creditors:

  (i) disclose the aggregate amount of debentures and other loans:

    (1) payable after more than five years;

    (2) payable by instalments, any of which fall due after more than five years;

  (ii) for (1) and (2) disclose the terms of repayment and rates of interest.

(b) Debentures during the year, disclose:

  (i) Class issued.

(ii) For each class:

- Amount issued
- Consideration received

17 *Accruals and deferred income*

	£'000
Government grants received	X
Credited to profit and loss account	(X)
	X

Note

Alternative presentation if not included as part of creditors, which saves dividing the accruals or deferred income amount between within and greater than one year.

18 *Called up share capital*

	£1 ordinary shares £'000	*6.2% preference shares* £'000
Authorised		
Number	X	X
Value	X	X
Allotted		
Number	X	X
Value	X	X

Notes

(a) Disclose number and nominal value for each class, both authorised and allotted.

(b) *Shares* **issued during the year**, disclose:

(i) Classes allotted.

(ii) For each class:

- Number and aggregate nominal value allotted
- Consideration received

19 *Reserves*

	Share premium £'000	*Revaluation* £'000	*General* £'000	*Profit and loss* £'000
At 1 January 20X5	X	X	X	X
Retained profit for the year	-	-	-	X
Revaluation	-	X	-	-
Transfers	-	-	X	X
At 31 December 20X5	X	X	X	X

20 *Contingent liabilities*

Note: governed by FRS 12 (see Chapter 10).

21 *Post balance sheet events*

Note: governed by SSAP 17 (see Chapter 10).

22 *Capital commitments*

	£'000
Amounts contracted but not provided for	X

Note

This figure is not included in the balance sheet as it is simply a note of future obligations to warn users of likely future capital expenditure.

Question 7

The best way to learn the format and content of published accounts and notes is to practice questions. However, you must start somewhere, so try to learn the above formats, then close this text and write out on a piece of paper:

(a) A standard layout for a balance sheet and profit and loss account.
(b) A list of notes to these accounts which are generally required.

Exam focus point

In the past the Examiner commented that in questions requiring the preparation of published financial statements, many marks were lost 'due to inexcusable errors such as the inclusion of balance sheet items in the profit and loss account, the treatment of a debit bank balance as a current liability, confusion over corporation tax adjustments and an inability to distinguish notes from workings.'

Make sure that you have practised a sufficient number of accounts preparation questions from the BPP *Practice and Revision Kit* before you sit the exam. The examiner places a high priority on this topic.

Filing exemptions for small and medium-sized companies

5.4 Small and medium-sized companies are allowed certain 'filing exemptions': the accounts they lodge with the Registrar of companies, and which are available for public inspection, need not contain all the information which must be published by large companies. This concession allows small and medium-sized companies to reduce the amount of information about themselves available to, say, trading rivals. It does **not** relieve them of their obligation to prepare full statutory accounts, because all companies, regardless of their size, must prepare full accounts for approval by the shareholders.

5.5 Small and medium-sized companies must therefore balance the expense of preparing two different sets of accounts against the advantage of publishing as little information about themselves as possible. Many such companies may decide that the risk of assisting their competitors is preferable to the expense of preparing accounts twice over, and will therefore not take advantage of the filing exemptions.

5.6 A company qualifies as a small or medium company in a particular financial year if, for that year, two or more of the following conditions are satisfied.

IMPORTANT

The following is important for your studies

	Small	Medium
Turnover (This amount must be adjusted proportionately in the case of an accounting period greater or less than 12 months)	≤ £2.8m	≤ £11.2m
Balance sheet total (ie total assets before deduction of any liabilities)	≤ £1.4m	≤ £5.6 m
Average number of employees	≤ 50	≤ 250

5.7 **Public companies** can **never** be **entitled** to the **filing exemptions** whatever their size; nor can banking and insurance companies; nor can companies which are authorised persons under the Financial Services Act 1986; nor can members of groups containing any of these exceptions.

5.8 The form and content of the abbreviated accounts are contained in separate schedules of the Act: Schedule 8A for small companies and Schedule 245A for medium-sized companies. **Small companies** may file an **abbreviated balance sheet** showing only the items which, in the statutory format, are denoted by a **letter or Roman number**. They are not required to file either a profit and loss account or a directors' report. No details need be filed of the **emoluments of directors**. Only **limited notes** to the accounts are required.

5.9 The only exemptions allowed to **medium-sized companies** are in the profit and loss account. **Turnover need not be analysed** between a company's **different classes of businesses**, or its **different geographical markets**. The profit and loss account may begin with the figure of gross profit (or loss) by amalgamation of items 1, 2, 3 and 6 in Format 1, or of items 1 to 5 in Format 2.

5.10 If a small or medium-sized company files 'abbreviated accounts' a **statement** by the **directors** must appear above the **director's signature** on the balance sheet. The statement must be that the financial statements have been prepared in **accordance** with the **special provisions** of Part VII of the Act relating to small or (as the case may be) medium-sized companies.

5.11 Abbreviated accounts must be accompanied by a **special report of the company's auditors** stating that, in their opinion, the directors are **entitled to deliver** abbreviated accounts and those accounts are **properly prepared.** The text of the auditors' report on the full statutory accounts must be included as a part of this special report. A **true and fair view** is **still required,** however; if the shorter-form financial statements fail to give a true and fair view because of the use of exemptions, or for any other reason, the auditors should qualify their audit report in the normal way.

The FRSSE

5.12 In December 1996 the ASB published an Exposure Draft of the *Financial Reporting Standard for Smaller Entities* (FRSSE) and this was published in final form in November 1997. This represents a major simplification of financial reporting for smaller entities.

5.13 At present preparers and auditors of small entities' accounts need to refer to the complete range of accounting standards, many of whose provisions are not relevant to smaller entities. The FRSSE provides preparers and auditors with a single reference point, a **single comprehensive accounting standard** containing the measurement and disclosure requirements most relevant to their circumstances.

5.14 The FRSSE is applicable to all companies that satisfy the definition of a small company in companies legislation and would also be available to other entities that would meet that definition if they were companies. A company that chooses to comply with the FRSSE is exempt from all other accounting standards and UITF Abstracts. The FRSSE contains in a simplified form the requirements from existing accounting standards that are relevant to the majority of smaller entities.

5.15 In order to keep the FRSSE as user-friendly as possible some of the requirements in accounting standards relating to more complex transactions, eg the treatment of convertible debt in FRS 4 *Capital instruments*, have not been included, as they do not affect most smaller entities. Where guidance is needed on a matter not contained in the proposed FRSSE, regard should be paid to existing practice as set out in the relevant accounting standards.

Summary financial statements

5.16 CA 1989 amended CA 1985 so that **listed companies** need not send all their members their full financial statements but can instead send them summary financial statements (SFSs). All members who want to receive full financial statements are still entitled to them, however.

5.17 An SFS must:

(a) State that it is only a summary of information in the company's annual accounts and the directors' report.

(b) Contain a statement by the company's auditors of their opinion as to whether the summary financial statement is consistent with those accounts and that report and complies with the relevant statutory requirements.

(c) State whether the auditors' report on the annual accounts was unqualified or qualified, and if it was qualified set out the report in full together with any further material needed to understand the qualification.

5.18 SFSs must be derived from the company's annual accounts and the directors' report and the form and content are specified by regulations made by the Secretary of State.

The key figures from the full statements must be included along with the review of the business and future developments shown in the directors' report. Comparative figures must be shown.

6 THE DIRECTORS' REPORT

6.1 Attached to every balance sheet there must be a directors' report (s 234 CA 1985). CA 1985 states specifically what information must be included.

6.2 The directors' report is largely a **narrative report**, but certain figures must be included in it. The purpose of the report is to give the users of accounts a more complete picture of the state of affairs of the company.

6.3 The directors' report is expected to contain a fair review of the development of the business of the company during that year and of its position at the end of it. No guidance is given on the form of the review, nor the amount of detail it should go into.

6.4 S 234 CA 1985 also requires the report to show the amount, if any, recommended for dividend.

6.5 Other disclosure requirements are as follows.

(a) The principal activities of the company in the course of the financial year, and any significant changes in those activities during the year.

(b) Where significant, an estimate should be provided of the difference between the book value of land held as fixed assets and its realistic market value.

(c) Information about the company's policy for the employment for disabled persons:

(i) For giving fair consideration to applications for jobs from disabled persons.

(ii) For continuing to employ (and train) people who have become disabled whilst employed by the company.

(iii) For the training, career development and promotion of disabled employees.

(Companies with fewer than 250 employees are exempt from (c).)

(d) The names of persons who were directors at any time during the financial year.

(e) For those persons who were directors at the year end, the interests of each (or of their spouse or infant children) in shares or debentures of the company:

(i) At the beginning of the year, or at the date of appointment as director, if this occurred during the year.

(ii) At the end of the year.

If a director has no such interests at either date, this fact must be disclosed. (The information in (e) may be shown as a note to the accounts instead of in the directors' report.)

(f) Political and charitable contributions made, **if these together exceeded more than £200 in the year**, giving:

(i) **Separate totals** for political contributions and charitable contributions.

(ii) The amount of each separate political contribution **exceeding £200**, and the name of the recipient.

(g) Particulars of any important events affecting the company or any of its subsidiaries which have occurred since the end of the financial year (significant 'post-balance sheet events').

(h) An indication of likely future developments in the business of the company and of its subsidiaries.

(i) An indication of the activities (if any) of the company and its subsidiaries in the field of research and development.

(j) Particulars of purchases (if any) of its own shares by the company during the year, including reasons for the purchase.

(k) Particulars of other acquisitions of its own shares during the year (perhaps because shares were forfeited or surrendered, or because its shares were acquired by the company's nominee or with its financial assistance).

6.6 Note that the 1985 Act requires details of important post balance sheet events to be explained in the directors' report. The requirements of SSAP 17 (see Chapter 10), which should be considered in conjunction with the 1985 Act, are either for the accounts themselves to be altered, or for the amount of the adjustment to results to be disclosed in a note to the accounts.

6.7 A further requirement relating to the directors' report is contained in the Employment Act 1982. The requirement relates to any company employing on average **more than 250 people each week**. The directors of such a company must state in their report what action has been taken during the financial year to introduce, maintain or develop arrangements aimed at:

(a) **Employee information,** providing employees systematically with information on matters of concern to them.

(b) **Employee consultation,** consulting employees or their representatives on a regular basis so that the views of employees can be taken into account in making decisions which are likely to affect their interest.

(c) **Employee involvement,** encouraging the involvement of employees in the company's performance through an employees' share scheme or by some other means.

(d) **Company performance,** achieving common awareness on the part of all employees of the financial and economic factors affecting the performance of the company.

6.8 It should be noted that these provisions do not mean that any such action must be taken, only that if it is taken it must be disclosed in the directors' report. Moreover, wide discretion is granted to the directors in deciding what needs to be disclosed, since no definition is given of such terms as 'matters of concern to them' or 'decisions which are likely to affect their interests'.

Creditor payment policy

6.9 A recent amendment to CA 1985 requires companies to disclose details of the company's policy on the **payment of creditors**. This disclosure requirement applies if:

(a) The company was at any time during the year a public company.

(b) The company did not qualify as a small or medium-sized company under s 247 and was at any time within the year a member of a group of which the parent company was a public company.

6.10 The directors' report needs to state, with respect to the financial year immediately following that covered by the report:

(a) Whether in respect of some or all of its suppliers (ie those classified as 'trade creditors') it is the company's policy to **follow any code or standard** on payment practice, and if so, the name of the code or standard, and the place where information about, and copies of, the code or standard can be obtained.

(b) Whether in respect of some or all of its suppliers, it is the company's policy to:

(i) **Settle the terms** of payment with those suppliers when agreeing the terms of each transaction.

(ii) Ensure that those suppliers are **made aware** of the terms of payment.

(iii) **Abide by** the terms of payment.

(c) Where the company's policy is **not** as mentioned in either of the two paragraphs above, in respect of some or all of its suppliers, what its policy is with respect to the payment of those suppliers.

If the company's policy is different for different suppliers or classes of suppliers, the directors' must identify the suppliers or classes of suppliers to which the different policies apply.

7 OTHER ITEMS IN THE ANNUAL REPORT

The auditors' report

7.1 The annual accounts of a limited company must be audited by persons independent of the company. In practice, this means that the members of the company appoint a firm of Chartered Accountants or Chartered Certified Accountants to investigate the accounts prepared by the company and report as to whether or not they show a true and fair view of the company's results for the year and its financial position at the end of the year. The audit report is governed by auditing regulations. The work of the external auditors is examined in more detail in Chapter 13.

7.2 When the auditors have completed their work they must prepare a report explaining the work that they have done and the opinion they have formed. In simple cases they will be able to report that they have carried out their work in accordance with auditing standards and that, in their opinion, the accounts show a true and fair view and are properly prepared in accordance with the Companies Act 1985. This is described as an **unqualified audit report**.

7.3 Sometimes the auditors may disagree with the directors on a point concerned with the accounts. If they are unable to persuade the directors to change the accounts, and if the item at issue is material, it is the auditors' duty to prepare a **qualified report**, setting out the matter(s) on which they disagree with the directors.

7.4 The financial statements to which the auditors refer in their report comprise the:

(a) Profit and loss account.
(b) Balance sheet.
(c) Notes to the accounts.
(d) Cash flow statement.

In addition they must consider whether the information given in the **directors' report is consistent** with the audited accounts. If they believe it is not consistent then they must state that fact in their report. Note that the cash flow statement is not mentioned outright.

7.5 The auditors' report is included as a part of the company's published accounts. It is addressed to the **members of the company** (not to the directors).

The chairman's report

7.6 Most large companies include a chairman's report in their published financial statements. This is purely **voluntary** as there is no statutory requirement to do so.

7.7 The chairman's report is not governed by any regulations and is often unduly optimistic. Listed companies now include an Operating and Financial Review (OFR) in the annual report: see Chapter 12. This has been introduced to encourage more meaningful analysis.

Question 8

In between now and your examination obtain as many sets of company accounts or annual reports as you can. (You may like to use the Financial Times Free Annual Report Service for this purpose – look at the share price pages of the FT for information. Alternatively, you could access the FT website.) Read through the whole of each report and compare the format of the accounts and the disclosure of the notes with the contents of this chapter, and with the rest of this Study Text.

Note. Ignore the consolidated accounts and the information about the 'group' or 'group companies'.

Chapter roundup

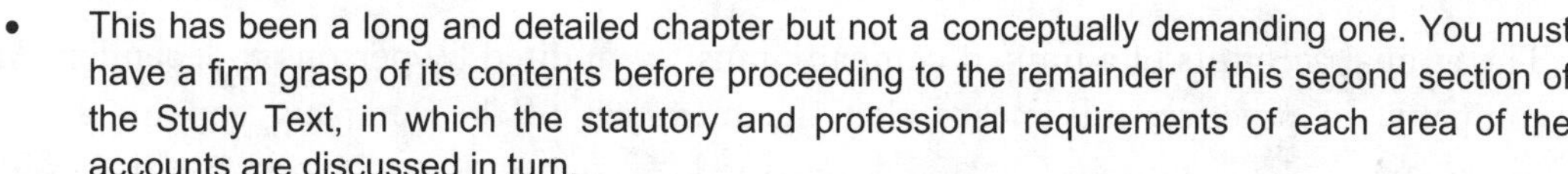

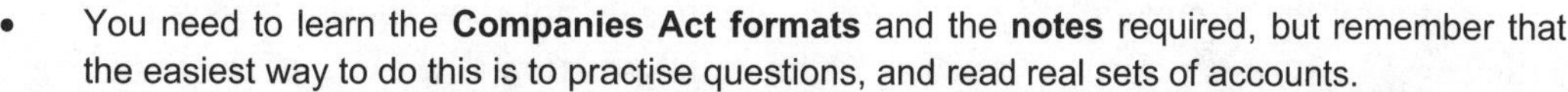

- This has been a long and detailed chapter but not a conceptually demanding one. You must have a firm grasp of its contents before proceeding to the remainder of this second section of the Study Text, in which the statutory and professional requirements of each area of the accounts are discussed in turn.
- You need to learn the **Companies Act formats** and the **notes** required, but remember that the easiest way to do this is to practise questions, and read real sets of accounts.
- You will appreciate the **contents** of the auditors' report, the directors' report, the chairman's report and the OFR if you read some real annual reports.
- After you have finished each of the following chapters, up to and including Chapter 11, **refer back** to the contents of this chapter to consider how the figures and disclosures required by any SSAP or FRS fits in with the formats and disclosure requirements of the Companies Act.

Quick quiz

1 The two bedrocks of accounting are:

A Accruals, prudence
B Prudence, consistency
C Consistency, accruals
D Going concern, accruals

2 An estimation technique is the method used to establish the estimated monetary amounts associated with the selected measurement bases.

True ☐

False ☐

3 What does CA 1985 say about a 'true and fair view'?

4 The period allowed for layout and delivery of accounts.

- Private companies .... months
- Public companies.............. months

5 List the disclosure requirements of UITF Abstract 7.

6 Turnover is defined by the Companies Act as the amounts derived from the provision of goods and services falling within the company's ordinary activities after deduction of which of the following?

A Carriage inwards
B Trade discounts
C VAT
D Carriage out
E Other sales taxes
F Stock losses

7

	Small company	*Medium company*
Turnover	....	....
Total assets	....	....
Average number of employees	....	....

8 List eight disclosures required in the directors report.

9 Companies must disclose their creditor payment policy in the financial statements.

True ☐

False ☐

10 The chairman's report is a statutory requirement.

True ☐

False ☐

Quick quiz answers

1 D (See para 1.4 and 1.5)

2 True, see paragraph 1.20

3 See paragraph 2.1

4 Ten, seven

5 See paragraph 3.8

6 B, C and E (4.12)

7

	Small company	*Medium company*
Turnover	≤£2.8m	≤£11.2m
Total assets	≤£1.4m	≤£5.6m
Average number of employees	≤50	≤250

8 See paragraphs 6.4 and 6.5

9 False, Only if they are a public company or they fail to meet the requirements for small or medium companies.

10 False.

Now try the question below from the Exam Question Bank

Number	Level	Marks	Time
Scenario B: Q1	Exam	26	47 mins

Chapter 3

REPORTING FINANCIAL PERFORMANCE

Topic list		Syllabus reference	Ability required
1	**FRS 3 *Reporting financial performance***	(ii), (iii)	Evaluation
2	**Exceptional and extraordinary items**	(ii)	Application
3	**Structure of the profit and loss account**	(ii)	Application
4	**FRS 3 statement and notes**	(ii)	Application
5	**FRS 14 *Earnings per share***	(iii)	Evaluation
6	**Prior period adjustments**	(ii)	Application
7	**SSAP 25 *Segmental reporting***	(ii)	Application

Introduction

FRS 3 Reporting financial performance introduced radical changes to the format of the profit and loss account and the associated notes to the accounts. Of major importance to you at this stage are the definitions of extraordinary and exceptional items and prior period adjustments. You may be asked to produce a statement of total recognised gains and losses, but the adjustments you would be required to make would be limited to those relating to property revaluations and simple goodwill transactions.

FRS 14 *EPS* is a demanding standard and you should work through this section slowly to ensure you understand how to calculate the relevant figures. We have included FRS 14 in this chapter because it ties in to FRS 3 (FRS 3 restricts the use of extraordinary items thus preventing manipulation of the EPS figure), but also because it is a very important performance indicator, as we will see in Part D of this text.

SSAP 25 is a straightforward standard – learn the definitions and formats.

Learning outcomes covered in this chapter

- **Explain** and apply the rules for reporting performance
- **Explain** the accounting rules contained in Financial Reporting Standards which provide guidance as to the appropriate treatment of certain transactions
- **Identify, apply** and **evaluate** the accounting treatment of significant transactions

Syllabus content covered in this chapter

- Reporting Performance (FRS 3); the measurement of income, the 'layered effect', exceptional and extraordinary items, prior year adjustments and the Statement of Total Recognised Gains and Losses (STGL) and the Reconciliation of Movements in Shareholders Funds. Segmental reporting (SSAP 25).
- Earnings per share (FRS 14 and FRS 3) to include the effect of bonus issues, rights issues and convertible stock.

1 FRS 3 REPORTING FINANCIAL PERFORMANCE

1.1 FRS 3 represents an attempt by the ASB to improve the **quality** of financial information provided to shareholders. In particular it was an attempt to move away from the high profile of the earnings per share. The main elements of the FRS are as follows.

(a) **New structure** of the profit and loss account
(b) **Extraordinary** items
(c) Statement of total recognised gains and losses
(d) Other **new** disclosures
(e) Earnings per share

2 EXCEPTIONAL AND EXTRAORDINARY ITEMS

2.1 A company may experience events or undertake transactions which are 'out of the ordinary', ie they are the result of something that the company does not usually do. FRS 3 lays down the rules for dealing with 'out of the ordinary' items and how they are shown in the profit and loss account. FRS 3 restricts the way companies can manipulate these figures.

Exceptional items

Exam focus point

This appeared in a MCQ in the May 2003 paper. Remember the MCQ section is worth 20 percent of the total marks of your paper.

KEY TERMS

FRS 3 defines **exceptional items** as:

'Material items which derive from events or transactions that fall **within** the ordinary activities of the reporting entity and which **individually** or, if of a **similar** type, in **aggregate**, need to be disclosed by virtue of their **size or incidence** if the financial statements are to give a **true and fair view**.'

The definition of **ordinary activities** is important.

'Any activities which are undertaken by a reporting entity **as part of its business** and such related activities in which the reporting entity engages in furtherance of, incidental to, or arising from these activities. Ordinary activities include the effects on the reporting entity of any event in the various environments in which it operates including the political, regulatory, economic and geographical environments **irrespective** of the frequency or unusual nature of the event.'

2.2 There are two types of exceptional item and their accounting treatment is as follows.

(a) Firstly, there are three categories of exceptional items, so called super exceptionals, which must be shown **separately on the face of the profit and loss account** after operating profit and before interest and allocated appropriately to discontinued and continued activities.

(i) Profit or loss on the **sale** or termination **of an operation**

(ii) **Costs of a fundamental reorganisation** or restructuring that has a material effect on the nature and focus of the reporting entity's operations

(iii) Profit or loss on **disposal of fixed assets**

For both items (i) and (iii) profit and losses may not be offset within categories.

(b) All other items should be allocated to the appropriate statutory format heading and attributed to continuing or discontinued operations as appropriate. If the item is sufficiently material that it is needed to show a true and fair view it must be disclosed on the face of the profit and loss account.

2.3 In both (a) and (b) an adequate description must be given in the notes to the accounts to enable its nature to be understood.

2.4 FRS 3 does not give examples of the type of transaction which is likely to be treated as exceptional. However, its predecessor on the subject, SSAP 6, gave a useful list of examples of items which if of a sufficient size might normally be treated as exceptional.

(a) Abnormal charges for bad debts and write-offs of stock and work in progress
(b) Abnormal provisions for losses on long-term contracts
(c) Settlement of insurance claims

Exam focus point

'Super exceptionals' frequently appears as an item in the compulsory accounts preparation question.

Extraordinary items

2.5 The ASB publicly stated that it does not envisage extraordinary items appearing on a company's profit and loss account after the introduction of FRS 3. Its decline in importance has been achieved by tightening of the definition of an extraordinary item.

KEY TERM

Extraordinary items are defined as material items possessing a high degree of abnormality which arise from events or transactions that fall outside the ordinary activities of the reporting entity and which are not expected to recur.

2.6 An example given by the chairman of the ASB was that 'if the Martians landed and destroyed a company's factory, that could be treated as an extraordinary item'. Extraordinary items are therefore very rare!

2.7 Extraordinary items should be shown on the face of profit and loss account before **dividends** and other **minority interests** (for group accounts). Tax associated with the extraordinary item should be shown **separately**. A description of the extraordinary items should be given in the notes to the accounts.

3 STRUCTURE OF THE PROFIT AND LOSS ACCOUNT

3.1 All statutory headings from turnover to operating profit must be subdivided between that arising from continuing operations and that arising from discontinued operations. In addition, turnover and operating profit must be further analysed between that from existing and that from newly acquired operations. Only figures for turnover and operating profit need be shown on the face of the profit and loss account; all additional information regarding costs may be relegated to a note.

PROFIT AND LOSS EXAMPLE 1	*20X3*	*20X3*	*20X2 as restated*
	£m	£m	£m
Turnover			
Continuing operations	550		500
Acquisitions	50		
	600		
Discontinued operations	175		190
		775	690
Cost of sales		(620)	(555)
Gross profit		155	135
Net operating expenses		(104)	(83)
Operating profit			
Continuing operations	50		40
Acquisitions	6		
	56		
Discontinued operations	(15)		12
Less 20X2 provision	10		
		51	52
Profit on sale of properties in continuing operations		9	6
Provision for loss on operations to be discontinued			(30)
Loss on disposal of discontinued operations	(17)		
Less 20X2 provision	20		
		3	
Profit on ordinary activities before interest		63	28
Interest payable		(18)	(15)
Profit on ordinary activities before taxation		45	13
Tax on profit on ordinary activities		(14)	(4)
Profit on ordinary activities after taxation		31	9
Extraordinary items – included only to show positioning		-	-
Profit for the financial year		31	9
Dividends		(10)	(3)
Retained profit for the financial year		21	6
Earnings per share		39p	10p
Adjustments (to be itemised and an adequate description to be given)		Xp	Xp
Adjusted earnings per share		Yp	Yp

Note. Reason for calculating the adjusted earnings per share to be given.

PROFIT AND LOSS ACCOUNT EXAMPLE 2 (to operating profit line)

	Continuing operations 20X3	*Acquisitions 20X3*	*Discontinued of operations 20X3*	*Total 20X3*	*Total 20X2 as restated*
	£m	£m	£m	£m	£m
Turnover	550	50	175	775	690
Cost of sales	(415)	(40)	(165)	(620)	(555)
Gross profit	135	10	10	155	135
Net operating expenses	(85)	(4)	(25)	(114)	(83)
Less 20X2 provision			10	10	
Operating profit	50	6	(5)	51	52
Profit on sale of properties	9			9	6
Provision for loss on operations to be discontinued					(30)
Loss on disposal of the discontinued operations			(17)	(17)	
Less 20X2 provision	-	-	20	20	
Profit on ordinary activities before interest	59	6	(2)	63	28

Thereafter example 2 is the same as example 1.

NOTES TO THE FINANCIAL STATEMENTS

Note required in respect of profit and loss account example 1

	20X3			*20X2 (as restated)*		
	Continuing	*Discontinued*	*Total*	*Continuing*	*Discontinued*	*Total*
	£m	£m	£m	£m	£m	£m
Cost of sales	455	165	620	385	170	555
Net operating expenses						
Distribution costs	56	13	69	46	5	51
Administrative expenses	41	12	53	34	3	37
Other operating income	(8)	0	(8)	(5)	0	(5)
	89	25	114	75	8	83
Less 20X2 provision	0	(10)	(10)			
	89	15	104			

The total figures for continuing operations in 20X3 include the following amounts relating to acquisitions: cost of sales £40 million and net operating expenses £4 million (namely distribution costs £3 million, administrative expenses £3 million and other operating income £2 million).

Note required in respect of profit and loss account example 2

	20X3			*20X2 (as restated)*		
	Continuing	*Discontinued*	*Total*	*Continuing*	*Discontinued*	*Total*
	£m	£m	£m	£m	£m	£m
Turnover				500	190	690
Cost of sales				385	170	555
Net operating expenses						
Distribution costs	56	13	69	46	5	51
Administrative expenses	41	12	53	34	3	37
Other operating income	(8)	0	(8)	(5)	0	(5)
	89	25	114	75	8	83
Operating profit				40	12	52

The total figure of net operating expenses for continuing operations in 20X3 includes £4 million in respect of acquisitions (namely distribution costs £3 million, administrative expenses £3 million and other operating income £2 million).

Discontinued operations

Exam focus point

This topic appeared in a MCQ in the May 2003 exam.

KEY TERMS

A **discontinued operation** is one which meets **all** of the following conditions.

(a) The sale or termination must have been completed before the **earlier of 3 months** after the year end or the date the financial statements are **approved**. (Terminations not completed by this date may be disclosed in the notes.)

(b) Former activity must have **ceased permanently**.

(c) The sale or termination has a material effect on the **nature and focus** of the entity's operations and represents a **material reduction** in its operating facilities resulting either from:

(i) Its **withdrawal** from a **particular market** (class of business or geographical).

(ii) A **material reduction in turnover** in its continuing markets.

(d) The assets, liabilities, results of operations and activities are clearly distinguishable, physically, operationally and for financial reporting purposes.

Accounting for the discontinuation

3.2 (a) *Results*

The results of the discontinued operation up to the date of sale or termination or the balance sheet date should be shown **under each of the relevant profit and loss account headings.**

(b) *Profit/loss on discontinuation*

The profit or loss on discontinuation or costs of discontinuation should be **disclosed separately** as an exceptional item after operating profit and before interest.

(c) *Comparative figures*

Figures for the previous year must be **adjusted** for any activities which have become discontinued in the current year.

Acquisitions

3.3 **Acquisitions** include most **holdings acquired by a group** (beyond the scope of your syllabus), as well as unincorporated businesses purchased. However, **start-ups** are **not acquisitions.**

Question 1

Gupta plc's profit and loss account for the year ended 31 December 20X8, with comparatives, is as follows.

	20X8	*20X7*
	£'000	£'000
Turnover	200,000	180,000
Cost of sales	(60,000)	(80,000)
Gross profit	140,000	100,000
Distribution costs	(25,000)	(20,000)
Administration expenses	(50,000)	(45,000)
Operating profit	65,000	35,000

During the year the company sold a material business operation with all activities ceasing on 14 February 20X9. The loss on the sale of the operation amounted to £2.2m. The results of the operation for 20X7 and 20X8 were as follows.

	20X8	*20X7*
	£'000	£'000
Turnover	22,000	26,000
Profit/(loss)	(7,000)	(6,000)

In addition, the company acquired an unincorporated business which contributed £7m to turnover and an operating profit of £1.5m.

Required

Prepare the profit and loss account and related notes for the year ended 31 December 20X8 complying with the requirements of FRS 3 as far as possible.

Answer

	20X8		*20X7*	
	£'000	£'000	£'000	£'000
Turnover				
Continuing operations				
(200 – 22 – 7)/(180 – 26)		171.0		154
Acquisitions		7.0		-
		178.0		154
Discontinued		22.0		26
		200.0		180
Cost of sales		(60.0)		(80)
Gross profit		140.0		100
Distribution costs		(25.0)		(20)
Administration expenses (50 – 2.2)		(47.8)		(45)
Operating profit				
Continuing operations * (bal)	72.7		41	
Acquisitions	1.5		-	
	74.2		41	
Discontinued	(7.0)		(6)	
		67.2		35
Exceptional item		(2.2)		-
		65.0		35

* ie 65.0 + 2.2 + 7.0 – 1.5 = 72.7; 35 + 6 = 41

Note to the profit and loss account

	20X8			*20X7 (as restated)*		
	Continuing £'000	*Discontinued* £'000	*Total* £'000	*Continuing* £'000	*Discontinued* £'000	*Total* £'000
Cost of sales	X	X	60.0	X	X	80

Net operating expenses						
Distribution costs	X	X	25.0	X	X	20
Administration expenses	X	X	47.8	X	X	45
	X	X	72.8	X	X	65

4 FRS 3 STATEMENT AND NOTES

4.1 FRS 3 introduced a new statement and a variety of new notes to expand the information required in published accounts which we saw in Chapter 2.

Statement of recognised gains and losses

4.2 This statement is required by FRS 3 to be presented with the same prominence as the profit and loss account, balance sheet and cash flow statement, ie as a **primary statement**.

4.3 The statement will include all gains and losses occurring during the period and so would typically include the following.

	£
Profit for the year (per the profit and loss account)	X
Items taken directly to reserves	
Surplus on revaluation of fixed assets	X
Surplus/deficit on revaluation of investment properties	X
Total recognised gains and losses for the year	X
Prior period adjustments (see later)	(X)
Total gains and losses recognised since last annual report	X

4.4 At a glance, it seems that all this new statement does is to reconcile the opening and closing net assets of a business. This is, however, not so since FRS 3 requires that **transactions with shareholders are to be excluded**, ie:

- Dividends paid and proposed
- Share issues and redemptions

Since these transactions do not represent either gains or losses.

4.5 Where the profit or loss for the year is the **only** recognised gain or loss, **a statement** to that effect should be given immediately below the profit and loss account.

Realised and distributable profits

4.6 At this point it may be worth pointing out that, just because gains and losses are 'recognised' in this statement, they are not necessarily 'realised', or 'distributable', ie as a dividend. An example of realised profits might be profits resulting from sale proceeds already received.

This area is covered in more detail in Chapter 11.

Question 2

Can you think of two other types of gains and losses which might be recognised during a period but which are not realised and do not pass through the profit and loss account?

Answer

(a) Gains or losses arising on the translation of foreign currency, for example with overseas investments

(b) Gains or losses on long-term trade investments

4.7 Under CA 1985:

(a) The **distribution** of **unrealised profits** to shareholders is **prohibited.**

(b) **Only** profits **realised** at the balance sheet date shall be **included** in the **profit and loss** account.

(c) Similarly, **transfers from a revaluation reserve** to the profit and loss account are only permitted if they represent a transfer of **realised** profits.

4.8 Generally speaking, realised profits and losses have been recognised in the profit and loss account; unrealised profits and loses may be recognised in the balance sheet. FRS 3 argues that users of accounts need to know about the unrealised movements. The statement brings all the information together.

4.9 However, since the 1985 Act states that there is an **overriding requirement** to **give a true and fair view**, the directors may include an **unrealised profit in the profit and loss account** where there are **special reasons** for doing so.

4.10 If unrealised profits are thus recognised in the profit and loss account, **particulars** of this **departure** from the **statutory accounting principle**, the **reasons** for it and its **effect** are required to be given in a note to the accounts.

4.11 For example, SSAP 9 states that turnover and profits should be recognised on **long-term contracts** as soon as their outcome is foreseeable with reasonable certainty. With the introduction of the Companies Act 1985, there was some doubt as to whether this practice should be allowed to continue, on the grounds that 'attributable' profit might not be 'realised'. However, the CCAB takes the view that, since **attributable profits** in SSAP 9 are based on the principle of **reasonable certainty**, they may be regarded as realised profits within the context of the 1985 Act (see Chapter 7).

4.12 The Companies Act 1985 states that **unrealised profits may not be distributed** to shareholders. **However** there is **no legal requirement to distinguish between distributable and non-distributable profits in a published balance sheet.**

4.13 The **CCAB's guidance** note on distributable profits attempts to make some **clarification** about how distributable profits (realised profits less realised losses) should be determined. The following points were included in the note.

4.14 If an **asset is revalued**, the **surplus is unrealised profit** and is **not taken through the profit and loss account**. The double entry is:

DEBIT	Asset account
CREDIT	Revaluation reserve

with the amount of the increase in valuation. The **gain on revaluation** of an asset is **recognised** in the **statement of total recognised gains and losses** (STRGL), but it is not **realised.**

4.15 The 1985 Act states that certain **provisions** are to be considered as **realised losses**. These provisions are specified as '... any amount written off by way of providing for depreciation or diminution in value of assets', and '... any amount retained as reasonably necessary for the purpose of providing for any liability or loss which is likely to be incurred, or certain to be incurred but uncertain as to amount or as to the date on which it will arise'.

4.16 **Development costs** are **realised losses** in the **year** in which the costs are **incurred, unless** the costs are **capitalised** (in accordance with **SSAP 13** *Accounting for research and development* and the Companies Act 1985) in which case the development costs are **written off** as realised losses over a **number of years** (see Chapter 6).

Reconciliation of movements in shareholders' funds

4.17 This reconciliation is required by FRS 3 to be included in the notes to the accounts. What the reconciliation aims to do is to pull together financial performance of the entity as is reflected in:

(a) The **profit and loss** account.

(b) **Other movements** in shareholders' funds as determined by the statement of total recognised gains and losses.

(c) **All other changes** in shareholders' funds not recognised in either of the above.

4.18 The typical contents of the reconciliation would be as follows.

	£
Profit for the financial year	X
* Dividends	(X)
	X
Other recognised gains and losses (per statement of total recognised gains and losses)	X
* New share capital	X
Net addition to shareholders' funds	X
Opening shareholders' funds	X
Closing shareholders' funds	X

* Items not appearing in the statement of recognised gains and losses

Question 3

Extracts from Zoe Ltd's profit and loss account for the year ended 31 December 20X8 were as follows.

	£'000
Profit after tax	512
Dividend	(120)
Retained profit	392

During the year the following important events took place.

(a) Assets were revalued upward by £110,000.
(b) £300,000 share capital was issued during the year.
(c) Certain stock items were written down by £45,000.
(d) Opening shareholders' funds at 1 January 20X1 were £3,100,000.

Show how the events for the year would be shown in the statement of recognised gains and losses and the reconciliation of movements in shareholders funds.

Answer

STATEMENT OF RECOGNISED GAINS AND LOSSES

	£'000
Profit after tax	512
Asset revaluation	110
	622

RECONCILIATION OF MOVEMENTS IN SHAREHOLDERS' FUNDS

	£'000
Profit after tax	512
Dividend	(120)
	392
Other recognised gains and losses (622 – 512)	110
New share capital	300
Net addition to shareholders' funds	802
Opening shareholders' funds	3,100
Closing shareholders' funds	3,902

(*Note:* The stock write down is a normal trading item and does not need to be disclosed in either of the above statements.)

Note of historical cost profits and losses

4.19 If a company has adopted any of the **alternative accounting** rules as regards **revaluation of assets** then the **reported** profit figure per the profit and loss account may **deviate** from the **historical** cost profit figure. If this deviation is material then the financial statements must include a reconciliation statement after the statement of recognised gains and losses or the profit and loss account. The profit figure to be reconciled is profit before tax; however, the retained profit for the year must also be **restated.**

4.20 Note that FRS 3 **requires** the profit or loss on the disposal of a revalued asset to be calculated by reference to the difference between proceeds and the **net carrying amount** (ie the revalued figure less depreciation). The profit or loss based on historical cost will appear in the note of historical cost profits.

Question 4

Sase Ltd reported a profit before tax of £162,000 for the year ended 31 December 20X6. During the year the following transactions in fixed assets took place.

(a) Asset A with a book value of £40,000 was revalued to £75,000. The remaining useful life is estimated to be five years.

(b) Asset B (with a five year useful life at the date of revaluation) was revalued upwards by £20,000 (book value £30,000) and was sold for £48,000 one year after its revaluation.

Show the reconciliation or profit to historical cost profit for the year ended 31 December 20X1.

Answer

RECONCILIATION OF PROFIT TO HISTORICAL COST PROFIT
FOR THE YEAR ENDED 31 DECEMBER 20X6

	£'000
Reported profit on ordinary activities before taxation	162
Realisation of property revaluation gains (20 – 20/5)*	16
Difference between historical cost depreciation charge and the actual depreciation charge of the year calculated on the revalued amount (75,000 – 40,000)/5	7
	185

* When asset B was revalued last year, £20,000 would have been credited to revaluation reserve. At the end of that year the annual transfer of £20,000 ÷ 5 years would have been made to profit and loss reserve, leaving £16,000 in revaluation reserve. This year, with asset B being sold, the related revaluation reserve credit balance becomes realised (see exam focus point below).

Exam focus point

The annual transfer from revaluation reserve to profit and loss reserve reflects the technical requirement strictly. However, this is not required for Paper 6 purposes.

5 FRS 14 EARNINGS PER SHARE (EPS)

Exam focus point

In the compulsory section of the May 2001 exam, candidates were required to disclose the EPS for a company and to discuss why the EPS ratio is unique in having its own accounting standard.

The November 2002 paper required an explanation of the purpose and limitations of the EPS ratio.

The May 2003 exam required the calculation of EPS to get to a P/E ratio.

KEY TERM

Earnings per share is a way of calculating the return on each ordinary share in the year. It is basically earnings (profit after tax and preference dividends) divided by number of shares.

Role of EPS

5.1 Earnings per share (EPS) is widely used by investors as a **measure of a company's performance** and is of particular importance in:

(a) Comparing the results of a company over a period of time.

(b) Comparing the performance of one company's equity shares against the performance of another company's equity, and also against the returns obtainable from loan stock and other forms of investment.

The purpose of any earnings yardstick is to achieve as far as possible clarity of meaning, comparability between one company and another, one year and another, and attributablity of profits to the equity shares. FRS 14 *Earnings per share* goes some way to ensuring that all these aims are achieved.

5.2 FRS 14 applies to all companies who have publicly traded shares or who are in the process of issuing shares publicly. However, where companies present EPS on a voluntary basis, FRS 14 **must** be adopted.

5.3 The ASB stated that earnings per share (EPS) was not a priority, but the development of new **international standards** on the area led to efforts to adopt a similar approach.

5.4 The following key terms may be useful for the remainder of this section.

KEY TERMS

- **Equity instrument:** any instrument that evidences a residual interest in the assets of an entity after deducting all of its liabilities.
- **Fair value:** the amount for which an asset could be exchanged, or a liability settled, between knowledgeable, willing parties in an arm's length transaction.
- **Financial instrument**: any contract that gives rise to both a financial asset of one entity and a financial liability or equity instrument of another entity.
- **Ordinary shares:** any equity instrument that is subordinate to all other classes of equity instruments.
- **Potential ordinary share:** a financial instrument or other contract that may entitle its holder to ordinary shares.
- **Warrants or options**: financial instruments that give the holder the right to purchase ordinary shares. *(FRS 14)*

Basic EPS

5.5 The standard has been developed with the user of the accounts in mind. The ASB have actively discouraged reliance on EPS, preferring a more rounded approach. Despite this EPS is a popular measure of profitability. The aim of the standard is to provide a consistent approach to EPS which will allow:

- Comparisons between entities' results
- Comparison of an entity's results over the years

KEY TERM

EPS is profit in pence attributable to each equity share.

The basic EPS calculation is:

$$\frac{\text{Earnings}}{\text{Issued ordinary shares}}$$

KEY TERMS

Earnings are the net profits after tax, interest, minority earnings and dividends on other classes of shares (also after extraordinary items, but in practice, these are rare).

Issued ordinary shares are all ordinary shares in circulation during the year. The weighted average approach is taken to calculate this amount.

Changes to ordinary share numbers

Share issues at market value

5.6 The following example will show how this issue is treated.

- The weighted average number for the period is used

- There is no retrospective effect

5.7 EXAMPLE: WEIGHTED AVERAGE NUMBER OF SHARES

Consider the following issues and buy-backs of shares. What is the weighted average number of shares?

	Issued shares	*Shares bought back*	*Balance*
1 January 20X9	20,000	-	20,000
31 March 20X9 Issue of new shares for cash	4,000	-	24,000
1 July 20X9 Purchase of shares for cash	-	8,000	16,000
31 December 20X9 Year end balance	24,000	8,000	16,000

5.8 SOLUTION

Weighted average

$(20{,}000 \times 3/12) + (24{,}000 \times 3/12) + (16{,}000 \times 6/12) = 19{,}000$

or

$20{,}000 + (4{,}000 \times 9/12) - (8{,}000 \times 6/12) = 19{,}000$

5.9 There are a number of **events** which will **alter** the **number of ordinary shares issued** by a company.

- Bonus issues
- Bonus elements (ie rights issues)
- Share splits
- Share consolidation

5.10 These events must be reflected in the EPS calculations. The basic EPS should reflect issues of ordinary shares from the date consideration is receivable. An event should be included in the diluted EPS calculation even if it occurs after the balance sheet date. All events must be allowed for up to the date of approval of the accounts.

Bonus issues

5.11 A bonus issue involves an increase in the issued shares without a corresponding increase in capital. The adjustment for bonus issues should be made back to the earliest possible period. This means that

(a) The issue is included for the full year.
(b) The issue applies to the prior year.

5.12 EXAMPLE: BONUS ISSUE

	20X8	*20X9*
Net profit 31 December	£3,000	£4,500
Ordinary shares until 30 June 20X9	500	

Bonus issue 1 July 20X9: one share for every two ordinary shares held at 30 June 20X9

5.13 SOLUTION

Bonus issue $500 \times 1/2 = 250$

EPS for 20X9 $\dfrac{£4{,}500}{(500 + 250)} = 600\text{p}$

Adjusted EPS for 20X8 $\dfrac{\pounds 3{,}000}{(500+250)} = 400\text{p}$

Note that, as the bonus issue involved no consideration, it is treated as though it had occurred at the **earliest period reported**.

Rights issues

5.14 A rights issue usually involves shares issued for an exercise price, that is, less than the fair value of the currently issued shares. The current year's ordinary shares are multiplied by an adjustment factor:

$$\frac{\text{Fair value of current shares}}{\text{Theoretical ex-rights value per share}}$$

Note that fair value is the average price of the ordinary shares during the period.

5.15 EXAMPLE: RIGHTS ISSUE

	20X7	*20X8*	*20X9*
	£	£	£
Net profit as at 31 December	24,000	30,400	36,000
Shares before the rights issue	100,000		

The rights issue is to be one share for every five currently held (giving 20,000 new shares). Exercise price £1.00. The last date to exercise rights is 1 April 20X8.

The fair value of an ordinary share before the issue is £2.20.

5.16 SOLUTION

Theoretical ex-rights value per share is

$$\frac{\text{Fair value of current shares + Amount received from exercise of rights}}{\text{Number of current shares + Number of shares issued}}$$

$$\frac{(\pounds 2.20 \times 100{,}000\text{ shares}) + (\pounds 1.00 \times 20{,}000)}{100{,}000\text{ shares} + 20{,}000\text{ shares}} = \frac{\pounds 220{,}000 + \pounds 20{,}000}{120{,}000} = \frac{\pounds 240{,}000}{120{,}000}$$

Theoretical ex-rights value per share = £2

Adjustment factor

$$\frac{\text{Fair value of current shares}}{\text{Theoretical ex-rights value per share}} = \frac{\pounds 2.20}{\pounds 2.00} = 1.1$$

Earnings per share

	20X7	*20X8*	*20X9*
20X7 EPS as originally stated: £24,000/100,000 shares	24.0p		
20X7 EPS restated for rights issue: £24,000/(100,000 shares × 1.1)	21.8p		
20X8 EPS allowing for rights issue: $\dfrac{\pounds 30{,}400}{(100{,}000 \times 1.1 \times 3/12) + (120{,}000 \times 9/12)}$		25.9p	
20X9 EPS £36,000/120,000			30.0p

Note that the adjustment factor is used on the original number of shares. Once the rights issue has taken place, the new number of shares (in this case 120,000) is included. For 20X8 the weighted average principle is applied.

Contingently issuable shares

5.17 Contingently issuable shares are issued after certain conditions have been fulfilled. They are not included in the basic EPS calculation until all the criteria have been met fully.

Part paid shares

5.18 If shares are part paid, then only the element which has been paid up is included in the calculation.

Alternative EPS

5.19 It should be noted that the adjustments covered so far affect the number of shares in the EPS calculation. This figure is the **denominator.**

KEY TERM

The **denominator** is the number of shares which are deemed to be entitled to the earnings of the entity.

5.20 The **standard's emphasis** is strongly upon the **weighted average number** of ordinary shares as opposed to the earnings figure. Many companies provide alternative EPS figures. The standard is very clear on this.

(a) The **basic EPS** and the **diluted EPS** must have the **same prominence** as **any other EPS** figure disclosed.

(b) The **weighted average** ordinary shares may only be calculated on the **basis prescribed** by the standard.

(c) The **reason** for the **alternative calculation** should be **disclosed**.

(d) The alternative calculation must be calculated on a **consistent basis,** year on year.

5.21 Alternative EPS calculations will therefore only have an alternative earnings figure; the **numerator.**

KEY TERM

The **numerator** is the earnings figure used in the EPS calculation.

5.22 If this amount is **different** from the **reported net profit** of the entity then a **reconciliation** must be provided to show **how** the **numerator** has been **derived.**

5.23 The EPS calculation in simple terms is therefore:

$$\frac{\text{Numerator}}{\text{Denominator}}$$

5.24 A favoured alternative EPS is the **headline EPS.**

'Headline' EPS

5.25 The ASB effectively destroyed the analysts' favourite EPS figure with the publication of FRS 3 and the subsequent publication of FRS 14, making clear that it did not believe anyone should rely on a single earnings figure. FRS 3 did allow for an EPS, but the figure was calculated after every conceivable expense, including extraordinary items if companies are able to identify any in future. The publication of FRS 3 drew loud protests from some investment houses, which felt that the new EPS figure would prove **volatile and confusing** to users. This is the EPS taken up by FRS 14.

5.26 The Institute of Investment Management and Research (IIMR) set up a sub-committee to investigate whether a definition for some kind of maintainable earnings could be developed. The sub-committee concluded that a standard measure for maintainable earnings, which could be used as a basis for forecasts, was not feasible, as too much **conjecture and subjectivity** are involved. This view falls in line with the ASB's.

5.27 Instead, the IIMR defines a **'headline' figure for earnings** which, it acknowledges, 'is inferior to maintainable earnings as a basis for forecasts', but is nevertheless robust and factual. 'The number is justified by its practical usefulness, even if it cannot encapsulate the company's performance in itself.'

5.28 The headline earnings figure **includes** all the trading profits and losses for the year, including interest, and profits and losses arising from operations discontinued or acquired at any point during the year. **Excluded** from the figure are profits or losses from the sale or termination of a discontinued operation, from the sale of fixed assets or businesses or from any permanent diminution in their value or write-off (except for assets acquired for resale). Abnormal trading items (any defined by FRS 3 as extraordinary or exceptional), says the IIMR, should be included in the figure but prominently displayed in a note if they are significant.

5.29 When the IIMR's original ED was published, the *Financial Times* announced that it would use the method to calculate **price/earnings ratios**, and Extel also announced that it would use the figure. The statement was specifically not directed at companies, but many are expected to take up the definition. A large number of listed companies already disclose an EPS figure in addition to the one required by FRS 3 (and 14).

5.30 As with all EPS figures which are offered as an alternative to the FRS 3 and 14 figure, a **reconciliation** of the two EPS figures must be shown. Also, the alternative method must be applied consistently from year to year. No companies are *required* to produce the IIMR figure.

Example of 'headline' EPS

5.31 An **example** of the reconciliation between EPS as calculated under FRS 3 and 14 and 'headline' EPS might be as follows.

	20X6	*20X5*
	pence	pence
EPS as required by FRS 14	62.5	57.3
Exceptional items		
Classification of restructuring costs	-	4.8
Sale of property adjustments	13.8	3.1
'Headline' EPS	76.3	65.2

Diluted EPS

Exam focus point

You should pay particular attention to this area as it may cause problems in the exam.

In the May 2001 paper, candidates were asked to define diluted EPS and discuss why it is important to disclose this figure, where applicable.

5.32 At the end of an accounting period a company may have securities which do not have a claim to equity earnings, but they may do **in the future**.

- **Separate classes of equity share** not yet entitled to a share of equity earnings, but becoming so at a future date
- **Convertible loan stock** or **convertible preference shares** which enable their holders to exchange their securities at a later date for ordinary shares at a predetermined rate
- **Options** or **warrants**

5.33 These securities have the potential effect of increasing the number of equity shares ranking for dividend and so diluting or 'watering down' the EPS. These securities may be **dilutive potential ordinary shares.**

KEY TERM

A **dilutive** potential ordinary share is one which decreases the share of net profit, or increases the loss shared.

5.34 The diluted EPS gives users of the accounts a view on the potential ordinary shares of the entity. There is the potential to forecast the future EPS from the amounts given. Again, the ASB is careful to point out that a number of measures should be used in order to assess the returns from an entity, stating that no one measure is accurate enough to rely on.

Pro forma calculations

5.35 The following are the simple pro forma calculations for the three main sets of securities.

(a) **Shares not yet ranking for dividend**

(i) *Earnings*

	£
Earnings	X

(ii) *Number of shares*

	No
Basic weighted average	X
Add shares that will rank in future periods	X
Diluted number	X

(b) **Convertible loan stock or preference shares**

(i) *Earnings*

	£
Earnings	X
Add back loan stock interest net of CT (or preference dividends) 'saved'	X
	X

(ii) *Number of shares*

	No
Basic weighted average	X
Add additional shares on conversion (using terms giving maximum dilution available after the year end)	X
Diluted number	X

(c) **Options or warrants**

(i) *Earnings*

	£
Earnings	X

(ii) *Number of shares*

	No
Basic weighted average	X
Add additional shares issued at nil consideration	X
Diluted number	X

Share options

5.36 A share option allows the purchase of shares at a favourable amount which is less than the fair value of existing shares. The calculation of diluted EPS includes those shares deemed as issued for no consideration. For this purpose, the following calculation is used.

$$\frac{\text{Shares under option} \times \text{exercise price}}{\text{Fair value of ordinary shares}}$$

5.37 This gives the number of shares that are to be excluded from the EPS calculation. This will become more clear in the following example.

5.38 EXAMPLE: EFFECTS OF SHARE OPTIONS ON DILUTED EARNINGS PER SHARE

Net profit for 20X9	£1,000,000
Weighted average number of ordinary shares for 20X9	10 million
Average fair value of one ordinary share	£2.40
Weighted average number of shares under option during 20X9	3 million
Exercise price for shares under option in 20X9	£2.00

5.39 SOLUTION

	Shares	*Net profit*	*EPS*
Net profit for 20X9		£1,000,000	
Weighted average shares for 20X9	10m		
Basic EPS			10p
Number of shares on option	3m		
Number of shares that would have been issued at fair value: (3m × £2)/£2.40	(2.5m)		
Diluted EPS	10.5m	£1,000,000	9.5p

Note that the net profit has not been increased. This is because the calculation only includes shares deemed to be issued for no consideration.

Convertible bonds

5.40 In cases where the issue of shares will affect earnings, the numerator should be adjusted accordingly. This occurs when bonds are converted. Interest is paid out on the bond. When conversion takes place this interest is no longer payable.

5.41 EXAMPLE: CONVERTIBLE BONDS

Net profit	£500
Ordinary shares in issue	1,000
Basic EPS	50p
Convertible 15% bonds	200

Each block of 5 bonds is convertible to 8 ordinary shares. The tax rate (including any deferred tax) is 40%.

5.42 SOLUTION

Interest expense relating to the bonds 200 @ 15% =	£30
Tax @ 40%	£12
Adjusted net profit £500 + £30 – £12 =	£518
Number of ordinary shares resulting from the bond conversion	320
Number of ordinary shares used for the diluted EPS calculation 1,000 + 320 =	1,320

Diluted EPS $\frac{£518}{1{,}320} = 39.2\text{p}$

5.43 Earnings should be adjusted for savings or expenses occurring as a result of conversion. Other examples of this are:

(a) Preference dividends saved when preference shares are converted.

(b) Additional liability on a profit sharing scheme as a result of higher profits (ie if conversion of bonds increases profit, a higher amount will be payable to members of a profit related pay scheme).

Ranking dilative securities

Exam focus point

CIMA suggests that dilution must also be addressed from the perspective of every class of potential share and that some of these may have the capacity to dilute, whereas others not. CIMA reassures that 'any computational exam questions will avoid this by having only one category of potential shares'.

The following material is therefore provided only for information and in the interests of completeness – for practical use and for later papers.

5.44 The approach prescribed by FRS 14 involves including only dilutive potential ordinary shares. Antidulutive shares are not to be included. This prudent approach recognises potential reduction of earnings but not increases.

5.45 In considering whether potential ordinary shares are dilutive or antidiluative, each issue or series of potential ordinary shares is considered separately rather than in any aggregate. The sequence in which potential ordinary shares are considered may affect whether they are dilutive. Therefore, in order to maximise the dilution of basic earnings per share, each issue or series of potential ordinary shares is considered in sequence from the most dilutive to the lease dilutive.

Limitations of EPS

5.46 EPS on its own is not all that informative. It must be seen in the context of several other matters.

(a) EPS is used for comparing results of a company over time. Is its EPS growing? What is the rate of growth? Is the rate of growth increasing or decreasing?

(b) Is there likely to be a significant dilution of EPS in the future, perhaps due to the exercise of share options or warrants, or the conversion of convertible loan stock into equity?

(c) EPS should not be used in a cavalier fashion to compare the earning of one company with another. For example, if A plc has an EPS of 12p for its 10,000,000 10p shares and B plc has an EPS of 24p for its 50,000,000 25p share, we must take account of the numbers of shares. When earnings are used to compare one company's shares with another, this is done using the P/E ratio or perhaps the yearning yield.

(d) If EPS is to be a reliable basis for comparing results, it must be calculated consistently.

5.47 Remember that:

(a) EPS is a figure based on past data

(b) It is easily manipulated by changes in accounting policies, changes in estimation techniques and by mergers or acquisitions.

5.48 The role of EPS in management bonus formula or calculatations makes it particularly susceptible to manipulation. The attention given to EPS as a performance measure by City analysts might arguably be disproportionate to its true benefit. Investors should be more concerned with future earnings, but of course estimates of these are more difficult to reach than the readily available figure.

Disclosure

5.49 Note the following.

(a) FRS 14 requires that **basic EPS** and **diluted EPS** are disclosed on the face of the profit and loss account, even if the amounts are negative. Comparative figures are also required.

(b) A basic and diluted EPS figure is required for every set of ordinary shares with different rights.

(c) The standard requires inclusion of all potential ordinary shares which will have a dilutive effect on the diluted EPS, regardless of materiality.

(d) The nil basis EPS is no longer required as this information can be derived from other disclosures in the financial statements.

(e) EPS need only be presented in the consolidated results of a group where the parent's results are shown as well.

Exam focus point

The purpose of any earnings yardstick is to achieve as far as possible clarity of meaning, comparability between one company and another, one year and another, and attributability of profits to the equity shares. FRS 14 *Earnings per share* goes some way to ensuring that all these aims are achieved.

6 PRIOR PERIOD ADJUSTMENTS

Exam focus point

This topic appeared in an MCQ in the May 2003 exam.

6.1 When the financial statements of a company are compiled, certain items (eg accruals, provisions) represent best estimates at a point in time. Further evidence received in the following year may suggest that previous estimates were incorrect. In most cases the 'error' will not be significant in size and so as a result the difference should be dealt with in the current year's accounts.

KEY TERMS

Prior period adjustments are therefore defined by FRS 3 as:

'Material adjustments applicable to prior periods arising from changes in accounting policy or from the correction of fundamental errors. They do not include normal recurring adjustments or corrections of accounting estimates made in prior periods.'

A **fundamental error** is an error which is so significant that the truth and fairness of the financial statements is not achieved.

6.2 A **change in accounting policy** requires a prior period adjustment based on the fundamental accounting concept of **consistency**. For users of the financial statements to make meaningful comparisons of a company's results it is important that the current year's and the last year's comparatives are prepared on the same basis. Therefore if for any reason a company changes its accounting policy they must go back and represent last year's accounts on the same basis.

6.3 Reasons for a **change in accounting policy** are:

(a) To show a truer and fairer view.
(b) Introduction of, or change to, standards or legislation.

6.4 The following accounting treatment should be used to make a prior period adjustment.

(a) Restate the prior year profit and loss account and balance sheet.

(b) Restate the opening reserves balance.

(c) Include the adjustment in the reconciliation of movements in shareholders' funds.

(d) Include a note at the foot of the statement of total recognised gains and losses of the current period.

Question 6

Kanu Ltd was established on 1 January 20X0. In the first three years' accounts deferred development expenditure was carried forward as an asset in the balance sheet. During 20X3 the directors decided that for the current and future years, all development expenditure should be written off as it is incurred. This decision has not resulted from any change in the expected outcome of development projects on hand, but rather from a desire to favour the prudence concept. The following information is available.

(a) Movements on the deferred development account.

Year	*Deferred development expenditure incurred during year*	*Transfer from deferred development expenditure account to P & L account*
	£'000	£'000
20X0	525	-
20X1	780	215
20X2	995	360

(b) The 20X2 accounts showed the following.

	£'000
Retained reserves b/f	2,955
Retained profit for the year	1,825
Retained profits carried forward	4,780

(c) The retained profit for 20X3 after charging the actual development expenditure for the year was £2,030,000.

Required

Show how the change in accounting policy should be reflected in the statement of reserves in the company's 20X3 accounts.

Ignore taxation.

Answer

If the new accounting policy had been adopted since the company was incorporated, the additional profit and loss account charges for development expenditure would have been:

	£'000
20X0	525
20X1 (780 – 215)	565
	1,090
20X2 (995 – 360)	635
	1,725

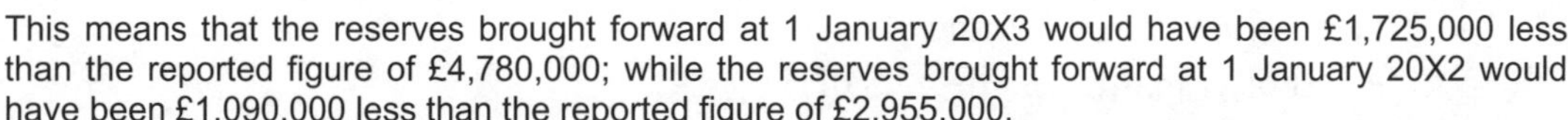

This means that the reserves brought forward at 1 January 20X3 would have been £1,725,000 less than the reported figure of £4,780,000; while the reserves brought forward at 1 January 20X2 would have been £1,090,000 less than the reported figure of £2,955,000.

The statement of reserves in Kanu Ltd's 20X3 accounts should, therefore, appear as follows.

STATEMENT OF RESERVES (EXTRACT)

		Comparative (previous year) figures	
	20X3	*20X2*	
	£'000	£'000	
Retained profits at the beginning of year			
Previously reported	4,780	2,955	
Prior year adjustment (note 1)	1,725	1,090	
Restated	3,055	1,865	
Retained profits for the year	2,030	1,190	(note 2)
Retained profits at the end of the year	5,085	3,055	

Notes

1 The accounts should include a note explaining the reasons for and consequences of the changes in accounting policy. (See above workings for 20X3 and 20X2.)

2 The retained profit shown for 20X2 is after charging the additional development expenditure of £635,000.

7 SSAP 25 SEGMENTAL REPORTING

Exam focus point

The compulsory statutory accounts preparation question for the May 2002 paper revolved around segmental reporting.

A MCQ on SSAP25 appeared on the May 2003 paper.

7.1 SSAP 25 *Segmental reporting* builds on the CA 1985 requirements to provide limited segmental analyses (given in Chapter 2).

(a) Where a company has **two or more classes of business,** it must show in a note the amount of **turnover and operating profit** attributable to each class of business.

(b) Where a company operates in **more than one geographical market,** it must show in a note the amount of **turnover** attributable to each market.

Any or all of these analyses can be omitted on grounds of commercial sensitivity (their publication would be 'seriously prejudicial' to the interests of the reporting entity), but the directors must then state that these analyses would have been published but for these considerations.

7.2 SSAP 25 applies only to an entity which is one of the following.

(a) A public company or has a public limited company as a subsidiary undertaking.

(b) A banking or insurance company or group.

(c) Exceeds the criteria, multiplied in each case by 10, for defining a medium-sized company under s 248 of the Companies Act 1985, as amended from time to time by statutory instrument. (The criteria for defining a medium-sized company are given in Chapter 2.)

7.3 The purpose of disclosing segmental information is to separately identify those areas which:

- Earn varying rates of return
- Are subject to different degrees of risk
- Experience different rates of growth
- Have different potentials for future development

7.4 SSAP 25 extends the Companies Act requirements on analysis of turnover as follows:

- The **result** as well as turnover must be disclosed for all segments
- 'Result' for these purposes is **profit or loss** before tax
- Each segment's **net assets** should be disclosed (so that return on capital employed can be calculated)
- Segmental turnover must be analysed between sales to **customers** outside the group and **inter-segment** sales/transfers (where material)

Like CA 1985, SSAP 25 requires analysis by two types of segment, **class of business** and **geographical market**. Comparative figures should be provided.

Definitions

KEY TERM

The SSAP defines a **class of business** as a distinguishable component of an entity that provides a separate product or service or a separate group of related products or services.

7.5 Factors to take into account in making this distinction are the nature of the products or services and production processes, markets distribution channels, organisation of activities and legislative framework relating to any part of the business.

KEY TERM

SSAP 25 defines a **geographical segment** as a geographical area comprising an individual country or a group of countries in which an entity operates, or to which it supplies products or services.

7.6 A geographical analysis should help the user of the financial statements to assess the extent to which an entity's operations are subject to factors such as:

- Expansionist or restrictive **economic** climates
- Stable or unstable **political** regimes
- **Exchange control** regulations
- **Exchange rate** fluctuations

7.7 SSAP 25 requires that turnover should be analysed by origin and by destination unless the two amounts are not materially different, which should then be stated.

Identifying segments

7.8 Identifying segments could be difficult and the SSAP suggests as a rule of thumb that a segment should normally be regarded as material if its third party turnover is ≥ 10% of the entity's total third party turnover or its profit is ≥ 10% of the combined results of all segments in profit (or its loss is ≥ 10% of the combined results of all loss making segments) or its net assets are ≥ 10% of total net assets of the entity. The aim is to inform users of the accounts about activities earning a different rate of return from the rest of the business; or subject to different degrees of risk; or experiencing different growth rates; or with different potential for future development.

Common costs

7.9 Common costs should be treated in the way that the directors deem most appropriate in pursuance of the objectives of segmental reporting. For internal accounting purposes, some companies routinely apportion common costs between divisions, segments and so on and others do not; the same considerations prompting that decision should be applied to segmental reporting.

7.10 EXAMPLE

Reproduced later in this section is the example given by SSAP 25 in its Appendix. Notice how the segmental results are reconciled to the entity's reported profit before taxation. This

is a requirement of the SSAP. The example shows a segmental analysis based on a consolidated profit and loss account. However, SSAP 25 also applies to companies which do not need to prepare group accounts. It is quite common for larger companies to operate through divisions or branches, and each of these could qualify as a segment, depending on the circumstances in each case. In both groups of companies and divisionalised single entity companies, there is frequently considerable trade between divisions.

Arguments against reporting by segment

7.11 Those who argue against this form of disclosure generally emphasise the practical problems, which include:

- **Identifying** segments for reporting purposes
- **Allocating** common income and costs among the different segments
- Reporting **inter-segment** transactions
- Providing information in such a way as to eliminate **misunderstanding** by investors
- Avoiding any **potential damage** that may be done to the reporting entity by disclosing information about individual segments

Question 7

The Leigh Group has three divisions (all based in the UK), A, B and C. Details of their turnover, results and net assets are given below.

	£'000
Division A	
Sales to B	304,928
Other UK sales	57,223
Middle East export sales	406,082
Pacific fringe export sales	77,838
	846,071
Division B	
Sales to C	31,034
Export sales to Europe	195,915
	226,949
Division C	
Export sales to North America	127,003

	Head office	*Division A*	*Division B*	*Division C*
	£'000	£'000	£'000	£'0000
Operational profit/(loss) before tax		162,367	18,754	(8,303)
Re-allocated costs from				
Head office		48,362	24,181	24,181
Interest costs		3,459	6,042	527
Fixed assets	49,071	200,921	41,612	113,076
Net current assets	47,800	121,832	39,044	92,338
Long-term liabilities	28,636	16,959	6,295	120,841
Deferred taxation	1,024	24,671	9,013	4,028

Required

Prepare a segmental report in accordance with SSAP 25 for publication in Bush's group.

Answer

Ignoring comparative figures, Leigh plc's segmental report would look like this.

CLASSES OF BUSINESS

	Group	Division A	Division B	Division C
	£'000	£'000	£'000	£'000
Turnover				
Total sales	1,200,023	846,071	226,949	127,003
Inter-segment sales	335,962	304,928	31,034	-
Sales to third parties	864,061	541,143	195,915	127,003
Profit before taxation				
Segment profit/(loss)	172,818	162,367	18,754	(8,303)
Common costs **	96,724			
Operating profit	76,094			
Net interest	10,028			
Group profit before tax	66,066			
Net assets				
Segment net assets	427,016	281,123	65,348	80,545
Unallocated assets	67,211			
Total net assets	494,227			

GEOGRAPHICAL SEGMENTS

	Group	*United Kingdom*	*Middle East*	*Pacific fringe*	*Europe*	*North America*
Turnover						
Turnover by destination ***						
Sales to third parties	864,061	57,223	406,082	77,838	195,915	127,003

* Turnover, profit, net interest and net assets should be the same as those shown in the consolidated accounts.

** Common costs and unallocated assets are those items in the consolidated accounts which cannot reasonably be allocated to any one segment nor does the group wish to apportion them between segments. An example of a common cost is the cost of maintaining the holding company share register, and an example of an unallocated asset might be the head office building.

*** Turnover by destination must be disclosed in accordance with the Companies Act 1985. If Leigh's divisions were not all in the UK, then another analysis would be required by SSAP 25 on the same lines as that shown for classes of business but analysed between the geographical origins of turnover.

CLASSES OF BUSINESS

	Industry A		Industry B		Other Industries		Group	
	20X2	20X1	20X2	20X1	20X2	20X1	20X2	20X1
	£'000	£'000	£'000	£'000	£'000	£'000	£'000	£'000
Turnover								
Total sales	33,000	30,000	42,000	38,000	26,000	23,000	101,000	91,000
Inter-segment sales	(4,000)	-	-	-	(12,000)	(14,000)	(16,000)	(14,000)
Sales to third parties	29,000	30,000	42,000	38,000	14,000	9,000	85,000	77,000
Profit before taxation								
Segment profit	3,000	2,500	4,500	4,000	1,800	1,500	9,300	8,000
Common costs							(300)	(300)
Operating profit							9,000	7,700
Net interest							(400)	(500)
							8,600	7,200
Group share of the profit before taxation of associated undertakings	1,000	1,000	1,400	1,200	-	-	2,400	2,200
Group profit before taxation							11,000	9,400
Net assets								
Segment net assets	17,600	15,000	24,000	25,000	19,400	19,000	61,000	59,000
Unallocated assets*							3,000	3,000
							64,000	62,000
Group share of the net assets of associated undertakings	10,200	8,000	8,800	9,000	-	-	19,000	17,000
Total net assets							83,000	79,000

* Unallocated assets consist of assets at the group's head office in London amounting to £2.4 million 20X1 : £2.5 million) and at the group's regional office in Hong Kong amounting to £0.6 million (20X1: £0.5 million).

GEOGRAPHICAL SEGMENTS

	United Kingdom		*North America*		*Far East*		*Other*		*Grou*	
	20X2	20X1	20X2	20X1	20X2	20X1	20X2	20X1	20X2	20X1
	£'000	£'000	£'000	£'000	£'000	£'000	£'000	£'000	£'000	£'000
Turnover										
Turnover by destination										
Sales to third parties	34,000	31,000	16,000	14,500	25,000	23,000	10,000	8,500	85,000	77,000
Turnover by origin										
Total sales	38,000	34,000	29,000	27,500	23,000	23,000	12,000	10,500	102,000	95,000
Inter-segment sales	-	-	(8,000)	(9,000)	(9,000)	(9,000)	-	-	(17,000)	(18,000)
Sales to third parties	38,000	34,000	21,000	18,500	14,000	14,000	12,000	10,500	85,000	77,000
Profit before taxation										
Segment profit	4,000	2,900	2,500	2,300	1,800	1,900	1,000	900	9,300	8,000
Common costs									(300)	(300)
Operating profit									9,000	7,700
Net interest									(400)	(500)
									8,600	7,200
Group share of the profit before taxation of associated undertakings	950	1,000	1,450	1,200	-	-	-	-	2,400	2,200
Group profit before taxation									11,000	9,400
Net assets										
Segment net assets	16,000	15,000	25,000	26,000	16,000	15,000	4,000	3,000	61,000	59,000
Unallocated assets*									3,000	3,000
									64,000	62,000
Group share of the net assets of associated undertakings	8,500	7,000	10,500	10,000	-	-	-	-	19,000	17,000
Total net assets									83,000	79,000

* Unallocated assets consist of assets at the group's head office in London amounting to £2.4 million (20X1 : £2.5 million) and at the group's regional office in Hong Kong amounting to £0.6 million (20X1 : £0.5 million).

Chapter roundup

- FRS 3 *Reporting financial performance* has introduced radical changes to the profit and loss account of large and medium sized companies.
- You must know the FRS 3 **definitions** of:
  - extraordinary items
  - exceptional items
  - prior period adjustments
  - discontinued operations
  - total recognised gains and losses
- You must know the **format** of the statement of total recognised gains and losses, the reconciliation of movements in shareholders' funds and the note on historical cost profits and losses, and understand their contents and purpose.
- You must learn:
  - the effect on EPS of: a new issue of shares; a rights issue; a bonus issue;
  - how to calculate **fully diluted EPS**;
  - the **disclosure** requirements of FRS 14.

  The only way to do this is by working through the examples a number of times and repeated question practice.
- Disclosure of the basic EPS and diluted EPS on the face of the profit and loss is required, along with comparatives for both figures. This is the case even if the figures are negative.
- Other EPS figures can be disclosed in the accounts.
  - These must use the same basis for calculating the denominator
  - The reason for the method used must be disclosed
  - They must be consistent year on year
  - The required EPS figures should have the same prominence within the accounts
- The denominator is calculated by finding the weighted average number of ordinary shares in issue in the year.
- Any effect that conversion to ordinary shares has on the earnings figure must be reflected in the calculation of the diluted EPS.
- Only dilutive shares are included in the diluted EPS. Anti-dilutive shares are ignored.
- *SSAP 25* is primarily a disclosure statement concerned to improve the quality of information provided by published accounts. You must be able to prepare a **segmental analysis** and if necessary to use the results to help with interpretation of the accounts as well as to discuss the advantages and limitations of segmental reporting.
- **Prior period adjustments** will only occur in two types of situation.
  - In cases of fundamental error
  - When an accounting policy is changed

  Make sure that you can account for a prior period adjustment.

Quick quiz

1 Ordinary activities are undertaken by a reporting entity as part of its ....

2 Which of the following exceptional items must be shown on the face of the profit and loss account per FRS 3?

A Loss on disposal of manufacturing equipment
B Profit on the sale of a branch
C A significant insurance claim settlement
D The cost of restructuring the entity so that its focus and the nature of its operations are materially different

E A write off of 40% of the year end stock due to unforeseen obsolescence
F A provision for a major loss on a long term contract

3 Give an example of an extraordinary event if you can.

4 A company's year end is 31 December 20X1. The financial statements are approved on 10 February 20X2. A large foreign operation is sold on the 11th February. Should the operation be treated as a discontinued operation?

5 How should a discontinued activity be accounted for?

6 Draw up a proforma statement of total recognised gains and losses.

7 The movement in the reconciliation of movements in shareholders funds is:

Profit /loss for the financial year + Other recognised gains/losses – Dividends + New share capital

True ☐

False ☐

8 To what companies does FRS 14 apply?

A Companies in the process of issuing shares publicly
B Companies with publicly traded shares
C Any company which discloses an EPS figure
D All of the above

9 The following accounting treatment should be used to make a prior period of adjustment.

- Restate the prior year .... and ....
- Restate the .... balance.
- Include the adjustment in the ....
- Include a .... at the foot of the statement ....

10 What figure prefixes the following as the rule of thumb for identifying a segment under SSAP 25?

- .... of the entities total third party turnover
- .... of the combined profit of all profit making segments
- .... of the net assets of the entity

Answers to quick quiz

1 Business. (see para 2.1)

2 All of them. (2.2-2.4)

3 The ASB dopes not envisage any extraordinary items appearing on the company's profit and loss account after the introduction of FRS 3.

4 No. The sale is after the accounts were approved. Disclosure in a note can be made. (3.1)

5 The **results** of the discontinued activity should be shown along with profit/loss on discontinuation (exceptional item) and comparatives. (3.2)

6 Compare yours to that in paragraph 4.3.

7 True (4.17/4.18)

8 D. (5.2)

9 Refer to paragraph 6.4

10 $\geq$ 10%. (7.8)

Now try the question below from the Exam Question Bank

Number	Level	Marks	Time
2	Introductory	n/a	36 mins

Chapter 4

CASH FLOW STATEMENTS

Topic list		Syllabus reference	Ability required
1	FRS 1 *Cash flow statements*	(ii)	Application
2	Preparing a cash flow statement	(ii)	Application
3	Interpretation of cash flow statements	(ii)	Application

Introduction

You have already covered basic cash flow accounting in your Stage 1 studies. Here, the study of cash flow statements revolves around FRS 1, which governs the content and disclosure of cash flow statements in company accounts.

FRS 1 was the first standard produced by the Accounting Standards Board.

This chapter adopts a systematic approach to the preparation of cash flow statements in examinations; you should learn this method and you will then be equipped for any problems which might arise in the exam itself.

When you get to the chapter on the interpretation of accounts in Part D, remember to refer back to this chapter so that you can consider the information provided by cash flow statements.

You must be aware that you will be required to:

- Answer questions on cash flow statements that require a knowledge of FRS 1
- Explain the role of cash flow statements and interpret their content

Learning outcome in this chapter

- **Prepare** a cash flow statement in a form suitable for publication

Syllabus content covered in this chapter

- The preparation of cash flow statements (FRS 1)

1 FRS 1 CASH FLOW STATEMENTS

1.1 FRS 1 sets out the structure of a cash flow statement and it also sets the minimum level of disclosure.

Exam focus point

Examination questions are likely to be computational, but an element of discussion and interpretation may be required. Consider this and remember cashflows as you work through Part D of this text.

There were computational questions in November 2001 and May 2002. November 2001 also included a discursive element on cash management.

Because of the standard way in which a cash flow statement is prepared, you could earn a lot of easy marks if you are prepared to do enough practice to enable you to complete them quickly and accurately.

Objective

1.2 The FRS begins with the following statement.

> 'The objective of this FRS is to ensure that reporting entities falling within its scope:
>
> (a) Report their cash generation and cash absorption for a period by highlighting the significant components of cash flow in a way that facilitates comparison of the cash flow performance of different businesses.
>
> (b) And provide information that assists in the assessment of their liquidity, solvency and financial adaptability.'

Scope

1.3 The FRS applies to all financial statements intended to give a true and fair view of the financial position and profit or loss (or income and expenditure), except those of various exempt bodies in group accounts situations or where the content of the financial statements is governed by other statutes or regulatory regimes. In addition, small companies are excluded as defined by companies legislation.

Format of the cash flow statement

1.4 The format of a cash flow statement for a company should follow the format from FRS 1 which is discussed and illustrated in this chapter.

1.5 A cash flow statement should list its cash flows for the period classified under the following standard headings:

- Operating activities (using either the direct or indirect method)
- Returns on investments and servicing of finance
- Taxation
- Capital expenditure and financial investment
- Acquisitions and disposals
- Equity dividends paid
- Management of liquid resources
- Financing

The last two headings can be shown in a single section provided a subtotal is given for each heading. Acquisitions and disposals are not on your syllabus; the heading is included here for completeness.

1.6 Individual categories of **inflows** and **outflows** under the standard headings should be disclosed separately either in the cash flow statements or in a note to it unless they are

allowed to be shown net. Cash inflows and outflows may be shown net if they relate to the management of liquid resources or financing and the inflows and outflows either:

- Relate in substance to a single financing transaction (unlikely to come up in Paper 6)
- Are due to short maturities and high turnover occurring from rollover or reissue (for example, short-term deposits): *see below, paragraph 1.27

The requirement to show cash inflows and outflows separately does not apply to cash flows relating to operating activities.

1.7 Each cash flow should be classified according to the substance of the transaction giving rise to it.

Links to other primary statements

1.8 Because the information given by a cash flow statement is best appreciated in the context of the information given by the other primary statements, the FRS requires two reconciliations, between:

- **Operating profit** and the net cash flow from operating activities
- The movement in **cash in** the period and the movement in **net debt**

Neither reconciliation forms part of the cash flow statement but each may be given either adjoining the statement or in a separate note.

1.9 The **movement in net debt** should identify the following components and reconcile these to the opening and closing balance sheet amount:

- The cash flows of the entity
- Other non-cash changes
- The recognition of changes in market value and exchange rate movements

Definitions

1.10 The FRS includes the following important definitions (only those of direct concern to your syllabus are included here). Note particularly the definitions of cash and liquid resources.

KEY TERMS

(a) An **active market** is a market of sufficient depth to absorb the investment held without a significant effect on the price. (This definition affects the definition of liquid resources below.)

(b) **Cash** is cash in hand and deposits repayable on demand with any qualifying financial institution, less overdrafts from any qualifying financial institution repayable on demand. Deposits are repayable on demand if they can be withdrawn at any time without notice and without penalty or if a maturity or period of notice of not more than 24 hours or one working day has been agreed. Cash includes cash in hand and deposits denominated in foreign currencies.

(c) **Cash flow** is an increase or decrease in an amount of cash.

(d) **Liquid resources** are current asset investments held as readily disposable stores of value. A readily disposable investment is one that is both:

(i) Disposable by the reporting entity without curtailing or disrupting its business.

- Readily convertible into known amounts of cash at or close to its carrying amount
- Traded in an active market

(e) **Net debt** is the borrowings of the reporting entity less cash and liquid resources. Where cash and liquid resources exceed the borrowings of the entity reference should be to 'net funds' rather than to 'net debt'.

(f) **Overdraft** is a borrowing facility repayable on demand that is used by drawing on a current account with a qualifying financial institution.

Exam focus point

Do ensure you fully understand the above definitions because questions may be phrased in a way that assumes knowledge of them.

Classification of cash flows by standard heading

1.11 The FRS looks at each of the cash flow categories in turn.

Operating activities

1.12 Cash flows from operating activities are in general the cash effects of transactions and other events relating to operating or trading activities, normally shown in the profit and loss account in arriving at operating profit. They include cash flows in respect of operating items relating to provisions, whether or not the provision was included in operating profit.

1.13 A reconciliation between the operating profit reported in the profit and loss account and the net cash flow from operating activities should be given either adjoining the cash flow statement or as a note. The reconciliation is not part of the cash flow statement: if adjoining the cash flow statement, it should be clearly labelled and kept separate. The reconciliation should disclose separately the movements in stocks, debtors and creditors related to operating activities and other differences between cash flows and profits.

Returns on investments and servicing of finance

1.14 These are receipts resulting from the ownership of an investment and payments to providers of finance and non-equity shareholders (eg the holders of preference shares).

1.15 Cash inflows from returns on investments and servicing of finance include:

- Interest received, including any related tax recovered
- Dividends received

1.16 Cash outflows from returns on investments and servicing of finance include:

- Interest paid (even if capitalised), including any tax deducted and paid to the relevant tax authority
- Cash flows that are treated as finance costs (this will include issue costs on debt and non-equity share capital)

- The interest element of finance lease rental payments
- Dividends paid on non-equity shares of the entity

Taxation

1.17 These are cash flows to or from taxation authorities in respect of the reporting entity's revenue and capital profits. VAT and other sales taxes are discussed below.

(a) Taxation cash inflows include cash receipts from the relevant tax authority of tax rebates, claims or returns of overpayments.

(b) Taxation cash outflows include cash payments to the relevant tax authority of tax.

Capital expenditure and financial investment

1.18 These cash flows are those related to the acquisition or disposal of any fixed asset other than one required to be classified under 'acquisitions and disposals' (discussed below), and any current asset investment not included in liquid resources (also dealt with below). If no cash flows relating to financial investment fall to be included under this heading the caption may be reduced to 'capital expenditure'.

1.19 The cash inflows here include receipts from:

- Sales or disposals of property, plant or equipment
- The repayment of the reporting entity's loans to other entities

1.20 Cash outflows in this category include:

- Payments to acquire property, plant or equipment
- Loans made by the reporting entity

Acquisitions and disposals

1.21 These cash flows are related to the acquisition or disposal of any trade or business, or of an investment in an entity that is either an associate, a joint venture, or a subsidiary undertaking (these group matters are beyond the scope of your syllabus).

(a) Cash inflows here include receipts from sales of trades or businesses.
(b) Cash outflows here include payments to acquire trades or businesses.

Equity dividends paid

1.22 The cash outflows are dividends paid on the reporting entity's equity shares.

Management of liquid resources

1.23 This section should include cash flows in respect of liquid resources as defined above. Each entity should explain what it includes as liquid resources and any changes in its policy. The cash flows in this section can be shown in a single section with those under 'financing' provided that separate subtotals for each are given.

1.24 Cash inflows include:

- Withdrawals from short-term deposits not qualifying as cash in so far as not netted under *above (paragraph 1.9)
- Inflows from disposal or redemption of any other investments held as liquid resources

1.25 Cash outflows include:

- Payments into short-term deposits not qualifying as cash in so far as not netted under *above (paragraph 1.9)
- Outflows to acquire any other investments held as liquid resources

Financing

1.26 Financing cash flows comprise receipts or repayments of principal from or to external providers of finance. The cash flows in this section can be shown in a single section with those under 'management of liquid resources' provided that separate subtotals for each are given.

1.27 Financing cash inflows include:

- Receipts from issuing shares or other equity instruments
- Receipts from issuing debentures, loans and from other long-term and short-term borrowings (other than overdrafts)

1.28 Financing cash outflows include:

- Repayments of amounts borrowed (other than overdrafts)
- The capital element of finance lease rental payments
- Payments to reacquire or redeem the entity's shares
- Payments of expenses or commission on any issue of equity shares

Exceptional and extraordinary items and cash flows

1.29 Where cash flows relate to items that are classified as exceptional or extraordinary in the profit and loss account they should be shown under the appropriate standard headings according to the nature of each item. The cash flows relating to exceptional or extraordinary items should be identified in the cash flow statement or a note to it and the relationship between the cash flows and the originating exceptional or extraordinary item should be explained.

1.30 Where cash flows are **exceptional** because of their **size or incidence** but are not related to items that are treated as exceptional or extraordinary in the profit and loss account, sufficient disclosure should be given to explain their cause and nature.

Value added tax and other taxes

1.31 Cash flows should be shown net of any attributable value added tax or other sales tax unless the tax is irrecoverable by the reporting entity. The net movement on the amount payable to, or receivable from the taxing authority should be allocated to cash flows from operating activities unless a different treatment is more appropriate in the particular circumstances concerned. Where restrictions apply to the recoverability of such taxes, the irrecoverable amount should be allocated to those expenditures affected by the restrictions. If this is impracticable, the irrecoverable tax should be included under the most appropriate standard heading.

1.32 Taxation cash flows other than those in respect of the reporting entity's revenue and capital profits and value added tax, or other sales tax, should be included within the cash flow statement under the same standard heading as the cash flow that gave rise to the taxation cash flow, unless a different treatment is more appropriate in the particular circumstances concerned.

Material non-cash transactions

1.33 Material transactions not resulting in movements of cash of the reporting entity should be disclosed in the notes to the cash flow statement if disclosure is necessary for an understanding of the underlying transactions.

Comparative figures

1.34 Comparative figures should be given for all items in the cash flow statement and such notes thereto as are required by the FRS with the exception of the note to the statement that analyses changes in the balance sheet amount making up net debt.

1.35 EXAMPLE: SINGLE COMPANY

The following example is provided by FRS 1 for a single company.

XYZ LIMITED
CASH FLOW STATEMENT FOR THE YEAR ENDED 31 DECEMBER 20X6

Reconciliation of operating profit to net cash inflow from operating activities

	£'000
Operating profit	6,022
Depreciation charges	899
Increase in stocks	(194)
Increase in debtors	(72)
Increase in creditors	234
Net cash inflow from operating activities	6,899

CASH FLOW STATEMENT

	£'000
Net cash inflow from operating activities	6,889
Returns on investments and servicing of finance (note 1)	2,999
Taxation	(2,922)
Capital expenditure (note 1)	(1,525)
	5,441
Equity dividends paid	(2,417)
	3,024
Management of liquid resources (note 1)	(450)
Financing (note 1)	57
Increase in cash	2,631

Reconciliation of net cash flow to movement in net debt (note 2)

	£'000	£'000
Increase in cash in the period	2,631	
Cash to repurchase debenture	149	
Cash used to increase liquid resources	450	
Change in net debt*		3,230
Net debt at 1.1.X6		(2,903)
Net funds at 31.12.X6		327

*In this example all changes in net debt are cash flows.

The reconciliation of operating profit to net cash flows from operating activities can be shown in a note.

NOTES TO THE CASH FLOW STATEMENT

1 *Gross cash flows*

	£'000	£'000
Returns on investments and servicing of finance		
Interest received	3,011	
Interest paid	(12)	
		2,999
Capital expenditure		
Payments to acquire intangible fixed assets	(71)	
Payments to acquire tangible fixed assets	(1,496)	
Receipts from sales of tangible fixed assets	42	
		(1,525)
Management of liquid resources		
Purchase of treasury bills	(650)	
Sale of treasury bills	200	
		(450)
Financing		
Issue of ordinary share capital	211	
Repurchase of debenture loan	(149)	
Expenses paid in connection with share issues	(5)	
		57

Note. These gross cash flows can be shown on the face of the cash flow statement, but it may sometimes be neater to show them as a note like this.

2 *Analysis of changes in net debt*

	As at 1 Jan 20X6 £'000	*Cash flows* £'000	*Other changes* £'000	*At 31 Dec 20X6* £'000
Cash in hand, at bank	42	847		889
Overdrafts	(1,784)	1,784		
		2,631		
Debt due within 1 year	(149)	149	(230)	(230)
Debt due after 1 year	(1,262)		230	(1,032)
Current asset investments	250	450		700
Total	(2,903)	3,230	-	327

Question 1

Close the book for a moment and jot down the format of the cash flow statement.

2 PREPARING A CASH FLOW STATEMENT

2.1 In essence, preparing a cash flow statement is very straightforward. You should therefore simply learn the format given above and apply the steps noted in the example below. Note that the following items are treated in a way that might seem confusing, but the treatment is logical if you think in terms of **cash**.

(a) Increase in stock is treated as **negative** (in brackets). This is because it represents a cash **outflow**; cash is being spent on stock.

(b) An increase in debtors would be treated as **negative** for the same reasons; more debtors means less cash.

(c) By contrast an increase in creditors is **positive** because cash is being retained and not used to pay off creditors. There is therefore more of it.

2.2 EXAMPLE: PREPARATION OF A CASH FLOW STATEMENT

Kitty Ltd's profit and loss account for the year ended 31 December 20X8 and balance sheets at 31 December 20X7 and 31 December 20X8 were as follows.

KITTY LIMITED
PROFIT AND LOSS ACCOUNT FOR THE YEAR ENDED 31 DECEMBER 20X8

	£'000	£'000
Sales		720
Raw materials consumed	70	
Staff costs	94	
Depreciation	118	
Loss on disposal	18	
		300
Operating profit		420
Interest payable		28
Profit before tax		392
Taxation		124
		268
Dividend		72
Profit retained for year		196
Balance brought forward		490
		686

KITTY LIMITED
BALANCE SHEETS AS AT 31 DECEMBER

	20X8		*20X7*	
	£'000	£'000	£'000	£'000
Fixed assets				
Cost		1,596		1,560
Depreciation		318		224
		1,278		1,336
Current assets				
Stock	24		20	
Trade debtors	76		58	
Bank	48		56	
	148		134	
Current liabilities				
Trade creditors	12		6	
Taxation	102		86	
Proposed dividend	30		24	
	144		116	
Working capital		4		18
		1,282		1,354
Long-term liabilities				
Long-term loans		200		500
		1,082		854
Share capital		360		340
Share premium		36		24
Profit and loss		686		490
		1,082		854

During the year, the company paid £90,000 for a new piece of machinery.

Required

Prepare a cash flow statement for Kitty Ltd for the year ended 31 December 20X8 in accordance with the requirements of FRS 1 (revised).

2.3 SOLUTION

Step 1. Set out the proforma cash flow statement with all the headings required by FRS 1 (revised). You should leave plenty of space. Ideally, use three or more sheets of paper, one for the main statement, one for the notes (particularly if you have a separate note for the gross cash flows) and one for your workings. It is obviously essential to know the formats very well.

Step 2. Complete the reconciliation of operating profit to net cash inflow as far as possible. When preparing the statement from balance sheets, you will usually have to calculate such items as depreciation, loss on sale of fixed assets and profit for the year (see Step 4).

Step 3. Calculate the figures for tax paid, dividends paid, purchase or sale of fixed assets, issue of shares and repayment of loans if these are not already given to you (as they may be). Note that you may not be given the tax charge in the profit and loss account. You will then have to assume that the tax paid in the year is last year's year-end provision and calculate the charge as the balancing figure.

Step 4. If you are not given the profit figure, open up a working for the profit and loss account. Using the opening and closing balances, the taxation charge and dividends paid and proposed, you will be able to calculate profit for the year as the balancing figure to put in the statement.

Step 5. You will now be able to complete the statement by slotting in the figures given or calculated.

KITTY LIMITED
CASH FLOW STATEMENT FOR THE YEAR ENDED 31 DECEMBER 20X8

Reconciliation of operating profit to net cash inflow

	£'000
Operating profit	420
Depreciation charges	118
Loss on sale of tangible fixed assets	18
Increase in stocks	(4)
Increase in debtors	(18)
Increase in creditors	6
Net cash inflow from operating activities	540

CASH FLOW STATEMENT

	£'000	£'000
Net cash flows from operating activities		540
Returns on investment and servicing of finance		
Interest paid		(28)
Taxation		
Corporation tax paid (W1)		(108)
Capital expenditure		
Payments to acquire tangible fixed assets (W2)	(90)	
Receipts from sales of tangible fixed assets (W2)	12	
Net cash outflow from capital expenditure		(78)
		326
Equity dividends paid (24 + 72 – 30)		(66)
		260
Financing		
Issues of share capital (360 + 36 – 340 – 24)	32	
Long-term loans repaid (500 – 200)	(300)	
Net cash outflow from financing		(268)
Decrease in cash		(8)

NOTES TO THE CASH FLOW STATEMENT

Analysis of changes in net debt

	At 1 Jan 20X8	*Cash flows*	*At 31 Dec 20X8*
	£'000	£'000	£'000
Cash in hand, at bank	56	(8)	48
Debt due after 1 year	(500)	300	(200)
Total	(444)	292	(152)

Workings

1 *Corporation tax paid*

	£'000
Opening CT payable	86
Charge for year	124
Net CT payable at 31.12.X8	(102)
Paid	108

2 *Fixed asset disposals*

COST

	£'000		£'000
At 1.1.X7	1,560	At 31.12.X8	1,596
Purchases	90	Disposals	54
	1,650		1,650

ACCUMULATED DEPRECIATION

	£'000		£'000
At 31.1.X8	318	At 1.1.X7	224
Depreciation on disposals	24	Charge for year	118
	342		342

NBV of disposals	30
Net loss reported	(18)
Proceeds of disposals	12

Exam focus point

Usually cash flow statements represent straightforward marks for a lot of number crunching.

Once you have set up a proforma try to work through your answer in a confident, relaxed but brisk manner. Avoid panicking over any part you can't do as a lot of it stands alone and you can get marks for what you have done.

Alternative methods

2.4 FRS 1 allows two possible layouts for a cash flow statement in respect of operating activities:

- The **indirect method**, which is the one we have used so far
- The **direct method**

2.5 Under the **direct method** the operating element of the cash flow statement should be shown as follows.

	£'000
Operative activities	
Cash received from customers	X
Cash payments to suppliers	(X)
Cash paid to and on behalf of employees	(X)
Other cash payments	(X)
Net cash flow from operating activities	X

2.6 Points to note are as follows.

(a) The reconciliation of operating profits and cash flows is still required (by note).

(b) **Cash received from customers** represents cash flows received during the accounting period in respect of sales.

(c) **Cash payments to suppliers** represents cash flows made during the accounting period in respect of goods and services.

(d) **Cash payments to and on behalf of employees** represents amounts paid to employees including the associated tax and national insurance. It will, therefore, comprise gross salaries, employer's National Insurance and any other benefits (eg pension contributions).

Exam focus point

The Paper 6 examiner has suggested that where the direct method is used, the reconciliation of operating profits and cash flows is still required by way of note. Hence, there is unlikely to be any benefit in opting for the direct method.

However, in practice, there are companies like Marks and Spencer, who nevertheless use the direct method. Obviously, the direct method may be used where the company wishes to provide its shareholders with the information shown by this approach, in spite of any extra effort that may be involved.

Question 2

The summarised accounts of Rene plc for the year ended 31 December 20X8 are as follows.

RENE PLC
BALANCE SHEET AS AT 31 DECEMBER 20X8

	20X8		20X7	
	£'000	£'000	£'000	£'000
Fixed assets				
Tangible assets		628		514
Current assets				
Stocks	214		210	
Debtors	168		147	
Cash	7		-	
	389		357	
Creditors: amounts falling due within one year				
Trade creditors	136		121	
Tax payable	39		28	
Dividends payable	18		16	
Overdraft	-		14	
	193		179	
Net current assets		196		178
Total assets less current liabilities		824		692
Creditors: amounts falling due after more than one year				
10% debentures		(80)		(50)
		744		642
Capital and reserves				
Share capital (£1 ords)		250		200
Share premium account		70		60
Revaluation reserve		110		100
Profit and loss account		314		282
		744		642

RENE PLC
PROFIT AND LOSS ACCOUNT
FOR THE YEAR ENDED 31 DECEMBER 20X8

	£'000
Sales	600
Cost of sales	(319)
Gross profit	281
Other expenses (including depreciation of £42,000)	(194)
Profit before tax	87
Tax	(31)
Profit after tax	56
Dividends	(24)
Retained profit for the year	32

You are additionally informed that there have been no disposals of fixed assets during the year. New debentures were issued on 1 January 20X8. Wages for the year amounted to £86,000.

Required

Produce a cash flow statement using the direct method suitable for inclusion in the financial statements, as per FRS 1 (revised 1996).

Answer

RENE PLC
CASH FLOW STATEMENT
FOR THE YEAR ENDED 31 DECEMBER 20X8

	£'000	£'000
Operating activities		
Cash received from customers (W1)	579	
Cash payments to suppliers (W2)	(366)	
Cash payments to and on behalf of employees	(86)	
		127
Returns on investments and servicing of finance		
Interest paid		(8)
Taxation		
UK corporation tax paid (W5)		(20)
Capital expenditure		
Purchase of tangible fixed assets (W6)	(146)	
Net cash outflow from capital expenditure		(146)
		(47)
Equity dividends paid (W4)		(22)
Financing		
Issue of share capital	60	
Issue of debentures	30	
Net cash inflow from financing		90
Increase in cash		21

NOTES TO THE CASHFLOW STATEMENT

1 *Reconciliation of operating profit to net cash inflow from operating activities*

	£'000
Operating profit (87 + 8)	95
Depreciation	42
Increase in stock	(4)
Increase in debtors	(21)
Increase in creditors	15
	127

2 Reconciliation of net cash flow to movement in net debt

	£'000
Net cash inflow for the period	21
Cash received from debenture issue	(30)
Change in net debt	(9)
Net debt at 1 January 20X8	(64)
Net debt at 31 December 20X8	(73)

3 Analysis of changes in net debt

	At 1 January 20X8 £'000	*Cash flows* £'000	*At 31 December 20X8* £'000
Cash at bank	-	7	7
Overdrafts	(14)	14	-
		21	
Debt due after 1 year	(50)	(30)	(80)
Total	(64)	(9)	(73)

Workings

1 *Cash received from customers*

DEBTORS CONTROL ACCOUNT

	£'000		£'000
B/f	147	Cash received (bal)	579
Sales	600	C/f	168
	747		747

2 *Cash paid to suppliers*

CREDITORS CONTROL ACCOUNT

	£'000		£'000
Cash paid (bal)	366	B/f	121
C/f	136	Purchases (W3)	381
	502		502

3 *Purchases*

	£'000
Cost of sales	319
Opening stock	(210)
Closing stock	214
Expenses (194 – 42 – 86 – 8 debenture interest)	58
	381

4 *Dividends*

DIVIDENDS

	£'000		£'000
∴ Dividends paid	22	Balance b/f	16
Balance c/f	18	Dividend for year	24
	40		40

5 *Taxation*

TAXATION

	£'000		£'000
∴ Tax paid	20	Balance b/f	28
Balance c/f	39	Charge for year	31
	59		59

6 *Purchase of fixed assets*

	£'000
Opening fixed assets	514
Less depreciation	(42)
Add revaluation (110 – 100)	10
	482
Closing fixed assets	628
Difference = additions	146

Note

Remember that a loss on disposal is calculated as net book value less proceeds, not original cost less proceeds. Do not forget to calculate the accumulated depreciation on the disposed asset. With respect to dividends, remember that dividends paid should be deducted as a cash outflow whereas dividends proposed should be added back to the retained profit.

3 INTERPRETATION OF CASH FLOW STATEMENTS

Exam focus point

Often you may get a cash flow statement to prepare but along with it comes a little question for 5 marks or so. These tend not to recur in terms of content, but are designed to test whether you really understand what a cash flow is, what the various parts mean, its advantages and limitations. To prepare for a very much unseen and probably unpredictable question, you could try to talk a friend through a cash flow statement on the basis that they will ask you probing questions as you go along.

3.1 In this section we will try to cover a number of points that may be useful in addressing a discursive question on cash flow statements.

3.2 Cash management is an important part of **business survival**. A business can be profitable but will hit trouble if it lacks **cash to pay its debts**.

3.3 Cash flow statements **eliminate** the **impact** of the **accruals** basis of accounting. The effects of **provisions** are **excluded**.

3.4 It may be easier to **compare** the cash flows of **different companies** instead of profits. This avoids the impact of different **accounting policies** and **estimation techniques**, but not the implications of different **business practices** eg one hotel may employ its own in-house cleaners whereas another hotel may contract out its cleaning tasks.

3.5 Cash flow statements could deliver more accurate **messages to shareholders and employees**. There may be profits but perhaps not the cash for high dividends or optimistic wage claims. Stakeholders expectations can therefore be managed better.

3.6 A review of the cash flow statement can give an idea of **where the money is coming from**. Is the company generating enough cash from **operating activities**? Or does the company have to rely on **borrowings** and **sales of fixed assets**?

3.7 Like profitability, cash flow needs to be reviewed over a **number of years**. As always, **trends** are **important**.

3.8 Cash flow statements **avoid** the consequences of **revaluations** of fixed assets.

3.9 Cash flow statements can themselves be susceptible to **window dressing/manipulation**.

- **Holding back** on **payments** to make the cash flow look better.
- **Selling off assets, borrowing** more money or **issuing new shares** can be used to cover for lack of cash flow from operations.
- Making a **special effort** to **collect debtors** before the period end.
- **Transactions** themselves can be arranged in a **cash flow advantageous manner** eg lease or hire an asset to spread payments rather than one-off acquisitions.

3.10 Because of the above, it may be helpful to **review** the **cash flow** from the **various sources against** the **liabilities** shown in the **balance sheet**. for example, is the level of cash flow from operations adequate to cover current liabilities?

3.11 From a business management perspective, cautious concentration on cash may lead businesses to be **commercially risk averse** and **not maximise profitability**.

3.12 **Idle cash** is unlikely to provide as profitable returns as compared to those that can be earned on good commercial activities or projects.

3.13 Acquisitions of **fixed assets** may adversely affect cash flow, but are nevertheless **important for long term growth** of a business.

3.14 Profit is good measure of commercial performance whereas cash provides information on financial adaptability and liquidity. **In the long-term, positive cash flow will depend on the business being profitable.**

3.15 Cash flow statements are historic. Whether they can be predictive depends on the stability of the business itself. Their effectiveness as a management tool is more likely to be enhanced when **used** in **conjunction** with cash flow **forecasts** into the future.

3.16 From an in-house management accountant's perspective, the cash flow statement should be used in conjunction with **other management** tools such as the **business strategy**, the **business plan, management accounts, investment appraisal reports** and **cash flow forecasts**.

Question 3

Can you think of some possible disadvantages of cash flow accounting?

Answer

The main disadvantages of cash accounting are essentially the advantages of accruals accounting (proper matching of related items). There is also the practical problem that few businesses keep historical cash flow information in the form needed to prepare a historical cash flow statement and so extra record keeping is likely to be necessary.

Why FRS 1 was revised

3.17 FRS 1 was revised, at least in part, because of certain criticisms. We will look at these briefly.

3.18 The original FRS 1 included 'cash equivalents' with cash. Cash equivalents were highly liquid investments with a maturity date of less than three months from the date of acquisitions (netted off against similar advances from banks). The inclusion of cash equivalents was criticised because it did not reflect the way in which businesses were managed: in particular, the requirement that to be a cash equivalent an investment had to be within three months of maturity was considered unrealistic. In the revised FRS, only cash in hand and deposits repayable on demand, less overdrafts, are included in 'cash'.

3.19 To distinguish the management of assets similar to cash (which previously might have been classed as 'cash equivalents') from other investment decisions, the revised FRS has a section dealing separately with the cash flows arising from the management of liquid resources.

3.20 The new note required by FRS 1 (revised) reconciling movement in net debt gives additional information on company performance, solvency and financial adaptability.

Chapter roundup

Cash flow statements were made compulsory for companies because it was recognised that accounting profit is not the only indicator of a company's performance. FRS 1 *Cash flow statements* was revised in October 20X6.

- Cash flow statements concentrate on the **sources** and **uses** of cash and are a useful indicator of a company's liquidity and solvency.
- You need to learn the **format** of the statement; setting out the format is an essential first stage in preparing the statement but it will only really sink in with more question practice.
- Remember the **step-by-step preparation** procedure and use it for all the questions you practise.
- Note that you may be expected to **analyse** or **interpret** a cash flow statement; this is raised again in Chapter 12.

Quick quiz

1 List the aims of a cash flow statement.

2 The standard headings in the FRS1 cashflow are:

- O.................. a................
- R.................. on i.................. and s.................... of f..................
- T....................
- C.................. e...................... and f.................. i....................
- A..................... and d....................
- E...................... d....................... p......................
- M..................... of l..................... r....................
- F....................

3 Liquid resources are current asset investments which will mature or can be redeemed within three months of the year end.

True ☐

False ☐

4 Why are you more likely to encounter the indirect method as opposed to the direct method?

5 List five advantages of cash flow accounting.

Answers to quick quiz

1 Comparability and assessment of liquidity, solvency and financial adaptability.

2 See paragraph 1.8.

3 False. See the definition in paragraph 1.13(d) if you are not sure about this.

4 The indirect method utilises figures which appear in the financial statements. The figures required for the direct method may not be readily available. (see para 2.7)

5 See paragraph 3.9

Now try the question below from the Exam Question Bank

Number	Level	Marks	Time
3	Exam level	25	45 mins

Part C

Accounting standards

Chapter 5

FIXED ASSETS: TANGIBLE ASSETS

Topic list		Syllabus reference	Ability required
1	Statutory provisions relating to all fixed assets	(iii)	Evaluation
2	FRS 15 *Tangible fixed assets*	(iii)	Evaluation
3	Revaluation	(iii)	Evaluation
4	SSAP 19 *Accounting for investment properties*	(iii)	Evaluation
5	FRS 11 *Impairment of fixed assets and goodwill*	(iii)	Knowledge

Introduction

You have already looked at fixed assets and the principles of depreciation in your Foundation studies. If you are in any doubt about the various methods of depreciation which can be used and the related calculations, you should refer back to your Foundation study material.

The other two standards covered in this chapter are quite straightforward. Learn their main provisions and make sure that you can carry out the relevant exercises.

In Section 1, before we look at individual accounting standards, we will consider the disclosure requirements relating to fixed assets laid down by the Companies Act. Refer to Chapter 2 to put these requirements into context. Remember that these provisions apply to **all** fixed assets. We will look at **intangible** fixed assets in Chapter 6.

Learning outcomes covered in this chapter

- **Explain** the accounting rules contained in Financial Reporting Standards which provide guidance as to the appropriate treatment of certain transactions
- **Identify**, **apply** and **evaluate** the accounting treatment of significant transactions

Syllabus content covered in this chapter

- Tangible fixed assets (FRS 15 and FRS 11) – the calculation of depreciation and the effect of revaluations, changes to economic useful life, impairment values, repairs, improvements and disposals. (Note: For FRS 11 no value in use calculations are required only a knowledge of basic principles.)
- Investment properties (SSAP 19).

1 STATUTORY PROVISIONS RELATING TO ALL FIXED ASSETS

1.1 The standard balance sheet format of CA 1985 divides fixed assets into three categories:

(a) **Intangible assets** (BI in the CA 1985 format).
(b) **Tangible assets** (BII).
(c) **Investments** (BIII).

1.2 In this chapter we will deal with the general rules of the CA 1985 relating to *all* fixed assets. These may be considered under two headings.

(a) **Valuation:** the amounts at which fixed assets should be stated in the balance sheet.

(b) **Disclosure:** the information that should be disclosed in the accounts regarding:

- Valuation of fixed assets
- Movements on fixed asset accounts during the year.

Valuation of fixed assets

Cost

1.3 The two key ways of acquiring a tangible fixed asset are either by purchase or by self-production.

1.4 **Purchased asset: Its cost is simply the purchase price plus any expenses incidental to its acquisition.**

1.5 **Asset produced by a company for its own use:** This should be included at 'production cost' which *must* include:

- **Cost of raw materials**
- **Consumables** used
- Other **attributable direct costs** (such as labour)

Production cost **may** additionally **include:**

- **A reasonable proportion of indirect costs**
- **Interest** on any capital borrowed to **finance production** of the asset.

The amount of capitalised interest must however be disclosed in a note to the accounts.

Depreciation

1.6 The '**cost**' of any fixed asset having a limited economic life, whether purchase price or production cost, **must be reduced by provisions for depreciation** calculated to write off the cost, less any residual value, **systematically over the period of the asset's useful life.** This very general requirement is supplemented by the more detailed provisions of FRS 15 *Tangible fixed assets* which is dealt with in the next section.

1.7 Any provision for **impairment** should be disclosed on the **face of the profit and loss account or by way of note.** Where a provision becomes **no longer necessary**, because the conditions giving rise to it have altered, it should be **written back**, and again **disclosure** should be made.

(Impairment is covered in more detail later in the text).

Fixed assets valuation: alternative accounting rules

1.8 Although the Companies Act 1985 maintains **historical cost** principles as the **normal basis** for the preparation of accounts, **alternative bases** allowing for **revaluations** and **current cost accounting are permitted provided that:**

(a) The **items affected** and the **basis of valuation** are **disclosed** in a note to the accounts;

(b) The **historical cost** in the current and previous years is **separately disclosed** in the balance sheet or in a note to the accounts. Alternatively, the difference between the revalued amount and historical cost may be disclosed.

KEY TERM

Using the **alternative accounting rules**, the appropriate value of any fixed asset (ie its **current cost or market value**), rather than its purchase price or production cost, **may be included in the balance sheet.**

1.9 Here is a diagram to help clarify the options available under CA 1985, schedule 4.

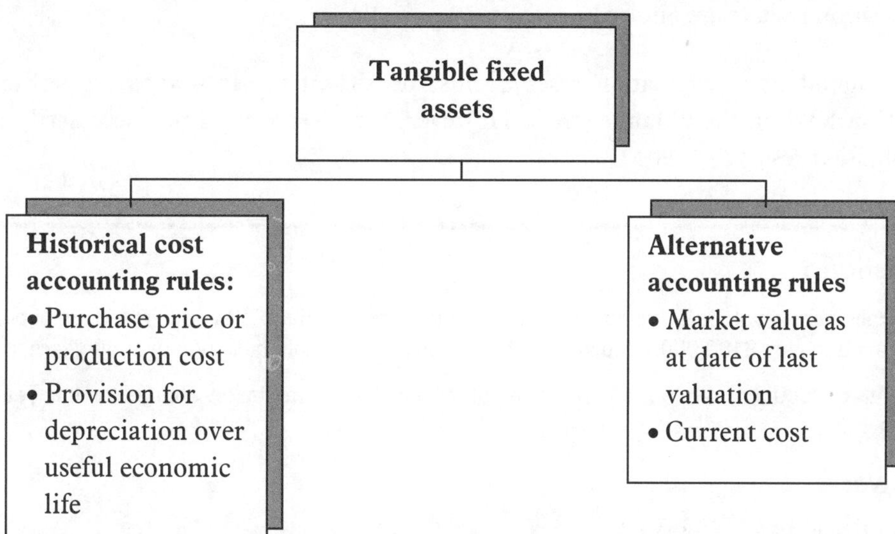

1.10 **Where appropriate, depreciation may be provided on the basis of the new valuation(s),** such depreciation being referred to in the Companies Act 1985 as the '**adjusted amount**' of depreciation. For profit and loss account purposes, **FRS 15** (see below) specifically states that depreciation must be charged on the **revalued amount** and that the ***whole* charge** must be taken to the **profit and loss account**.

Revaluation reserve

KEY TERM

Where the value of any fixed asset is determined by using the **alternative accounting rules**, the amount of **profit or loss arising** must be credited or (as the case may be) debited to a separate reserve, the **revaluation reserve.** (Revised asset value – net book value prior to revaluation: Transfer to revaluation reserve)

1.11 The **depreciation** written off **prior to** the **revaluation** should not be **written back** to the **profit and loss account**. CA 1985 also allows any potential deferred tax on a surplus to be taken to revaluation reserve. (See Chapter 8).

1.12 The revaluation reserve **must be reduced** to the extent that the amounts standing to the credit of the reserves are, in the opinion of the **directors** of the company, **no longer necessary** for the purposes of the accounting policies adopted by the company.

Uses of revaluation reserve

1.13 However, the Companies Act 1985 states that an amount **may be transferred** from the revaluation reserve to the profit and loss account ie debit revaluation reserve and credit profit and loss reserve, if the amount:

- Was previously charged to profit and loss account
- Represents realised profit (for example on disposal of a fixed asset)

1.14 The revaluation reserve may also be used for a **bonus issue** of shares. No other debits to revaluation reserve are allowed.

1.15 The amount of a revaluation reserve must be shown under a **separate sub-heading** in **position KIII** on the **balance sheet**. However, the reserve need not necessarily be called a 'revaluation reserve'.

Question 1

Studivation Ltd revalued a freehold building on 31 March 20X5 to £300,000. The original purchase cost 10 years ago was £180,000. Studivation Ltd depreciates freehold buildings over 40 years.

Show the accounting entries for the revaluation and the depreciation charge for the year ended 31 March 20X6.

Answer

			£	£
(a)	*Revaluation*			
	DEBIT	Fixed asset cost (£300,000 – £180,000)	120,000	
	DEBIT	Accumulated depreciation (£180,000 ÷ 40 × 10)	45,000	
	CREDIT	Revaluation reserve		165,000
(b)	*Depreciation charge*			
	DEBIT	Depreciation (£300,000 ÷ 30)	10,000	
	CREDIT	Accumulated depreciation		10,000

Fixed assets: Companies act disclosures

1.16 **Notes to the accounts** must show, for **each class** of **fixed assets**, an analysis of the **movements** on both **costs** and **depreciation provisions**. Refer back to the note on fixed assets in Chapter 2.

1.17 Where any **fixed assets** of a company (other than listed investments) are included in the accounts at an alternative accounting valuation, the **following information** must also be given:

(a) The **years** (so far as they are known to the directors) in which the assets were **severally valued** and the **several values**.

(b) In the case of assets that have been **valued** during the **financial period**, the **names** of the **persons** who valued them or particulars of their **qualifications** for doing so and (whichever is stated) the **bases of valuation** used by them.

1.18 A **note to the accounts** must **classify land and buildings** under the headings of:

(a) **Freehold property.**

(b) **Leasehold property,** distinguishing between:

(i) **Long leaseholds,** in which the **unexpired term** of the lease at the balance sheet date is **not less than 50 years.**

(ii) **Short leaseholds** which are all leaseholds other than long leaseholds.

2 FRS 15 TANGIBLE FIXED ASSETS

Exam focus point

FRS 15 is likely to come up in the examination as part of a question.

The standard itself is quite straightforward but you will be expected to apply it. This is likely to involve being able to interpret working at various given scenarios.

KEY TERM

Tangible fixed assets have **physical substance** and are held for:

- Use in the production or supply of goods or services
- Rental to others
- Administration purposes

on a **continuing basis** in the **reporting entity's activities.**

They are held to **earn revenue** by their **use, not** from their **resale.**

Objective

2.1 FRS 15 deals with accounting for the initial measurement, valuation and depreciation of tangible fixed assets. It also sets out the information that should be disclosed to enable readers to understand the impact of the accounting policies adopted in relation to these issues.

Initial measurement

Exam focus point

Initial measurement and tested in the November 2002 are May 2003 papers. These required the ability to understand and interpret given information with a FRS 15 perspective.

There was also a 7 mark question on the treatment of decommissioning costs included in the May 2003 paper.

2.2 A tangible fixed asset should **initially be measured at cost.**

> **KEY TERM**
>
> **Cost** is purchase price plus any costs directly attributable to bringing the asset into working condition for its intended use.

Directly attributable costs

2.3 Directly attributable costs include:

- **Direct labour** costs of using **own employees**
- **Acquisition costs,** eg stamp duty, import duties
- Cost of **site preparation** and clearance
- Initial **delivery and handling** costs
- **Installation** costs
- **Professional fees** eg legal and architect's fees
- The estimated cost of **dismantling and removing** the asset and restoring the site, to the extent that it is recognised as a provision under FRS 12 *Provisions, contingent liabilities and contingent assets* (discussed in Chapter 11). The fact that the prospect of such expenditures emerges only some time after the original capitalisation of the asset (eg because of legislative changes) does not preclude their capitalisation.

2.4 Administration and other general overhead costs and employee costs not related to the specific tangible fixed asset are not directly attributable costs.

2.5 In general terms, directly attributable costs can be regarded as incremental costs that would have been avoided only if the tangible fixed asset had not been constructed as required.

Abnormal costs

2.6 Costs such as those arising from design error, wasted materials, industrial disputes, idle capacity or production delays are considered to be **abnormal** and **not directly attributable** to bringing the asset into **working condition** and its **intended use**. This approach is consistent with SSAP 9. They should therefore should **not be capitalised** as part of the cost of the asset.

Start-up or commissioning period

2.7 The costs associated with a **start-up** or **commissioning period** should be **included** in the cost of the tangible fixed asset **only where** the **asset is available for use** but **incapable** of operating at **normal levels without** such a **start-up** or **commissioning period.**

2.8 The costs of an **essential commissioning period** are included as part of the **cost of bringing the asset up to its normal operating potential,** and **therefore** as **part** of its **cost.**

However, there is no justification for regarding costs relating to other start-up periods, where the asset is available for use but not yet operating at normal levels.

Question 2

Halliday Inn has been is being built and opens for business in January 20X9. Demand is expected to build up slowly and high levels of room occupancy are only likely to be achieved over a period of several months.

Should any of the costs incurred in the run up to optimal occupancy of hotel be capitalised.

Answer

No. The hotel is able to operate at normal levels immediately on opening without necessarily having to go through a start up period in a slack season.

Question 3

Duncan Donatz Ltd has constructed a high speed machine for making holes of different shapes in doughnuts.

The machine is to be commissioned in two stages:

(1) *Test run phase.* This phase is designed to ensure that the shapes are punched properly and the process operates smoothly and efficiently. During this run in phase, output will be restricted to test runs.

(2) *Demand building phase*. During this phase output is expected to be low because the company is trying to achieve product acceptance of a different innovative type of doughnut. However, the machine is capable of operating at a normal level of output.

How should the costs relating to these two start up phases be treated?

Answer

Phase 1. The relevant costs should be capitalised together with the cost of machine because the machine is **not capable** of operating at normal levels without such a start up or commissioning period.

Phase 2. Costs associated with this period should be written off to profit and loss account. The machine is now capable of operating at normal levels and the low volumes are due to market factors.

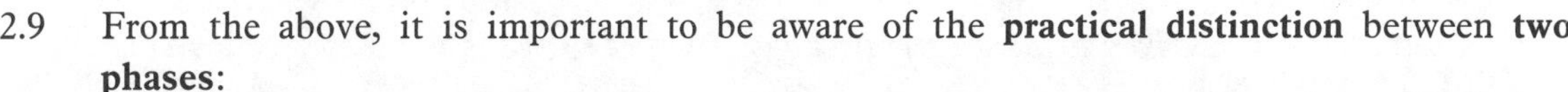

2.9 From the above, it is important to be aware of the **practical distinction** between **two phases**:

(a) **Essential start-up** and **commissioning** phase, without which the asset is **incapable** of operating at normal levels.

(b) **Demand building phase** when output is built up to **full utilisation.**

2.10 Remember that the FRS 15 approach differs from the SSAP 9 approach to initial recognition. FRS 15 works on an **incremental cost approach,** whereas **SSAP 9** is based on **total absorption costing basis** and therefore does not prohibit recognition of general overheads.

Finance costs

Exam focus point

The capitalisation of finance costs appeared in the May 2002 exam paper. It could appear again soon.

2.11 Finance costs directly attributable to the construction of a fixed asset **may be capitalised** if it is **company policy** to do so. However, this **policy must be applied consistently**.

2.12 All finance costs that are **directly attributable** to the construction of a tangible fixed asset should be **capitalised** as part of the **cost of the asset**.

KEY TERM

Directly attributable finance costs are those that would have been **avoided** if there had been **no expenditure on the asset**.

2.13 If finance costs are capitalised, capitalisation should start when:

- Finance **costs** are being **incurred**
- Expenditure on the **asset** is being **incurred**
- **Activities** necessary to get the **asset ready** for use are **in progress**

2.14 **Capitalisation** of finance costs should **cease** when the asset is **ready for use**.

Subsequent expenditure

2.15 After a tangible fixed asset has been brought into use, in practice, there is likely to be **further money spent**.

(a) **Revenue expenditure** which should be **written off** to the profit and loss account.
(b) **Capital expenditure** which should be debited to **tangible fixed assets**.

Expenditure to be written off to profit and loss account

GENERAL RULE

Subsequent expenditure to ensure that a tangible fixed asset maintains its previously assessed standard of performance should be written off to profit and loss account as it is incurred.

Question 4

Yummy Foods Ltd has to regularly service and overhaul its labelling machines to ensure that the labels are properly aligned and the tins roll off the production line efficiently, in accordance with the company's production targets.

How should these cost be treated?

Answer

Such expenditure ensures that the machinery sustains its originally assessed standard of performance. Without such expenditure, the useful economic life or residual value is likely to be reduced and in consequence the depreciation charge would increase.

Hence the expenditure is effectively 'repairs and maintenance' to be expensed in the profit and loss account.

Expenditure to be capitalised

2.16 FRS 15 specifies three scenarios where subsequent expenditure should be capitalised.

(a) It **enhances** the **economic benefits** over and **above previously assessed standards of performance.**

(b) A **component** of an asset that has been treated **separately** for **depreciation purposes** (because it has a substantially different useful economic life from the rest of the asset) has been **restored** or **replaced.**

(c) The expenditure related to a **major inspection** or **overhaul** that **restores economic benefits** that have been consumed and reflected in the depreciation charge.

Enhancement of economic benefits

2.17 FRS 15 offers two ways of **enhancing** the **economic benefits** that a tangible fixed asset might deliver:

(a) Mod**ifying the asset** to increase its capacity.

Eg a hotel reduces its non-productive communal areas to give it more bedrooms.

(b) **Upgrading the asset** to achieve a substantial **improvement** in the **quality** of the product or service provided to customers.

Eg a hotel reupholsters its fabric furniture with leather to improve the quality of service provided to its guests.

Replacement of separately depreciated component

2.18 In these circumstances, the component is disposed of and replaced by a new asset.

Question 5

Safeair Ltd treats its aircraft engines separately for depreciation purposes. The engine on one of its aircraft caught fire on take off and has had to be replaced.

How should the cost of the replacement engine be treated?

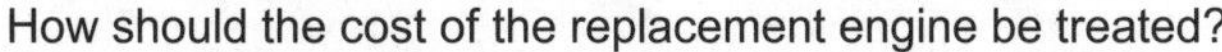

Answer

The new engine should be capitalised as a fixed asset addition with the destroyed engine taken to disposal account and expensed via the profit and loss account.

Major overhauls and inspections

2.19 In addition to routine repairs and maintenance, some assets also require substantial expenditure every few years on major overhauls or inspections. Some examples found in practice are aircraft airworthiness inspections, ocean liner refits, theme park ride overhauls, refurbishment of kiln linings and replacing roofs of buildings.

Question 6

Safeair Ltd is required by law to overhaul its aircraft once every three years. Unless the overhauls are done, the aircraft cannot be flown.

How should the costs of the overhauls be treated?

Answer

The cost of the overhaul is capitalised when incurred because it restores the economic benefits flowing from the tangible fixed assets. The carrying amount representing the cost of benefits consumed is removed from the balance sheet.

Depreciation

Exam focus point

The important point to note is that depreciation is the allocation of cost (or revalued amount), less estimated residual value, over expected useful life. It is not intended as a process of valuing assets. Depreciation is consistent with the FRS 18 accruals basis of accounting: the cost is spread over the periods to which the cost relates, rather than being charged to the period when the payment is made. This is in keeping with what the ASB statement of principles refers to as 'time matching'.

Purpose of depreciation

2.20 As noted earlier, the Companies Act 1985 requires that all fixed assets having a limited economic life should be depreciated. **FRS 15** provides a useful discussion of the **purpose of depreciation** and supplements the statutory requirements in important ways.

KEY TERM

Depreciation is defined in FRS 15 as the measure of the cost or revalued amount of the **economic benefits** of the tangible fixed asset that have been **consumed during the period**.

Consumption includes:

- Wearing out
- Using up
- Other reduction in the useful economic life

of a tangible fixed asset, whether arising from:

- Use
- Effluxion (passage) of time
- Obsolescence through either:
  - changes in technology
  - reduction in demand for the goods and services produced by the asset.

2.21 This definition includes

- **Amortisation** of **assets** with a **pre-determined life**, such as a **leasehold**
- **Depletion** of **wasting assets** such as **mines**.

General requirements

2.22 FRS 15 specifies the following general rules regarding depreciation.

(a) The depreciable amount of a tangible fixed asset should be allocated on a **systematic basis** over its **useful economic life**

(b) The depreciation method used should **reflect** as fairly as possible the **pattern** in which the asset's **economic benefits** are **consumed** by the company

(c) The depreciation charge for each period should be recognised as an **expense** in the profit and loss account.

Methods of depreciation

2.23 A **variety of methods** can be used to **allocate** the **depreciable amount** of a tangible fixed asset. **No specific method is stipulated.**

2.24 FRS 15 mentions two common methods of depreciation.

(a) **Straight-line**. This method assumes that equal amounts of economic benefit are consumed in each year of the asset's life. Therefore the asset is written off in **equal instalments** over its **estimated useful economic life.**

(b) **Reducing balance**. Here the **depreciation rate** is applied to the **opening net book value**. This method charges more depreciation in the early years of an asset's life than in later years. In later years, there is likely to be more spent on repairs and maintenance.

2.25 There are the methods you may encounter in practice.

(a) **Sum of digits**. Like reducing balance, this loads the charges towards the earlier years.

(b) **Machine hours**. This method is suited to assets that depreciate primarily through use rather than passage of time. Typical examples are delivery lorries, mines and quarries. Here the asset is consumed depending on factors such as mileage travelled or tonnage extracted.

2.26 The closest FRS 15 gets to making a recomendation is to suggest that where the pattern of consumption of an asset's economic benefits is uncertain, straight-line method of depreciation is usually adopted. In practice this is the most widely used method.

Factors affecting depreciation

2.27 FRS 15 outlines the factors to be considered in determining the useful economic life, residual value and depreciation method of an asset.

(a) The **expected usage** of the asset by the entity, assessed by reference to the asset's **expected capacity** or **physical output**

(b) The **expected physical deterioration** of the asset through use or **effluxion of time**; this will depend upon the **repair and maintenance programme** of the entity both when the asset is in **use** and when it is **idle**

(c) **Economic or technological obsolescence**, for example arising from **changes** or **improvements** in **production**, or a change in the **market demand** for the product or **service output** of that asset

(d) **Legal or similar limits** on the **use of the asset**, such as the **expiry dates** of related leases

Review of useful economic life

GENERAL RULE

The **useful economic life** of a tangible fixed asset should be **reviewed** at the **end of each reporting period** and revised if expectations are significantly different from previous estimates.

2.28 If **useful economic life** is **revised**, the **carrying amount** (ie book value) of the tangible fixed asset at the date of revision is **depreciated** over the **revised remaining useful economic life** from that point onwards.

2.29 Remember that the useful economic life of a tangible fixed asset is an **accounting estimate,** not an accounting policy. In such cases, the standard accounting practice is **not to restate previous years' figures** when estimates are revised. (ie the opening balances on profit and loss account and accumulated deprecation are not adjusted.)

2.30 The approach is to depreciate the carrying amount of the tangible fixed asset over the remaining useful economic life, beginning in the period in which the change is made. (Eg Book value is £24,000 and the remaining useful economic life is revised from 2 years to 4 years. Instead of charging £12,000 a year for the next 2 years, £6,000 per annum would be written off for the next 4 years.)

2.31 However, if future results could be materially distorted, the adjustment to accumulated deprecation should be recognised in the accounts in accordance with FRS 3 (normally as an exceptional item).

Exam focus point

The May 2003 paper included a 5 mark question on accounting treatment for a change in expected UEL.

Revision of residual value

GENERAL RULE

Where the residual value is material, it should be reviewed at the end of each period to take account of **expected technological changes,** but still based on prices prevailing at the date of acquisition (or revaluation).

2.31 This involves a revision to an accounting estimate and should be accounted for prospectively rather than retrospectively, ie amend future depreciation write offs but do not restate any opening balances brought forward from last year.

Revision of method of depreciation

GENERAL RULE

A change in depreciation method is permissible only on the grounds that the new method will give a **fairer presentation** of the results and of the financial position.

2.32 The depreciation method is an **accounting estimate**. Therefore, a change of method is not a change of accounting policy.

2.33 The carrying amount (ie book value) of the asset is depreciated on the new method over the remaining useful economic life, beginning in the period in which the change is made.

Two or more components of a fixed asset

GENERAL RULE

Where the tangible fixed asset comprises two or more major components with substantially different useful economic lives, each component should be accounted for separately for depreciation purposes and depreciated over its useful economic life.

2.34 Examples include:

- Land and buildings
- The structure of a building and items within the structure, such as general fittings

2.35 Freehold land usually has an indefinite life, unless subject to depletion (eg a quarry). Buildings have a limited life and are therefore depreciated.

2.36 In effect, the asset is treated as though it were several different assets for depreciation purposes. FRS 15 also requires component depreciation if subsequent expenditure on replacing a component is to be capitalised.

Non-depreciation

GENERAL RULE

For tangible fixed assets other than non-depreciable land, the **only grounds** for not charging depreciation are that the depreciation charge and accumulated depreciation are **immaterial**.

The depreciation charge and accumulated depreciation are immaterial if they would **not reasonably influence** the **decisions** of a **user** of the accounts.

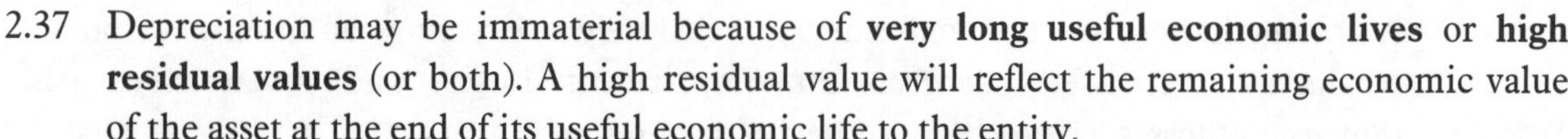

2.37 Depreciation may be immaterial because of **very long useful economic lives** or **high residual values** (or both). A high residual value will reflect the remaining economic value of the asset at the end of its useful economic life to the entity.

2.38 The above rules come into play in relation to what are known as '**trophy assets**'.

- **Top quality** buildings in desirable areas
- **Antique** fixtures and fittings
- **Historic** buildings

2.39 This approach was also advocated by the hotel, catering and public house industry on the grounds that their assets were regularly maintained and refurbished and therefore their useful economic life were not restricted.

2.40 However, where entities have avoided changing depreciation on the grounds of immateriality, they will nevertheless be required to perform impairment reviews under FRS 11. In practice, the **impairment review route** may prove **costly** and **counter-productive**, when the profit and loss account has nevertheless and **inevitably to suffer a hit** resulting from an impairment loss.

Impairment requirements

2.41 The application of impairment reviews in relation specifically to trophy assets has been touched as above. **Generally** tangible fixed assets other than non depreciable land, should be **reviewed for impairment** at the **end of the reporting** period where:

- **No depreciation** is charged on the **grounds** that it would be **immaterial.**
- The **estimated remaining useful economic life exceeds 50 years.**

The review should be in accordance with FRS 11 *Impairment of fixed assets and goodwill,* which will be discussed in more detail later.

Depreciation on revalued assets

2.42 Many companies **carry fixed assets** in their balance sheets at **revalued amounts,** particularly in the case of freehold buildings. When this is done, the **depreciation charge** should be calculated **on the basis of the revalued amount** (not the original cost).

Disclosure requirements of FRS 15

2.43 The following information should be sclosed separately in the financial statements for each class of tangible fixed assets.

(a) The depreciation methods used.

(b) The useful economic lives or the depreciation rates used.

(c) Total depreciation charged for the period.

(d) Where material, the financial effect of a change during the period in either the estimate of useful economic lives or the estimate of residual values.

(e) The cost or revalued amount at the beginning of the financial period and at the balance sheet date.

(f) The cumulative amount of provisions for depreciation or impairment at the beginning of the financial period and at the balance sheet date.

(g) A reconciliation of the movements, separately disclosing additions, disposals, revaluations, transfers, depreciation, impairment losses, and reversals of past impairment losses written back in the financial period.

(h) The net carrying amount at the beginning of the financial period and at the balance sheet date.

2.44 Where there has been a change in the depreciation method used, the effect, if material, should be disclosed in the period of change. The reason for the change should also be disclosed.

3 REVALUATION

Exam focus point

The November 2001 exam included an entire question on the FRS 15 revaluation rules.

- Reasons for keeping valuations up to date
- Rational for choice of treatments
- Calculation of depreciation
- Impact on accounting ratios.

Policy basis

3.1 Before FRS 15, companies could pick and choose which of their assets they wished to revalue and when. This allowed companies to massage their balance sheet figures through the inclusion of meaningless **out of date valuations**, thereby **hindering comparability** between companies from year to year. FRS 15 puts a stop to this '**cherry picking**'.

BASIC REQUIREMENTS

An entity may adopt a policy of **revaluing tangible fixed assets**. Where this policy is adopted **it must be applied consistently** to all assets of the same class.

Where an asset is revalued its carrying amount should be its **current value** as at the balance sheet date, current value being the **lower of replacement cost and recoverable amount**. The recoverable amount, in turn, is the **higher** of **net realisable value** and **value in use.**

3.2 A **class of fixed assets** is 'a category of tangible fixed assets having a similar nature, function or use in the business of an entity'. (FRS 15)

KEY TERMS

Replacement cost. The cost at which an **identical asset** could be **purchased** or **constructed**.

Recoverable amount. The higher of net realisable value and value in use.

Net realisable value. The **amount** at which an **asset could be disposed of**, less any **direct selling costs.**

Value in use. The **present value** of **future cash flows** obtainable as result of an asset's **continued use, including** those resulting from **ultimate disposal**.

3.3 The above basic requirements can be summarised by the following diagram.

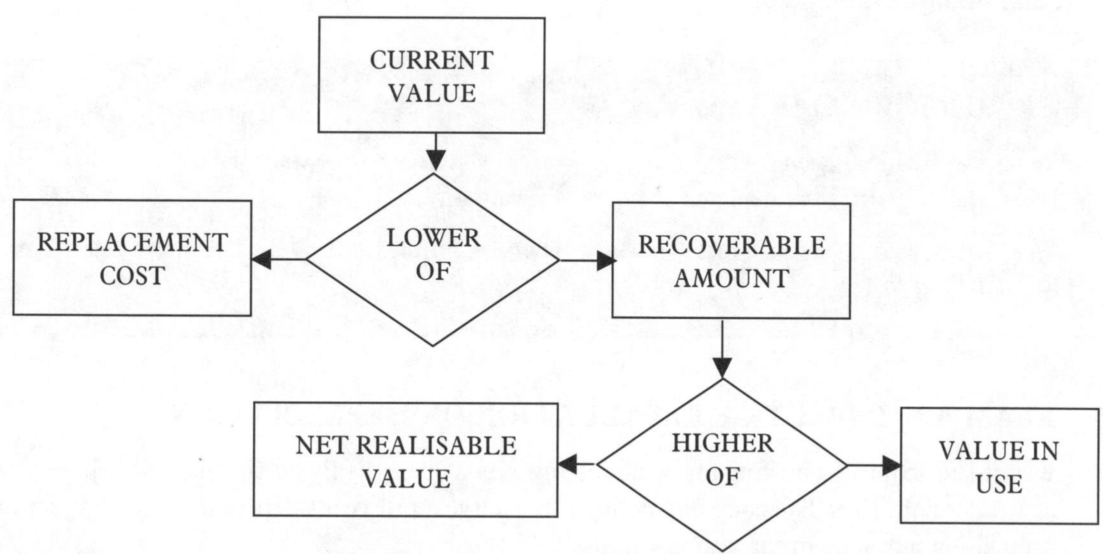

Frequency of valuation

Genereal rule

3.4 The valuation of properties should be done on the basis of a 5 year cycle.

(a) A **full valuation** every **5 years**

(b) An **interim valuation** in **year 3 of the five-year cycle**.

(c) An **interim valuation also in years 1, 2 and 4** of the **five-year cycle** should also be done where it is likely that there has been a **material change in value**.

Portfolios of non-specialised properties

3.5 For non-specialised properties, eg factories, warehouses, shops and offices, there is another alternative. A **full valuation** may be performed on a **rotation basis** designed to cover all the properties over a **five-year cycle**. An **interim valuation** on the **remaining four-fifths** of the portfolio should be done where it is likely that there has been a **material change** in value.

This approach is appropriate only where the property portfolio is held by the entity under either of **two specified scenarios**.

(a) The portfolio consists of a number of **broadly similar properties** whose characteristics are such that their values are likely to be affected by the **same market factors**.

(b) The portfolio can be divided on a **continuing basis** into **five groups of a broadly similar spread**.

Valuers

3.6 FRS 15 specifies who may carry out a **full valuation**.

(a) A qualified external valuer (eg a surveyor, who is independent of the company), or
(b) A qualified internal valuer, but subject to review by a qualified external valuer.

3.7 An **interim valuation** may be done by an internal or external, qualified valuer.

Depreciation on revalued assets

BASIC REQUIREMENTS

Where an asset has been revalued, the depreciation charge is based on the revaluation amount, less residual value, from the date of revaluation.

The asset's residual value should also be re-estimated on revaluation, based on values prevailing at that date.

3.8 EXAMPLE: IMPACT OF REVALUATION ON DEPRECIATION

Kevin Ltd acquires a buffing machine costing £100,000 on 1 July 20X4, which it depreciates at 10% straight line. The company policy is to charge a full year's depreciation in the year of acquisition but none in the year of disposal.

When the directors came to prepare the accounts for the year ended 31 December 20X7, the directors decided to obtain a full professional valuation, to be incorporated into the financial statements.

Yasmin, Nicole and Associates, Chartered Surveyors, valued the asset at £108,000.

It is now 31 December 20X9. Show the entries in the relevant accounts in the book of Kevin Ltd.

3.9 SOLUTION

PLANT AND EQUIPMENT

		£			£
1.7.X4	Cost of buffing machine	100,000	31.12.X7	Balance c/d	108,000
31.12.X7	Revaluation reserve (W3)	8,000			
		108,000			108,000
1.1.X8	Balance b/d	108,000			

PROVISION FOR DEPRECIATION

		£			£
1.7.X7	Revaluation reserve (W3)	40,000	31.12.X4	Charge for year (W1)	10,000
			31.12.X5	Charge for year (W1)	10,000
			31.12.X6	Charge for year (W1)	10,000
			31.12.X7	Charge for year (W1)	10,000
		40,000			40,000
			31.12.X8	Charge for year (W2)	18,000
			31.12.X9	Charge for year (W2)	18,000

DEPRECIATION CHARGE

		£			£
31.12.X4	Provision (W1)	10,000	31.12.X4	Tfr to P+L a/c	10,000
31.12.X5	Provision (W1)	10,000	31.12.X5	Tfr to P+L a/c	10,000
31.12.X6	Provision (W1)	10,000	31.12.X6	Tfr to P+L a/c	10,000
31.12.X7	Provision (W1)	10,000	31.12.X7	Tfr to P+L a/c	10,000
31.12.X8	Provision (W2)	18,000	31.12.X8	Tfr to P+L a/c	18,000
31.12.X9	Provision (W2)	18,000	31.12.X9	Tfr to P+L a/c	18,000

REVALUATION RESERVE

		£			£
31.12.X8	Add'l depn to P+L a/c*	8,000	31.12.X7	Adj. On buffing machine (W3)	48,000
31.12.X9	Add'l depn to P+L a/c*	8,000			
Note: These adjustments go directly to P+L reserve, avoiding the current year's P+L account.			*Note:* This adjustment will be done via STRG.		

PROFIT AND LOSS RESERVE (depreciation adjustments only)

					£
			31.12.X8	Depn adj *	8,000
			31.12.X9	Depn adj *	8,000

Exam focus point

* You do not need to be able to do these adjustment for your Paper 6 exam. However, it does come into the picture when we discuss distributable profits in Chapter 11.

Workings

1 £100,000 ÷ 10 years = £10,000 per annum.

2 £108,000 ÷ 6 years = 18,000 per annum.

3 *Revaluation of buffing machine*

	£
Cost	100,000
Accumulated depreciation to 31.12.X7	(40,000)
Net book value at 31.12.X7	60,000
Revaluation increase	48,000
Valuation as at 31.12.X7	108,000

4 SSAP 19 ACCOUNTING FOR INVESTMENT PROPERTIES Pilot Paper

4.1 The introduction of SSAP 12, with its requirement that all fixed assets including freehold buildings (though excluding freehold land) should be depreciated, caused a stir amongst property investment companies who feared that their reported profits would be severely reduced. The lobby was sufficiently strong to result in the publication of a separate standard for such properties.

Exam focus point

The definition of investment properties was tested in the May 2003 paper.

Definition of investment properties

4.2 SSAP 19 defines an investment property as follows.

KEY TERM

'.... An **investment property** is an interest in land and/or buildings:

(a) In respect of which **construction** work and **development** have been **completed**

(b) Which is held for its **investment potential,** any **rental income** being **negotiated** at **arm's length.**

'....The following are **exceptions** from the definition:

(a) A property which is **owned** and **occupied** by a company for its **own purposes** is not an investment property.

(b) A property **let to** and **occupied** by **another group company** is not an investment property for the purposes of its own accounts or the group accounts.'

Question 7

Lucy Limited and its subsidiaries are engaged in manufacturing of sweets and confectionery in Luton. It owns three properties which are held in a different ways.

(a) **Broadacres** is its factory and office building.

(b) **Kandikorna** is a retail premises let to Darren Limited a subsidiary which deals directly with the public.

(c) **High Standards** is an office block which is let to a firm of accountants on an arms length rental basis.

Identify which properties are investment properties.

Answer

(a) Broadacres is **not** an **investment property** because it is owned and **occupied** by Lucy Limited for its **own purposes**.

(b) Kandikorna is **not** an **investment property** because it is let and **occupied** by **another group company**.

(a) High Standards is an **investment company** because it **meets the criteria** for being classified as an investment property.

Justification for special approach to investment properties

4.3 Investment properties, as defined, are **not held** to be **consumed within** the **operations** of an enterprise, but instead for their **investment potential.**

4.4 The sale of an investment property is also unlikely to materially impact on the manufacturing or trading operations of an enterprise.

4.5 What is of **prime importance** to users of accounts, regarding investment properties, is their **current value** and any **changes in their current value**, rather than a systematic calculation of annual depreciation.

Accounting treatment

4.6 Per **SSAP 19**, investment properties should not be depreciated. Instead they should be **revalued annually** at their **open market value** and the aggregate **surplus** or **deficit** arising transferred to **investment revaluation reserve** (IRR) via the STRGL.

4.7 There may be circumstances where the **deficit** relating to an **individual investment property** is expected to be **permanent**. In such case, the deficit should be charged in the **profit and loss account** for the period.

4.8 Sometimes an investment property is held on a **lease** with a relatively **short unexpired term**, ie 20 years or less. Here the **carrying value** of lease must be **depreciated** over its **useful economic life** in accordance with the approach set out in **FRS 15**, the charge going to profit and loss account. The objective is to avoid the situation whereby the rentals received for such short leases are credited to profit and loss accounts whilst on the other hand any annual movements arising from revaluation's are processed to investment revaluation reserve via STRGL. Under these requirements, both debit (depreciation) and credit (rental income) would be processed to the profit and loss account.

4.9 SSAP 19 specifies various criteria for determining open market value.

(a) The valuation **need not** be made by **qualified** or **independent valuers.**

(b) However, **disclosure** is required regarding:

- The **names** and **qualifications** of the valuers
- The **basis** of valuation used
- **Whether** the person making the valuation is an **employee** or **officer** of the company.

(c) Sometimes investment properties represent a **substantial proportion** of the **total assets** of a **major enterprise** (eg a listed company). In these instances, their **valuation** would normally be carried out:

(i) **Annually** by a **qualified person** having **recent experience** of valuing **similar properties**

(ii) At least every **five years** by an **external valuer**.

4.10 The carrying value of investment properties and investment revaluation reserve should be disclosed prominently in the accounts.

4.11 Investment properties can be owned by **ordinary trading companies as well as property investment companies.** If the assets of a company consist wholly or mainly of investment properties, this fact should also be disclosed.

4.12 Further points to note about SSAP 19 are as follows.

(a) SSAP 19 acknowledges that exemption from depreciation for investment property is **contrary** to the depreciation rules in the **Companies Act 1985**. This departure is considered permissible because the Act states that compliance with the rules is a subordinate requirement to the '**overriding purpose of giving a true and fair view**'.

Where the true and fair override is invoked the notes to the accounts must disclose particulars of that departure, the reasons for it, and its effect. (See chapter 3).

(b) SSAP 19 **does not apply to immaterial items.**

Disposals

4.13 **SSAP 19 does not deal with the problem of accounting for the disposal of investment properties. However, FRS 3** *Reporting financial performance* **states the following** in relation to the disposal of any revalued fixed assets.

(a) The **profit or loss** on **disposal** of an **asset** should be accounted for as the **difference** between the **sale proceeds** and the **net carrying amount**.

(b) Any **revaluation surplus** remaining is now **realised**, so FRS 3 requires this to be transferred to the **profit and loss reserve**.

Diminution in value: Amendment to SSAP 19

4.14 Previously, under SSAP 19, any deficit on the IRR had to be taken to the profit and loss account. In other words, where the value of one or more investment property fell so far that the total IRR was insufficient to cover the deficit, then the excess was taken to the profit and loss account. SSAP 19 has now been amended as follows.

(a) **Any diminution in value which is considered permanent should be charged to the profit and loss account.**

(b) **Where diminution is temporary, a temporary IRR deficit is allowed.**

Question 8

Compare the accounting treatment of land and buildings as laid down by FRS 15 with the accounting treatment of investment properties as laid down by SSAP 19 and explain why a building owned for its investment potential should be accounted for differently from one which is occupied by its owners.

Answer

FRS 15 requires that all fixed assets should be depreciated, including freehold buildings. The only exception to this is freehold land which need only be depreciated if it is subject to depletion, for example, quarries or mines.

Where a property is revalued, depreciation should be charged so as to write off the new valuation over the estimated remaining useful life of the building.

SSAP 19, by contrast, recognises that there is a **conceptual difference** between *investment properties* and other fixed assets. Such properties are not depreciated and are carried in the balance sheet at open market value, re-assessed every year. An external valuation should be made at least once every five years.

Changes in the value of an investment property should not be taken to the profit and loss account. In other words, a company **cannot claim profit** on the **unrealised gains on revaluation** of such properties. The revaluation should be disclosed as a movement on an 'investment revaluation reserve'. Should this reserve show a **debit balance** (a loss) the **full amount** of the balance should be removed by charging it to the **profit and loss account**.

SSAP 19 acknowledges that there is a difference between investment properties and other fixed assets, including non-investment properties. Investment properties are held 'not for consumption in the business operations but as investments, the disposal of which would not materially affect any manufacturing or trading operations of the enterprise'.

It follows from this that the item of prime importance is the current value of the investment properties and changes in their current value rather than a calculation of systematic annual depreciation should be reported.

---

5 FRS 11 IMPAIRMENT OF FIXED ASSETS AND GOODWILL

5.1 FRS 11 *Impairment of fixed assets and goodwill*, was published in July 1998. It sets out the principles and methodology for accounting for impairments of fixed assets and goodwill.

5.2 It would be unnecessarily onerous for all fixed assets and goodwill to be tested for impairment every year. In general, fixed assets and goodwill need be **reviewed for impairment only if there is some indication that impairment has occurred.**

5.3 Impairment might occur owing to a variety of factors.

(a) Something happening to the fixed asset itself.
(b) Something adverse has happened within the company environment
(c) Something happening in the external environment.

5.4 The following diagram summarises the indicators of impairment which are discussed at length in FR 11.

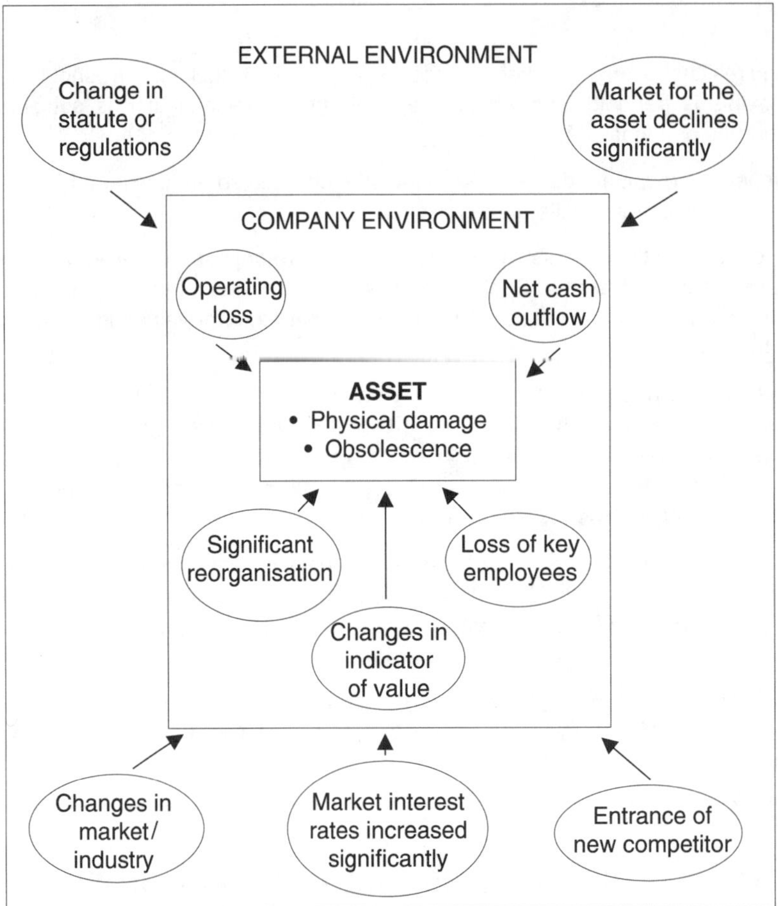

5.5 Where possible, **the test for impairment** should be done at the **individual asset level.** However, impairment can often be tested only for groups of assets because the cash flows upon which the calculation is based do not arise from the use of a single asset. In these cases, **impairment** is measured for the **smallest group** of assets (the **income-generating unit**) that produces a largely **independent income stream,** subject to constraints of **practicality** and **materiality**.

5.6 Impairment is measured by **comparing the carrying value of the fixed asset or income-generating unit with its recoverable amount.** The recoverable amount is the higher of the amounts that can be obtained from selling the fixed asset or income-generating unit (net **realisable value**) or using the fixed asset or income-generating unit (**value in use**).

5.7 The above issues can be summarised by the following diagram.

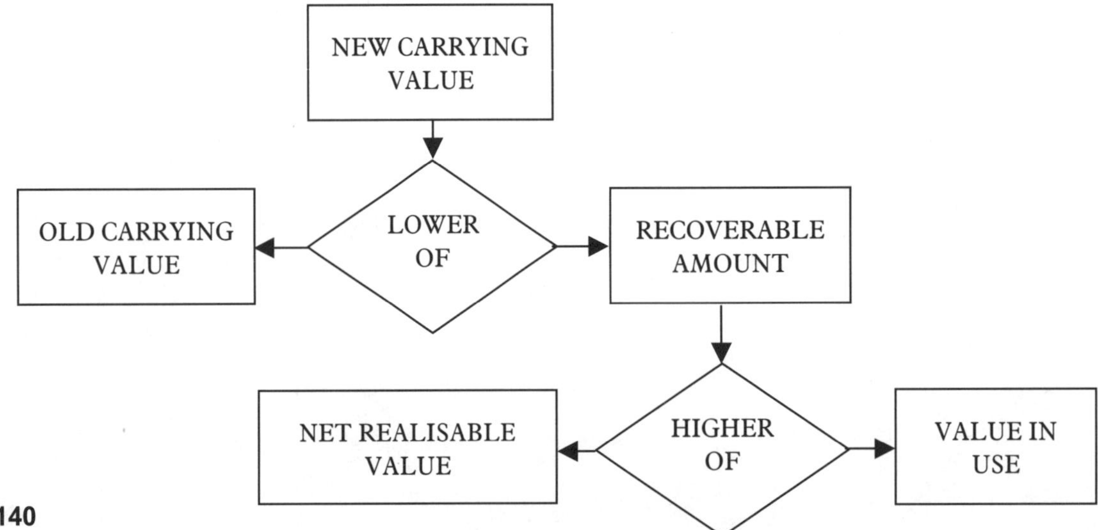

Question 9

Determine the impairment loss relating to one of Goody Goods Limited's fixed assets for the following four scenarios.

	Scenario 1	*Scenario 2*	*Scenario 3*	*Scenario 4*
	£'000	£'000	£'000	£'000
• Carrying amount	750	750	900	900
• Net realisable value *	800	600	800	600
• Value in use **	600	800	600	800

Answer

• Recoverable amount	* 800	** 800	* 800	** 800
• Carrying amount	750	750	900	900
• Impairment	Nil	Nil	100	100

5.8 **Net realisable value** is the **expected proceeds** of selling the fixed asset or income-generating unit less any **direct selling costs. Value in use** is calculated by **discounting** the **expected cash flows** arising from the use of fixed asset or assets in the income-generating unit at the rate of return that the market would expect from an equally risky investment.

5.9 In some cases a detailed calculation of value in use will not be necessary. A simple estimate may be sufficient to demonstrate that either value in use is higher than carrying value or value in use is lower than net realisable value, in which case impairment is measured by reference to net realisable value.

5.10 The **reversal** of past impairment losses is recognised when the **recoverable amount** of a **tangible fixed asset** has **increased because of a change in economic conditions** or in the expected use of the asset. Increases in the recoverable amount of **goodwill and intangible assets** are recognised **only** when an **external event** caused the recognition of the impairment loss in previous periods, and subsequent external events clearly and **demonstrably reverse** the effects of that event in a way that was not foreseen in the original impairment calculations.

5.11 **Impairment losses** are recognised in the **profit and loss account**, unless they arise on a previously revalued fixed asset. Impairment losses on **revalued fixed assets** are recognised in the **statement of total recognised gains and losses** until the **carrying value** of the asset falls **below depreciated historical cost** unless the impairment is clearly caused by a consumption of economic benefits, in which case the loss is recognised in the profit and loss account. **Impairments below depreciated historical cost** are recognised in the **profit and loss account**.

Chapter roundup

- A number of accounting regulations on the valuation and disclosure of **fixed assets** are contained in the Companies Act 1985.
- In the case of **tangible fixed assets**, these regulations are supplemented by the provisions of FRS 15 and SSAP 19 on investment properties.
- **SSAP 19** conflicts with the statutory requirement to depreciate all fixed assets with a limited economic life, by stating that investment properties need not ordinarily be depreciated. Companies taking advantage of this provision will need to justify their departure from statute as being necessary to provide a true and fair view.
- Remember that Section 1 of this chapter lists the statutory requirements applying to **all** fixed assets, including the intangible assets and investments dealt with in the next chapter.
- You should now go back to **Chapter 2** and consider how the accounting treatments and disclosure requirements of these three standards fit in to the published accounts formats and notes and the CA 1985 requirements.

Quick quiz

1 Which of the following elements can be included in the production cost of a fixed asset?

A Labour
B Raw materials
C Electricity and fuel used
D Interest on loan taken out to finance production of the asset

2 The revaluation reserve can be reduced when a fixed asset is disposed of.

True ☐

False ☐

3 Define depreciation.

4 When the method of depreciation is changed this constitutes a change of accounting policy and an adjustment should be made to the depreciation charged in previous year.

True ☐

False ☐

5 When are investment properties (as defined by SSAP 19) subject to depreciation?

Answers to quick quiz

1 All of them. (see para 1.5)

2 True. (1.13)

3 See paragraph 2.20

4 False. (2.32 – 2.33)

5 When the property is subject to a lease which has 20 years or less to run. (4.8)

Now try the questions below from the Exam Question Bank

Number	Level	Marks	Time
4	Exam level	15	27 mins
5	Introductory	n/a	27 mins
Scenario B: 2a	Exam level	18	32 mins

Chapter 6

FIXED ASSETS: INTANGIBLE ASSETS AND INVESTMENTS

	Topic list	Syllabus reference	Ability required
1	**Intangible assets: the requirements of the Companies Act 1985**	-	**Knowledge**
2	**SSAP 13 *Accounting for research and development***	(iii)	**Application**
3	**Introduction to goodwill (May 2003, onwards)**	-	**Knowledge**
4	**FRS 10: Goodwill and intangible assets (May 2003, onwards)**	-	**Knowledge**
5	**Investments**	-	**Knowledge**

Introduction

We will look at intangible assets in this chapter, the main categories of which are R & D costs and goodwill.

Accounting for research and development according to SSAP 13 is relatively straightforward, but you must learn the definitions of the types of research and development as these determine the accounting treatment.

The treatment of investments is addressed only briefly here, again because the absence of group accounts from the syllabus limits the areas we can cover.

Learning outcomes covered in this chapter

- **Explain** the accounting rules contained in Financial Reporting Standards which provide guidance as to the appropriate treatment of certain transactions
- **Identify, apply** and **evaluate** the accounting treatment of significant transactions

Syllabus content covered in this chapter

- Research and development (SSAP 13) – arguments for and against capitalisation and the criteria to be met before development expenditure can be capitalised.
- Goodwill (excluding goodwill arising on consolidation) and intangible fixed assets (FRS 10 and FRS 11) recognition, valuation, amortisation and impairment. (May 2003 exams)

1 INTANGIBLE ASSETS: THE REQUIREMENTS OF THE COMPANIES ACT 1985

1.1 The statutory balance sheet format lists the following **intangible fixed assets** (item BI in the format).

(a) Development costs
(b) Concessions, patents, licences, trade marks and similar rights and assets

(c) Goodwill
(d) Payments on account

1.2 With regard to concessions, patents, licences, trade marks etc the Companies Act states that such items should only be treated, and disclosed, as assets if they were:

- **Acquired** for valuable consideration
- **Created** by the company itself

1.3 With regard to development costs, the Act states that such costs may only be treated as an asset in the balance sheet (rather than being written off immediately) in 'special circumstances'. The Act does not define these circumstances and this is a case where a SSAP goes further than statute. SSAP 13 (see below) lays down strict criteria for determining when such expenditure may be treated as an asset. The Act merely states that, if it is so treated, the following disclosures must be made by way of note.

(a) The period over which the amount of the costs originally capitalised is being or is to be written off.

(b) The reasons for capitalising the development costs.

1.4 With regard to goodwill, the Act implicitly makes a distinction between **inherent** goodwill and **purchased** goodwill. The distinction will be explained when we come to look at FRS 10 *Goodwill and intangible assets*, but for now it is enough to say that the Act does not permit **inherent** goodwill to be included as an asset in the balance sheet. The difficulties of valuing such goodwill are in any case so great that very few companies have ever carried it in their balance sheets. However, several listed companies have capitalised **brands** which were developed in-house.

1.5 **Purchased** goodwill may be treated as an asset in the balance sheet. If it is so treated (rather than being written off immediately), it must be written off systematically over a period chosen by the directors. The period chosen must not exceed the useful economic life of the goodwill. Disclosure should be made of the period chosen and of the reasons for choosing that period.

1.6 This statutory requirement to amortise any goodwill capitalised does not extend to goodwill arising on consolidation. Even so, companies have to amortise consolidation goodwill to comply with the stricter requirements of FRS 10.

2 SSAP 13 ACCOUNTING FOR RESEARCH AND DEVELOPMENT

2.1 In many companies, especially those which produce food, or 'scientific' products such as medicines, or 'high technology' products, the expenditure on research and development (R & D) is considerable. When R & D is a large item of cost, its accounting treatment may have a significant influence on the profits of a business and its balance sheet valuation.

Exam focus point

SSAP 13 was tested in November 2001 by way of four 5 mark questions. The standard is also handy for slipping in as part of a statutory accounts preparation question.

Definitions

KEY TERMS

SSAP 13 defines research and development expenditure as falling into one or more of the following categories.

(a) **Pure research** is original research to obtain new scientific or technical knowledge or understanding. There is **no clear commercial end** in view and such research work does not have a practical application. Companies and other business entities might carry out this type of research in the hope that it will provide new knowledge which can subsequently be exploited.

(b) **Applied research** is original research work which also seeks to obtain new scientific or technical knowledge, but which has a **specific practical aim** or application (for example research on improvements in the effectiveness of toothpastes or medicines). Applied research may develop from 'pioneering' pure research, but many companies have full-time research teams working on applied research projects.

(c) **Development** is the use of existing scientific and technical knowledge to **produce** new (or substantially improved) **products or systems**, prior to starting commercial production operations.

Accounting treatment

2.2 The dividing line between each of these categories will often be indistinct in practice, and some expenditure might be classified as research or as development. It may be even more difficult to distinguish development costs from production costs. For example, if a prototype model of a new product is developed and then sold to a customer, the costs of the prototype will include both development and production expenditure.

2.3 SSAP 13 states that, although there may be practical difficulties in isolating research costs and development costs, there is a difference of principle in the method of accounting for each type of expenditure.

(a) Expenditure on pure and applied research is usually a continuing operation which is necessary to ensure a company's survival. One accounting period does not gain more than any other from such work, and it is therefore appropriate that research costs should be written off as they are incurred (in the year of expenditure). This conforms with CA 1985, which seems not to envisage the capitalisation of research expenditure in any circumstances.

(b) The development of new and improved products is different, because development expenditure is incurred with a particular commercial aim in view and in the reasonable expectation of earning profits or reducing costs. In these circumstances it is appropriate that development costs should be deferred (capitalised) and matched against the future revenues.

2.4 SSAP 13 attempts to restrict indiscriminate deferrals of development expenditure and states that development costs may only be deferred to future periods, when the following criteria are met.

(a) There must be a **separately** defined development project, with project **expenses** clearly identifiable.

(b) The expected outcome of the project must have been assessed, and there should be reasonable certainty that it is:

(i) **Commercially** viable, having regard to market conditions, competition, public opinion and consumer and environmental legislation

(ii) **Technically** feasible

(c) The **overall profits** from the developed product or system should reasonably be expected to cover the past and future development costs.

(d) The company should have adequate **resources** to complete the development project.

If **any** of these conditions are not satisfied the development costs should be written off in the year of expenditure.

A useful mnemonic to remember these conditions by is **SECTOR**, made up of the words in **bold**.

2.5 Where development expenditure is deferred to future periods, its **amortisation** should begin with the commencement of production, and should then be written off on a systematic basis over the period in which the product is expected to be sold. If the accounting policy of deferral of development expenditure is adopted it should be consistently applied to all projects that meet the criteria.

2.6 Deferred development expenditure should be reviewed at the end of every accounting period. If the conditions which justified the deferral of the expenditure no longer apply or are considered doubtful, the deferred expenditure, to the extent that it is now considered to be irrecoverable, should be written off. Development expenditure once written off can now be reinstated, if the uncertainties which had led to its being written off no longer apply. This was not permitted by the original SSAP 13, but has been amended because the CA 1985 **does** permit the reinstatement of costs previously written off.

2.7 EXAMPLES

Examples given by SSAP 13 of activities that would normally be **included** in R & D.

- Experimental, theoretical or other work aimed at the discovery of new knowledge or the advancement of existing knowledge
- Searching for applications of that knowledge
- Formulation and design of possible applications for such work
- Testing in search for, or evaluation of, product, service or process alternatives
- Design, construction and testing of pre-production prototypes and models and development batches
- Design of products, services, processes or systems involving new technology or substantially improving those already produced or installed
- Construction and operation of pilot plants

2.8 Examples of activities that would normally be **excluded** from research and development.

- Testing and analysis either of equipment or product for purposes of quality or quantity control

- Periodic alterations to existing products, services or processes even though these may represent some improvement
- Operational research not tied to a specific research and development activity
- Cost of corrective action in connection with break-downs during commercial production
- Legal and administrative work in connection with patent applications, records and litigation and the sale or licensing of patents
- Activity, including design and construction engineering, relating to the construction, relocation, rearrangement or start-up of facilities or equipment other than facilities or equipment whose sole use is for a particular research and development project
- Market research

SSAP 13 states that a company can defer **market research** expenditure under the accruals concept (if it is prudent so to do) but it must be disclosed entirely separately from deferred development expenditure.

Exclusions

2.9 The above provisions of SSAP 13 do **not** extend to the following cases.

(a) Expenditure on tangible fixed assets acquired or constructed to provide facilities for research and/or development activities should be capitalised and depreciated over their useful lives in the usual way. However, the depreciation may be capitalised as part of deferred development expenditure if the development work for which the assets are used meets the criteria given in Paragraph 2.4 above.

(b) Expenditure incurred in locating mineral deposits in extractive industries is outside the scope of SSAP 13.

(c) Expenditure incurred where there is a firm contract.

- To carry out development work on behalf of third parties on such terms that the related expenditure is to be fully reimbursed
- To develop and manufacture at an agreed price which has been calculated to reimburse expenditure on development as well as on manufacture

is not to be treated as deferred development expenditure.

Any such expenditure which has not been reimbursed at the balance sheet date should be included in work in progress.

Disclosure requirements

2.10 The Companies Act 1985 does **not** require disclosure of the total amount of R & D expenditure during an accounting period, but SSAP 13 requires that all large companies (defined below) should disclose the total charged in the profit and loss account, distinguishing between **current year** expenditure and **amortisation** of deferred development expenditure.

2.11 SSAP 13 requires the following companies to disclose R & D expenditure.

- Public companies
- Special category companies (ie banking and insurance companies)

- Holding companies with a plc or special category company as a subsidiary
- Companies who satisfy the criteria, multiplied by 10, for defining a medium-sized company (see Chapter 2)

This means that, currently, a **private company will be exempted** if it is not itself (and does not control) a special category company and it meets two of the following criteria.

- **Turnover ≤ £112 million**
- **Total assets** (before deduction of current or long-term liabilities) ≤ **£56 million**
- ≤ **2,500 employees**

2.12 Where deferred development costs are included in a company's balance sheet the following information must be given in the notes to the accounts.

(a) Movements on deferred development expenditure, and the amount brought forward and carried forward at the beginning and end of the period.

(b) The accounting policy used to account for R & D expenditure should be clearly explained.

These requirements are, of course, **additional** to those contained in the CA 1985 given in Section 1 of this chapter.

Alternative accounting treatments

2.13 There has generally been little disagreement on the treatment of research expenditure. However, the treatment of development expenditure is more controversial.

2.14 The principal argument **in favour** of deferral of development expenditure stems from the accruals concept: expenditure on development creates an asset, the existence of which will lead to future benefits. Those who argue in favour of this concept believe that the return on capital employed (see Chapter 12) will only give a true measure of the profitability of the company if deferred development expenditure is included in capital employed. They also point out that it is common practice to capitalise patent rights acquired from other firms, that the products which are subject to the patent rights will usually have involved some development costs and that there is no reason for treating internally generated technological expertise in a manner different from that bought in.

2.15 The arguments **against** deferral stem from the uncertainty inherent in any development project. When a development project is started there is a possibility that

- It will not be a technical success
- A technically successful project will, for other reasons, not be followed by full scale implementation
- An implemented project will not be a commercial success

2.16 The standard has been criticised on the grounds that, where the conditions discussed above are satisfied, companies have the **option** of whether or not to defer development expenditure. It should be remembered, however, that it would be impossible to force companies to carry forward development expenditure, since the criteria are highly subjective. It appears that the majority of companies incurring development expenditure write it off immediately.

Question 1

In connection with SSAP 13 Accounting for research and development:

(a) Define 'applied research' and 'development'.

(b) Explain why it is considered necessary to distinguish between applied research and development expenditure and how this distinction affects the accounting treatment.

(c) State whether the following items are included within the SSAP 13 definition of research and development, and give your reasons:

(i) Market research
(ii) Testing of pre-production prototypes
(iii) Operational research
(iv) Testing in search of process alternatives

Answer

(a) **Applied research** expenditure is expenditure on original investigations which are carried out in order to gain new scientific or technical knowledge, but which also have a specific practical aim or objective. An example might be research into a disease with the intention of finding a cure or a vaccine.

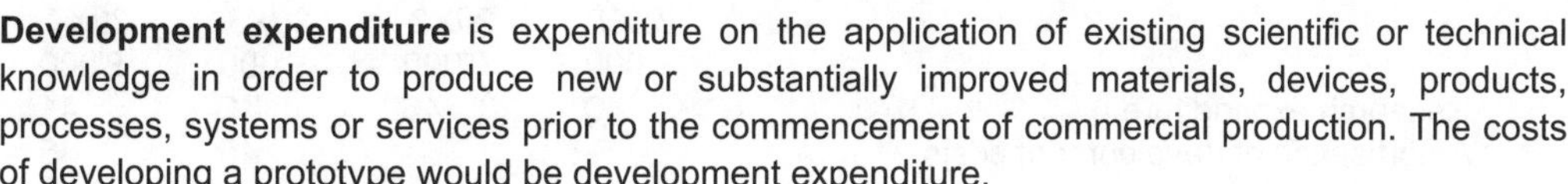

Development expenditure is expenditure on the application of existing scientific or technical knowledge in order to produce new or substantially improved materials, devices, products, processes, systems or services prior to the commencement of commercial production. The costs of developing a prototype would be development expenditure.

(b) SSAP 13 considers that:

'pure and applied research can be regarded as part of a continuing operation required to maintain a company's business and its competitive position. In general, no one particular period rather than any other will be expected to benefit and therefore it is appropriate that these costs should be written off as they are incurred.'

This is in accordance with the matching concept which requires that revenue and costs are 'matched with one another **so far as their relationship can be established or justifiably assumed**' (SSAP 2, Paragraph 14 – SSAP 2 has now been superseded by FRS 18) and also with the prudence concept.

This has the affect that applied research costs must be written off as incurred but development expenditure can be deferred (that is, capitalised as an intangible asset) and amortised over the life of the product, service, process or system developed. This treatment is only permissible if the project meets certain criteria designed to ensure that deferral is prudent.

(c) (i) Market research is not normally considered to be research and development activity. It is specifically excluded in the SSAP. This is presumably because it does not depart from routine activity and it does not contain an appreciable element of innovation.

(ii) Testing of prototypes is included in SSAP 13's list of activities normally to be considered as research and development. A prototype must be constructed and tested before full-scale production can be risked and so it is an essential stage in the development process.

(iii) 'Operational research not tied to a specific research and development activity' is an activity which SSAP 13 considers should not normally be included in research and development. 'Operational research' is presumably used here to denote the branch of applied mathematics which includes techniques such as linear programming and network analysis. The implication is that routine use of such techniques (to improve production efficiency, for example) does not fall within SSAP 13's jurisdiction, in spite of the use of the word 'research'.

(iv) 'Testing in search for, or evaluation of, product, service or process alternatives' is considered to be research and development work by SSAP 13. It would fall within the definition of applied research.

Question 2

Fredericks plc incurs the following expenditure in years 20X1-20X5.

	Research	*Development*
	£'000	£'000
20X1	40	65
20X2	45	70
20X3	49	-
20X4	41	-
20X5	43	-

You are told that Fredericks plc capitalises development expenditure when appropriate. The item developed in 20X1 and 20X2 goes on sale on 1 January 20X3 and it will be three years from then until any competitor is expected to have a similar product on the market.

Required

Show the profit and loss account and balance sheet extracts for all five years.

Answer

PROFIT AND LOSS ACCOUNT (EXTRACTS)

	20X1	*20X2*	*20X3*	*20X4*	*20X5*
	£'000	£'000	£'000	£'000	£'000
Research expenditure	40	45	49	41	43
Amortisation of development costs	-	-	45	45	45

BALANCE SHEET (EXTRACT)

	20X1	*20X2*	*20X3*	*20X4*	*20X5*
Intangible fixed assets	£'000	£'000	£'000	£'000	£'000
Development costs	65	135	135	135	135
Amortisation	-	-	(45)	(90)	(135)
Net book value	65	135	90	45	-

3 INTRODUCTION TO GOODWILL

KEY TERM

It is usual for the value of a business as a going concern to differ from the aggregate **fair value** of its separable net assets. The difference, which may be positive or negative, is described as **goodwill**.

3.1 By definition, goodwill is an asset which cannot be realised separately from the business as a whole.

3.2 There are many factors which may explain why goodwill arises. Examples are a skilled management team, good labour relations and a strategic location. These factors are intangible and it is difficult to place a money value on them. For this reason, it is not usual to show goodwill as an asset in the balance sheet; any amount at which it was valued would be arbitrary and subject to fluctuations.

Inherent goodwill and purchased goodwill

3.3 It is generally agreed that goodwill of a kind exists in every business. However, the **only time** when **goodwill is valued** and may be disclosed as an asset in the balance sheet is when

one business acquires another as a going concern. This is because there is then a positive indication available of the value of goodwill acquired.

3.4 For example, suppose that Bakon acquires the business of Hegg for £120,000 in cash at a time when the balance sheets of the two businesses are as follows.

	Bakon	*Hegg*
	£	£
Tangible fixed assets	500,000	66,000
Net current assets	220,000	33,000
Capital and reserves	720,000	99,000

3.5 Assuming that the book values of Hegg's assets equate to their market values it is clear that Bakon values Hegg's goodwill at £21,000 since he is willing to pay £120,000 for assets which separately have a value of £99,000. Bakon's balance sheet after the acquisition might appear as follows.

	£
Purchased goodwill	21,000
Tangible fixed assets	566,000
Net current assets £(220,000 + 33,000 – 120,000)	133,000
Capital and reserves	720,000

3.6 The goodwill acquired from Hegg is described as **purchased goodwill** because Bakon paid cash for it in buying the business of Hegg as a going concern. It is likely that Bakon's business also has goodwill, but because its value has not been evidenced in a purchase transaction it would be unacceptable, under existing accounting conventions, to disclose it as an asset in Bakon's balance sheet. Goodwill which is presumed to exist, but which has not been evidenced in a purchase transaction, is called **non-purchased or inherent goodwill.**

Negative goodwill

KEY TERM

Negative goodwill arises when the price paid for a business is less than the fair value of the separable net assets acquired. This might happen, for example, if the vendor needed cash quickly and was forced to sell at a bargain price.

4 FRS 10 GOODWILL AND INTANGIBLE ASSETS

Exam focus point

Goodwill is relatively new to the syllabus and it is only natural that the examiner will want to reflect this change on papers set.

4.1 The FRS applies to all financial statements except those entities applying the Financial Reporting Standard for Smaller Entities which do not prepare consolidated accounts.

4.2 The requirements of the FRS apply to all intangible assets except those specifically addressed by another accounting standard, eg SSAP 13. Oil and gas exploration and development costs are also exempt.

4.3 Although it is framed around the purchase of a subsidiary undertaking, it also applies to the acquisition of unincorporated entities.

Objective

4.4 The objective stated by the FRS is to ensure that

- Capitalised goodwill and intangible assets are **charged in the P&L** account as far as possible in the periods in which they are depleted
- Sufficient information is disclosed in the financial statements to enable users to determine the impact of goodwill and intangible assets on the financial position and performance of the reporting entity

Definitions

4.5 The FRS introduces a variety of new definitions, some of which relate to terms used above.

KEY TERMS

Class of intangible assets: a group of intangible assets that have similar nature or function in the business of the entity.

Identifiable assets and liabilities: the assets and liabilities of an entity that are capable of being disposed of or settled separately, without disposing of a business of the entity.

Purchased goodwill: the difference between the fair value of the consideration paid for an acquired entity and the aggregate of the fair values of that entity's identifiable assets and liabilities. Positive goodwill arises when the fair value of the consideration paid exceeds the aggregate fair values of the identifiable assets and liabilities. Negative goodwill arises when the aggregate fair values of the identifiable assets and liabilities of the entity exceed the fair value of the consideration paid.

Residual value: the net realisable value of an asset at the end of its useful economic life. Residual values are based on prices at the date of acquisition (or revaluation) of the asset and do not take account of expected future price changes.

Useful economic life: the useful economic life of an intangible asset is the period over which the entity expects to derive economic benefit from that asset. The useful economic life of purchased goodwill is the period over which the value of the underlying business is expected to exceed the values of its identifiable net assets.

(FRS 10)

4.6 FRS 10 also includes definitions of the following terms.

- Impairment
- Intangible assets
- Net realisable value
- Readily ascertainable market value
- Recoverable amount
- Value in use

Initial recognition

Goodwill

4.7 Positive purchased goodwill should be **capitalised** and classified as an asset on the balance sheet.

4.8 Internally generated goodwill **should not** be capitalised.

Intangible assets

4.9 An intangible asset purchased separately from a business should be capitalised at cost.

4.10 Where an intangible asset is acquired as part of the acquisition of a business the treatment depends on whether its value can be measured reliably on its initial recognition.

(a) If its value **can be measured** reliably, it should initially be recorded at its **fair value**. (The fair value should not create or increase any negative goodwill arising on the acquisition unless the asset has a readily ascertainable market value.)

(b) If the value of the asset **cannot be measured** reliably, the intangible asset must be subsumed within the amount of the **purchase price** attributed to goodwill.

Non-purchased intangibles

4.11 FRS 10 states that companies may capitalise **non-purchased** ('internally-developed') intangibles but only to the extent that they have a 'readily ascertainable market value'. This is an important definition that implies that:

- The asset must be a member of a group of **homogenous assets** (ie they are all of the same kind), which are equivalent in all material respects
- There is an **active market** for that group of assets, evidenced by frequent transactions

4.12 Examples given by the FRS of intangibles that may meet these conditions include certain operating licences, franchises and quotas. The FRS goes on to say that intangibles such as brands and publishing titles are not equivalent in all material aspects – in fact they are all unique – and so do not have readily ascertainable market values. They are therefore not examples of non-purchased intangibles that can be capitalised.

Exam focus point

The treatment of internally developed brands and publishing titles is a neat little topic that an examiner might slip into a paper

Approach to amortisation and impairment

4.13 The approach of the FRS to amortisation reflects the wish to charge goodwill to the profit and loss account only to the extent that the carrying value of the goodwill is not supported by the current value of the goodwill within the acquired business.

4.14 The approach is based on a combination of:

- **Amortising** over a limited period on a systematic basis
- An annual **impairment review**

4.15 The first task is to decide whether or not the goodwill or intangible has a limited useful economic life.

Assets with a limited useful economic life

Amortisation

4.16 The FRS states that, where goodwill and intangible assets are regarded as having limited useful economic lives they should be amortised on a systematic basis over those lives.

4.17 The standard gives little guidance on how to predict an asset's useful economic life, which can be very difficult for goodwill and intangibles as it is impossible to see them actually wearing out. It does, however, give examples of relevant considerations, which include certain economic and legal factors relating to the asset. An intangible may, for example, be linked to a product with a specific lifespan, or there may be time periods attached to legal rights (eg patents).

4.18 There is a rebuttable presumption that the useful economic lives of purchased goodwill and intangible assets are limited to periods of 20 years or less. This presumption may be rebutted and a useful economic life regarded as a longer period or indefinite only if:

(a) The **durability** of the acquired business or intangible asset **can be demonstrated** and justifies estimating the useful economic life to exceed 20 years

(b) The goodwill or intangible asset is capable of **continued measurement** (so that annual impairment reviews will be feasible)

Question 3

The circumstances where an indefinite useful economic life longer than 20 years may be legitimately presumed are limited. What factors determine the durability of goodwill?

Answer

FRS 10 mentions the following.

(a) The nature of the business
(b) The stability of the industry in which the acquired business operates
(c) Typical lifespans of the products to which the goodwill attaches
(d) The extent to which the acquisition overcomes market entry barriers that will continue to exist
(e) The expected future impact of competition on the business

---

4.19 Uncertainty about the length of the useful economic life is not a good reason for choosing one that is unrealistically short or for adopting a 20 year useful economic life by default.

4.20 In amortising an intangible asset, a residual value may be assigned to that asset only if such residual value can be measured reliably. **No residual value** may be assigned to **goodwill**. In practice, the residual value of an intangible asset is often insignificant.

4.21 The method of amortisation should be chosen to reflect the expected pattern of depletion of the goodwill or intangible asset. A straight-line method should be chosen unless another method can be demonstrated to be more appropriate.

4.22 Whatever the useful economic life chosen, the company should be able to justify it. It should be reviewed annually and revised if appropriate.

Impairment review

4.23 In addition to the amortisation, the asset should have an impairment review (see below) after the first year to ensure that its performance was as expected.

4.24 If this review shows that results are as predicted, no other review is required unless events or changes in the future indicate that the value of the goodwill or intangible may not be recoverable.

4.25 If the review shows that the post-acquisition performance is poorer than anticipated, a full review is required in accordance with FRS 11 *Impairment of fixed assets and goodwill* (see Chapter 5).

4.26 Goodwill and intangible assets that are amortised over a period exceeding 20 years from the date of acquisition should be reviewed for impairment at the end of each reporting period.

Assets with an indefinite useful economic life

No amortisation

4.27 Where goodwill and intangible assets are regarded as having indefinite useful economic lives, they should not be amortised.

4.28 'Indefinite' is not the same as 'infinite', it means merely that no limit can be fixed for it.

Important!

If the option not to amortise is taken, this constitutes a departure from the Companies Act and will need to be justified by invoking the **true and fair override**.

Impairment review

4.29 Goodwill and intangible assets that are not amortised (because their useful economic life is deemed to be indefinite) should be reviewed for impairment at the end of each reporting period.

4.30 If an impairment loss is recognised, the revised carrying value, if being amortised, should be amortised over the current estimate of the remaining useful economic life.

4.31 If goodwill arising on consolidation is found to be impaired, the carrying amount of the investment held in the accounts of the parent undertaking should also be reviewed for impairment.

4.32 The emphasis on impairment reviews is a key feature of the new FRS. The ASB believes that a formal requirement to monitor the value of acquired goodwill and intangible assets using standardised methods and to report any losses in the financial statements will enhance the quality of the information provided to users of financial statements.

Reversal of impairment

4.33 Normally, once an impairment review has identified a loss, this cannot be restored at a later date. However, if the loss was caused by an external event that later reversed in a way that was not foreseen, the original impairment loss may be restored. An example of this might be: if a direct competitor came on to the market, leading to an impairment loss, and then the competitor did not survive or produced a different product from the one originally envisaged.

Revaluation

4.34 Goodwill may not be revalued, except in the circumstances described above, ie the reversal of an impairment. If an intangible asset has a readily ascertainable market value, it may be revalued to its market value.

4.35 Future amortisation should always be made on the revalued amount, just like depreciation for a revalued tangible fixed asset.

Negative goodwill

4.36 FRS 10 states that the investee's assets should be checked for impairment and the liabilities checked for understatement to ensure that the negative goodwill is justified. If indeed any negative goodwill remains after these tests, it needs to be disclosed consistently with positive goodwill.

4.37 Rather than being shown on the bottom half of the balance sheet as a capital reserve it is disclosed in the intangible fixed assets category, directly under positive goodwill, ie as a 'negative asset'. A sub-total of the net amount of positive and negative goodwill should be shown on the face of the balance sheet.

4.38 This presentation may seem a little odd. However, the ASB argues that negative goodwill does not meet the definition of a liability under the Statement of Principles and that this treatment is consistent with that of positive goodwill.

4.39 Negative goodwill should be recognised in the profit and loss account in the periods when the non-monetary assets acquired are depreciated or sold.

4.40 There are two important points to note.

(a) It would be strange for the investor to pay less than its fair value for the monetary items acquired. The value of cash, for example, is pretty universal. It is more likely that the negative goodwill represents a shortfall in the value of the non-monetary items.

(b) The benefit of the 'bargain' of getting these non-monetary items at less than fair value will only be realised when the non-monetary items themselves are realised.

Therefore it makes sense to credit the negative goodwill to the profit and loss account only when the non-monetary assets themselves are realised, and this is when they are either depreciated or sold.

Disclosures

4.41 FRS 10 requires various disclosures relating to the following.

- Recognition and measurement
- Amortisation of positive goodwill and intangible assets
- Revaluation
- Negative goodwill
- Impairment

4.42 The disclosure requirements are the same as for any other fixed asset, including the table showing a reconciliation of movements during the year, for every category of intangible assets (including goodwill), details of revaluations, accounting policies and details of amortisation charged.

4.43 Significant additional disclosure requirements include requirements to explain:

- The **bases of valuation** of intangible assets
- The **grounds** for believing a useful economic life to exceed 20 years or to be indefinite
- The **treatment** adopted of negative goodwill

Issues relating to FRS 10

4.44 The FRS 10 rules meant significant changes to the accounts of many companies. Over 95% of companies in the UK used to adopt the 'immediate write off' treatment permitted under SSAP 22. Some commentators suggested that some deals might not be done because of the tougher FRS 10 rules. This is probably an exaggeration, though FRS 10 might not be popular.

4.45 More seriously, reservations have been expressed about the thinking behind the standard by the firm Ernst & Young. The main observations are as follows.

(a) FRS 10 still **allows a choice** of accounting treatments. Companies can follow a regime that permits the goodwill to be carried as a permanent asset. This may allow some spurious assets to remain indefinitely in the balance sheet, potentially providing fuel for criticism of the profession in the next wave of accounting scandals.

(b) The impairment review, is **subjective**, not least in determining how the business is to be segmented. Forecasting cashflows is also problematic.

(c) The importance of **negative goodwill** has been **underestimated**. It is more likely to arise now that FRS 7 bans reorganisation provisions, thus raising the value of the net assets acquired.

(d) The treatment of negative goodwill is '**strange**'. It is a 'dangling credit' in the balance sheet and the profit and loss account treatment simply mirrors that required for depreciation without regard to the fact that this is a credit to the profit and loss account.

Exam focus point

The above discussion could lend itself to a small discursive question in an exam.

Section summary

4.46 (a) **Purchased goodwill and intangible assets** will both be **capitalised** as assets in the balance sheet. The option for goodwill of immediate write off to reserves, by-passing the profit and loss account, will no longer be available as it was under SSAP 22.

(b) Where goodwill and intangible assets have limited lives they will be **amortised** to the profit and loss account over their expected lives.

(c) Amortisation will not be required for assets that can be justified as having **indefinite lives**. They need to be written down only if their values drop below those in the balance sheet.

(d) There is a general presumption that the lives of goodwill and intangible assets will be **no more than 20 years**. A longer or indefinite life may be assigned only if the durability of the asset can be demonstrated and if it is possible to remeasure its value each year to identify any reduction.

(e) **Impairment reviews** must be performed annually where lives of **more than 20 years** are chosen. For lives of less than 20 years, they are required only in the year after acquisition, and in other years if there is some indication that the asset's value might have fallen below its recorded value.

Exam focus point

The June 2003 edition of *Financial Management* includes an excellent article on goodwill by David Burl.

Although the material covered is of a fairly high level, it may be wise to read through it. The Paper 6 examiner may have seen it and, although he is unlikely to set a question on it, it might possibly have stimulated some ideas for questions.

Perhaps you might find it beneficial to jot down say five key learning points from the article.

5 INVESTMENTS

5.1 The last category of fixed assets we need to consider is **investments**. Not all investments, however, are held by a company for the long term and it will be convenient to deal with fixed asset investments and current asset investments together.

KEY TERM

An **investment** can be defined as an asset that generates economic benefits in the form of distributions and/or appreciation in value.

5.2 Investments intended to be retained by a company on a continuing basis (for use in the company's activities) should be treated as fixed assets, while any other investments should be taken to be current assets.

5.3 The categories into which investments should be grouped and separately disclosed are given in the pro-forma balance sheet shown in Chapter 2.

Fixed asset investments

5.4 The provisions relating to fixed assets in general, which were given in the previous chapter, embrace investments which are held as fixed assets. But investments will not normally have a limited economic life, so that the requirement of systematic depreciation does not apply. Fixed asset investments will therefore be carried at cost less provisions for permanent diminutions in value with revaluations taken to a revaluation reserve

5.5 The **alternative accounting** rules allow the following bases of valuation, other than cost, for fixed asset investments.

(a) **Market value**: if this is higher than the stock exchange value, the latter should also be disclosed.

(b) **Directors' valuation**.

As always when advantage is taken of the alternative accounting rules, disclosure must be made of the items affected, the basis of valuation adopted and the comparable amounts determined according to the historical cost convention.

Current asset investments

5.6 Other current asset investments which are **readily marketable** investments should be shown at current market value, with increases or decreases in value taken to the profit and loss account.

5.7 Other current asset investments should be shown, in accordance with the prudence concept, at the lower of purchase price and net realisable value.

Listed vs unlisted

5.8 Investments, whether fixed assets or current assets, must be split between those listed on a recognised stock exchange and those which are unlisted. Shares dealt with on the Alternative Investment Market (AIM), are **not** 'listed', but they are 'quoted'. The amount of income from listed investments need not be shown in the profit and loss account, according to a recent amendment to CA 1985.

5.9 If the aggregate market value of investments listed on a recognised stock exchange differs from their carrying value in the balance sheet, the market value should be disclosed.

Substantial shareholdings

5.10 Where an investment comprises a substantial shareholding in another company there is further information which must be disclosed. This is to enable the company's members to obtain a proper appreciation of the nature of the investment.

(a) If a company owns **over 20%** of the equity shares in another company or the investment exceeds 20% of the investing company's assets, then the **name and nationality** of the company should be disclosed. For each class of shares held, the identity of the class and the proportion of the nominal value held must be given. These are called 'significant investments'.

(b) If **20% or more** of a company's shares are held, then the investing company must disclose its aggregate capital and reserves and profit or loss for the year.

(c) These requirements **do not apply** if the investment is to be treated as a **subsidiary, associate or joint venture**, nor if a 20% or greater investment is accounted for under the **equity method**. The equity method is outside your syllabus, but briefly it involves adding the investing company's share of an associated company's retained profit to the historical cost of the investment.

Chapter roundup

- This chapter has set out the **statutory accounting requirements** relating to intangible fixed assets and investments. These requirements are supplemented in the case of development costs by SSAP 13 and in the case of goodwill by FRS 10.
- *SSAP 13* is a standard which is generally accepted and well understood. You should ensure that you are very familiar with its provisions. Don't forget to learn the disclosure requirements.
- *FRS 10*, on the other hand, is a complex standard. You should be aware of the Key provisions within FRS 10.
- Go back now to **Chapter 2** and consider how the accounting treatments and disclosure requirements discussed in this chapter fit in with the published accounts formats and notes.

Quick quiz

1 Patents can only be treated as assets in a company's accounts if they are:

- .... for valuable consideration
- .... by the company itself

2 What are the criteria which must be met before development expenditure can be deferred?

- S......................
- C......................
- O......................
- E......................
- T......................
- R......................

3 Development expenditure written off may be reinstated if the uncertainties which led to the write-off no longer apply.

True ☐

False ☐

4 Peggy buys Sandra's business for £30,000. The business assets are a bar valued at £20,000, stocks at £3,000 and debtors of £3,000. How much is goodwill valued at?

5 How should negative goodwill be accounted for under FRS10?

Answers to quick quiz

1 Acquired, created (see para 1.2)

2 **S**eparately defined project. **E**xpenses identifiable. **C**ommercially viable, **T**echnically feasible, **O**verall profitability, **R**esources to complete it. (2.4)

3 True. (2.6)

4 £30,000 – £20,000 – £3,000 – £3,000 = £4,000 (3.5)

5 It should be disclosed in the intangible fixed assets category. (4.37)

Now try the question below from the Exam Question Bank

Number	Level	Marks	Time
6	Introductory	n/a	20 mins

Chapter 7

STOCKS AND WORK IN PROGRESS

	Topic list	Syllabus reference	Ability required
1	**Stocks and short-term work in progress**	(iii)	Evaluation
2	**Long-term contract work in progress**	(iii)	Evaluation
3	**Standard costing and marginal costing systems**	(iii)	Evaluation

Introduction

You have encountered stocks and stock valuation in your Foundation studies. Stock valuation has a direct impact on a company's gross profit and it is usually a material item in a company's accounts. This is therefore an important subject area. If you have any doubts about accounting for stocks and methods of stock valuation you would be advised to go back to your Foundation study material and revise this topic.

Section 1 of this chapter goes over some of this ground again, concentrating on the effect of SSAP 9. Section 2 goes on to discuss a new area, long-term contract work in progress. You should find this topic fairly logical as long as you work through the examples and question carefully.

Standard costing and marginal costing systems are considered briefly in Section 3, but these topics are more closely related to your cost accounting studies.

Learning outcomes covered in this chapter

- **Explain** the accounting rules contained in Financial Reporting Standards which provide guidance as to the appropriate treatment of certain transactions.
- **Identify, apply** and **evaluate** the accounting treatment of significant transactions.

Syllabus content covered in this chapter

- Stocks and long term contracts (SSAP 9) to cover methods of determining cost, NRV, the inclusion of overheads, and the measurement of profit on uncompleted contracts.

1 STOCKS AND SHORT-TERM WORK IN PROGRESS

1.1 In most businesses the value put on stock is an important factor in the determination of profit. Stock valuation is, however, a highly subjective exercise and consequently there is a wide variety of different methods used in practice. The CA 1985 regulations and SSAP 9 *Stocks and long-term contracts* requirements were developed to achieve greater uniformity in the valuation methods used and in the disclosure in financial statements prepared under the historical cost convention.

1.2 SSAP 9 defines stocks and work in progress as:

- **Goods** or other assets purchased **for resale**
- **Consumable stores**

- **Raw materials** and components purchased for incorporation into products for sale
- **Products and services** in intermediate stages of completion
- **Long-term contract balances**
- **Finished goods**

1.3 In published accounts, the Companies Act 1985 requires that these stock categories should be grouped and disclosed under the following headings:

- **Raw materials and consumables**
- **Work in progress**
- **Finished goods and goods for resale**
- **Payments on account** (presumably intended to cover the case of a company which has paid for stock items but not yet received them into stock)

1.4 A distinction is also made in SSAP 9 between:

- Stocks and work in progress other than long-term contract work in progress
- Long-term contract work in progress.

We will look at long-term contracts later in the chapter, but first we must consider how stock is to be valued.

Exam focus point

The November 2001 Paper asked for the problems associated with determining NRV, as well as for a calculation of closing stock. The November 2002 and May 2003 papers also included questions on the treatment of closing stocks under SSAP 9 as part of a compulsory question.

Determination of the cost of stock

1.5 To determine profit, costs should be matched with related revenues. Since the cost of unsold stock and work in progress at the end of an accounting period has been incurred in the expectation of future sales revenue, it is appropriate to carry these costs forward in the balance sheet, and to charge them against the profits of the period in which the future sales revenue is eventually earned. How to do this is the problem.

1.6 However if there is no reasonable expectation of sufficient future revenue to cover cost incurred (eg as a result of deterioration, obsolescence or a change in demand) the irrecoverable cost should be charged to revenue in the year under review. Thus the fundamental rule of stock valuation is that stocks normally need to be stated at **cost** or, if lower, at **net realisable value.**

1.7 The comparison of cost and net realisable value should be made separately for each item of stock, but if this is impracticable, similar categories of stock item can be grouped together.

1.8 This valuation principle is backed by CA 1985. However, CA 1985 (under its alternative accounting rules) also allows stocks to be stated at their **current cost.** If historical costs are used in determining purchase price or production cost, the difference between the historical cost and the current cost valuations must be stated.

1.9 Of **cost** and **net realisable value** the latter is the easier to define, though not necessarily the easier to ascertain in practice, since the amount of subjective judgement involved is high.

SSAP 9 defines **net realisable value** as the actual or estimated selling price (net of trade but before settlement discounts) **less**:

- All further **costs to completion**
- And all **costs** to be incurred in **marketing, selling and distributing**

1.10 The cost of stocks is harder to determine.

(a) Cost is the expenditure which has been incurred in the **normal course of business** in bringing the product or service to its **present location and condition**. This expenditure should include, in addition to the cost of purchase, such **costs of conversion** as are appropriate to that location and condition.

(b) **Cost of purchase** comprises **purchase price** including **import duties, transport** and **handling costs** and any other **directly attributable costs,** less **trade discounts,** rebates and subsidies.

(c) **Cost of conversion** comprises:

- Costs which are **specifically attributable** to units of production, eg direct labour, direct expenses and sub-contracted work
- **Production overheads**
- **Other overheads,** if any, **attributable** in the particular circumstances of the business to bringing the product or service to its present location and condition

1.11 CA 1985 also allows (but, unlike SSAP 9, does not **require**) the inclusion of production overheads in the valuation of stock.

1.12 **Production overheads** are those overheads incurred in respect of materials, labour or services for production, based on the **normal level of activity,** taking one year with another. When allocating production overheads to the valuation of stock, care must be taken to **exclude all abnormal overheads** such as **exceptional spoilage, idle capacity and other losses** which are **avoidable under normal conditions.**

1.13 CA 1985 additionally permits the inclusion of **interest payable** on capital borrowed to finance the production of the asset, to the extent that it accrues in respect of the **period of production.** Any interest so included must be **disclosed in a note to the accounts.** Such capitalisation of interest would also be an allowable addition to cost under SSAP 9 if it fell within the scope of Paragraph 1.10 (c) (iii) above.

1.14 One further point to note concerns the determination of cost of purchase or purchase price. SSAP 9 states the following **general principle regarding cost of purchase.**

> 'The methods used in allocating costs to stocks need to be selected with a view to providing the fairest possible approximation to the expenditure actually incurred.'

1.15 When prices are fluctuating it is sometimes difficult to decide on the cost of each item of stock. Therefore there are various methods of estimating the cost of goods still in stock at the year end. Appendix 1 to SSAP 9 mentions the following specific methods which may satisfy the general principle.

- Job costing
- Batch costing
- Process costing
- Standard costing
- Unit cost

- Average cost
- FIFO (first in, first out)

1.16 In the UK, the Inland Revenue accepts FIFO, average cost and (in the case of many retailing companies) 'selling price less normal gross profit margin' as stock valuation methods in arriving at taxable profit. It does **not** accept LIFO.

Exam focus point

In an exam, you might be given a situation in which there is not sufficient information to make a final decision. In this kind of scenario, you need to explain the options available and to identify gaps in the available knowledge that prevent you from reaching a conclusive answer.

1.17 FIFO and LIFO: a comparison

Bruce, a retailer commenced business on 1 January 20X5, with a capital of £500. He decided to specialise in a single product line and by the end of June 20X5, his purchases and sales of this product were as follows.

	PURCHASES		*SALES*	
	Units	*Unit price*	Units	*Unit price*
		£		£
January	30	5.00	20	7.00
February	-	-	5	7.20
April	40	6.00	25	8.00
May	25	6.50	30	8.50
June	20	7.00	20	9.00
	115		100	

(a) What is the retailer's gross profit for the period

(i) If stock is valued using LIFO

(ii) If stock is valued using FIFO

(b) Assuming that all purchases and sales are made for cash and that there are no other transactions for the period, draw up balance sheets as at 30 June 20X5, showing:

- Stock valued on a FIFO basis
- Stock valued on a LIFO basis

1.18 SOLUTION

(a) (i) *LIFO basis*

	SALES			*COST OF SALES*		
	Units	*Unit price*	*Total*	Units	*Unit price*	*Total*
		£	£		£	£
January	20	7.00	140.00	20	5.00	100.00
February	5	7.20	36.00	5	5.00	25.00
April	25	8.00	200.00	25	6.00	150.00
May	30	8.50	255.00	25	6.50	162.50
				5	6.00	30.00
June	20	9.00	180.00	20	7.00	140.00
	100		811.00	100		607.50
Closing stock				10	6.00	60
				5	5.00	25
				15		85

		£
Sales		811.00
Less cost of sales		607.50
Gross profit		203.50

(ii) *FIFO basis*

	£	£
Sales		811.00
Purchases	692.50	
Less closing stock 15 @ 7.00	105.00	
		587.50
		223.50

(b) BALANCE SHEETS AS AT 30 JUNE 20X5

	(i) *LIFO basis*	*(ii)* *FIFO basis*
	£	£
Original capital	500.00	500.00
Profit	203.50	223.50
	703.50	723.50
Stock	85.00	105.00
Cash	618.50	618.50
	703.50	723.50

1.19 In a time of rising prices LIFO (which uses the most current costs) will tend to give a more realistic measure of profit, but results in an outdated stock valuation being disclosed in the balance sheet. The exercise below is good revision.

When NRV > cost

1.20 There are various key situations which might lead to net realisable value being less than cost.

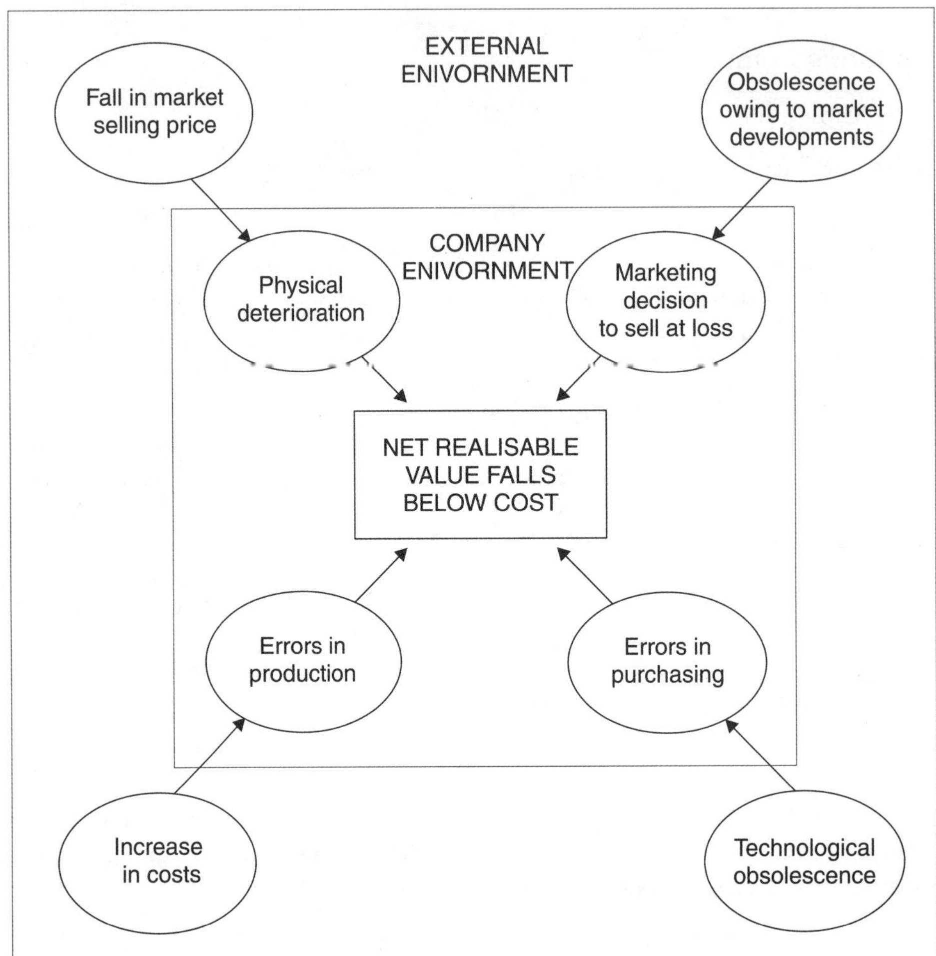

1.21 The comparison of cost and net realisable value should strictly be done in respect of each item of stock separately. In practice, it may be necessary to resort to a more broad brush approach and assign individual stock items to broad categories containing similar items.

Question 1

Modern Electronics Ltd has the following stock at its year end of 31 December 20X8.

	Purchase price	*Attributable manufacturing overheads*	*Attributable non-manufacturing overheads*	*Total cost*	*Net realisable value*
	£ million	£ million	£ million	£ million	£ million
Current stock	55	10	5	70	90
Obsolete stock	20	6	4	30	15
Total				100	105

Answer

	Purchase price	*Attributable production overheads*	*Total relevant cost*	*Net realisable value*	*Lower of cost and net realisable value*
	£ million	£ million	£ million	£ million	£ million
Current stock	55	10	65	90	65
Obsolete stock	20	6	26	15	15
Total			91	105	80

Exam focus point

The November 2002 paper included a question similar to the one above on NRV.

Question 2

On 1 November 20X2 a company held 300 units of finished goods item no 9639 in stock. These were valued at £12 each. During November 20X2 three batches of finished goods were received into store from the production department as follows.

Date	*Units received*	*Production cost per unit*
10 November	400	£12.50
20 November	400	£14
25 November	400	£15

Goods sold out of stock during November were as follows.

Date	*Units sold*	*Selling price per unit*
14 November	500	£20
21 November	500	£20
28 November	100	£20

What was the profit from selling stock item 9639 in November 20X2, applying the following principles of stock valuation:

(a) FIFO?
(b) LIFO?
(c) Cumulative weighted average costing?

Ignore administration, sales and distribution costs.

Answer

(a) *FIFO*

Date	*Issue costs*	*Issue cost total* £	*Closing stock* £
14 November	300 units × £12 plus		
	200 units × £12.50	6,100	
21 November	200 units × £12.50 plus		
	300 units × £14	6,700	
28 November	100 units × £14	1,400	
Closing stock	400 units × £15		6,000
		14,200	6,000

(b) *LIFO*

Date	*Issue costs*	*Issue cost total* £	*Closing stock* £
14 November	400 units × £12.50 plus		
	100 units × £12	6,200	
21 November	400 units × £14 plus		
	100 units × £12	6,800	
28 November	100 units × £15	1,500	
Closing stock	300 units × £15 plus		
	100 units × £12		5,700
		14,500	5,700

(c) *Cumulative weighted average cost*

		Unit cost	Balance in stock	Total cost of sales	Closing stock
		£	£	£	£
1 November Opening stock	300	12	3,600		
10 November	400	12.50	5,000		
	700	12.286	8,600		
14 November	500	12.286	6,143	6,143	
	200	12.286	2,457		
20 November	400	14	5,600		
	600	13.428	8,057		
21 November	500	13.428	6,714	6,714	
	100	13.428	1,343		
25 November	400	15	6,000		
	500	14.686	7,343		
28 November	100	14.686	1,469	1,469	
30 November	400	14.686	5,874	14,326	5,874

Summary: profit

	FIFO	LIFO	Weighted average
	£	£	£
Opening stock	3,600	3,600	3,600
Cost of production	16,600	16,600	16,600
	20,200	20,200	20,200
Closing stock	6,000	5,700	5,874
Cost of sales	14,200	14,500	14,326
Sales (1,100 × £20)	22,000	22,000	22,000
Profit	7,800	7,500	7,674

2 LONG-TERM CONTRACT WORK IN PROGRESS — Pilot paper

Exam focus point

The November 2002 paper included a full question on SSAP 9 based on a shipbuilding company. The May 2003 paper included a scenario based on the construction of a leisure centre on which two MCQs were set.

Introduction

2.1 The most controversial aspect of SSAP 9 is its approach to the valuation of work in progress for incomplete long-term contracts.

KEY TERM

A **long-term contract** is defined as: 'a contract entered into for the design, manufacture or construction of a **single substantial asset** or the provision of a service (or of a combination of assets or services which together constitute a **single project**) where the time taken substantially to complete the contract is such that the **contract activity** falls into **different accounting periods**.'

Usually long-term contracts will **exceed one year** in duration, although a **sufficiently material contract** whose activity **straddles a balance sheet date** should still be accounted for as a **long-term contract even if it will last in total less than a year**. This is to ensure that the accounts for **both accounting periods** involved will still give a **true and fair view** of the activities of the company.

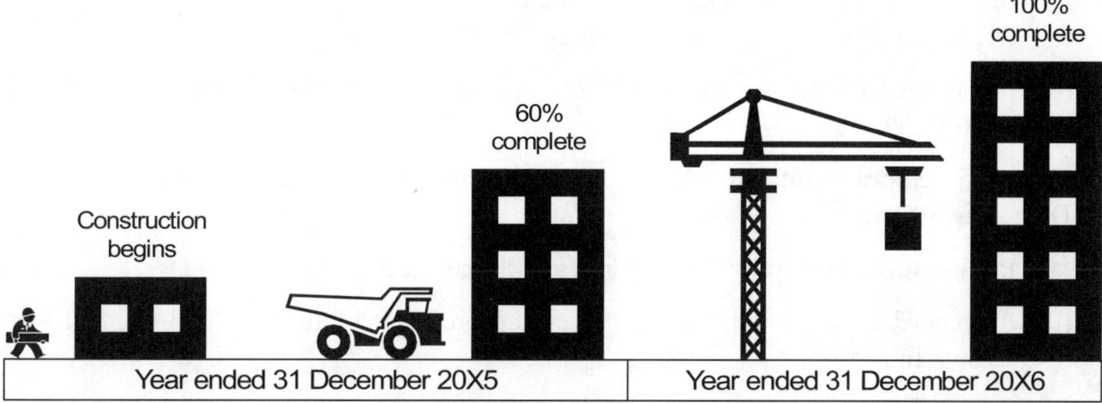

2.2 The existence of a proper **contract** is **important**, because it provides a basis of **reasonable certainty** whereby it is nevertheless **prudent** to **allow recognition** of **profits before completion of work.** In the absence of a contract, there would be uncertainty and this would trigger a need for caution and prudence to be exercised.

Exam focus point

Part of a question ion the November 2003 paper required the candidate to explain how the booking of profit under long-term contract accounting is compatible with the desirable feature of prudence as envisaged by FRS 18.

The underlying problem

2.3 It is the following requirement which causes the greatest controversy around SSAP 9.

> 'Separate consideration needs to be given to long-term contracts. Owing to the **length of time** taken to complete such contracts, to defer recording turnover and taking profit into account until completion may result in the profit and loss account reflecting not so much a **fair view** of the results of the **activity** of the company **during the year** but rather the results relating to contracts that have been completed in the year. It is therefore appropriate to take **credit** for **ascertainable turnover** and **profit** while contracts are **in progress** ....'

Some companies might prefer to value work in progress on long-term contracts at cost, and to **defer taking any profit** on the contract into the profit and loss account **until the contract had been completed**. This policy may be considered **prudent**, but there may be an **underlying management motive** to **defer profits** and **tax liabilities.**

2.4 EXAMPLE: LONG-TERM CONTRACTS

A numerical example might help to illustrate the problem. Suppose that a contract is started on 1 January 20X5, with an estimated completion date of 31 December 20X6. In the first year, to 31 December 20X5:

(a) Costs incurred amounted to £600,000.

(b) Half the work on the contract was completed.

(c) The final contract price is £1,500,000.

(d) Certificates of work completed have been issued, to the value of £750,000. (*Note.* It is usual, in a long-term contract, for a qualified person such as an architect or engineer to inspect the work completed, and if it is satisfactory, to issue certificates. This will then be the notification to the customer that progress payments are now due to the contractor. Progress payments are commonly the amount of valuation on the work certificates issued, minus a precautionary retention of 10%.).

(e) It is estimated with reasonable certainty that further costs to completion in 20X6 will be £600,000.

What is the contract profit in 20X5, and what entries would be made for the contract at 31 December 20X5 if:

(a) Profits are deferred until the completion of the contract.

(b) A proportion of the estimated turnover and profit is credited to the profit and loss account in 20X5?

2.5 SOLUTION

(a) If profits were deferred until the completion of the contract in 20X6, the turnover and profit recognised on the contract in 20X5 would be nil, and the value of work in progress on 31 December 20X5 would be £600,000. SSAP 9 takes the view that this policy is unreasonable, because in 20X6, the total profit of £300,000 would be recorded. Since the contract revenues are earned throughout 20X5 and 20X6, a profit of nil in 20X5 and £300,000 in 20X6 would be contrary to the matching concept of accounting.

(b) It is fairer to recognise turnover and profit throughout the duration of the contract.

As at 31 December 20X5 turnover of £750,000 should be matched with cost of sales of £600,000 in the profit and loss account, leaving an attributable profit for 20X5 of £150,000.

The only balance sheet entry as at 31 December 20X5 is a debtor of £750,000 recognising that the company is owed this amount for work done to date. No balance remains for stock, the whole £600,000 having been recognised in cost of sales.

Definitions

Exam focus point

Long-term contract accounting is very much of a practical area. Make sure you read the question carefully to ensure you pick up the little nuances in the examiner's requirements.

2.6 SSAP 9 gives some other important definitions, as well as that of long-term contracts themselves given above.

KEY TERMS

'**Attributable profit**. That part of the total profit currently estimated to arise over the duration of the contract, after allowing for estimated remedial and maintenance costs and increases in costs so far as not recoverable under the terms of the contract, that fairly reflects the profit attributable to that part of the work performed at the accounting date. (There can be no attributable profit until the profitable outcome of the contract can be assessed with reasonable certainty.)

Foreseeable losses. Losses which are currently estimated to arise over the duration of the contract (after allowing for estimated remedial and maintenance costs and increases in costs so far as not recoverable under the terms of the contract). This estimate is required irrespective of:

- Whether or not work has yet commenced on such contracts
- The proportion of work carried out at the accounting date
- The amount of profits expected to arise on other contracts

Payments on account. All amounts received and receivable at the accounting date in respect of contracts in progress.'

Approach for calculating turnover and profit to be taken

2.7 The SSAP 9 rules for calculating the turnover and profit to be taken on incomplete long-term contracts follow directly from the definitions given above and are as follows.

(a) **Turnover** and **profit** must reflect the proportion of the work carried out at the accounting date (and allow for any known inequalities in profitability in the various stages of a contract).

(b) Where the outcome of a contract cannot be **foreseen with reasonable certainty**, so that the expected profit cannot be reasonably assessed, it is prudent *not* to take up any profit. (This will be especially appropriate in the case of long-term contracts in their early stages.) However, 'in such circumstances, if no loss is expected it may be appropriate to show as turnover a proportion of the total contract value using a zero estimate of profit' (SSAP 9).

(c) If there is an **expected loss** on a contract, provision must be made for the **whole of the loss** as soon as it is foreseen (so none of the loss should be deferred). This has the effect of reducing the value of WIP to its net realisable value. For example, if a contract is 75% complete, and:

- Costs incurred to date are £300,000
- Further costs to completion are expected to be £100,000
- The contract price is £360,000

in addition to a suitable proportion of costs incurred, then the full expected loss of £40,000 should be charged against profit in the current period.

Exam focus point

The November 2002 paper asked candidates to discuss the SSAP 9 approach for recognising losses in full, as soon as they can be foreseen, in relation to the Statement of Principles.

Treatment of other costs

2.8 The **estimated future costs** must take into account **estimated costs of rectification and guarantee work** and any possible increases in wages, prices of raw materials etc, so far as these are **not recoverable** from the **customer** under the terms of the contract.

2.9 **Interest payable** for finance etc must be **excluded** from **costs unless specifically attributable** to the **contract.**

Estimating attributable profit

2.10 There are generally two alternative formulae for determining the estimated attributable profit for the year.

- Work certified basis
- Costs incurred basis

(a) $\text{Attributable profit} = \dfrac{\text{Work certified to date}}{\text{Total contract price}} \times \text{Estimated total profit}$

(b) $\text{Attributable profit} = \dfrac{\text{Cost of work completed to date}}{\text{Total costs}} \times \text{Estimated total profit}$

2.11 Care should be exercised in adopting a costs incurred basis eg if there is high initial outlay or perhaps the expensive items only go in towards the end of the contract. The examiner may therefore provide a tailored formula for the specific exam question which you will need to interpret and apply on the day.

An extra prudent approach

2.12 Some companies feel that it is more prudent to take credit for profit only in respect of the cash which has been received from the customer. Hence, the figure for attributable profit obtained above, is subjected to a further fraction.

$$\text{'Extra prudent' attributable profit} = \frac{\text{Cash received}}{\text{Work certified to date}} \times \text{Attributable profit as above.}$$

2.13 With a little bit of basic maths, the above can be expressed as:

$$\text{'Extra prudent' attributable profit} = \frac{\text{Cash received}}{\text{Total contract price}} \times \text{Estimated total profit}$$

Exam focus point

The extra prudent approach might well not be required by the examiner. It is shown here to demonstrate what some companies use in practice. Read the question carefully to understand the examiner's requirements.

Available guidance

2.14 SSAP 9 does not provide any guidance on how to work out cost of sales, but focuses instead on the approach to determining attributable profit.

2.15 The amount of turnover and profit on a long-term contract to be recognised in an accounting period is found using a cumulative approach ie deduct figure for total at end of last year from total at end of this year to get figure for the current year.

	£
Cumulative turnover/attributable profit	X
Less any turnover/attributable profit taken into account in previous years	X
Turnover/profit to be recognised in current period	X

2.16 **Estimates of total profit may change** from one year to another. Therefore, attributable profits have to be **recalculated** at the end of **each period**. Remember that at an **early stage** in the contract, in order to show a **true and fair view** of activity in the period, an **appropriate proportion of turnover** should be recorded in the profit and loss account but, on grounds of **prudence, no profit** should be recorded until the overall result of the contract is more certain.

Using a step by step approach

2.17 In valuing long-term WIP and the other disclosures required under SSAP 9, an organised approach is essential. The following suggested method breaks the process down into five logical steps.

Step 1. Compare the contract value and the total costs expected to be incurred on the contract. If a loss is foreseen (that is, if the costs to date plus estimated costs to completion exceed the contract value) then it must be charged against profits. If a loss has already been charged in previous years, then only the difference between the loss as previously and currently estimated need be charged (or credited).

Step 2. Using the percentage completed to date (or other formula given in the question), calculate turnover attributable to the contract for the period (for example percentage complete × total contract value, less of course, turnover taken in previous periods).

Step 3. Calculate the cost of sales on the contract for the period.

	£
Total contract costs × percentage complete (or follow instructions in question)	X
Less any costs charged in previous periods	(X)
	X
Add foreseeable losses in full (not previously charged)	X
Cost of sales on contract for the period	X

Step 4. Deduct the cost of sales for the period as calculated above (including any foreseeable loss) from work in progress at cost up to the total balance on the account. If the cost of sales transfer exceeds this balance, then show the excess as a provision for liabilities and charges or as an accrual.

Step 5. Calculate **cumulative** turnover on the contract (the total turnover recorded in respect of the contract in the profit and loss accounts of all accounting periods since the inception of the contract). Compare this with total progress payments to date.

(a) If turnover exceeds payments on account, an 'amount recoverable on contracts' is established and separately disclosed within debtors.

(b) If payments on account exceed cumulative turnover then the excess is:

- First deducted from any remaining balance on work in progress
- Any balance is disclosed within creditors

Double entry

2.18 The accounting double entry for a long-term contract is as follows.

(a) *During the year*

(i) DEBIT Contract account (WIP)
CREDIT Cash/creditors

Being costs incurred

(ii) DEBIT Trade debtors
CREDIT Debtors: amounts recoverable on contracts

Being progress payments invoiced

(iii) DEBIT Bank
CREDIT Trade debtors

Being cash received

(b) *At year end*

(i) DEBIT Debtors: amounts recoverable on contracts
CREDIT Turnover (P&L)

Being turnover recognised

(ii) DEBIT Cost of sales (P&L)
CREDIT Contract account

Being costs matched against turnover

(iii) DEBIT Provisions on long-term contracts (P&L)
CREDIT Provision for future losses (B/S)

Being a provision for future losses

Summary of accounting treatment

2.19 The following summarises the accounting treatment for long-term contracts – **make sure that you understand it.**

Profit and loss account

(a) **Turnover and costs**

(i) Turnover and associated costs should be recorded in the profit and loss account 'as contract activity progresses'.

(ii) Include an 'appropriate proportion of total contract value as turnover' in the profit and loss account.

(iii) The costs incurred in reaching that stage of completion are matched with this turnover, resulting in the reporting of results which can be attributed to the proportion of work completed.

(iv) Turnover is the 'value of work carried out to date'.

(b) **Attributable profit**

(i) It must reflect the proportion of work carried out.

(ii) It should take into account any known inequalities in profitability in the various stages of a contract.

Balance sheet

(a) **Stocks**

	£
Costs to date	X
Less transfer to profit and loss a/c	(X)
	X
Less foreseeable losses	(X)
	X
Less payments on account in excess of turnover	(X)
WIP	X

(b) **Debtors**

	£
Cumulative turnover recognised	X
Less payments on account	(X)
Amount recoverable on contracts	X

(c) **Creditors**. Where payments on account exceed both cumulative turnover and net WIP the excess should be included in creditors under 'payments on account'.

(d) **Provisions**. To the extent foreseeable future losses exceed WIP, the losses should be provided.

Question 3

Chopra Helicopters Ltd is engaged in long-term contracts for the construction of large helicopters. At the end of September 20X3 there are two uncompleted contracts on the books, details of which are as follows.

CONTRACT	*A*	*B*
Date commenced	1.9.X3	1.4.X1
Expected completed date	23.12.X3	23.12.X3
	£	£
Final contract price	70,000	290,000
Costs to 30.9.X3	21,000	210,450
Value of work certified to 30.9.X3	20,000	230,000
Progress payments invoiced to 30.9.X3	20,000	210,000
Cash received to 30.9.X3	18,000	194,000
Estimated costs to completion at 30.9.X3	41,000	20,600

Required

Prepare calculations showing the amounts to be included in the balance sheet at 30 September 20X3 in respect of the above contracts.

Answer

Contract A is a short-term contract and will be included in the balance sheet as work in progress at cost less amounts received and receivable £(21,000 – 20,000) ie £1,000.

Contract B is a long-term contract and will be included in the balance sheet at cost plus attributable profit less amounts received and receivable.

The estimated final profit is:

		£
Final contract price		290,000
Less:	cost to date	(210,450)
	estimated future costs	(20,600)
		58,950

The attributable profit is found as follows.

$$\text{Estimated final profit} \times \frac{\text{Work certified}}{\text{Total contract work}} \times \frac{\text{Cash received}}{\text{Invoiced amounts}}$$

$$\pounds 58{,}950 \times \frac{230{,}000}{290{,}000} \times \frac{194{,}000}{210{,}000}$$

Attributable profit = £43,191

In this instance, the company has adopted the extra prudent approach and applied the cash received fraction. Remember, however, this might not be asked for in the exam.

Long-term contract work in progress

CONTRACT B

	£
Costs to date	210,450
Attributable profit	43,191
Anticipated loss	-
	253,641
Progress payments received and receivable	210,000
	43,641

PROFITABLE AND LOSS-MAKING CONTRACTS

2.20 Students sometimes find accounting for long-term contracts quite confusing, particularly where contracts are loss-making. We can look at the differences between profitable and loss-making contracts in more depth.

Profitable contracts

2.21 PROFIT AND LOSS ACCOUNT (EXTRACT)

	£
Turnover	X
Cost of sales	(X)
Attributable profit	X

2.22 BALANCE SHEET (EXTRACT)

	£
Current assets	
Stock: long-term contracts	
Costs to date	X
Less P&L a/c cost of sales	(X)
Less excess payments on account	(X)
	X
Debtors: amounts recoverable on contracts	£
Sales value of work: turnover	X
Less progress payments invoiced	(X)
	X
Debtors: trade debtors	£
Progress payments invoiced less cash received	X
Current liabilities	£
Payments on account (when payments received are in excess of turnover which cannot be offset against stock balance)	X

Loss-making contracts

2.23 PROFIT AND LOSS ACCOUNT (EXTRACT)

	£
Turnover	X
Cost of sales	(X)
	(X)
Provision for loss (balancing figure to give)	(X)
Total foreseeable loss	(X)

2.24 BALANCE SHEET (EXTRACT)

	£
Current assets	
Stock: long-term contracts	
Costs incurred	X
Less cost of sales	(X)
Less provision for loss	(X)
Less negative debtors balance	(X)
Positive/nil balance	X
Debtors: amounts recoverable on contracts	£
Sales value of work	X
Less progress payments invoiced	(X)
Positive/nil balance	X
Debtors: trade debtors	£
Progress payments invoiced less cash received	X
Current liabilities	£
Payments on account	
Negative debtor balance not relieved against stock	X
Provision for liabilities and charges	£
Provision for loss not offset against stock balance	X

2.25 The following comprehensive exercise should make things clearer.

Question 4

Pablo plc has two contracts in progress, the details of which are as follows.

	Bella (profitable)	*Donna (loss-making)*
	£'000	£'000
Total contract price	300	300
Costs incurred to date	90	150
Estimated costs to completion	135	225
Progress payments invoiced and received	116	116

Required

Show extracts from the profit and loss account and the balance sheet for each contract, assuming they are both:

(a) 40% complete
(b) 36% complete

Answer

(a) *Bella contract*

(i) *40% complete*

	£'000
Profit and loss account	
Turnover (40% × 300)	120
Cost of sales (40% × 225)	90
Gross profit	30
Balance sheet	
Debtors (120 – 116)	4
WIP (90 – 90)	-

(ii) *36% complete*

	£'000
Profit and loss account	
Turnover (36% × 300)	108
Cost of sales (36% × 225)	81
Gross profit	27
Balance sheet	
Debtors (108 – 116 = –8)	-
WIP (90 – 81 – 8*) =	1

* Set off excess payments on account against WIP.

(b) *Donna contract*

(i) *40% complete*

Working

	£'000	£'000
Total contract price		300
Less: costs to date	150	
estimated costs to completion	225	
		375
Foreseeable loss		(75)

	£'000
Profit and loss account	
Turnover (40% × 300)	120
Cost of sales (40% × 375)	(150)
	(30)
Provision for future losses (bal fig)	(45)
Gross loss	(75)

Balance sheet	£'000
Debtors (120 – 116)	4
WIP (150 – 150)	-
Provision for future losses	(45)

(ii) 36% complete

	£'000
Profit and loss account	
Turnover (36% × 300)	108
Cost of sales (36% × 375)	(135)
	(27)
Provision for future losses (balancing figure)	(48)
Gross loss	(75)
Balance sheet	
Debtors (108 – 116 = –8)	-
WIP (150 – 135 – 48* = –33)	-
Creditors: payments on account	8
Provisions: provisions for future losses	33

* Set off provision for losses before excess payments on account.

Exam focus point

Are you completely satisfied with your skills in doing long-term contract accounting? Are you completely comfortable with the disclosure requirements? If not, consider any necessary reworking till you have it really mastered.

3 STANDARD COSTING AND MARGINAL COSTING SYSTEMS

3.1 When a company's financial accounts and cost accounts are integrated into a single set of accounts, there will be a single set of records for inventory. For cost and management accounting purposes, stocks might be valued at marginal cost or standard cost. However, when the financial accounts are prepared, the stock values will then need to be adjusted so as to conform with the valuation method used to prepare the financial accounts. In other words, there might be a requirement at the end of an accounting period to convert stock values from marginal cost to full cost (to include an element of fixed production overheads) or from standard cost to 'actual' cost (with 'actual' cost defined as FIFO or weighted average cost).

3.2 The Appendix to SSAP 9 makes the following recommendations.

(a) When accounts are prepared on a marginal costing basis, some overheads (variable overheads) might be included in stock values. However, it will then be necessary to add on to marginal costs an appropriate proportion of production overhead costs not already included in marginal cost (in other words, a proportion of fixed production overheads).

(b) The allocation of overheads included in the valuation of stocks and work in progress needs to be based on the **company's normal level of activity**, taking one year with another. In deciding what activity level is 'normal' the factors to be considered are:

(i) The output capacity of the plant under prevailing working conditions (for example single shift, double shift).

(ii) Budgeted output for the current year and future years.

(iii) Actual output for the current year and previous years.

3.3 Temporary changes in output volume may be ignored, but permanent changes should lead to a revision of what is considered the 'normal level' of output.

3.4 For further information on standard and marginal costing, you should refer to your cost accounting studies.

Chapter roundup

- The *Companies Act 1985* requires that the balance sheet should show stocks (CI) sub-divided as follows.

Stocks
Raw materials and consumables
Work in progress
Finished goods and goods for resale
Payments on account (of purchases)

- Stocks must be valued at the lower of **cost** and **net realisable value**. Learn the definitions of these terms.
- The rules for calculating accounting entries on **long-term contracts** can be summarised as follows.
  - Turnover taken on long-term contracts should be debited to 'Amounts recoverable on contracts' (and credited to the profit and loss account)
  - The amount at which long-term contract work in progress is stated in accounts should be cost, less cost of sales to date, including any foreseeable losses
  - Progress payments received and receivable should first be credited to 'Amounts recoverable on contracts' and then to any remaining balance on work in progress
  - Any remaining balance of progress payments should be disclosed within creditors
- **Marginal costing** is not acceptable for stock valuation in published accounts.
- At this stage of your studies the most difficult aspect of SSAP 9 to be mastered is the valuation and disclosure of **long-term contracts**. You must be able both to calculate all the balances to be included in accounts and to discuss the reasons for SSAP 9's provisions.
- However, don't overlook the SSAP 9 and CA 1985 provisions on valuation and disclosure of **stocks** and **short-term work in progress**. Perhaps the most likely exam topic is the valuation of stocks at net realisable value, so learn the difference between cost and NRV and the circumstances when NRV is likely to be used.
- Go back to **Chapter 2** and consider how the accounting treatments and disclosure requirements discussed in this chapter fit in with the published accounts formats and notes.

Quick quiz

1 Net realisable value = Selling price **less** .... **less** ....

2 Which stock costing methods are permissible under SSAP 9?

A FIFO, LIFO, average cost, unit cost
B Unit cost, job cost, batch cost, LIFO
C Process costing, unit cost LIFO, average cost
D Job costing, average cost, FIFO, unit cost.

3 Any expected loss on a long-term contract must be recognised, in full, in the year it was identified.

True ☐

False ☐

4 List the five steps to be taken when valuing long-term contracts.

5 Which items in the profit and loss and balance sheet are potentially affected by long term contracts?

Answers to quick quiz

1 Net realisable value = selling price **less** costs to completion **less** costs to market, sell and distribute.

2 D, LIFO is not an acceptable costing method (see paras 1.15, 1.16)

3 True. (2.6(c))

4 See paragraph 2.12.

5 Profit and loss: turnover and cost of sales. Balance sheet: stocks, debtors, creditors and provisions (2.14)

Now try the questions below from the Exam Question Bank

Number	Level	Marks	Time
7	Exam level	20	36 mins
8	Exam level	20	36 mins
9	Exam level	20	36 mins
10	Exam level	20	36 mins

Chapter 8

TAXATION IN COMPANY ACCOUNTS

	Topic list	Syllabus reference	Ability required
1	Corporation tax	(iii)	Application
2	Income tax	(iii)	Application
3	FRS 19 *Deferred tax*	(iii)	Application
4	Taxation in company accounts	(iii)	Application
5	Disclosure requirements	(iii)	Application

Introduction

You should read and work through this chapter very carefully. There are plenty of exercises here – make sure that you attempt each one yourself without referring to the solution immediately.

Some of the topics discussed in this chapter are more straightforward than others. You may have noticed that SSAP 5 *Accounting for VAT* is not included in the chapter. This is because you should already be familiar with VAT from your Foundation studies. Go back and revise this area if you are not.

In relation to corporation tax you must be able to calculate the relevant tax figures and know how they should be disclosed in the accounts according to FRS 16.

Deferred taxation is probably the most difficult topic in this chapter. Concentrate on trying to understand the logic behind the tax and the reasons why the FRS 19 approach has been adopted.

The more complicated numerical aspects of deferred tax are unlikely to be examined in this paper.

Learning outcomes covered in this chapter

- **Explain** the accounting rules contained in Financial Reporting Standards which provide guidance as to the appropriate treatment of certain transactions
- **Identify, apply** and **evaluate** the accounting treatment of significant transactions

Syllabus content covered in this chapter

- Tax in financial accounts (FRS 16), and deferred taxation (FRS 19) (timing differences, the full provision method and the partial provision method).

Exam focus point

The compulsory statutory accounts preparation question inevitably includes parts requiring the settling up of the figures for corporation tax and deferred tax, given estimated figures.

1 CORPORATION TAX

1.1 Companies are required to pay **corporation tax** on their taxable profits. The **taxable profits** of a company are essentially its **net profit before dividends, adjusted for certain items where the tax treatment differs from the accounts treatment.**

1.2 The **rate** at which companies are charged to corporation tax **depends on the level of their profits.** Companies with small profits currently pay corporation tax at a rate of 20%; other companies currently pay at a rate of 30%.

1.3 The amount of tax to which a company is assessed on its profit for an accounting period is called its **tax liability** for that period. Under current legislation, a company must pay its tax liability nine months after the end of the relevant accounting period. However, if profits exceed £1.5m companies must pay quarterly instalments starting 6 months and 13 days after the start of the accounting period.

1.4 EXAMPLE: MAINSTREAM CORPORATION TAX

Tabitha Ltd supplies the following information.

	£
Year to 30 June 20X6	
Dividend received	10,000
Year to 30 June 20X7	
Trading profits	100,000
Dividend received	20,000
Dividend paid for the year	35,000

Assuming that the rate of corporation tax is 30%, calculate the mainstream corporation tax liability for the year to 30 June 20X7.

1.5

	£
Corporation tax: 30% × £100,000	30,000
Mainstream corporation tax liability	30,000

2 INCOME TAX

2.1 A company pays corporation tax, not income tax. However, **when a company pays certain expenses** (debenture interest, patent royalties) **it must deduct income tax at a specified rate and pay this to the Revenue**; the company is thus a collector of taxes. The recipient receives the net income (ie he or she has suffered tax deducted at source). For debenture interest, the income tax rate applied is 20%.

2.2 For example, a company pays debenture interest of £100,000.

		£	£
DEBIT	Profit and loss account	100,000	
CREDIT	Debenture holder		80,000
	Inland revenue control		20,000

2.3 When a company **receives** such interest net of basic rate income tax, it is not liable for the tax that it has paid. If a company received £80,000 in debenture interest, the entry to 'gross up' the interest is would be as follows.

		£	£
DEBIT	Inland Revenue control (£80,000 × 20/80)	20,000	
CREDIT	Interest received		20,000

With the tax credit

2.4 **Gross debenture interest received is treated as taxable profit for corporation tax and gross debenture interest paid is treated as a tax allowable expense.** The company may reclaim the tax 'paid' on debenture interest received in the following order.

(a) Set off income tax suffered against income tax payable to the Revenue.
(b) Set the excess against the year's mainstream corporation tax liability (no limit).
(c) Reclaim a refund from the Revenue.

Exam focus point

In the exam the examiner would give detailed instructions if grossing up of this sort was required. If a question involved debenture interest receivable, then the examiner would normally assume that all figures were gross and any tax recoverable had already been offset against tax collected from interest payable. The following question demonstrates both grossing up and offset.

Question 1

Hilary Ltd presents the following information for the year to 31 March 20X8.

	£
Trading profit (equal to taxable trading profit)	700,000
Debenture interest received (gross)	30,000
Debenture interest paid (gross)	20,000
Dividend paid	20,000

Assuming that the rate of corporation tax is 30%, the rate of income tax on debenture interest is 20%, calculate the mainstream corporation tax liability for the year to 31 March 20X8 and show the ledger accounts recording this information.

Answer

(a)

	£
Trading profit	700,000
Debenture interest received	30,000
	730,000
Debenture interest paid	20,000
Taxable profit	710,000

	£
Corporation tax at 30%	213,000
Less income tax 20% × £(30,000 – 20,000)	2,000
Mainstream corporation tax liability	211,000

(b)

DEBENTURE INTEREST RECEIVED ACCOUNT

	£		£
Profit and loss account	30,000	Bank account	24,000
		Income tax account	6,000
	30,000		30,000

DEBENTURE INTEREST PAID ACCOUNTS

	£		£
Bank account	16,000	Profit and loss account	20,000
Income tax account	4,000		
	20,000		20,000

DIVIDENDS PAID ACCOUNT

	£		£
Bank account	20,000	Profit and loss account	20,000

PROFIT AND LOSS ACCOUNT

	£		£
Debenture interest paid	20,000	Trading profit	700,000
Corporation tax	213,000	Debenture interest received	30,000
Dividends paid	20,000		
Balance c/f	477,000		
	730,000		730,000

INCOME TAX ACCOUNT

	£		£
Debenture interest received account		Debenture interest paid account	4,000
	6,000	Corporation tax	2,000
	6,000		6,000

CORPORATION TAX ACCOUNT

	£		£
		Profit and loss account	213,000
Income tax account	2,000		
Balance c/f	211,000		
	213,000		213,000

3 FRS 19 DEFERRED TAX 5/01

Exam Focus Point

This section may seem quite complicated. Do not worry about the numbers too much, but remember that you must be able to **explain** the purpose of the deferred tax balance. The May 2001 exam included a ten mark question on the disclosures required for deferred tax and the reasons for them.

3.1 You may already be aware from your studies of taxation that accounting profits and taxable profits are not the same. There are several reasons for this but they may conveniently be considered under two headings.

(a) **Permanent differences** arise because certain expenditure, such as entertainment of UK customers, is not allowed as a deduction for tax purposes although it is quite properly deducted in arriving at accounting profit. Similarly, certain income (such as UK dividend income) is not subject to corporation tax, although it forms part of accounting profit.

(b) **Timing differences** arise because certain items are included in the accounts of a period which is different from that in which they are dealt with for taxation purposes.

Deferred taxation is the tax attributable to timing differences.

KEY TERM

Deferred tax. Estimated future tax consequences of transactions and events recognised in the financial statements of the current and previous periods.

3.2 Deferred taxation is therefore a means of ironing out the tax inequalities arising from timing differences.

(a) In years when **corporation tax is saved** by timing differences such as accelerated capital allowances, a charge for deferred taxation is made in the P&L account and a provision set up in the balance sheet.

(b) In years when **timing differences reverse**, because the depreciation charge exceeds the capital allowances available, a deferred tax credit is made in the P&L account and the balance sheet provision is reduced.

Deferred tax is the subject of a new standard, FRS 19 *Deferred tax.* Before we look at the detailed requirements of FRS 19, we will explore some of the issues surrounding deferred tax.

3.3 You should be clear in your mind that the tax actually payable to the Inland Revenue is the **corporation tax liability**. The credit balance on the deferred taxation account represents an estimate of tax saved because of timing differences but expected ultimately to become payable when those differences reverse.

3.4 FRS 19 identifies the main categories in which timing differences can occur.

(a) **Accelerated capital allowances.** Tax deductions for the cost of a fixed asset are accelerated or decelerated, ie received before or after the cost of the fixed asset is recognised in the profit and loss account.

(b) **Pension liabilities** are accrued in the financial statements but are allowed for tax purposes only when paid or contributed at a later date.

(c) **Interest charges or development costs** are capitalised on the balance sheet but are treated as revenue expenditure and allowed as incurred for tax purposes.

(d) **Intragroup profits in stock**, unrealised at group level, are reversed on consolidation (not relevant for this syllabus).

(e) **Revaluations.** An asset is revalued in the financial statements but the revaluation gain becomes taxable only if and when the asset is sold.

(f) **Unrelieved tax losses.** A tax loss is not relieved against past or present taxable profits but can be carried forward to reduce future taxable profits.

(g) **Unremitted earnings of subsidiaries.** The unremitted earnings of subsidiary and associated undertakings and joint ventures are recognised in the group results but will be subject to further taxation only if and when remitted to the parent undertaking (not relevant for this syllabus).

3.5 Deferred taxation is therefore an accounting convention which is introduced in order to apply the accruals concept to income reporting where timing differences occur. However, **deferred tax assets** are not included in accounts as a rule, because it would not be prudent, given that the recovery of the tax is uncertain.

Basis of provision

3.6 A comprehensive tax allocation system is one in which deferred taxation is computed for every instance of timing differences: **full provision**. The opposite extreme would be the **nil provision** approach ('**flow through** method'), where only the tax payable in the period would be charged to that period.

SSAP 15

3.7 SSAP 15, the forerunner of FRS 19, rejected both these approaches and prescribed a middle course, called **partial provision.**

> 'Tax deferred or accelerated by the effect of timing differences should be accounted for to the extent that it is probable that a liability or asset will crystallise. Tax deferred or accelerated by the effect of timing differences should not be accounted for to the extent that it is probable that a liability or asset will not crystallise.'

3.8 The **probability** that a liability or asset would crystallise was assessed by the directors on the basis of **reasonable assumptions**. They had to take into account all relevant information available up to the date on which they approved the financial statements, and also their intentions for the future. Ideally, financial projections of future plans had to be made for a number (undefined) of years ahead. The directors' judgement had to be exercised with prudence.

3.9 If a company predicted, for example, that capital expenditure would **continue at the same rate** for the foreseeable future, so that capital allowances and depreciation would remain at the same levels, then no originating or reversing differences of any significance to the continuing trend of the tax charge would arise and so no change to the provision for deferred tax needed to be made (unless there were other significant timing differences).

The three different methods compared

3.10 Under the **flow-through method**, the tax liability recognised is the expected legal tax liability for the period (ie no provision is made for deferred tax). The main **advantages** of the method are that it is straightforward to apply and the tax liability recognised is closer to many people's idea of a 'real' liability than that recognised under either full or partial provision.

3.11 The main **disadvantages** of flow-through are that it can lead to large fluctuations in the tax charge and that it does not allow tax relief for long-term liabilities to be recognised until those liabilities are settled. The method is not used internationally.

3.12 The **full provision method** has the **advantage** that it is consistent with general international practice. It also recognises that each timing difference at the balance sheet date has an effect on future tax payments. If a company claims an accelerated capital allowance on an item of plant, future tax assessments will be bigger than they would have been otherwise. Future transactions may well affect those assessments still further, but that is not relevant in assessing the position at the balance sheet date. The **disadvantage** of full provision is that, under certain types of tax system, it gives rise to large liabilities that may fall due only far in the future. The full provision method is the one prescribed by FRS 19.

3.13 The **partial provision method** addresses this disadvantage by providing for deferred tax only to the extent that it is expected to be paid in the foreseeable future. This has an obvious intuitive appeal, but its effect is that deferred tax recognised at the balance sheet date includes the tax effects of future transactions that have not been recognised in the financial statements, and which the reporting company has neither undertaken nor even committed to undertake at that date. It is difficult to reconcile this with the ASB's *Statement of Principles*, which defines assets and liabilities as arising from past events.

Exam focus point

You need to understand the concept of deferred tax, it is unlikely that you will need to perform detailed calculations.

3.14 It is important that you understand the issues properly so consider the example below.

3.15 EXAMPLE: THE THREE METHODS COMPARED

Suppose that Kim plc begins trading on 1 January 20X7. In its first year it makes profits of £5m, the depreciation charge is £1m and the capital allowances on those assets is £1.5m. The rate of corporation tax is 33%.

3.16 SOLUTION: FLOW THROUGH METHOD

The tax liability for the year is 33% £(5.0 + 1.0 – 1.5)m = £1.485m. The potential deferred tax liability of 33% × (£1.5m – £1m) is completely ignored and no judgement is required on the part of the preparer.

3.17 SOLUTION: FULL PROVISION

The tax liability is £1.485m again, but the debit in the P&L account is increased by the deferred tax liability of 33% × £0.5m = £165,000. The total charge to the P&L account is therefore £1,650,000 which is an effective tax rate of 33% on accounting profits (ie 33% × £5.0m). Again, no judgement is involved in using this method.

3.18 SOLUTION: PARTIAL PROVISION

Is a deferred tax provision necessary under partial provision? It is now necessary to look ahead at future capital expenditure plans. Will capital allowances exceed depreciation over the next few years? If *yes*, no provision for deferred tax is required. If *no*, then a reversal is expected, ie there is a year in which depreciation is greater than capital allowances. The deferred tax provision is made on the maximum reversal which will be created, and any not provided is disclosed by note.

If we assume that the review of expected future capital expenditure under the partial method required a deferred tax charge of £82,500 (33% × £250,000), we can then summarise the position.

Summary

3.19 The methods can be compared as follows.

Method	*Provision*	*Disclosure*
	£	£
Flow-through	-	-
Full provision	165,000	-
Partial provision	82,500	82,500

Note that under he partial provisions method the amount of the full timing difference ($33^1/_3$ × £500,000) that is not provided for must be disclosed (33% × £250,000).

FRS 19 *Deferred tax*

3.20 In December 2000 the ASB published FRS 19. The FRS replaced SSAP 15 and comes into effect for accounting periods ending on or after 23 January 2002, although earlier adoption is encouraged. It requires entities to provide for tax timing differences on a **full, rather than partial provision basis.**

Objective

3.21 The objective of FRS 19 is to ensure that:

(a) Future tax consequences of past transactions and events are recognised as liabilities or assets in the financial statements

(b) The financial statements disclose any other special circumstances that may have an effect on future tax charges.

Scope

3.22 The FRS applies **to all financial statements that are intended to give a true and fair view** of a reporting entity's financial position and profit or loss (or income and expenditure) for a period. The FRS applies to taxes calculated on the basis of taxable profits, including withholding taxes paid on behalf of the reporting entity.

3.23 Reporting entities applying the Financial Reporting Standard for Smaller Entities **(FRSSE)** currently applicable are **exempt** from the FRS.

Recognition of deferred tax assets and liabilities

REMEMBER!

Deferred tax should be recognised in respect of **all timing differences that have originated but not reversed by the balance sheet date.**

Deferred tax should **not be recognised on permanent differences.**

Question 2

Can you remember some examples of timing differences?

Answer

- Accelerated capital allowances
- Pension liabilities accrued but taxed when paid
- Interest charges and development costs capitalised but allowed for tax purposes when incurred
- Unrealised intra-group stock profits reversed on consolidation
- Revaluation gains
- Tax losses
- Unremitted earnings of subsidiaries, associates and joint ventures recognised in group results

KEY TERM

Permanent differences. Differences between an entity's taxable profits and its results as stated in the financial statements that arise because certain types of income and expenditure are non-taxable or disallowable, or because certain tax charges or allowances have no corresponding amount in the financial statements.

Allowances for fixed asset expenditure

3.24 Deferred tax **should be recognised** when the **allowances** for the cost of a fixed asset are **received before or after the cost of the fixed asset is recognised in the profit and loss account.** However, if and when **all conditions** for retaining the allowances have been met, the **deferred tax should be reversed.**

3.25 If an asset is not being depreciated (and has not otherwise been written down to a carrying value less than cost), the timing difference is the amount of capital allowances received.

3.26 Most capital allowances are received on a **conditional basis**, ie they are repayable (for example, via a balancing charge) if the assets to which they relate are sold for more than their tax written-down value. However, some, such as industrial buildings allowances, are repayable only if the assets to which they relate are sold within a specified period. Once that period has expired, all conditions for retaining the allowance have been met. At that point, deferred tax that has been recognised (ie on the excess of the allowance over any depreciation) is reversed.

Question 3

An industrial building qualifies for an IBA when purchased in 20X1. The building is still held by the company in 20Z6. What happens to the deferred tax?

Answer

All the conditions for retaining tax allowances have been met. This means that the timing differences have become permanent and the deferred tax recognised should be reversed. Before the 25 year period has passed, deferred tax should be provided on the difference between the amount of the industrial building allowance and any depreciation charged on the asset.

Measurement – discounting

3.27 Reporting entities are **permitted but not required** to discount deferred tax assets and liabilities to reflect the time value of money.

3.28 The ASB believes that, just as other long-term liabilities such as provisions and debt are discounted, so too in principle should long-term deferred tax balances. The FRS therefore permits discounting and provides guidance on how it should be done. However, the ASB stopped short of making discounting mandatory, acknowledging that there is as yet **no internationally accepted methodology** for discounting deferred tax, and that for some entities **the costs might outweigh the benefits.** Entities are encouraged to select the more appropriate policy, taking account of factors such as materiality and the policies of other entities in their sector.

Question 4

Can you think of a situation where it might be appropriate to discount deferred tax liabilities?

Answer

Where the reversal is fairly slow, for example with industrial buildings allowances.

3.29 Discounting should be **applied consistently** to all tax flows on timing differences where the effect is expected to be **material** and where the **tax flows have not already been discounted**.

3.30 **No account** should be taken of **future timing differences** including future tax losses.

3.31 The **scheduling of the reversals** should take account of the **remaining tax effect of transactions already reflected in the financial statements,** for example tax losses at the balance sheet date.

3.32 The **discount rate** should be the **post tax return** that could be obtained at the balance sheet date on **government bonds** with **similar maturity dates** and in **currencies similar to those of the deferred tax assets or liabilities.** It may be possible to use average rates without introducing material errors.

Presentation

3.33 In the **balance sheet** classify:

- Net deferred tax liabilities as 'provisions for liabilities and charges'
- Net deferred tax assets as debtors, as a separate subhead if material.

3.34 Balances are to be **disclosed separately** on the face of the balance sheet **if** so **material** as to distort the financial statements.

3.35 In the **profit and loss account** classify as part of **tax on profit or loss on ordinary activities.**

Disclosures

3.36 FRS 19 has detailed disclosures relating to deferred tax, which are best learnt by studying the illustrative example below, taken from the Appendix.

IMPORTANT!

Note in particular that the FRS requires information to be disclosed **about factors affecting current and future tax charges. A key element** of this is a requirement to disclose a **reconciliation of the current tax charge for the period to the charge that would arise if the profits reported in the financial statements were charged at a standard rate of tax.**

The May 2002 exam sought an explanation as to why this reconciliation is helpful to readers of financial statements.

3.37 EXAMPLE: DISCLOSURES

The following illustrates how the disclosures required by the FRS could be presented in the notes to the accounts. The reconciliation of the tax charge, illustrated as a reconciliation of monetary amounts in note 1 (b) below, could alternatively be given as a reconciliation of the standard rate of tax to the effective rate.

1 TAX ON PROFIT ON ORDINARY ACCOUNTS

(a) *Analysis of charge in period*

	20X9		*20X8*	
	£m	£m	£m	£m
Current tax				
UK corporation tax on profits of the period	40		26	
Adjustments in respect of previous periods	4		(6)	
		44		20
Foreign tax		12		16
Total current tax (note 1(b))		56		36
Deferred tax				
Origination and reversal of timing differences	67		60	
Effect of increased tax rate on opening liability	12		-	
Increase in discount	(14)		(33)	
Total deferred tax (note 2)		65		27
Tax on profit on ordinary activities		121		63

(b) *Factors affecting the tax charge for period*

The tax assessed for the period is lower than the standard rate of corporation tax in the UK (31 per cent). The differences are explained below.

	20X9	*20X8*
	£m	£m
Profit on ordinary activities before tax	361	327
Profit on ordinary activities multiplied by standard rate of corporation tax in the UK of 31% (20X8: 30%)	112	98
Effects of		
Expenses not deductible for tax purposes (primarily goodwill amortisation)	22	10
Capital allowances for period in excess of depreciation	(58)	(54)
Utilisation of tax losses	(17)	(18)
Rollover relief on profit on disposal of property	(10)	-
Higher tax rates on overseas earnings	3	6
Adjustments to tax charge in respect of previous periods	4	(6)
Current tax charge for period (note 1 (a))	56	36

(c) *Factors that may affect future tax charges*

Based on current capital investment plans, the group expects to continue to be able to claim capital allowances in excess of depreciation in future years but at a slightly lower level than in the current year.

The group has now used all brought-forward tax losses, which have significantly reduced tax payments in recent years.

No provision has been made for deferred tax on gains recognised on revaluing property to its market value or on the sale of properties where potentially taxable gains have been rolled over into replacement assets. Such tax would become payable only if the property were sold without it being possible to claim rollover relief. The total amount unprovided for is £21 million. At present, it is not envisaged that any tax will become payable in the foreseeable future.

The group's overseas tax rates are higher than those in the UK primarily because the profits earned in country X are taxed at a rate of 45 per cent. The group expects a reduction in future tax rates following a recent announcement that the rate of tax in that country is to reduce to 40 per cent.

No deferred tax is recognised on the unremitted earnings of overseas subsidiaries, associates and joint ventures. As the earnings are continually reinvested by the group, no tax is expected to be payable on them in the foreseeable future.

2 PROVISION FOR DEFERRED TAX

	31.12.20X9	*31.12.20X8*
	£m	£m
Accelerated capital allowances	426	356
Tax losses carried forward	-	(9)
Undiscounted provision for deferred tax	426	347
Discount	(80)	(66)
Discounted provision for deferred tax	346	281
Provision at start of period	281	
Deferred tax charge in profit and loss account for period (note 1)	65	
Provision at end of period	346	

Problems

3.38 The FRS makes a significant change. It will have the effect of **increasing the liabilities** reported by entities that at present have **large amounts of unprovided deferred tax** arising from capital allowances in excess of depreciation.

3.39 Criticisms that may be made of the FRS 19 approach include the following.

(a) The provisions on **discounting** are somewhat **confusing.**

(b) The standard is **complicated,** and there is **scope for manipulation and inconsistency**, since discounting is optional.

(c) It is **open to question whether deferred tax is a liability** as defined in the *Statement of Principles*. It is not, strictly speaking, a present obligation arising as a result of a past event. However, it is being recognised as such under the FRS.

(d) Arguably the flow-through or **nil provision method is closer to the ASB definition,** but this method, although much simpler, has been rejected to bring the standard closer to the IAS.

3.40 **Section summary**

- Deferred tax is tax relating to timing differences.
- Full provision must be made for tax timing differences.
- Discounting is allowed but not required.

Exam focus point

The May 2002 paper included 20 mark question on deferred tax including advice to directors on recognition of a deferred tax asset.

4 TAXATION IN COMPANY ACCOUNTS

4.1 We have now looked at the 'ingredients' of taxation in company accounts. There are **two** aspects to be learned:

- Taxation on profits in the **profit and loss account**
- Taxation payments due, shown as a liability in the **balance sheet**

Taxation in the profit and loss account

4.2 The tax on profit on ordinary activities is calculated by aggregating:

- **Corporation tax** on taxable profits
- **Transfers** to or from **deferred taxation**
- Any **underprovision or overprovision** of corporation tax on profits of previous years

4.3 When corporation tax on profits is calculated for the profit and loss account, the calculation is only an **estimate** of what the company thinks its tax liability will be. In subsequent dealings with the Inland Revenue, a **different** corporation tax charge might eventually be agreed.

The **difference** between the estimated tax on profits for one year and the actual tax charge finally agreed for the year is made as an **adjustment** to taxation on profits in the **following year**, resulting in the disclosure of either an underprovision of tax or an overprovision of tax.

Question 5

In the accounting year to 31 December 20X3, Darren Ltd made an operating profit before investment income and taxation of £110,000.

Corporation tax on the operating profit has been estimated as £45,000.

In the previous year (20X2) corporation tax on 20X2 profits had been estimated as £38,000 but it was subsequently agreed at £40,500 with the Inland Revenue.

A transfer to the deferred taxation account of £16,000 will be made in 20X3.

Required

(a) Calculate the tax on profits for 20X3 for disclosure in the accounts.
(b) Calculate the amount of mainstream corporation tax payable on 30 September 20X4.

Answer

(a)

	£
Corporation tax on profits	45,000
Deferred taxation	16,000
Underprovision of tax in previous year £(40,500 – 38,000)	2,500
Tax on profits for 20X3	63,500

(b)

	£
Tax payable on 20X3 profits	45,000
Mainstream corporation tax liability	45,000

Taxation in the balance sheet

4.4 It should already be apparent from the previous examples that the corporation tax charge in the profit and loss account will not be the same as corporation tax liabilities in the balance sheet.

4.5 In the balance sheet, there are several items which we might expect to find.

(a) **Income tax may be payable** in respect of (say) interest payments paid in the last accounting return period of the year, or accrued.

(b) If no corporation tax is payable (or very little), then there might be an **income tax recoverable asset** disclosed in current assets (income tax is normally recovered by offset against the tax liability for the year).

(c) There will usually be a **liability for mainstream corporation tax,** possibly including the amounts due in respect of previous years but not yet paid.

(d) We may also find a **liability on the deferred taxation account.** Deferred taxation is shown under 'provisions for liabilities and charges' in the balance sheet.

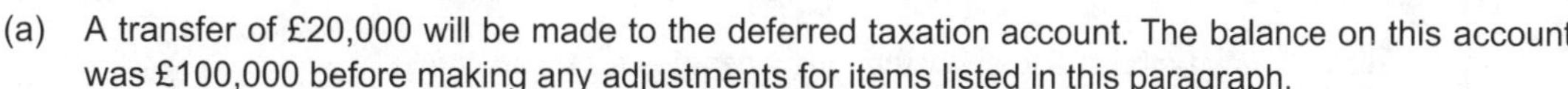

Question 6

For the year ended 31 July 20X4 Gary Ltd made taxable trading profits of £1,200,000 on which corporation tax is payable at 30%.

(a) A transfer of £20,000 will be made to the deferred taxation account. The balance on this account was £100,000 before making any adjustments for items listed in this paragraph.

(b) The estimated tax on profits for the year ended 31 July 20X3 was £80,000, but tax has now been agreed with the Inland Revenue at £84,000 and fully paid.

(c) Mainstream corporation tax on profits for the year to 31 July 20X4 is payable on 1 May 20X5.

(d) In the year to 31 July 20X4 the company made a capital gain of £60,000 on the sale of some property. This gain is taxable at a rate of 30%.

Required

(a) Calculate the tax charge for the year to 31 July 20X4.
(b) Calculate the tax liabilities in the balance sheet of Gary as at 31 July 20X4.

Answer

(a) *Tax charge for the year*

			£
(i)	Tax on trading profits (30% of £1,200,000)		360,000
	Tax on capital gain		18,000
	Deferred taxation		20,000
			398,000
	Underprovision of taxation in previous years £(84,000 – 80,000)		4,000
	Tax charge on ordinary activities		402,000

(ii) *Note.* The profit and loss account will show the following.

	£	£
Operating profit (assumed here to be the same as taxable profits)		1,200,000
Profit from sale of asset (exceptional)		60,000
Profit on ordinary activities before taxation		1,260,000
Tax on profit on ordinary activities		402,000
Retained profits for the year		858,000

(b) *Taxation in the balance sheet*

	£
Deferred taxation	
Balance brought forward	100,000
Transferred from profit and loss account	20,000
	120,000

The mainstream corporation tax liability is as follows.

Payable on 1 May 20X5	£
Tax on ordinary profits (30% of £1,200,000)	360,000
Tax on capital gain (30% of £60,000)	18,000
Due on 1 May 20X5	378,000

Summary

	£
Creditors: amounts falling due within one year	
Mainstream corporation tax, payable on 1 May 20X5	378,000
Provisions for liabilities and charges	
Deferred taxation	120,000

Note. It may be helpful to show the journal entries for these items.

		£	£
DEBIT	Tax charge (profit and loss account)	402,000	
CREDIT	Corporation tax creditor		*382,000
	Deferred tax		20,000

* This account will show a debit balance of £4,000 until the underprovision is recorded, since payment has already been made: (360,000 + 18,000 + 4,000).

5 DISCLOSURE REQUIREMENTS

CA 1985

5.1 The CA 1985 requires that the '**tax on profit or loss on ordinary activities**' **is disclosed** on the face of the profit and loss account or in a note to the accounts. In addition, the **notes** to the profit and loss account **must state**:

(a) The **basis** on which the charge for UK corporation tax and UK income tax is computed. Particulars are required of any special circumstances affecting the tax liability for the current or future financial years.

(b) The **amounts** of the charge for:

- UK corporation tax (showing separately the amount, if greater, of UK corporation tax before any double taxation relief)
- UK income tax
- Non-UK taxation on profits, income and capital gains

(*Note.* The same details must be given, if relevant, in respect of the 'tax on extraordinary profit or loss'.)

5.2 The CA 1985 also requires certain disclosures in respect of deferred tax.

(a) Deferred tax should be shown in the balance sheet under the heading '**provisions for liabilities and charges**' and in the category of provision for 'taxation, including deferred taxation'. The amount of any provision for taxation other than deferred taxation must be disclosed. The provision for taxation is different from tax liabilities which are shown as creditors in the balance sheet.

(b) **Movements** on reserves and provisions must be disclosed, including provisions for deferred tax

- The amount of the provision at the **beginning** of the year and the end of the year
- The amounts **transferred** to or from the provision during the year
- The **source/application** of any amount so transferred

FRS 16

5.3 FRS 16 *Current tax* supplements and extends these CA 1985 provisions requiring that a company's ***profit and loss account*** should disclose separately (if material):

(a) The **amount** of the UK corporation tax specifying:

- The **charge for corporation tax** on the income of the year (stating the rate used to make the provision)
- **Transfers** to or from the deferred taxation account
- The **relief** for overseas taxation

(b) The **total overseas taxation** relieved and unrelieved.

5.4 FRS 16 also requires that in respect of the **profit and loss account**, taxed receipts and payments should be included at the gross amounts (including the income tax deducted at source).

FRS 19

5.5 FRS 19 requires that **deferred** tax relating to the ordinary activities of the enterprise should be **shown separately** as a part of the tax on profit or loss on ordinary activities, either on the face of the profit and loss account, or by note.

5.6 **Adjustments** to deferred tax arising from changes in tax rates and tax allowances should normally be **disclosed separately** as part of the tax charge for the period.

5.7 The **deferred tax liabilities and assets**, should be **disclosed in the balance sheet or notes**. They should be disclosed separately on the face of the balance sheet if the amounts are so material that the absence of disclosure would affect interpretation of the Financial Statements.

Chapter roundup

- The disclosure requirements relating to company taxation are very detailed and **must be learned**. The best way is to practise on past exam questions.
- **FRS 19** requires full provision for **deferred** tax.

  °It is unlikely that complicated numerical questions will be set in the exam so concentrate on **understanding** deferred tax.
- You must also be able to prepare the **notes to the accounts** on tax for publication. This means mastering the disclosure requirements of FRS 16, FRS 19 and the CA 1985.

Quick quiz

1 The due date of payment of corporation tax for a company with profits of less than £1.5m is:

A Twelve months after the company's financial statements have been filed at Companies House
B Nine months after the end of the relevant accounting period
C Nine months after the company's financial statements have been filed at Companies House
D Twelve months after the end of the relevant accounting period

2 Debenture interest paid can be reclaimed in the following ways.

- Set off against ....
- Set the excess off against the ....
- .... a .... from the revenue

3 Temporary differences are the same as timing differences

True ☐

False ☐

4 What are the three bases under which deferred tax can be computed?

5 Which method does FRS 19 require to be used?

6 Under FRS 19 deferred tax assets and liabilities may/must be discounted. (Delete as applicable.)

7 Tax on profit on ordinary activities is the aggregate of:

.... + ... + ...

8 List the disclosure requirements set out by the CA 1985.

Answers to quick quiz

1 B (see para 1.3)

2 Against: income tax payable; the year's mainstream corporation tax liability and reclaim a refund. (2.4)

3 False. Timing differences include permanent differences. (3.1)

4 The nil provision basis, the full provision basis and the partial provision basis. (3.10)

5 Full provision. (3.20)

6 May. (3.27)

7 Corporation tax on taxable profits, transfers to/from deferred tax, under/over provisions form previous years.

8 See paragraphs 5.1 and 5.2.

Now try the question below from the Exam Question Bank

Number	Level	Marks	Time
11	Exam level	20	36 mins

Chapter 9

CREDIT SALES, LEASES AND HIRE PURCHASE

Topic list		Syllabus reference	Ability required
1	Types of lease and HP agreement	(iii)	Evaluation
2	Lessees	(iii)	Evaluation
3	Lessors	(iii)	Evaluation
4	FRS 5 *Reporting the substance of transactions*	(iii)	Knowledge

Introduction

Leasing transactions are extremely common so this is an important practical subject. Lease accounting is regulated by SSAP 21, which was introduced because of abuses in the use of lease accounting by companies. These companies effectively 'owned' an asset and 'owed' a debt for its purchase, but showed neither the asset nor the liability on the balance sheet because they were not required to do so. This is an example of 'off balance sheet finance', so it is closely associated with the principles of FRS 5.

You may be required to:

- Discuss the reasons for the different accounting treatments of operating and finance leases, from the perspectives of both the lessee and the lessor
- Answer questions that involve preparation of the relevant ledger accounts and extracts from the financial statements
- Show an awareness of the relevance of the interest rate implicit in a lease and the net present value of the minimum lease payment

Learning outcomes covered in this chapter

- **Explain** the accounting rules contained in Financial Reporting Standards which provide guidance as to the appropriate treatment of certain transactions
- **Identify, apply** and **evaluate** the accounting treatment of significant transactions

Syllabus content covered in this chapter

- Lease and hire purchase contracts (SSAP 21) – operating leases and finance leases in the books of the lessor and lessee
- The principle of substance over form (FRS 5) and its application to transactions for sale and repurchase agreements and consignment stock (May 2003, and onwards)

1 TYPES OF LEASE AND HP AGREEMENT Pilot paper, 5/01

Exam focus point

The pilot paper examined SSAP 21 in relation to the *Statement of Principles* and the way the treatment of finance leases applies to the definition of assets and liabilities. The May 2001 exam looked to the criteria used to define a lease as finance or operating and how this would affect the financial statements and the calculation of ratios, in particular gearing.

The May 2003 paper asked candidates to:

- Explain the meaning of a finance lease
- Identify whether a particular example should be treated as an operating lease or a finance lease
- Calculate financial statement figures

Bits of SSAP 21 sometimes appear as part of a larger accounts preparation question.

1.1 Where goods are acquired other than on immediate cash terms, arrangements have to be made in respect of the future payments on those goods. In the simplest case of credit sales, the purchaser is allowed a period of time (say one month) to settle the outstanding amount and the normal accounting procedure in respect of debtors/creditors will be adopted. However, in recent years there has been considerable growth in hire purchase and leasing agreements.

1.2 SSAP 21 Accounting for leases and hire purchase contracts standardises the accounting treatment and disclosure of assets held under lease or hire purchase.

1.3 In a leasing transaction there is a contract between the lessor and the lessee for the hire of an asset. The lessor retains legal ownership but conveys to the lessee the right to use the asset for an agreed period of time in return for specified rentals. SSAP 21 recognises two types of lease.

KEY TERMS

(a) A **finance lease** transfers substantially all the risks and rewards of ownership to the lessee. Although strictly the leased asset remains the property of the lessor, in substance the lessee may be considered to have acquired the asset and to have financed the acquisition by obtaining a loan from the lessor.

(b) An **operating lease** is any lease which is not a finance lease. An operating lease has the character of a rental agreement with the lessor usually being responsible for repairs and maintenance of the asset. Often these are relatively short-term agreements with the same asset being leased, in succession, to different lessees.

1.4 A **finance lease** is very similar in substance to a **hire purchase agreement**. (The difference in law is that under a hire purchase agreement the customer eventually, after paying an agreed number of instalments, becomes entitled to exercise an option to purchase the asset. Under a leasing agreement, ownership remains forever with the lessor.)

1.5 In this chapter the **user** of an asset will often be referred to simply as the **lessee**, and the **supplier** as the **lessor**. You should bear in mind that identical requirements apply in the case of hirers and vendors respectively under hire purchase agreements.

1.6 To expand on the statement in Paragraph 1.3(a) above, a finance lease should be presumed if at the inception of a lease the **present value of the minimum lease payments** amounts to substantially all (normally 90% or more) of the **fair value of the leased asset.**

The present value should be calculated by using the **interest rate implicit in the lease.**

1.7 Some of these terms need to be explained.

KEY TERMS

(a) The **minimum lease payments** are the minimum payments over the remaining part of the lease term plus any residual amounts guaranteed by the lessee or by a party related to the lessee.

(b) **Fair value** is the price at which an asset could be exchanged in an arm's length transaction.

(c) The **interest rate implicit in the lease** is the discount rate that, at the inception of a lease, when applied to the amounts which the lessor expects to receive and retain, produces an amount equal to the fair value of the leased asset.

(d) The **lease term** is the period for which the lessee has contracted to lease the asset and any further terms for which the lessee has the option to continue to lease the asset, with or without further payment, which option it is reasonably certain at the inception of the lease that the lessee will exercise.

Accounting for leases: lessees and lessors

1.8 **Operating leases** do not really pose an accounting problem. Payments by the lessee are charged to the lessee's and credited to the lessor's profit and loss account. The lessor treats the leased asset as a fixed asset and depreciates it in the normal way.

1.9 For assets held under **finance leases or hire purchase** this accounting treatment would not disclose the reality of the situation. If a lessor leases out an asset on a finance lease, the asset will probably never be seen on his premises or used in his business again. It would be inappropriate for a lessor to record such an asset as a fixed asset. In reality, what the lessor owns is a stream of cash flows receivable from the lessee. The asset is a debtor rather than a fixed asset.

1.10 Similarly, a lessee may use a finance lease to fund the 'acquisition' of a major asset which he will then use in his business perhaps for many years. The substance of the transaction is that the lessee has acquired a fixed asset, and this is reflected in the accounting treatment prescribed by SSAP 21, even though in law the lessee never becomes the owner of the asset.

Exam focus point

Questions on leasing could involve a discussion of the reasons for the different accounting treatments of operating and finance leases, from the perspectives of both the lessor and the lessee. Practical questions could involve preparation of the relevant ledger accounts and/or extracts from the financial statements.

2 LESSEES

Accounting treatment

2.1 In light of the above, SSAP 21 requires that, when an asset changes hands under a finance lease or HP agreement, lessor and lessee should account for the transaction as though it were a credit sale. In the lessee's books therefore:

DEBIT Asset account
CREDIT Lessor (liability) account

2.2 The amount to be recorded in this way is the capital cost or fair value of the asset. This may be taken as the amount which the lessee might expect to pay for it in a cash transaction.

2.3 A variant approach which produces the same net result is to debit the asset account with the fair value, and to debit an **interest suspense account** with the total amount of interest or finance charges payable under the agreement and to credit a lessor account with the total amount (capital and interest) payable under the agreement. We will see later how this affects the year end accounting entries.

2.4 The asset should be **depreciated** over the shorter of:

- The lease term
- Its useful life

Apportionment of rental payments

2.5 When the lessee makes a rental payment it will comprise two elements.

(a) An **interest charge** on the finance provided by the lessor. This proportion of each payment is interest payable and interest receivable in the profit and loss accounts of the lessee and lessor respectively.

(b) A repayment of part of the **capital cost** of the asset. In the lessee's books this proportion of each rental payment must be debited to the lessor's account to reduce the outstanding liability. In the lessor's books, it must be credited to the lessee's account to reduce the amount owing (the debit of course is to cash).

2.6 The accounting problem is to decide what proportion of each instalment paid by the lessee represents interest, and what proportion represents a repayment of the capital advanced by the lessor. There are three methods you may encounter:

- The level spread method
- The sum-of-the-digits method
- The actuarial method

Exam focus point

An examination question should specify which method is to be used. In theory, the aim is that the profit and loss account finance charge should produce a constant rate of return on outstanding leasing obligations.

2.7 The **level spread method** is based on the assumption that finance charges accrue evenly over the term of the lease agreement. For example, if an asset with a fair value of £3,000 is being 'acquired' on a finance lease for five payments of £700 each, the total interest is

£(3,500 – 3,000) = £500. This is assumed to accrue evenly and therefore there is £100 interest comprised in each rental payment, the £600 balance of each instalment being the capital repayment.

The level spread method is over simple and takes no account of the commercial realities of the transaction. You should use it in the examination only if you are specifically instructed to or if there is insufficient information to use another method.

2.8 The **sum-of-the-digits** method approximates to the actuarial method, splitting the total interest (without reference to a rate of interest) in such a way that the greater proportion falls in the earlier years. The procedure is as follows.

(a) Assign a digit to each instalment. The digit 1 should be assigned to the final instalment, 2 to the penultimate instalment and so on.

(b) Add the digits. If there are twelve instalments, then the sum of the digits will be 78. For this reason, the sum of the digits method is sometimes called the *rule of 78*.

$$\text{Sum of the digits} = \frac{n \times (n+1)}{2}$$

(c) Calculate the interest charge included in each instalment. Do this by multiplying the total interest accruing over the lease term by the fraction:

$$\frac{\text{Digit applicable to the instalment}}{\text{Sum of the digits}}$$

2.9 The **actuarial method** is the most precise method. It derives from the assumption that the interest charged by a lessor company will equal the rate of return desired by the company, multiplied by the amount of capital it has invested. At the beginning of the lease the capital invested is equal to the fair value of the asset (less any initial deposit paid by the lessee). This amount reduces as each instalment is paid. The interest accruing is greatest in the early part of the lease term, and gradually reduces as capital is repaid. We will look at a simple example of the actuarial method.

2.10 EXAMPLE: APPORTIONMENT METHODS

On 1 January 20X8 Haldane Ltd, wine merchants, buys a small bottling and labelling machine from Weller Limited on hire purchase terms. The cash price of the machine was £7,710 while the HP price was £10,000. The HP agreement required the immediate payment of a £2,000 deposit with the balance being settled in four equal annual instalments commencing on 31 December 20X8. The HP charge of £2,290 represents interest of 15% per annum, calculated on the remaining balance of the liability during each accounting period. Depreciation on the plant is to be provided for at the rate of 20% per annum on a straight line basis assuming a residual value of nil.

You are required to show the breakdown of each instalment between interest and capital, using in turn each of the apportionment methods described above.

2.11 SOLUTION

In this example, enough detail is given to use any of the apportionment methods. In an examination question, you would normally be directed to use one method specifically.

(a) *Level spread method*

The £2,290 interest charges are regarded as accruing evenly over the term of the HP agreement. Each instalment therefore contains £2,290/4 = £572.50 of interest. The break down is then as follows.

	1st instalment	*2nd instalment*	*3rd instalment*	*4th instalment*
	£	£	£	£
Interest	572.50	572.50	572.50	572.50
Capital repayment (balance)	1,427.50	1,427.50	1,427.50	1,427.50
	2,000.00	2,000.00	2,000.00	2,000.00

(b) *Sum-of-the-digits method*

Each instalment is allocated a digit as follows.

Instalment	*Digit*
1st (20X8)	4
2nd (20X9)	3
3rd (20Y1)	2
4th (20Y2)	1
	10

The £2,290 interest charges can then be apportioned.

		£
1st instalment	£2,290 × 4/10	916
2nd instalment	£2,290 × 3/10	687
3rd instalment	£2,290 × 2/10	458
4th instalment	£2,290 × 1/10	229
		2,290

The breakdown is then as follows.

	1st instalment	*2nd instalment*	*3rd instalment*	*4th instalment*
	£	£	£	£
Interest	916	687	458	229
Capital repayment (balance)	1,084	1,313	1,542	1,771
	2,000	2,000	2,000	2,000

(c) *Actuarial method*

Interest is calculated as 15% of the outstanding *capital* balance at the beginning of each year. The outstanding capital balance reduces each year by the capital element comprised in each instalment. The outstanding capital balance at 1 January 20X8 is £5,710 (£7,710 fair value less £2,000 deposit).

	Total	*Capital*	*Interest*
	£	£	£
Capital balance at 1 Jan 20X8		5,710	
1st instalment (interest = £5,710 × 15%)	2,000	1,144	856
Capital balance at 1 Jan 20X9		4,566	
2nd instalment (interest = £4,566 × 15%)	2,000	1,315	685
Capital balance at 1 Jan 20Y1		3,251	
3rd instalment (interest = £3,251 × 15%)	2,000	1,512	488
Capital balance at 1 Jan 20Y2		1,739	
4th instalment (interest = £1,739 × 15%)	2,000	1,739	261
Capital balance at 1 Jan 20Y3	8,000	-	2,290

Interest suspense account

2.12 Where an interest suspense account is used (see Paragraph 2.3), the double entry for finance lease/HP instalments is as follows (assuming that the actuarial method is used to record the first instalment payable under the lease in the example above).

(a)	DEBIT	Asset account	£7,710	
		Interest suspense	£2,290	
	CREDIT	HP creditor		£10,000

Being entries required to record acquisition of asset on hire purchase

(b)	DEBIT	Lessor/HP creditor	£2,000	
	CREDIT	Bank		£2,000

Being instalment payment recorded in full

(c)	DEBIT	Interest payable/finance charges (P&L)	£856	
	CREDIT	Interest suspense account		£856

Being year end adjustment to ensure that the year's interest/finance charges are charged to the profit and loss account

2.13 The equivalent entries where a suspense account is not used might be as follows.

(a)	DEBIT	Asset account	£7,710	
	CREDIT	HP account		£7,710
(b)	DEBIT	HP creditor	£2,000	
	CREDIT	Bank		£2,000
(c)	DEBIT	Interest payable/finance charges (P & L)	£856	
	CREDIT	HP creditor		£856

Entry (c) ensures that the interest element is recorded and is an annual adjustment. It is, of course, possible to make the full correct entry as each instalment is paid:

DEBIT	Interest payable/finance charges (P & L)	£856	
	Lessor/HP creditor	£1,144	
CREDIT	Bank		£2,000

However, in practice in many companies the interest/finance charge calculation is only made annually when preparing published accounts.

2.14 Thus, at the year end, whatever system is used during the year, the balance on the lessor/HP creditor account (where appropriate, less the balance on the interest suspense account) will represent the outstanding capital liability. Future interest/finance charges are not a true liability as the capital could be paid off at any time, thus avoiding these charges.

Question 1

Red Buttons Ltd purchased a machine under a hire purchase agreement on 1 January 20X6. The agreement provided for an immediate payment of £2,000, following by five equal instalments of £3,056, each instalment to be paid on 30 June and 31 December respectively. The cash price of the machine was £10,000. Red Buttons estimated that it would have a useful economic life of five years, and its residual value would then be £1,000.

In apportioning interest to respective accounting periods, the company uses the 'sum of digits' method.

Required

(a) Write up the following ledger accounts for each of the three years to 31 December 20X6, 20X7 and 20X8 respectively:

(i) Machine hire purchase loan account
(ii) Machine hire purchase interest account

(b) Show the following balance sheet extracts relating to the machine as at 31 December 20X6, 20X7 and 20X8 respectively:

(i) Fixed assets: machine at net book value.

(ii) Creditors: amounts payable within one year – obligation under hire purchase contract.

(iii) Creditors: amounts falling due after more than one year – obligation under hire purchase Contract.

Answer

(a) (i)

MACHINE HIRE PURCHASE LOAN ACCOUNT

		£			£
20X6			*20X6*		
1.1	Bank	2,000	1.1	Machine	10,000
30.6	Bank	3,056	1.1	Machine interest	7,280
31.12	Bank	3,056			
31.12	Balance c/d	9,168			
		17,280			17,280
20X7			*20X7*		
30.6	Bank	3,056	1.1	Balance b/d	9,168
31.12	Bank	3,056			
31.12	Balance c/d	3,056			
		9,168			9,168
20X8			*20X8*		
30.6	Bank	3,056	1.1	Balance b/d	3,056

(ii)

MACHINE HIRE PURCHASE INTEREST ACCOUNT

		£			£
20X6			*20X6*		
1.1	Machine HP		31.12	Profit and loss a/c	4,368
	loan a/c	7,280	31.12	Balance c/d	2,912
		7,280			7,280
20X7			*20X7*		
1.1	Balance b/d	2,912	31.12	Profit and loss a/c	2,427
			31.12	Balance c/d	485
		2,912			2,912
20X8			*20X8*		
1.1	Balance b/d	485	31.12	Profit and loss a/c	485

Working

	£
Sum of the digits = 5 + 4 + 3 + 2 + 1 = 15 $\left(\text{or } \frac{5 \times 6}{2}\right)$	
(5 half year periods)	
Interest charge 20X6 = $7,280 \times \frac{5+4}{15}$ =	4,368
Interest charge 20X7 = $7,280 \times \frac{3+2}{15}$ =	2,427
Interest charge 20X8 = $7,280 \times \frac{1}{15}$ =	485
	7,280

(b) (i) Fixed assets: machines at net book value

		£
At 31.12.X6	Machines at cost	10,000
	Accumulated depreciation	3,600
	Net book value	6,400
At 31.12.X7	Machines at cost	10,000
	Accumulated depreciation	7,200
	Net book value	2,800
At 31.12.X8	Machines at cost	10,000
	Accumulated depreciation	9,000
	Residual value	1,000

Working

		£
Depreciation:	cost	10,000
	residual value	1,000
		9,000
Economic life (length of lease)		2½ years

Annual depreciation charge on a straight-line basis $= \frac{£9,000}{2½}$

= £3,600 per year

(ii) *Creditors: amounts payable within one year – obligation under hire purchase contract*

	£
At 31.12.X6	3,685
At 31.12.X7	2,571
At 31.12.X8	-

Workings

		£
31.12.X6	Balance per loan account	9,168
	Less due in 20X8	(3,056)
	Less interest element	(2,427)
		3,685
31.12.X7	Balance per loan account	3,056
	Less interest element	(485)
		2,571

(iii) *Creditors: amounts falling due after more than one year*

	£
At 31.12.X6	2,571
At 31.12.X7	-
At 31.12.X8	-

For working see (b)(ii) above.

Disclosure requirements for lessees

2.15 SSAP 21 requires lessees to disclose the following information.

(a) The gross amounts of assets held under finance leases* together with the related accumulated depreciation, analysed by class of asset. This information may be consolidated with the corresponding information for owned assets, and not shown separately. In that case, the net amount of assets held under finance leases* included in the overall total should also be disclosed.

(b) The amounts of obligations related to finance leases* (net of finance charges allocated to future periods). These should be disclosed separately from other obligations and liabilities and should be analysed between amounts payable in the next year, amounts payable in the second to fifth years inclusive from the balance sheet date and the aggregate amounts payable thereafter.

(c) The aggregate finance charges allocated for the period in respect of finance leases.*

* Including the equivalent information in respect of hire purchase contracts.

2.16 These disclosure requirements will be illustrated for Haldane Ltd (above example). We will assume that Haldane Ltd makes up its accounts to 31 December and uses the actuarial method to apportion finance charges. The company's accounts for the first year of the HP agreement, the year ended 31 December 20X8, would include the information given below.

BALANCE SHEET AS AT 31 DECEMBER 20X8 (EXTRACTS)

	£	£
Fixed assets		
Tangible assets held under hire purchase agreements		
Plant and machinery at cost	7,710	
Less accumulated depreciation (20% × £7,710)	1,542	
		6,168
Creditors: amounts falling due within one year		
Obligations under hire purchase agreements		1,315
Creditors: amounts falling due after more than one year		
Obligations under hire purchase agreements, falling due within two to five years £(1,512 + 1,739)		3,251

(Notice that only the outstanding **capital** element is disclosed under creditors. That is what is meant by the phrase 'net of finance charges allocated to future periods' in Paragraph 2.5(b) above.)

PROFIT AND LOSS ACCOUNT
FOR THE YEAR ENDED 31 DECEMBER 20X8

	£
Interest payable and similar charges	
Hire purchase finance charges	856

2.17 As noted above, SSAP 21 requires that leased assets should be depreciated over the shorter of the lease term and their useful lives; but assets acquired under HP agreements resembling finance leases should be depreciated over their **useful lives,** because such assets are legally the debtor's property. Haldane can therefore depreciate the machine over five years, not four years.

2.18 For **operating leases** the disclosure is simpler.

(a) The total of operating lease rentals charged as an expense in the profit and loss account should be disclosed, distinguishing between rentals payable for hire of plant and machinery and other rentals.

(b) Disclosure should be made of payments to which the lessee is committed under operating leases, analysed between those in which the commitment expires:

- Within a year from the balance sheet date
- In the second to fifth years inclusive
- Later than five years from the balance sheet date

Commitments in respect of land and buildings should be shown separately from other commitments.

3 LESSORS

Accounting treatment

3.1 In principle, accounting for a finance lease by a lessor is a mirror image of the entries for the lessee. The asset is recorded in the lessor's books as follows.

DEBIT	Lessee (debtor) account
CREDIT	Cash/creditors (purchase price of asset)

3.2 The income derived from the lease is spread over accounting periods so as to give a constant periodic rate of return for the lessor. The complex methods of achieving this are beyond the scope of your syllabus.

FRS 5: SALE AND LEASEBACK TRANSACTIONS

3.3 We mention FRS 5 in more detail in Section 4. Leases were a common form of off balance sheet finance before SSAP 21 was introduced. Ever since then, businesses have attempted to undertake types of arrangement whereby an asset is 'sold' but in fact the use is still retained.

3.4 FRS 5 states that where such a transaction is, in effect, a sale and leaseback, no profit should be recognised on entering into the arrangement and no adjustment made to the carrying value of the asset. As stated in the guidance notes to SSAP 21, this represents the substance of the transactions, 'namely the raising of finance secured on an asset that continues to be held and is not disposed of'.

Disclosure requirements for lessors

3.5 SSAP 21 requires lessors to disclose their net investments in (a) finance leases and (b) hire purchase contracts at each balance sheet date.

3.6 The accounts of Weller Ltd (example above) for the year ended 31 December 20X8 would show the information given below.

BALANCE SHEET AS AT 31 DECEMBER 20X8 (EXTRACTS)

	£
Current assets	
Debtors	
Net investment in finance leases (note)	4,566

NOTES TO THE BALANCE SHEET

Net investment in finance leases	£
Falling due within one year	1,315
Falling due after more than one year	3,251
	4,566

(The Companies Act 1985 requires amounts included as debtors to be separately disclosed if they fall due more than one year after the balance sheet date.)

3.7 SSAP 21 also requires disclosure by lessors of:

(a) The gross amounts of assets held for use in operating leases, and the related accumulated depreciation charges.

(b) The policy adopted for accounting for operating leases and finance leases and, in detail, the policy for accounting for finance lease income.

(c) The aggregate rentals receivable in respect of an accounting period in relation to finance leases and operating leases separately.

(d) The cost of assets acquired, whether by purchase or finance lease, for the purpose of letting under finance leases.

Question 2

Leisure Services Ltd, Stoke-on-Trent, are electrical wholesalers. On 2 May 20X3, they purchased on credit from TV Suppliers Ltd ten television sets for £1,600. They offered these for sale for cash at £240 each or on hire purchase for a cash deposit of £40 and eight quarterly instalments of £30 each, the first instalment being payable after three months. In the week ended 16 May 20X3 they sold two sets for cash and four on HP terms for which the cash deposits were paid at the time of sale.

On 1 December 20X3 Leisure Services Ltd installed one of their sets permanently on their own premises in a closed circuit television installation to detect theft.

You are required to prepare the necessary accounts (except cash and TV Suppliers Ltd) with dates and narrations in the ledger of Leisure Services Ltd to record the above transactions, balance them and prepare a trading account up to 31 December 20X3.

Note. The amount of HP interest earned in the period, calculated on the sum of the digits method, should be included in the trading account after sales.

Answer

Price structure

	£
Cost	160
Gross profit	80
Cash selling price	240
HP interest	40
HP selling price £(40 + (8 × 30))	280

With eight instalments, the sum of the digits is:

$$1 + 2 + ... + 7 + 8 = 36 \text{ (or } \frac{8 \times 9}{2} = 36)$$

Interest on the first instalment	= 8/36 × £40 = £9
Interest on the second instalment	= 7/36 × £40 = £8
Capital element in first instalment	= £(30 – 9) = £21
Capital element in second instalment	= £(30 – 8) = £22

Ledger accounts

FIXED ASSETS

20X3		£			
1 Dec	Purchases – closed circuit TV	160			

HP DEBTORS

20X3		£	*20X3*		£
16 May	Sales (4 × £240)	960	16 May	Bank: deposits	160
			16 Aug	Bank: 1st instalment (4 × £21)	84
			16 Nov	Bank: 2nd instalment (4 × £22)	88
			31 Dec	Balance c/f	628
		960			960

SALES

20X3		£	*20X3*		£
31 Dec	Trading account	1,440	16 May	HP debtors	960
				Cash (2 × £240)	480
		1,440			1,440

PURCHASES

20X3		£	20X3		£
2 May	Creditors	1,600	1 Dec	Fixed assets	160
			31 Dec	Trading account	1,440
		1,600			1,600

HP INTEREST RECEIVABLE

20X3		£	20X3		£
31 Dec	Trading account	68	16 Aug	Bank: 1st instalment (4 × £9)	36
			16 Nov	Bank: 2nd instalment (4 × £9)	32
		68			68

TRADING ACCOUNT TO 31 DECEMBER 20X3

	£	£
Sales		1,440
HP interest receivable		68
		1,508
Purchases	1,440	
Less closing stock (3 × £160)	480	
Cost of sales		960
Gross profit		548

Note. The inclusion of the HP interest receivable in the trading account is unusual, but is specifically required by the question. It would be more usual to show it as a credit in the profit and loss account.

Repossessions

3.8 Subject to various legal requirements, goods sold on hire purchase (but not credit sale) may be repossessed by the seller if the hirer fails to maintain his payments. The ledger accounts in respect of the hire purchase should be closed to a repossessions account which is credited with the value at which the item is brought back into stock and any penalty sums receivable. Any balance on the repossessions account represents the profit or loss on the repossession.

3.9 EXAMPLE: REPOSSESSIONS

Haldane, having paid amounts due in 20X8, decided to cease trading in January 20X9. Weller agreed to cancel the agreement on the payment of a penalty of £1,000 and took the plant into his stock at a value of £4,500. The ledger accounts would be as follows.

HP DEBTORS ACCOUNT

	£		£
Balance b/d	4,566	Repossessions a/c	4,566

REPOSSESSIONS ACCOUNT

	£		£
HP debtors a/c	4,566	Bank: penalty	1,000
P & L a/c: profit on repossession	934	Purchases: Plant taken into stock at valuation *	4,500
	5,500		5,500

* If the question does not give a valuation for the goods repossessed, then they can be taken into stock at the cost element in the outstanding debt:

$$\frac{6{,}168}{7{,}710} \times £4{,}566 = £3{,}653 \text{ in the above example.}$$

3.10 The total profit Weller earned from the abortive sale is as follows.

	£
Deposit/instalment received in 20X8	4,000
Penalty received in 20X9	1,000
	5,000
Plant in stock at valuation	4,500
	9,500
Cost of plant	6,168
	3,332

This has been accounted for as follows.

		£
20X8	Gross profit (£1,542) + interest earned (£856)	2,398
20X9	Profit on repossession	934
		3,332

4 FRS 5 REPORTING THE SUBSTANCE OF TRANSACTIONS

Exam focus point

FRS 5 became eligible for testing for the May 2003 paper onwards. As it did not make an appearance then, it would be wise to prepare for it showing up soon.

The problem of off balance sheet finance

4.1 Over the last decade the transactions undertaken by businesses have become more and more complex, often resulting in the divorce of legal title from access to the transaction's economic benefits and risks. Accounting for their legal form often meant that such transactions were not reflected on the balance sheet. This resulted in misleading accounting results and ratios. The **creative accounting** which has emerged over recent years occurred for two main reasons.

(a) Complex schemes were **deliberately engineered** by companies to ensure transactions were not reflected on the balance sheet, largely to manipulate gearing (ie borrowing) ratios.

(b) Apart from SSAP 2 (now superseded by FRS 18) and Schedule 4 of the Companies Act 1985, there was a lack of guidance for transactions not covered by a specific standard. This allowed companies to adopt a variety of accounting treatments.

4.2 The development of the ASB's *Statement of Principles* (see Chapter 1) will help to provide guidance. FRS 5 reinforces the recognition principles embodied in the *Statement of Principles* in a specific standard.

FRS 5

4.3 FRS 5 was issued by the ASB to tackle the problem of off balance sheet finance. It is a complex standard whose objective is to ensure that financial statements reflect the **commercial substance** of transactions and not just their legal form. SSAP 21 is an example of a standard which tackles this issue. The ASB felt that, rather than issue specific standards to deal with individual transactions, a general one was required to set out the principles of when commercial substance should apply.

4.4 For the majority of transactions the legal form and the commercial substance will be identical. However, three main features can be identified for situations where FRS 5 is most likely to apply.

(a) The **legal owner** is **not** the person **benefiting** from the asset.

(b) The transaction is part of a **series**. It will be necessary to view the series **as a whole** to determine the **substance.**

(c) The inclusion of **options and conditions** which are likely to be exercised.

Determining the substance of transactions

4.5 The first step is to establish whether a transaction changes the existing assets and liabilities of the company, either by creating new ones or altering the existing ones. In this context, the definitions of assets and liabilities are very important.

KEY TERMS

(a) **Assets** are rights or other access to future economic benefits controlled by the entity as a result of past transactions or events.

(b) **Liabilities** are an entity's obligation to transfer economic benefits as a result of past transactions or events.

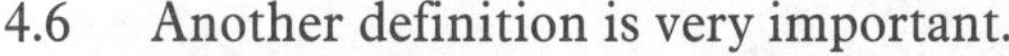

4.6 Another definition is very important.

KEY TERM

Recognition is the process of incorporating an item into the primary financial statements within the appropriate headings. It involves depiction of the item in words and by a monetary amount and the inclusion of that amount in the statement totals.

Exam focus point

For your examination, should a question arise on FRS 5 you should be able to apply it to a transaction to determine its accounting treatment. A typical question could require you to discuss alternative treatments for a transaction. The following may serve as a useful checklist of points to consider.

(a) FRS 5 'commercial substance over legal form'
(b) FRS 18 including the concepts of accruals and prudence
(c) Companies Act 1985 Schedule 4 fundamental principles
(d) Materiality
(e) Disclosure
(f) Truth and fairness
(g) Requirements of any relevant SSAP/FRS

The diagram on the following page should also help.

Interaction with other standards

4.7 The recognition criteria contained in FRS 5 will determine which assets and liabilities appear in the balance sheet. It will therefore influence the accounting treatment in future standards. In particular accounting for intangibles will be affected.

4.8 It is possible that a transaction will be covered by both FRS 5 and a specific standard. Where this overlap occurs the more detailed provisions should be followed unless commercial substance would not be reflected. Users should be guided by the 'spirit' and not the 'letter' of FRS 5.

Specific transactions

4.9 EXAMPLE: CONSIGNMENT STOCK

Suppose that Shantra Ltd owns a number of car dealerships in London. The terms of the arrangement between dealership and manufacturer are as follows.

(a) Legal title passes when the cars are either used by Shantra Ltd for demonstration purposes or sold to a third party.

(b) The price of the vehicles is fixed at the date of transfer.

(c) Shantra Ltd has no right to return the vehicle.

(d) Shantra Ltd pays a finance charge between delivery and the date legal title passes.

How should Shantra Ltd account for these transactions?

4.10 SOLUTION

We can determine the accounting treatment through a series of questions.

(a) What are the risks inherent in holding stock?

  (i) The risk that the value of the stock will fall below cost (obsolescence, damage etc).

  (ii) The risk that the market will depress and the stock will be sold at less than cost, or it will be unsaleable.

(b) What features of the arrangement indicate risk?

  (i) The price is fixed on transfer, so if the value falls, Shantra Ltd will bear the cost.

  (ii) If a car remains unsold, Shantra cannot return it to the manufacturer.

  (iii) Shantra Ltd must pay for each day a car is unsold, through a finance charge.

(c) On the basis of the above, how should Shantra Ltd account for the transactions?

  (i) The cars should be treated as trading stock and recognised on transfer at the fixed price.

  (ii) The finance charges may be expensed through the profit and loss account, but there may be an argument for capitalising such charges as part of the cost of bringing the asset to its current location and condition (SSAP 9).

Exam focus point

Remember that in testing accounting standards, the Examiner aims to test your understanding of the logic behind them. Scenarios are often presented and candidates are asked to discuss the implications of various standards for the accounting treatment in the financial statements. It is impossible to determine whether a particular treatment is within the spirit of a standard unless you understand fully why the standard was introduced.

Accounting treatment for the recognition of assets and liabilities

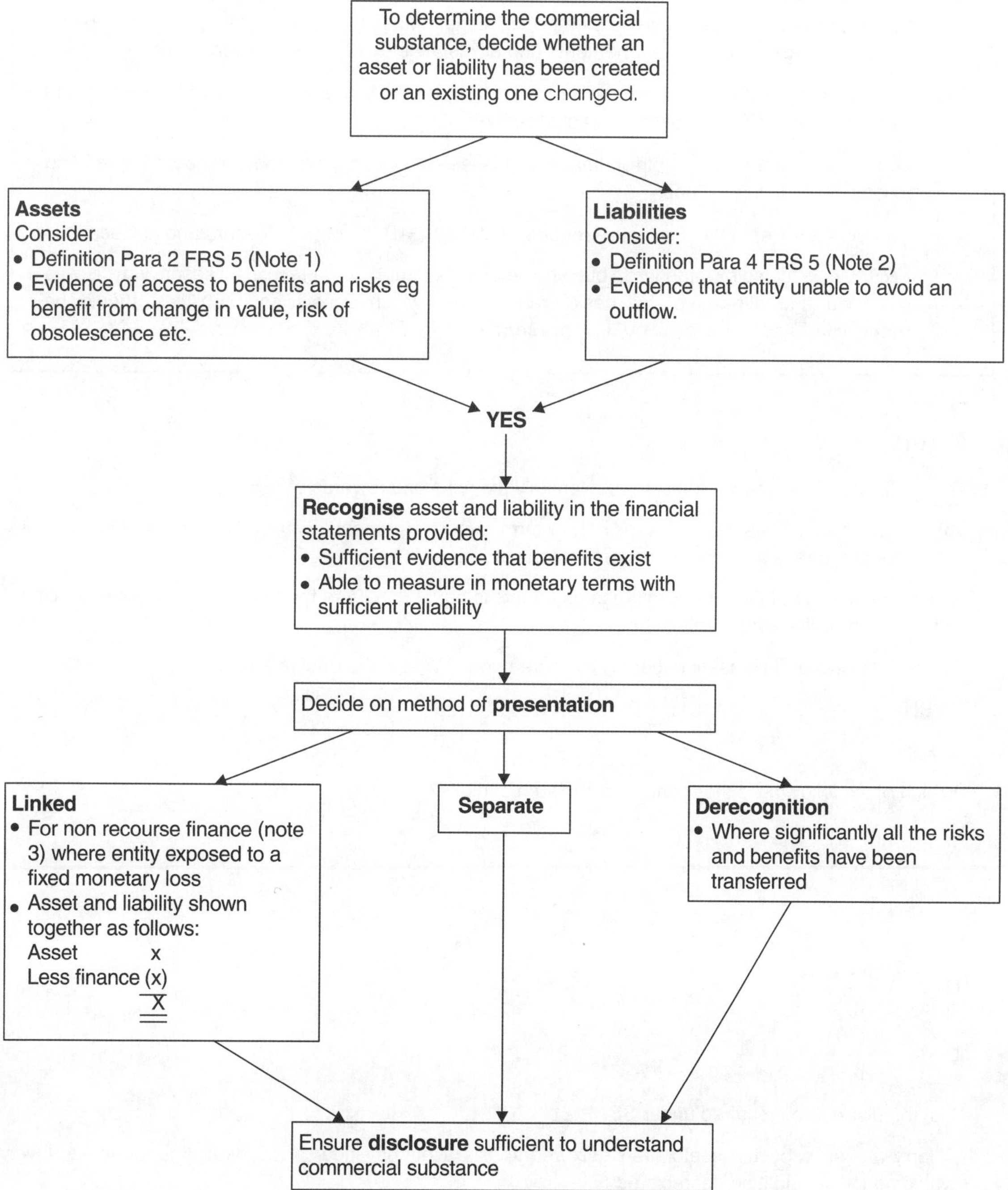

Notes

1 *Assets*: rights or other access to future economic benefits controlled by an entity as a result of past transactions or events.

2 *Liabilities*: an entity's obligations to transfer future economic benefits as a result of past transactions or events.

3 *Non-recourse finance*: there is no (or limited) recourse to the seller for losses.

Chapter roundup

- **Finance leases** are like **HP contracts**. In both cases assets acquired should be capitalised by the lessee and the interest element of instalments should be charged against profit. Operating leases are rental agreements and all instalments are charged against profit.
- You must learn (through repeated practice) how to apply the **level spread, actuarial** and **sum-of-the-digits** methods of interest allocation.
- **Lessor accounting** is a mirror image of lessee accounting, but the method of spreading income is not in this syllabus.
- You must also learn the disclosure requirements of SSAP 21 for both lessors and lessees.
- *FRS 5* is a complex standard, but you should be able to explain the reason why it was produced and determine, for basic transactions, which assets and liabilities should be **recognised** and how they should be **presented**.

Quick quiz

1 (a) ....leases transfer substantially the risks and rewards of ownership.

(b) ....leases are usually short-term rental agreements with the lessor being responsible for the repairs and maintenance of the asset.

2 The present value of the minimum lease payments is equal to 89% of the fair value of the leased asset. What type of lease is this likely to be?

3 A business acquires an asset under an HP agreement. What is the double entry?

DEBIT

CREDIT

4 Which of the following is the formula for the sum of digits?

A $\frac{n(n-1)}{2}$

B $\frac{n(n+1)}{2}$

C $\frac{2(n-1)}{n}$

D $\frac{2(n+1)}{n}$

5 List the disclosures required under SSAP 21.

6 A lorry has an expected useful life of six years. It is acquired under a four year finance lease. Over which period should it be depreciated?

7 A company leases a photocopier under an operating lease which expires in June 20X2. Its office is leased under an operating lease due to expire in January 20X3. How should past and future operating leases be disclosed in its 31 December 20X1 accounts?

8 A Company A brings in a debt factor. The terms of the agreement are that the factor pays Company A 90% of the value of the outstanding debtors. Interest is charged on this amount. The factor then collects the debts and reduces this amount accordingly. Company A is responsible for any uncollected debts. What is the substance of the transaction?

Answers to quick quiz

1 (a) Finance leases
(b) Operating leases

2 Per SSAP 21, an operating lease (see para 1.6)

3 DEBIT Asset account
CREDIT Lessor account

4 B (2.8)

5 See paragraph 2.15

6 The four year term. (2.17)

7 The total operating lease rentals charged though the profit and loss should be disclosed. The payments committed to should be disclosed analysing them between those leases which expire in the next year; in the second to fifth years and thereafter. (2.18)

8 The form is that Company A has sold its debtors to the factor. The substance is that Company A is still responsible for bad debts and the factor has provided a commercial loan with the debtors as security. (4.1-4.10)

Now try the questions below from the Exam Question Bank

Number	Level	Marks	Time
12	Exam level	20	36 mins
13	Exam level	20	36 mins

Chapter 10

MISCELLANEOUS STANDARDS

Topic list		Syllabus reference	Ability required
1	SSAP 17 *Accounting for post balance sheet events*	(iii)	Evaluation
2	FRS 12 *Provisions, contingent liabilities and contingent assets*	(iii)	Evaluation
3	SSAP 4 *Accounting for government grants*	(iii)	Evaluation
4	FRS 8 *Related party disclosures*	(ii)	Comprehension

Introduction

These topics are collected together under the title 'miscellaneous standards'. They are all very important, so don't skip over this chapter any of these standards can and will feature in an exam at some point.

In particular, FRS 12 is very important as it can affect many items in the accounts. Make sure you learn all the relevant definitions and understand the standard accounting treatment.

SSAP 4 and FRS 8 are fairly straightforward. Work through the sections and ensure you understand the key points.

Learning outcomes covered in this chapter

- **Explain** the accounting rules contained in Financial Reporting Standards which provide guidance as to the appropriate treatment of certain transactions
- **Identify, apply** and **evaluate** the accounting treatment of significant transactions
- **Explain** and **apply** the rules for the disclosure of related parties to a business

Syllabus content covered in this chapter

- Post balance sheet events (SSAP 17), provisions, contingent liabilities and contingent assets (FRS 12)
- Government grants (SSAP 4)
- The disclosure of related parties to a business (FRS 8)

1 SSAP 17 ACCOUNTING FOR POST BALANCE SHEET EVENTS

Exam focus point

SSAP 17 will often find its way into accounts preparation questions by way of a part question.

The May 2003 paper includes a significant question testing various aspects of SSAP 17.

1.1 SSAP 17 defines **post balance sheet events** as those events, both favourable and unfavourable, which occur between the balance sheet date and the date on which the financial statements are approved by the board of directors.

1.2 A distinction is made in SSAP 17 between **adjusting events** and **non-adjusting events.**

Adjusting events

KEY TERM

SSAP 17 defines **adjusting events** as post balance sheet events which provide additional evidence of conditions existing at the balance sheet date.

1.3 If they materially affect the amounts to be included, they need to be reflected in the financial statements. They include events which because of statutory or conventional requirements are reflected in financial statements.

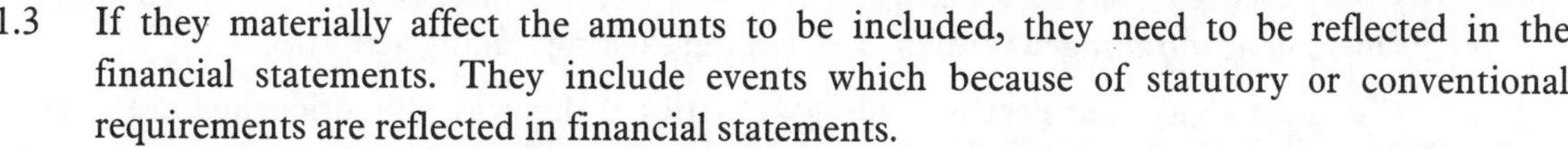

1.4 The second sentence of this definition refers to such events as:

- Resolutions relating to proposed **dividends** and amounts appropriated to reserves
- The effects of changes in **taxation** rates

1.5 An appendix to SSAP 17 cites a number of other post balance sheet events which normally should be classified as adjusting events.

(a) **Fixed assets**: the subsequent determination of the purchase price or of the sale proceeds of assets purchased or sold before the year end.

(b) **Property**: the valuation of a property which provides evidence of a permanent diminution in value.

(c) **Investments**: the receipt of a copy of the financial statements or other information in respect of an unlisted company which provides evidence of a permanent diminution in the value of a long-term investment.

(d) **Stocks**: the receipt of proceeds of sale or other evidence after the balance sheet date concerning the net realisable value of stock.

(e) **Work in progress**: the receipt of evidence that the previous estimate of accrued profit taken on a long-term contract was materially inaccurate.

(f) **Debtors**: the re-negotiation of amounts owing by debtors, or the insolvency of a debtor.

(g) **Claims**: amounts received or receivable in respect of insurance claims which were in the course of negotiation at the balance sheet date.

(h) **Discoveries**: the discovery of errors or frauds which show that the financial statements were incorrect.

1.6 Some events occurring after the balance sheet date, such as a deterioration in the company's operating results and in its financial position, may indicate a need to consider whether it is appropriate to use the *going concern* concept in the preparation of financial statements. Consequently such events may fall to be treated as adjusting events.

Non-adjusting events

KEY TERM

SSAP 17 defines **non-adjusting events** as events which arise after the balance sheet date and concern conditions which did not exist at that time.

1.7 Consequently they do not result in changes in amounts in financial statements. They may, however, be of such materiality that their disclosure is required by way of notes to ensure that financial statements are not misleading.

1.8 Again, a number of examples are given in the appendix:

- **Issues of shares** and debentures
- Purchases and sales of **fixed assets** and **investments**
- **Losses of fixed assets** or stocks as a result of a catastrophe such as fire or flood
- Opening **new trading activities** or extending existing trading activities
- **Closing** a significant **part of trading activities** if this was not anticipated at the year end
- **Decline in value of property and investments** held as fixed assets, if it can be demonstrated that the decline occurred after the year end
- **Government action**, such as nationalisation
- **Strikes** and other labour disputes

Accounting treatment and disclosure

1.9 Financial statements should be prepared on the basis of conditions existing at the balance sheet date and should also disclose the date on which they were approved by the board of directors (so that users can establish the duration of the 'post-balance sheet events period'). The standard is not intended to apply to events occurring after the date of board approval, but recommends that if such events are material the directors should consider publishing the relevant information so that users of financial statements are not misled.

1.10 SSAP 17 states that a material post balance sheet event requires changes in the amounts to be included in financial statements where it is either:

- An **adjusting** event
- Or it indicates that application of the **going concern concept** to the whole or a material part of the company is not appropriate

Separate disclosure of adjusting events is not normally required as they do no more than provide additional evidence in support of items in financial statements. However, in exceptional circumstances where a non-adjusting event is reclassified as an adjusting event, full disclosure of the adjustment is required.

1.11 CA 1985 requires that all liabilities and losses which have arisen or are likely to arise in respect of the financial year to which the accounts relate (or a previous financial year) shall be taken into account, including those that only become apparent between the balance sheet date and the date on which it is signed on behalf of the board of directors.

The Act therefore gives some statutory enforcement to the provisions in SSAP 17 in respect of adjusting post balance sheet events, but refers to 'liabilities and losses' only, and not to 'gains'.

1.12 SSAP 17 also requires that a material post balance sheet event should be disclosed where:

(a) It is a **non-adjusting event** of such materiality that its non-disclosure would affect the ability of the users of financial statements to reach a proper understanding of the financial position.

(b) Or it is the **reversal or maturity** after the year end of a transaction entered into before the year end, the substance of which was primarily to alter the appearance of the company's balance sheet (window dressing).

Exam focus point

Candidates have a tendency to take matters at their face value rather than question the motives and accounting significance behind them. A company may take out a long-term loan immediately prior to the year end and then repay it soon afterwards. You should realise that the balance sheet could give a misleading impression of the company's liquidity.

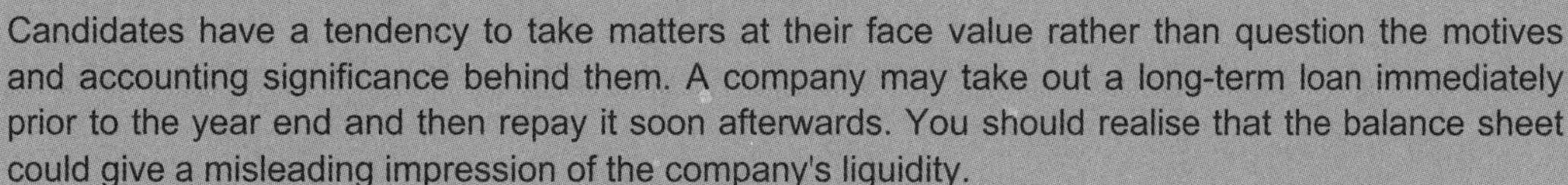

Do not get so caught up in describing bookkeeping implications that you miss the obvious.

1.13 In determining which non-adjusting events are of sufficient materiality to require disclosure, regard should be had to all matters which are necessary to enable users of financial statements to assess the financial position.

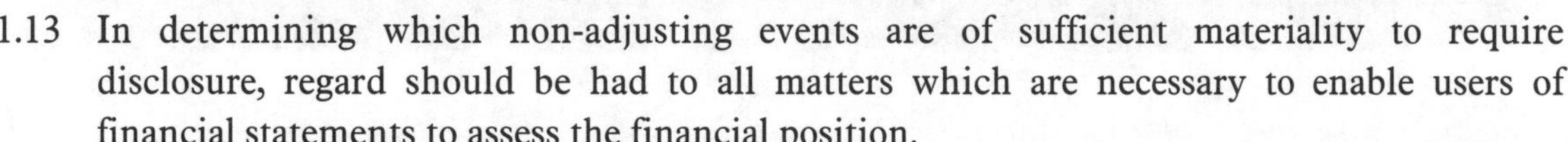

1.14 In respect of each post balance sheet event which is required to be disclosed the following two items of information should be given.

(a) The nature of the event.

(b) An estimate of the financial effect, or a statement that it is not practicable to make such an estimate. (*Note.* The estimate of the financial effect should be disclosed before taking account of taxation, and the taxation implications should be explained where necessary for a proper understanding of the financial position.)

1.15 CA 1985 requires that the directors' report should contain particulars of any important events affecting the company (or its subsidiaries) which have occurred since the end of the year.

Although this gives some statutory backing to the provisions of SSAP 17 in respect of non-adjusting post balance sheet events, it suggests the information be given in the directors' report rather than the notes to the accounts (as required by SSAP 17).

Question 1

Write out the list of items which SSAP 17 states should be:

(a) Adjusting
(b) Non-adjusting

Don't look back and cheat!

Answer

(a) See Paragraph 1.5.
(b) See Paragraph 1.8.

Exam focus point

Some candidates make the mistake of writing a general essay on SSAP 17. Always relate your answer to the context of the question. You may be required to provide a classification of certain items as adjusting or non-adjusting and give a discussion of the implications of these classifications for the accounting treatment required.

2 FRS 12 PROVISIONS, CONTINGENT LIABILITIES AND CONTINGENT ASSETS

2.1 As we have seen with regard to post balance sheet events, financial statements must include **all the information necessary for an understanding of the company's financial position**. Provisions, contingent liabilities and contingent assets are 'uncertainties' that must be accounted for consistently if we are to achieve this understanding.

Exam focus point

The May 2002 exam furnished four different claims for identification of accounting treatment, with due regard to FRS 12. There was also a significant question in the November 2003 paper.

This is a fairly practical area and is likely to appear in some guise in an exam.

Objective

2.2 FRS 12 *Provisions, contingent liabilities and contingent assets* aims to ensure that appropriate **recognition criteria** and **measurement bases** are applied to provisions, contingent liabilities and contingent assets and that **sufficient information** is disclosed in the **notes** to the financial statements to enable users to understand their nature, timing and amount.

Provisions

2.3 You will be familiar with provisions for depreciation and doubtful debts from your earlier studies. The sorts of provisions addressed by FRS 12 are, however, rather different.

2.4 Before FRS 12, there was no accounting standard dealing with provisions. Companies wanting to show their results in the most favourable light used to make large '**one off' provisions** in years where a high level of underlying profits was generated. Investors look for a constant return. They prefer to see steady profits not high profits in one year followed by a loss in the next.

2.5 These provisions, often known as '**big bath**' provisions, were then used to shield expenditure in future years when perhaps the underlying profits were not as good. In other words, **provisions were used for profit smoothing**.

IMPORTANT

The key aim of FRS 12 is to ensure that provisions are made only where there are valid grounds for them.

2.6 FRS 12 views a provision as a **liability**.

KEY TERMS

A **provision** is a **liability** of uncertain timing or amount.

A **liability** is an obligation of an entity to transfer economic benefits as a result of past transactions or events. *(FRS 12)*

2.7 The FRS distinguishes provisions from other liabilities such as trade creditors and accruals. This is on the basis that for a provision there is **uncertainty** about the timing or amount of the future expenditure. Whilst uncertainty is clearly present in the case of certain accruals the uncertainty is generally much less than for provisions.

Recognition

2.8 FRS 12 states that a provision should be **recognised** as a liability in the financial statements when:

- An entity has a **present obligation** (legal or constructive) as a result of a past event
- It is probable that a **transfer of economic benefits** will be required to settle the obligation
- A **reliable estimate** can be made of the obligation

Meaning of obligation

2.9 It is fairly clear what a legal obligation is. However, you may not know what a **constructive obligation** is.

KEY TERM

FRS 12 defines a **constructive obligation** as

'An obligation that derives from an entity's actions where:

- By an established pattern of past practice, published policies or a sufficiently specific current statement the entity has indicated to other parties that it will accept certain responsibilities
- As a result, the entity has created a valid expectation on the part of those other parties that it will discharge those responsibilities'

Question 2

In which of the following circumstances might a provision be recognised?

(a) On 13 December 20X9 the board of an entity decided to close down a division. The accounting date of the company is 31 December. Before 31 December 20X9 the decision was not communicated to any of those affected and no other steps were taken to implement the decision.

(b) The board agreed a detailed closure plan on 20 December 20X9 and details were given to customers and employees.

(c) A company is obliged to incur clean up costs for environmental damage (that has already been caused).

(d) A company intends to carry out future expenditure to operate in a particular way in the future.

Answer

(a) No provision would be recognised as the decision has not been communicated.

(b) A provision would be made in the 20X9 financial statements.

(c) A provision for such costs is appropriate.

(d) No present obligation exists and under FRS 12 no provision would be appropriate. This is because the entity could avoid the future expenditure by its future actions, maybe by changing its method of operation.

Probable transfer of economic benefits

2.10 For the purpose of the FRS, a transfer of economic benefits is regarded as '**probable**' if the event is **more likely than not** to occur. This appears to indicate a probability of more than 50%. However, the standard makes it clear that where there is a number of similar obligations the probability should be based on considering the population as a whole, rather than one single item.

2.11 EXAMPLE: TRANSFER OF ECONOMIC BENEFITS

If a company has entered into a warranty obligation then the probability of transfer of economic benefits may well be extremely small in respect of one specific item. However, when considering the population as a whole the probability of some transfer of economic benefits is quite likely to be much higher. If there is a **greater than 50% probability** of some transfer of economic benefits then a **provision** should be made for the **expected amount**.

Measurement of provisions

IMPORTANT

The amount recognised as a provision should be the best estimate of the expenditure required to settle the present obligation at the balance sheet date.

2.12 The estimates will be determined by the **judgement** of the entity's management supplemented by the experience of similar transactions.

2.13 Allowance is made for **uncertainty**. Where the effect of the **time value of money** is material, the amount of a provision should be the **present value** of the expenditure required to settle the obligation. An appropriate **discount** rate should be used.

Provisions for restructuring

2.14 One of the main purposes of FRS 12 was to target abuses of provisions for restructuring. Accordingly, FRS 12 lays down **strict criteria** to determine when such a provision can be made.

KEY TERM

FRS 12 defines a **restructuring** as:

A programme that is planned and is controlled by management and materially changes either:

- The scope of a business undertaken by an entity
- The manner in which that business is conducted

2.15 The FRS gives the following **examples** of events that may fall under the definition of restructuring.

- The **sale or termination** of a line of business
- The **closure of business locations** in a country or region or the **relocation** of business activities from one country or region to another
- **Changes in management structure**, for example, the elimination of a layer of management
- **Fundamental reorganisations** that have a material effect on the **nature and focus** of the entity's operations

2.16 The question is whether or not an entity has an obligation – legal or constructive – at the balance sheet date.

- An entity must have a **detailed formal plan** for the restructuring
- It must have **raised a valid expectation** in those affected that it will carry out the restructuring by starting to implement that plan or announcing its main features to those affected by it

IMPORTANT

A mere management decision is not normally sufficient. Management decisions may sometimes trigger off recognition, but only if earlier events such as negotiations with employee representatives and other interested parties have been concluded subject only to management approval.

2.17 Where the restructuring involves the **sale of an operation** then FRS 12 states that no obligation arises until the entity has entered into a **binding sale agreement.** This is because until this has occurred the entity will be able to change its mind and withdraw from the sale even if its intentions have been announced publicly.

Costs to be included within a restructuring provision

2.18 The FRS states that a restructuring provision should include only the **direct expenditures** arising from the restructuring, which are those that are both:

- **Necessarily entailed** by the restructuring
- Not associated with the **ongoing activities** of the entity

2.19 The following costs should specifically **not** be included within a restructuring provision.

- **Retraining** or relocating continuing staff
- **Marketing**

- **Investment in new systems** and distribution networks

Disclosure

2.20 Disclosures for provisions fall into two parts.

- Disclosure of details of the **change in carrying value** of a provision from the beginning to the end of the year
- Disclosure of the **background** to the making of the provision and the uncertainties affecting its outcome

Contingent liabilities

2.21 Now you understand provisions it will be easier to understand contingent assets and liabilities.

KEY TERM

FRS 12 defines a **contingent liability** as one of the following.

- A possible obligation that arises from past events and whose existence will be confirmed only by the occurrence or non-occurrence of one or more uncertain future events not wholly within the entity's control.
- A present obligation that arises from past events but is not recognised because:
  - It is not probable that a transfer of economic benefits will be required to settle the obligation
  - Or the amount of the obligation cannot be measured with sufficient reliability

2.22 As a rule of thumb, probable means more than 50% likely. **If an obligation is probable, it is not a contingent liability** – instead, a **provision is needed**.

Treatment of contingent liabilities

2.23 Contingent liabilities **should not be recognised in financial statements** but they **should be disclosed.** The required disclosures are:

- A brief description of the nature of the contingent liability
- An estimate of its financial effect
- An indication of the uncertainties that exist
- The possibility of any reimbursement

Exam focus point

The May 2002 paper included two 4 mark discussion questions on contingent liabilities. Little scenarios also have a habit of appearing as part of the compulsory accounts preparation question.

Contingent assets

KEY TERM

FRS 12 defines a **contingent asset** as:

A possible asset that arises from past events and whose existence will be confirmed by the occurrence of one or more uncertain future events not wholly within the entity's control.

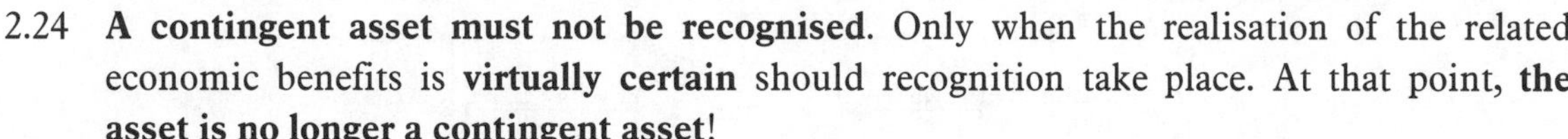

2.24 **A contingent asset must not be recognised**. Only when the realisation of the related economic benefits is **virtually certain** should recognition take place. At that point, **the asset is no longer a contingent asset**!

Disclosure: contingent liabilities

2.25 A **brief description** must be provided of all material contingent liabilities unless they are likely to be remote. In addition, provide

- An estimate of their **financial effect**
- Details of **any uncertainties**

2.26 *Disclosure: contingent assets*

Contingent assets must only be disclosed in the notes if they are **probable**. In that case a brief description of the contingent asset should be provided along with an estimate of its likely financial effect.

2.27 Try the question below to get the hang of FRS 12. But first, study the flow chart, taken from FRS 12, which is a good summary of its requirements.

Exam focus point

If you learn this flow chart you should be able to deal with most of the questions you are likely to meet in the exam.

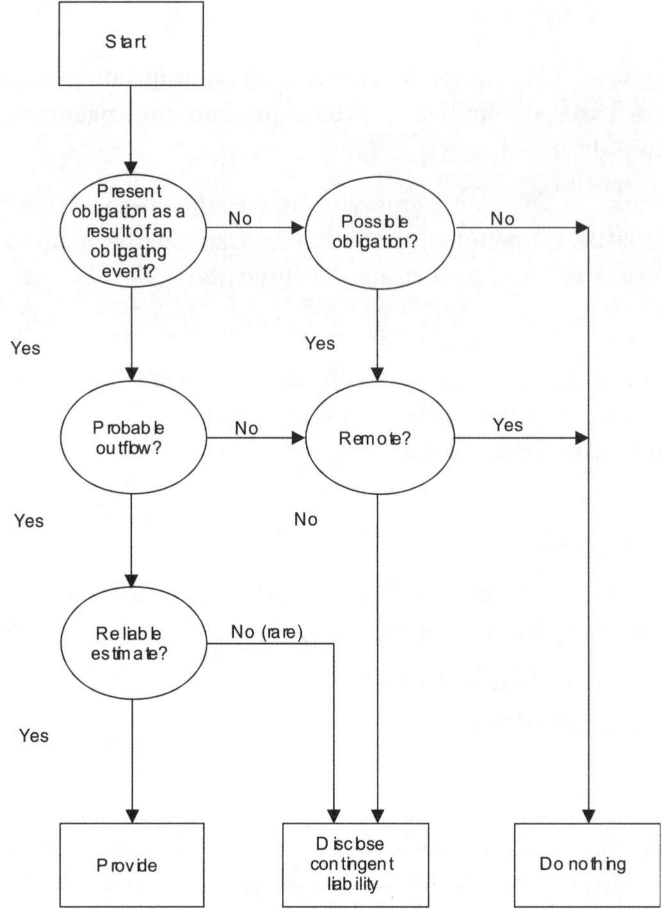

Question 3

During 20X9 Gomez Ltd gives a guarantee of certain borrowings of Moby Ltd, whose financial condition at that time is sound. During 20Y0, the financial condition of Moby Ltd deteriorates and at 30 June 20Y0 Moby Ltd files for protection from its creditors.

What accounting treatment is required:

(a) At 31 December 20X9?
(b) At 31 December 20Y0?

Answer

(a) At 31 December 20X9

There is a present obligation as a result of a past obligating event. The obligating event is the giving of the guarantee, which gives rise to a legal obligation. However, at 31 December 20X9 no transfer of economic benefits is probable in settlement of the obligation.

No provision is recognised. The guarantee is disclosed as a contingent liability unless the probability of any transfer is regarded as remote.

(b) At 31 December 20Y0

As above, there is a present obligation as a result of a past obligating event, namely the giving of the guarantee.

At 31 December 20Y0 it is probable that a transfer of economic events will be required to settle the obligation. A provision is therefore recognised for the best estimate of the obligation.

Section summary

2.28
- The objective of FRS 12 is to ensure that **appropriate recognition criteria** and measurement bases are applied to **provisions and contingencies** and that **sufficient information** is disclosed.
- The FRS seeks to ensure that provisions are **only recognised** when a **measurable obligation** exists. It includes detailed rules that can be used to ascertain when an obligation exists and how to measure the obligation.
- The standard attempts to **eliminate** the '**profit smoothing**' which has gone on before it was issued.

3 SSAP 4 ACCOUNTING FOR GOVERNMENT GRANTS

KEY TERM

Government grants are assistance provided by government to an enterprise.

(a) In the form of **cash** or **transfers** of **other assets**.

(b) In **return** for compliance with **certain conditions** relating to the operating activities of the enterprise.

Note: (Items such as free consultancy services are not grants)

3.1 In practice, the range of grants available is quite wide and may change regularly, reflecting changes in policy introduced by various governments. You therefore need to understand the general principles included in SSAP4 and be able to apply them to any scenario you encounter in your exams.

3.2 Note that for these purposes, government includes local, national or international government, agencies and similar bodies.

BASIC REQUIREMENTS

(a) Government grants should be recognised in the profit and loss account so as to match them with the expenditure towards which they are intended to contribute.

(b) Government grants should not be recognised in the profit and loss account until the conditions for this receipt have been compiled with and there is reasonable assurance that the grant will be received.

Revenue-based grants

3.3 These are given to **cover** some of the costs of various categories of **revenue expenditure**.

3.4 No particular problems arise in respect of revenue grants as they can be **credited** to **revenue** in the **same period** in which the **revenue expenditure** to which they **relate** is charged.

Capital-based grants

Exam focus point

The correct treatment of a grant received to offset the cost of purchasing a fixed asset was tested in May 2003.

3.5 These are given to **cover** a **proportion** of the **costs of certain** items of **capital expenditure** (for example buildings, plant and machinery), and may be **treated** in a **number of ways.**

(a) **Credit** the **full amount** of the capital grant to **profit and loss account.**

(b) **Credit** the **full amount** of the capital grant to a **non distributable reserve.**

3.6 In (a) there is an immediate impact on earnings and in (b) there is no impact on earnings. In both cases the concept of matching costs and revenues is not applied. The grant, like the depreciation cost of fixed assets, should apply to the full life of the assets and so should be spread over that period of time.

3.7 **SSAP 4 states that grants relating to fixed assets should be credited to revenue over the expected useful life of the assets and this can be done in one of two ways:**

(a) **By reducing the acquisition cost of the fixed asset** by the amount of the grant, and providing depreciation on the reduced amount.

(b) By **treating** the amount of the grant **as a deferred credit and transferring a portion of it to revenue** annually.

3.8 EXAMPLE: ACCOUNTING FOR GOVERNMENT GRANTS

Needham Limited receives a government grant towards the cost of a new grinder.

- Cost £100,000.
- Grant = 20%
- Expected life = four years
- Residual value = Nil.
- Expected profits of the company, before accounting for depreciation on the new machine or the grant = £50,000 per annum over expected life of the grinder.

The two alternative approaches outlined in SSAP 4 would give different accounts presentations.

3.9 SOLUTION

(a) *Reducing the cost of the asset approach*

	Year 1	*Year 2*	*Year 3*	*Year 4*	*Total*
	£	£	£	£	£
Profits					
Profit before depreciation	50,000	50,000	50,000	50,000	200,000
Depreciation*	(20,000)	(20,000)	(20,000)	(20,000)	(80,000)
Profit	30,000	30,000	30,000	30,000	120,000

*The depreciation charge on a straight line basis, for each year, is ¼ of £[100,000 – 20,000 (20%)] = £20,000.

Balance sheet at year end (extract)

	£	£	£	£
Fixed asset at cost	80,000	80,000	80,000	80,000
Accumulated depreciation	(20,000)	(40,000)	(60,000)	(80,000)
Net book value	60,000	40,000	20,000	-

(b) *Treating the grant as a deferred credit approach*

	Year 1	*Year 2*	*Year 3*	*Year 4*	*Total*
	£	£	£	£	£
Profits					
Profit before grant & dep'n	50,000	50,000	50,000	50,000	200,000
Depreciation	(25,000)	(25,000)	(25,000)	(25,000)	(100,000)
Grant	5,000	5,000	5,000	5,000	20,000
Profit	30,000	30,000	30,000	30,000	120,000

Balance sheet at year end (extract)

Fixed asset at cost	100,000	100,000	100,000	100,000
Accumulated depreciation	(25,000)	(50,000)	(75,000)	(100,000)
Net book value	75,000	50,000	25,000	-
Deferred income				
Government grant				
deferred credit	15,000	10,000	5,000	-

Assessment of alternative approaches

3.10 **The annual profits under both methods are the same, and both methods apply the matching concept in arriving at the profit figure.** Reducing the cost of the asset is simpler since, by reducing the depreciation charge, the amount of the grant is automatically credited to revenue over the life of the asset.

The **deferred credit method has the advantage of recording fixed assets at their actual cost, which allows for comparability and is independent of government policy.**

However, the netting off **method** may be in **conflict with the Companies Act 1985** in that the asset would no longer be carried at its purchase price or production cost.

3.11 **Legal opinion confirms the unacceptability of the netting off approach and hence the deferred credit method is preferable.**

3.12 Where the second method is used then **the amount of the deferred credit, if material, should be shown separately in the balance sheet.** SSAP 4 states that it should not be shown as part of the shareholders' funds and it is suggested that the amount should appear under the heading of '**Accruals and deferred income**' in the balance sheet.

3.13 The SSAP requires the **disclosure of the accounting policy** adopted for government grants **and** also requires disclosure of:

(a) The impact of government grants on the **company's profits** in the period **and/or** on its **financial position** generally.

(b) Any **potential liability** to repay grants.

(c) The nature of **government aid other than grants** which has materially affected profits in the period and an estimate of the impact, where possible.

3.14 A grant may be awarded to assist the financing of a project as a whole, where both capital and revenue expenditure are combined. In such cases the accounting treatment should be to match the grant with the relative proportions of revenue and capital expenditure incurred in the total project cost. For example, if two thirds of a project's costs are capital in nature and one third is revenue in nature, then any grant awarded against the whole project cost should be treated as one-third revenue-based and two thirds capital-based.

Exam focus point

This is another of those topics that lends itself to a question on how the treatment of capital based grants sits alongside the balance sheet driven approach to the accruals basis of accounting as envisaged by the ASB Statement of Principles and FRS 18.

Question 4

Rosemary plc is to receive a relocation grant of 30% of total expenses incurred. In 20X8 the company incurred the following costs associated with the relocation.

	£'000
Capital cost of factory	2,000
Training costs	200
Removal/relocation costs	300
	2,500

Required

Show the treatment of the government grant for 20X8.

Answer

	£'000
Grant received = 30% × 2,500 =	750
Capital expenditure	2,000
Revenue expenditure	500
	2,500

Revenue grant = $\frac{500}{2,500} \times 750 =$ 150

Capital grant = $\frac{2,000}{2,500} \times 750 =$ 600

750

		£'000	£'000
DEBIT	Cash	750	
CREDIT	P&L account		150
CREDIT	Deferred income		600

3.15 Section summary

The following accounting treatments apply.

(a) *Revenue-based grants*

DEBIT	Cash
CREDIT	P & L account

In the period in which the revenue expenditure to which the grant relates is charged.

(b) *Capital-based grants*

DEBIT	Cash
CREDIT	Accruals and deferred income

When the grant is received.

DEBIT	Accruals and deferred income
CREDIT	P & L account

Over the useful life of the related fixed asset.

3.16 Disclosure will be as follows.

(a) *Balance sheet: deferred income note*

	£
Balance at 1.1.20X0	X
Grants received during year	X
Transferred to profit and loss account	(X)
Balance at 31.12.20X0	X

(b) *Profit and loss account*: credit under 'other operating income'.

4 FRS 8 RELATED PARTY DISCLOSURES 5/01

Exam focus point

Related parties were examined in Section B of the May 2001 exam. Candidates were required to establish whether related parties existed and state which information they would need to make a final decision. Disclosure requirements and the need for them were also examined.

4.1 FRS 8 *Related party disclosures* makes it clear why a standard was required on this subject.

> 'In the absence of information to the contrary, it is assumed that a reporting entity has independent discretionary power over its resources and transactions and pursues its activities independently of the interests of its individual owners, managers and others. Transactions are presumed to have been undertaken on an arm's length basis, ie on terms such as could have obtained in a transaction with an external party, in which each side bargained knowledgeably and freely, unaffected by any relationship between them.
>
> These assumptions may not be justified when related party relationships exist, because the requisite conditions for competitive, free market dealings may not be present. Whilst the parties may endeavour to achieve arm's length bargaining the very nature of the relationship may preclude this occurring.'

4.2 FRS 8 can be summarised as follows.

(a) FRS 8 *Related party disclosures* requires the **disclosure** of:

(i) **Information on related party transactions**

(ii) The **name of the party controlling** the reporting entity and, if different, that of the ultimate controlling party whether or not any transactions between the reporting entity and those parties have taken place

Aggregated disclosures are allowed subject to certain restrictions.

Related parties are defined below.

FRS 8 is not long and the more detailed requirements are as follows.

Objective

4.3 The objective of FRS 8 is to ensure that financial statements contain the disclosures necessary to draw attention to the possibility that the reported financial position and results may have been affected by the existence of related parties and by material transactions with them. In other words, this is a standard which **is primarily concerned with disclosure**.

4.4 The definitions given in FRS 8 are fundamental to the effect of the standard.

DEFINITIONS

(a) **Close family** are those family members, or members of the same household, who may be expected to influence, or be influenced by, that person in their dealings with the reporting entity.

(b) **Control** means the ability of an undertaking to direct the financial and operating policies of another undertaking with a view to gaining economic benefits from its activities.

(c) **Key management** are those persons in senior positions having authority or responsibility for directing or controlling the major activities and resources of the reporting entity.

(d) **Persons acting in concert** comprise persons who, pursuant to an agreement or understanding (whether formal or informal), actively co-operative, whether through the ownership by any of them of shares in an undertaking or otherwise, to exercise control or influence over that undertaking.

4.5 The most important definitions are of *related parties* and *related party transactions.*

'Related parties

(a) Two or more parties are related parties when at any time during the financial period:

(i) one party has **direct or indirect control** of the other party; or

(ii) the parties are **subject to common control** from the same source; or

(iii) one party has **influence over the financial and operating policies** of the other party to an extent that that other party might be inhibited from pursuing at all times its own separate interests; or

(iv) the parties, in entering a transaction, are subject to **influence from the same source** to such an extent that one of the parties to the transaction has subordinated its own separate interests.

(b) For the avoidance of doubt, the following are **related parties** of the reporting entity:

(i) its ultimate and intermediate **parent undertakings**, subsidiary undertakings, and fellow subsidiary undertakings;

(ii) its **associates and joint ventures**;

(iii) the **investor or venturer** in respect of which the reporting entity is an associate or a joint venture;

(iv) **directors*** of the reporting entity and the directors of its ultimate and intermediate parent undertakings; and

(v) pension funds for the benefit of employees of the reporting entity or of any entity that is a related party of the reporting entity;

[* Directors include shadow directors, which are defined in companies legislation as persons in accordance with whose directions or instructions the directors of the company are accustomed to act.]

(c) and the following are **presumed to be related parties** of the reporting entity unless it can be demonstrated that neither party has influenced the financial and operating policies of the other in such a way as to inhibit the pursuit of separate interests:

(i) the **key management** of the reporting entity and the key management of its parent undertaking or undertakings;

(ii) a person owning or able to exercise control over **20 per cent or more of the voting rights** of the reporting entity, whether directly or through nominees;

(iii) each person **acting in concert** in such a way as to be able to exercise control or influence [in terms of part (a)(iii) of the definition of related parties, above] over the reporting entity; and

(iv) an entity managing or managed by the reporting entity under a **management contract**.

(d) Additionally, because of their relationship with certain parties that are, or are presumed to be, related parties of the reporting entity, the following are also presumed to be related parties of the reporting entity:

(i) **members of the close family** of any individual falling under parties mentioned in (a) – (c) above; and

(ii) partnerships, companies, trusts or other **entities** in which any individual or member of the close family in (a) – (c) above has a **controlling interest**.

Sub-paragraphs (b), (c) and (d) are not intended to be an exhaustive list of related parties.

Related party transaction
The transfer of assets or liabilities or the performance of services by, or for a related party irrespective of whether a price is charged.'

4.6 The most important point is in paragraph (a) of the definition of related parties because it defines in **general terms** what related party transactions are; the succeeding paragraphs of definition only add **some specifics**.

Scope

4.7 FRS 8 applies to all financial statements that are intended to give a true and fair view but it **excludes some transactions**; it does *not* require disclosure:

(a) Of **pension contributions** paid to a pension fund.

(b) Of **emoluments** in respect of services as an **employee** of the reporting entity.

4.8 Further types of transaction are also excluded as the FRS does not require disclosure of the relationship and transactions between the reporting entity and the parties listed in (a) to (d) below simply as a result of their role as:

(a) **Providers of finance** in the course of their business in that regard
(b) **Utility companies**
(c) **Government departments** and their sponsored bodies

- Even though they may circumscribe the freedom of action of an entity or participate in its decision-making process

(d) A **customer, supplier, franchiser, distributor** or **general agent** with whom an entity transacts a significant volume of business.

4.9 **FRS 8 then states the disclosures it requires, under two headings:**

(a) **Disclosure of control**
(b) **Disclosure of transactions and balances**

Disclosure of control

4.10 When the reporting entity is controlled by another party, there should be disclosure of the related party relationship and the name of that party and, if different, that of the ultimate controlling party. If the controlling party or ultimate controlling party of the reporting entity is not known, that fact should be disclosed. This information should be disclosed **irrespective of whether any transactions have taken place** between the controlling parties and the reporting entity.

Disclosure of transactions and balances

4.11 Financial statements should **disclose material transactions** undertaken by the reporting entity with a related party. Disclosure should be made **irrespective of whether a price is charged**. The disclosure should include:

(a) The **names** of the transacting parties

(b) A description of the **relationship** between the parties

(c) A description of the **transactions**

(d) The **amounts** involved

(e) **Any other elements** of the transactions necessary for an understanding of the financial statements

(f) The **amounts due** to or from related parties **at the balance sheet** date and provisions for doubtful debts due from such parties at that date

(g) **Amounts written off** in the period in respect of debts due to or from related parties

Transactions with related parties may be disclosed on an aggregated basis (aggregation of similar transactions by type of related party) unless disclosure of an individual transaction, or connected transactions, is necessary for an understanding of the impact of the transactions on the financial statements of the reporting entity or is required by law.

4.12 Further points of interest are made in the explanatory notes, particularly those on applying the definition of 'related party' given above.

(a) **Common control** is deemed to exist when **both parties are subject to control from boards having a controlling nucleus of directors in common.**

(b) The difference between control and influence is that **control brings with it the ability to cause the controlled party to subordinate its separate interests whereas the outcome of the exercise of influence is less certain.** Two related parties of a third entity are not necessarily related parties of each other.

4.13 Examples of such a situation of 'influence' rather than 'control' are given:

(a) Where two companies are associates of the same investor

(b) When one party is subject to control and another party is subject to influence from the same source

(c) Where two parties have a director in common

In these cases the two parties would not normally be treated as related parties unless it can be shown whether one or both parties have subordinated their own separate interests in entering into the transaction.

Disclosable related party transactions

4.14 The explanatory notes also give examples of related party transactions which would require disclosure:

(a) Purchases or sales of goods (finished or unfinished)
(b) Purchases or sales of property and other assets
(c) Rendering or receiving of services
(d) Agency arrangements
(e) Leasing arrangements
(f) Transfer of research and development
(g) Licence agreements
(h) Provision of finance (including loans and equity contributions in cash or in kind)
(i) Guarantees and the provision of collateral security
(j) Management contracts.

4.15 The *materiality* of related party transactions is also an important question because **only material related party transactions must be disclosed**. You should be familiar with the general definition of materiality, that transactions are material when disclosure might reasonably be expected to influence decisions made by the users of general purpose financial statements. In the case of related party transactions, materiality:

> 'is to be judged, not only in terms of their significance to the reporting entity, but also in relation to the other related party when that party is:
>
> (a) a director, key manager or other individual in a position to influence, or accountable for stewardship of, the reporting entity; or
>
> (b) a member of the close family of any individual mentioned in (a) above; or
>
> (c) an entity controlled by any individual mentioned in (a) or (b) above.'

Question 5

Which transactions are *excluded* by FRS 8?

Answer

See Paragraphs 4.7 and 4.8.

Current CA 1985 and Stock Exchange requirements

4.16 Some types of related party transactions are covered by existing statutory or Stock Exchange requirements, such as the provisions of the Companies Act 1985 covering transactions by directors and connected persons and 'Class IV' circulars which listed companies are required to send to shareholders when an acquisition or disposal of assets is made from or to a director, substantial shareholder or associate.

Chapter roundup

- *SSAP 17* amplifies the CA 1985 requirement to take account of **post balance sheet** liabilities and losses by distinguishing between adjusting and non-adjusting events and giving examples. It also requires disclosure of window dressing transactions. Where an otherwise non-adjusting event indicates that the going concern concept is no longer appropriate, then the accounts may have to be restated on a break-up basis. You should be able to define and discuss all these terms and apply them to practical examples.
- Under FRS 12 *a* **provision** should be recognised
  - When an entity has a **present obligation**, legal or constructive
  - It is probable that a **transfer of economic benefits** will be required to settle it
  - A **reliable estimate** can be made of its amount
- An entity **should not recognise a contingent asset or liability** but they **should be disclosed.**
- According to SSAP 4, the most appropriate treatment of government capital grants is to treat them as deferred income credited to the P+L account over the life of the related asset.
- *FRS 8* is primarily a **disclosure statement.** It is concerned with improving the quality of information provided by published accounts and also to strengthen their stewardship role.

Quick quiz

1 Define 'post balance sheet events'.

2 A property is valued and a permanent diminution in value is identified.

Adjusting event ☐

Non-adjusting event ☐

3 Stocks are lost in a fire.

Adjusting event ☐

Non-adjusting event ☐

4 A provision is a .... of .... timing or amount.

5 A programme is undertaken by management which converts the previously wholly owned chain of restaurants they ran into franchises. Is this restructuring?

6 Define contingent asset and contingent liability.

7 How can a government grant be accounted for?

(a) By reducing the acquisition cost.
(b) By treating the grant as a deferred credit.

8 Summarise the requirement of FRS 8.

9 Pension funds for the benefit of the employees of the reporting entity are deemed related parties by FRS 8.

True ☐

False ☐

Answers to quick quiz

1. Those events unfavourable and favourable which occur between the balance sheet date and the date of approval. (see para 1.1)
2. Adjusting. (1.5)
3. Non-adjusting. (1.8)
4. Liability of uncertain timing or amount. (2.6)
5. Yes. The manner in which the business is conducted has changed. (2.14)
6. Refer to paragraphs 2.21 and 2.23 respectively
7. Both. (3.4)
8. See paragraph 4.2.
9. True (4.5)

Now try the question below from the Exam Question Bank

Question to try	Level	Marks	Time
14	Exam level	20	36 mins

Chapter 11

SHARE CAPITAL TRANSACTIONS

Topic list		Syllabus reference	Ability required
1	**Historical cost accounting**	(ii)	Comprehension
2	**The issue and forfeiture of shares**	(ii)	Comprehension
3	**Ordinary and preference shares**	(ii)	Comprehension
4	**Debentures and loan stock**	(ii)	Comprehension
5	**FRS 4: Capital instruments**	(ii)	Comprehension
6	**Revenue recognition**	(ii)	Comprehension
7	**Distributable profits**	(ii)	Comprehension
8	**Redemption of shares**	(ii)	Comprehension

Introduction

You need to be able to explain historic cost accounting as it is the basis for the Financial Statements. Also ensure that you understand the concept of capital maintenance.

Accounting for share issues and forfeitures merely involves setting up the appropriate ledger accounts and then carrying out the proper double entry procedures. Do not try simply to rote learn these entries: understand the reasons behind them.

This chapter also deals with the legislation governing distributions and capital transactions. A certain amount of protection is afforded to the creditors of a company. This is to prevent shareholders being favoured over creditors.

Learning outcome covered in this chapter

- **Explain** and **apply** the rules governing share capital transactions

Syllabus content covered in this chapter

- The treatment in company accounts of shares, debentures, dividends and interest; the recognition of revenue, the distribution of profit and the maintenance of capital
- The issue and redemption of shares, including definitions and treatment of share issue and redemption costs, the share premium account, the capital redemption reserve and the purchase by a company of its own shares.

1 CAPITAL MAINTENANCE

Exam focus point

This chapter is important in its own right and is key to an accountant's work. Valuable marks are regularly involved in exam papers.

This section should also be studied carefully bearing in mind its impact on the analysis and interpretation of account to be covered later in this text.

Basic theoretical background

1.1 Capital maintenance is basically concerned with sustaining the equity of an entity and is subject to two key issues.

(a) The impact of inflation.
(b) What profits can be withdrawn.

1.2 EXAMPLE

Trailers Ltd is set up in Inflatiland (for illustrative purposes) with a share capital of £240,000 on 1 January 20X8 and purchases 40 caravans for £6,000 each. During the year it sold the original 40 caravans for £400,000 and purchased another further 30 caravans for £8,000 each, totalling £240,000. The official rate of inflation for the year is say 45%. Its accounts would look like the following.

TRADING ACCOUNT

	£	£
Sales		400,000
Purchases	480,000	
Closing stock	(240,000)	
Cost of sales		240,000
Profit		160,000

BALANCE SHEET

	£
Share capital	240,000
Retained profit	160,000
	400,000
Stocks	240,000
Cash	160,000
	400,000

How much of its profit can Trailers Ltd distribute while at the same time maintaining its equity:

- Operationally
- Financially

(a) *Operating capital maintenance*

The company began trading with 40 caravans but at the year end held only 30 caravans in stock.

Broadly, to maintain its operating capability, it would need to buy another 10 caravans. With inflation running at 45% this would probably entail further expenditure of £6,000 × 124% × 10 = £87,000 on 1 January 20X9.

Hence the profits Trailers could safely distribute would be £160,000 – £87,000 = £73,000. The key point here is that the response is driven by the need to maintain operating capability.

(b) *Financial capital maintenance*

A simple rough and ready measure might be to say that the company should maintain a level of equity in line with inflation ie £240,000 × 45% = £348,000.

Hence, Trailers could distribute £400,000 – £348,000 = £52,000 of its profits.

Notes. This is a very simple example to provide a flavour of the differences between operating capital maintenance and financial capital maintenance. Inflation accounting, as such, is a lot more complex and rigorous but is not part of the syllabus.

1.3 Currently, inflation is running at approximately 3% p.a. in the UK and hence is unlikely to present a problem. However, globally, there are countries where inflation is much higher.

1.4 As a point of passing interest, there is a **handy rule of thumb** which can be used to estimate how long it will take for a price level to double given a specific annual rate.

$$\text{Number of years for prices to double} = \frac{72}{\text{Average annual inflation rate}}$$

1.5 Hence, in the UK, it will take $\frac{72}{3}$ = 24 years for prices to double.

Limitations of historical cost accounting

1.6 **Fixed asset values are unrealistic**. This is especially so with property and in effect **unrealised holding gains** are not recognised, until the year of disposal.

1.7 **Accounting ratios may be unrealistic**. If net assets/capital employed are understated, accounting returns such as return on capital employed and asset utilisation could be misleading.

1.8 **Inter-company comparisons might be undermined**. For example, Company A may seem to be performing well because it is still coping with old virtually depreciated assets. Company B may be operating with expensive newly acquired assets. Company A's assets may need replacing soon, so there may well be questions about its financial adaptability if it does not have adequate reserves.

1.9 **Depreciation change is inadequate**. Under HCA, only the cost is spread over the economic life of the asset. Hence the performance statement will report rosier annual results, than if fixed assets and depreciation charges reflected revaluations.

1.10 **Trading performance may be overstated**. Sales revenue may be recognised on up-to-date selling prices but the cost of sales figure may include stocks brought forward from earlier periods included at out-of-date values. For example, an item of stock costing £100 is sold for £150 giving a recorded profit of £50. However this item is replenished at a cost of £120, suggesting that the make up of the recorded profit is probably:

	£
Holding gain	20
Trading profit	30
	50

Hence, trading profit includes holding gains on stock.

1.11 **Profits (or losses) on holdings of net monetary items are not shown**. For example £100 cash hold by a company on 1 January 20X6 could have purchased machine X. However, by 31 December 20X6, the price of the machine was £1,200. HCA do not tell the story of the loss on holding cash.

1.12 **Credit-worthiness is not enhanced**. If property is to be used as security to borrow money, current values rather than historical cost are more relevant to potential financiers.

1.13 **Comparisons over time are unrealistic**. This effectively reinforces the above. For example, if a company's sales are £1 million and £5 million in 1980 and 2005, respectively – which at first sight may seem impressive. However, the impact of inflation should be taken into consideration.

1.14 **The time effect of inflation on capital maintenance is not reflected**. As demonstrated above, profits may be distributed to the detriment of the long term viability of the business.

1.15 **The company may become a take-over target**. Understated asset values may lead to:

- Higher gearing ratios
- Lower assets per share value

Hence the company may be more susceptible to a take over bid.

Inflation accounting systems

1.16 These have been many developments in the history of the search for an alternative to HCA, mainly in the form of FREDs and reports. However, **as of today, there are no mandatory requirements in force.**

1.17 There are several systems of accounting for price changes, which are quite complex, but detailed knowledge is not required by the syllabus. The key systems fall into one of three categories.

(a) General price changes bases and in particular, **current purchasing power** (CPP).

(b) **Current value bases**. The basic principles of all these are:

(i) To show balance sheet items at some form of current value rather than historical cost.

(ii) To compute profits by matching the current value of costs at the date of consumption against revenue.

The current value of an item will normally be based on replacement cost, net realisable value or economic value.

(c) A **combination of these two systems**: suggestions of this type have been put forward by many writers and in particular in the ASC's *Handbook* on the subject.

The modified historical cost approach

1.18 As discussed in Chapter 4, CA 1985, Schedule 4 allows companies to apply both HCA rules and **alternative rules** subject to certain conditions. FRS 15 also sets out some requirements where a company would like to revalue tangible fixed assets.

KEY TERMS

Under modified HCA, fixed assets can be revalued to a current cost figure. Any excesses on re-evaluation over the historical cost is taken to a realisation reserve. Once the asset is disposed of, the unrealised holding gain can be released.

1.19 The modified HCA approach has several advantages.

- The financial statements produced are **easy to prepare, easy to read** and **easy to understand**.
- The mix and match approach is **practical**, albeit **pragmatic**. Revaluation of a class of fixed assets such as property but not plant and equipment is sensible.
- In periods of **low inflation**, cost can be a **useful** and **meaningful** figure. Moreover, it is relatively **simple to compare cost** figure between companies. Any impacts of inflation can be readily identified.

2 THE ISSUE AND FORFEITURE OF SHARES

Exam focus point

The November 202 paper required candidates to account for the issue and forfeiture of shares.

You could get discursive questions on share issues: benefits, impact on financial structure, impact on the accounting ratios, utilisation/purpose etc.

2.1 If you go back to Chapter 2, you will see that a company can increase its share capital by means of a **share issue**. Chapter 2 shows the disclosure requirements for such transactions. Here we will look at the **specific accounting entries** necessary for such an issue, including where a **share premium account is required** (when the price of the share is greater than its nominal value).

General rules and processes

2.2 The articles of association usually delegate the power to allot and issue shares to the directors as one of their management functions.

KEY TERM

As a general rule, if a company issues ordinary shares for **cash** it must first offer them to its existing ordinary shareholders in proportion to their shareholdings. This is called a **rights issue** because members may obtain new shares in right of their existing holdings.

2.3 The formal process for issuing new shares can be shown diagrammatically.

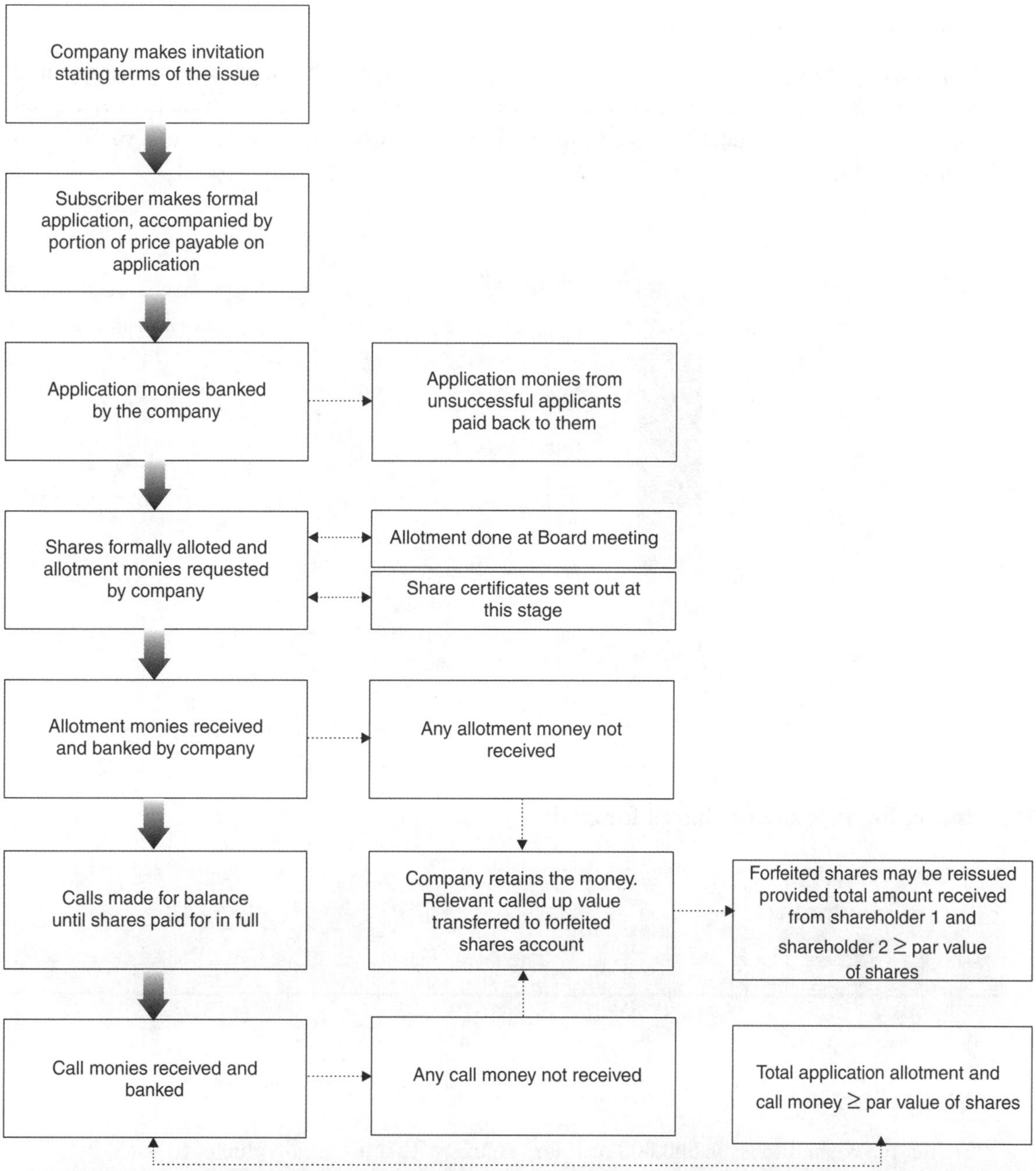

Company makes invitation stating terms of the issue

↓

Subscriber makes formal application, accompanied by portion of price payable on application

↓

Application monies banked by the company → Application monies from unsuccessful applicants paid back to them

↓

Shares formally alloted and allotment monies requested by company ↔ Allotment done at Board meeting ↔ Share certificates sent out at this stage

↓

Allotment monies received and banked by company → Any allotment money not received

↓

Calls made for balance until shares paid for in full | Company retains the money. Relevant called up value transferred to forfeited shares account → Forfeited shares may be reissued provided total amount received from shareholder 1 and shareholder 2 ≥ par value of shares

↓

Call monies received and banked → Any call money not received | Total application allotment and call money ≥ par value of shares

KEY TERM

Although a company may not allot shares for a consideration of less value than the nominal value of the shares, it is free to obtain a consideration of greater value. The excess of the consideration over the nominal value of the shares is **share premium** which must be credited to a statutory **share premium account** as part of the fixed capital.

2.4 Except when a rights issue is made to existing members, it is generally considered to be the duty of directors to obtain the highest possible price for the shares, and so to maximise the premium (if any). In practice the issue price will be set a little below the market price so as to offer some incentive to take up the offer. However, the price should not be too low so as to avoid diluting the value of the existing shares.

2.5 EXAMPLE

Goldenem Books plc is a successful publishing company whose shares are currently quoted on the stock exchange at 315 pence per share. The company wishes to raise further capital for expansion and has decided on a rights issue at 300 pence per share. Nominal value is 100 pence per share.

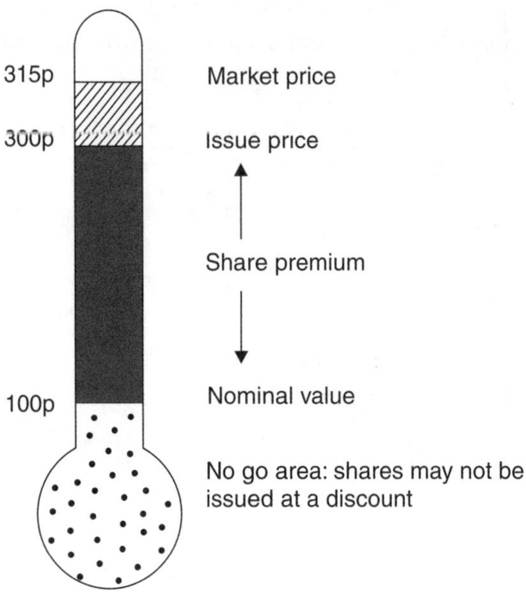

Accounting for an issue of shares for cash

Exam focus point

This area involves a lot of number crunching and fairly standard journal entries. Work through the examples enough time still you get them right in quick time.

2.6 EXAMPLE

Dalien plc wished to issue 500,000 ordinary shares with a nominal value of £1 each.

- 60p (including 10p premium) per share payable on application
- 20p on allotment and the final 30p on call, four months later.

The prospectus was published and applications for 600,000 shares were received. The directors rejected 'small' applicants for a total of 100,000 shares and allotted the remainder. Show the journal entries involved in respect of the issue, assuming that all cheques were banked on receipt.

2.7 SOLUTION

JOURNAL

(a)	DEBIT	Bank	£360,000	
	CREDIT	Application and allotment account		£360,000
		Being amounts received on application		

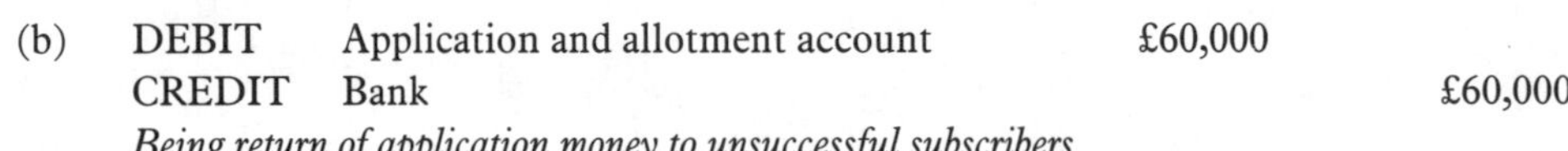

(b)	DEBIT	Application and allotment account	£60,000	
	CREDIT	Bank		£60,000
		Being return of application money to unsuccessful subscribers		

(c)	DEBIT	Application and allotment account	£400,000	
	CREDIT	Share capital account		£350,000
	CREDIT	Share premium account		£50,000
	Being allotment of shares			

(At this stage the total of the balances on the share capital account and share premium account shows the total amount receivable on application and allotment, while the debit balance on the application and allotment account records how much of that amount is still outstanding.)

(d)	DEBIT	Bank	£100,000	
	CREDIT	Application and allotment account		£100,000
	Being receipt of amounts due on allotment			

(This entry closes the application and allotment account.)

(e)	DEBIT	Call account	£150,000	
	CREDIT	Share capital account		£150,000
	Being the amount of the call on shares to make them fully paid			

(The share capital account is credited with the full amount due on the call, and the call account records the actual receipt of the money.)

(f)	DEBIT	Bank	£150,000	
	CREDIT	Call account		£150,000
	Being receipt of call money due			

2.8 If, in the example, shares had been allotted on a proportional basis, each subscriber would have received five-sixths of the number of shares applied for. There would therefore be no need for entry (b) above, and each subscriber's surplus application money would be applied to the amount due from him on allotment. Entry (c) above would remain the same, but entry (d) would be:

DEBIT	Bank	£40,000	
CREDIT	Application and allotment account		£40,000
Being receipt of amounts due on allotment			

2.9 EXAMPLE (CONTINUED)

After the call was made the money due on 10,000 of the shares was not received. The directors of Dalien plc (after due notice) forfeited the shares and subsequently reissued them at a price of 75p each. The journal entries (a) to (e) above would remain the same, but the subsequent entries would be:

(g)	DEBIT	Bank	£147,000	
	CREDIT	Call account		£147,000
	Being receipt of call money			

(If a balance sheet were drawn up at this stage, the debit balance on call account, being the £3,000 still receivable, would be shown as called up share capital not paid.)

(h)	DEBIT	Forfeiture account	£3,000	
	CREDIT	Call account		£3,000
	Being the forfeiture of the shares (The shares are now held by the company ready for re-issue.)			

When the shares are reissued the journal entries made are as follows.

(i)	DEBIT	Bank	£7,500	
	CREDIT	Forfeiture account		£7,500
	Being proceeds of reissue of shares			

(j) DEBIT Forfeiture account £4,500
CREDIT Share premium account £4,500
Being transfer of the premium on the reissued shares to share premium account.

(This is an additional premium obtained on the reissue of shares and is the excess of reissue price over the unpaid calls: 10,000 @ 45p.)

2.10 The combined example may be worked in ledger account form.

BANK ACCOUNT

	£		£
Application & allotment a/c	360,000	Application & allotment a/c	60,000
Application & allotment a/c	100,000	Balance c/d	554,500
Call a/c	147,000		
Forfeiture account	7,500		
	614,500		614,500

APPLICATION AND ALLOTMENT ACCOUNT

	£		£
Bank (100,000 @ 60p)	60,000	Bank (600,000 @ 60p)	360,000
Ordinary share capital a/c:		Bank (500,000 @ 20p)	100,000
(500,000 @ 70p)	350,000		
Share premium a/c:			
(500,000 @ 10p)	50,000		
	460,000		460,000

SHARE CAPITAL ACCOUNT: £1 ORDINARY SHARES

	£		£
Balance c/d	500,000	Application & allotment a/c	350,000
		Call a/c	150,000
	500,000		500,000

SHARE PREMIUM ACCOUNT

	£		£
Balance	54,500	Application & allotment a/c	50,000
		Forfeiture account	4,500
	54,500		54,500

CALL ACCOUNT

	£		£
Ordinary share capital a/c		Bank (490,000 @ 30p)	147,000
(500,000 @ 30p)	150,000	Forfeiture account	3,000
	150,000		150,000

FORFEITURE ACCOUNT

	£		£
Call a/c	3,000	Bank (10,000 @ 75p)	7,500
Share premium account	4,500		
	7,500		7,500

2.11 Dalien plc's balance sheets would be as follows.

(a) After the call (but before forfeiture)

	£
Current assets	
Debtors: called up share capital not paid	3,000
Cash at bank	547,000
	550,000

Capital and reserves	
Called up share capital: 500,000 £1 ordinary shares	500,000
Share premium account	50,000
	550,000

(b) After the forfeiture (but before reissue)

	£
Current assets	
Investments: own shares	3,000
Cash at bank	547,000
	550,000
Capital and reserves	
Called up share capital: 500,000 £1 ord shares fully paid	500,000
Share premium account	50,000
	550,000

After the reissue

	£
Current assets	
Cash at bank	554,500
Capital and reserves	
Called up share capital: 500,000 £1 ord shares fully paid	500,000
Share premium account	54,500
	554,500

Bonus issues

KEY TERM

A **bonus issue** is an issue of new shares to existing share holders in proportion to their existing shareholdings.

The new share capital is created by capitalising a part of existing reserves. This includes being able to use the share premium account.

The company's authority to make bonus issues of shares is governed by its own Articles of Association.

2.12 There are various key impacts of a bonus issue.

- The level of reserves available for distribution by way of dividends is reduced. However, in practice, the size of any bonus issue is unlikely to be so large as to adversely affect the company's dividend payment capability.
- The 'permanent capital' or 'creditors buffer' to satisfy creditors is increased.
- There will be more shares in issue which will have an arithmetical impact on the shares' market price. However, in practice the price is unlikely to go down proportionately because of the new issue. Market sentiment is likely to look favourably on a bonus issue and often the share price will effectively be boosted.

Exam focus point

The November 2002 paper asked candidates to identify the impact of a bonus issue on a company's capital structure as well as on the interests of shareholders and creditors

2.13 EXAMPLE

BUBBLES LIMITED
BALANCE SHEET (EXTRACT)

	£'000	£'000
Capital and reserves		
Share capital		
£1 ordinary shares (fully paid)		1,000
Reserves		
Share premium	500	
Undistributed profit	2,000	
		2,500
		3,500

Bubbles decided to make a '3 for 2' bonus issue (ie 3 new shares for every 2 already held). The double entry is as follows.

		£'000	£'000
DEBIT	Share premium	500	
	Undistributed profit	1,000	
CREDIT	Ordinary share capital		1,500

After the issue the balance sheet is as follows.

	£'000
Capital and reserves	
Share capital	
£1 ordinary shares (fully paid)	2,500
Reserves	
Undistributed profit	1,000
	3,500

1,500,000 new ('bonus') shares are issued to existing shareholders, so that if Mr X previously held 20,000 shares he will now hold 50,000. The total value of his holding should theoretically remain the same however, since the net assets of the company remain unchanged and his share of those net assets remains at 2% (50,000/2,500,000; previously 20,000/1,000,000).

Rights issues

KEY TERM

A **rights issue** is an offer of shares to existing shareholders in proportion to their existing holdings, usually at a price lower than the current market price.

Various courses of action are available to the shareholder.

- Take up or exercise the right
- Renounce the right and sell them on the market
- Renounce part of their right and take up the remainder
- Do nothing

Advantages of a rights issue

2.14 Rights issues are **cheaper** than **offers for sale** to the general public. This is partly because **no prospectus** is normally required, partly because the **administration** is **simpler** and partly because the cost of **underwriting** will be **less**. (Underwriters are financial institutions which agree (in exchange for a fee) to buy at the issue price, any shares not taken up. They provide protection against the issue being undersubscribed).

2.15 Rights issues are **more beneficial** to **existing shareholders** than issues to the general public. New shares are issues at a discount to the current market price, to make them attractive to investors. A rights issue **secures** the **discount** on the market price for existing shareholders, who may either keep the shares or sell them if they wish.

2.16 **Relative voting rights** are **unaffected** if shareholders all **take up their rights**.

2.17 The finance raised may be used to **reduce gearing** in book value terms by increasing share capital and/or to pay off long-term debt which will reduce gearing in market value terms.

Deciding the issue price for a rights issue

2.18 The offer price in a rights issue will be lower than the current market price of existing shares. The size of the discount will vary, and will; be larger for difficult issues. **The offer price** must **however be at or above the nominal value of the shares, so as not to contravene company law**.

2.19 A company making a rights issue must set a price which is low enough to secure the acceptance of shareholders, who are being asked to provide extra funds, but not too low, so as to avoid excessive dilution of the earnings per share.

Exam focus point

A question could ask for discussion on the effect of a rights issue, as well as calculations, eg of the effect on EPS.

2.20 The decision by individual shareholders as to whether they take up the offer will depend on:

- The expected rate of return on the investment (and the risk associated with it)
- The return obtainable from other investments (allowing for the associated risk)

2.21 EXAMPLE

Bubbles Ltd (above) decides to make a rights issue, shortly after the bonus issue. The terms are '1 for 5 @ £1.20' (one new share for every five already held, at a price of £1.20). Assuming that all shareholders take up their rights (which they are not obliged to) the double entry is as follows.

		£'000	£'000
DEBIT	Cash	600	
CREDIT	Ordinary share capital		500
CREDIT	Share premium		100

Mr X who previously held 50,000 shares will now hold 60,000, and the value of his holding should increase (theoretically at least) because the net assets of the company will increase. The new balance sheet will show:

£'000	£'000

Capital and reserves		
Share capital		
£1 ordinary shares		3,000
Reserves		
Share premium	100	
Undistributed profit	1,000	
		1,100
		4,100

The increase in funds of £600,000 represents the cash raised from the issue of 500,000 new shares at a price of £1.20 each.

Summary of procedure and accounting entries

2.22 The following procedure is followed for the issue and forfeiture of shares.

(a) **Application**: where potential shareholders apply for shares in the company and send cash to cover the amount applied for.

(b) **Allotment**: the company allocates shares to the successful applicants and returns cash to unsuccessful applicants.

(c) **Call**: where the purchase price is payable in instalments, the company will call for instalments on their due dates of payment.

(d) **Forfeiture**: if a shareholder fails to pay a call, his shares may be forfeited without the need to return the money he has paid. These forfeited shares may then be reissued to other shareholders.

2.23 The following summarises the relevant accounting entries.

(a) DEBIT Bank
CREDIT Application and allotment a/c
Application proceeds

(b) DEBIT Application and allotment a/c
CREDIT Bank
Money returned to over-subscribers

(c) DEBIT Bank
CREDIT Application and allotment a/c
Cash on allotment

(d) DEBIT Application and allotment a/c
CREDIT Share capital
CREDIT Share premium
Allotment of shares

(e) DEBIT Call a/c
CREDIT Share capital
Call of final instalment owed

(f) DEBIT Bank
CREDIT Call a/c
Cash receipts banked

(g) DEBIT Forfeiture a/c
CREDIT Call a/c
Forfeited shares

(h) DEBIT Bank
CREDIT Forfeiture a/c
Reissue forfeited shares

(i) DEBIT Forfeiture a/c
CREDIT Share premium a/c
Additional premium on reissue

Question 1

Mayke-a-Lot plc issued 50,000 £1 shares at £1.20 per share. Monies due were as follows.

On application	50p including premium
On allotment	30p
Call	40p

Applications were received amounting to £30,000 (ie for 60,000 shares).

At the call, 1,000 shares were forfeited. These were subsequently reissued for £1.10 cash.

Required

Write up the relevant ledger accounts for the above issue.

Answer

APPLICATION AND ALLOTMENT A/C

	£		£
Bank	5,000	Bank	30,000
Share capital	30,000	Bank	15,000
Share premium	10,000		
	45,000		45,000

BANK

	£		£
App & allot a/c	30,000	App & allot a/c	5,000
App & allot a/c	15,000		
Call	19,600		
Forfeiture a/c	1,100	C/d	60,700
	65,700		65,700

SHARE CAPITAL

	£		£
		App & allot	30,000
C/d	50,000	Call	20,000
	50,000		50,000

SHARE PREMIUM

	£		£
		App & allot a/c	10,000
C/d	10,700	Forfeiture a/c	700
	10,700		10,700

CALL A/C

	£		£
Share capital	20,000	Bank	19,600
		Forfeiture a/c	400
	20,000		20,000

INVESTMENT IN OWN SHARES

	£		£
Call a/c	400	Bank	1,100
Share premium	700		
	1,100		1,100

3 ORDINARY AND PREFERENCE SHARES

KEY TERMS

Ordinary shares

- Usually entitle the shareholder to vote at general meetings of the company.
- Are entitled to dividends, only after any preference dividends have been met.
- The actual dividend is decided on by the directors.
- Entitle the holder to receive any surplus net assets on winding up of the company, only after the entitlement of preference shareholders has been met. If there is not enough to fully meet the preference entitlement, there will obviously be nothing left for ordinary shareholders.

Preference shares

- Do not usually carry a vote at general meetings.
- The dividend usually represents a fixed percentage of nominal value.
- The dividend has priority to ordinary dividends.
- The dividend may be passed over if there are inadequate earnings. In such cases, the ordinary dividend would also be lost.
- If the preference shares are of a cumulative nature, any unpaid dividend will be carried forward for payment until available earnings permit.
- Entitlement to net assets on winding up is after creditors but before ordinary shareholders.

3.1 The above are the general characteristics of ordinary and preference shares. In practice, the actual rights attaching to each class will be set out in the Articles of Association.

Disadvantages of preference shares

3.2 Preference share have various disadvantages.

(a) They carry more **risk** than debt on **winding up**.

(b) **Interest** on debt attracts **relief for tax** purposes whereas preference dividends cannot be charged against taxable profits.

(c) The issue of preference shares does not restrict the company's **borrowing power,** at least in the sense that preference share capital is not secured against the assets of the business.

Exam focus point

Be clear in your mind where preference shares fit into the picture when you come to calculating accounting ratios.

3.3 From the point of view of the investor, preference shares are less attractive than loan stock.

(a) They cannot be secured on the company's assets.

(b) The dividend yield traditionally offered on preference dividends has been much too low to provide an attractive investment compared with the interest yields on loan stock in view of the additional risk involved.

KEY TERM

Loan stock is long-term debt capital raised by a company for which interest is paid, usually half yearly and at a fixed rate. Holders of loan stock are therefore long-term creditors of the company.

Advantages of preference shares

3.4 There are various benefits relating to preference shares

(a) **Dividends** do **not** have to be **paid** in a **year** in which **profits** are **poor**, while this is not the case with interest payments on long-term debt (loans or debentures)

(b) Since they do not normally carry voting rights, preference shares **avoid diluting** the **control** of **existing shareholders** while an issue of equity share would not.

(c) Unless they are redeemable, issuing preference share will **lower** the company's **gearing**. Redeemable preference share are normally treated as debts when gearing is calculated.

4 DEBENTURES AND LOAN STOCK

KEY TERM

Debentures are a form of loan stock, the written acknowledgement of a debt incurred by a company, normally containing provisions about the payment of interest and the eventual repayment of capital.

4.1 A **debenture trust deed** would includes clauses that protect the position of the debenture holder. A trustee (such as an insurance company or a bank) could intervene on behalf of debenture holders if the conditions of borrowing under which the debentures were issued are not being fulfilled. This might involve:

(a) **Failure to pay interest** on the due dates

(b) An attempt by the company to **sell off important assets** contrary to the terms of the loan.

(c) A company taking out **additional loans** and thereby **exceeding** previously agreed **borrowing limits** established either by the articles or by the terms of the debenture trust deed

4.2 **Advantages of debentures over preference shares**

(a) Debentures are a **cheaper form of finance** than preference shares because, unlike preference shares, debenture interest is tax-deductible.

(b) Debentures should be **more attractive** to investors because they will be **secured** on the assets of the company.

(c) Debentureholders **rank above preference shareholders** in the event of a liquidation.

(d) **Issue costs** should be **lower** for debentures than for preference shares.

5 FRS 4: CAPITAL INSTRUMENTS

5.1 The 1980's saw a financial environment which was sometimes described as one where 'anything goes'. Various types of hybrid financial instruments that had the characteristics both of equity and debt came into prominence. There was scope to present these in financial statements either as debt or equity, as might suit the individual company. To address these problems, the ASB issued FRS 4 *Capital instruments* in December 1993. The standard addresses how issuers should account for capital instruments.

KEY TERM

Capital instruments are instruments which are issued to raise finance. There are many different types. Common ones include bank loans, corporate bonds, convertible debt, ordinary shares, preference shares and options and warrants to subscribe for shares.

Distinguishing between debt and equity

5.2 One of the key users' ratios is the **gearing ratio**, ie the measure of the proportion of debt to equity. In order for this measure to be **meaningful** there must be **consistency** in the **allocation** of **financial instruments** between these two categories.

5.3 **Capital instruments** should be included in one of **three categories** in the balance sheet: liabilities, shareholders' funds or minority interests. The rules for distinguishing between debt and equity are based on the accounting model being developed in the ASB's *Statement of Principles*. They require:

(a) A company's **shares** to remain **in shareholders' funds**.

(b) Capital instruments to be reported as **liabilities** if they contain an '**obligation to transfer economic benefits**'.

(c) Capital instruments to be reported as **shareholders' funds** if they **do not contain an 'obligation to transfer economic benefits'**.

5.4 Some capital instruments have **features of both debt and equity**. The common example of such '**hybrid**' **instruments** is convertible debt, which is economically equivalent to conventional debt plus a warrant to acquire shares in the future.

5.5 If the individual components of such instruments are **physically separable**, the FRS requires that they should be accounted for separately. Where the components are **inseparable**, the instrument should be accounted for as a single instrument. Thus, for example, a convertible bond should not be notionally 'split' into debt and an option to acquire shares.

5.6 The rule for determining whether a capital instrument is a liability is widely drawn. **Convertible debt instruments** are **liabilities.**

5.7 The effect of applying these criteria is that **the classification of capital instruments will be consistent with their substance, rather than their legal form.**

Exam focus point

The November 2002 paper included a question requiring candidates to explain why certain types of share capital should be classified separately.

Disclosure: general

5.8 A fundamental part of FRS 4's approach on hybrid instruments and other less conventional forms of finance is to require issuers to make **considerable disclosure** about them.

5.9 In order to distinguish shares with debt characteristics from other share capital, the FRS contains a definition of a **'non-equity' shares.** Broadly speaking, these are shares that **contain preferential rights to participate in the company's profits or assets** (for example preference shares) or are redeemable.

5.10 The main new disclosure requirement is the analysis of the following items in the balance sheet.

Item	*Analysed between*	
Shareholders' funds	Equity interests	Non-equity interests
Liabilities	Convertible liabilities	Non-convertible liabilities

5.11 Such **analysis** is usually to be given on the **face** of the **balance sheet. Dividends** to shareholders should be **analysed similarly** in the **profit and loss account.** Considerable disclosure is also required about the rights and terms of each class of non-equity share and convertible debt.

5.12 The overall effect is to provide the users of financial statements with quite a **detailed analysis of shareholders' funds** showing the amounts pertaining to **each separate class of share** and a **summary of the rights of the holders.**

Exam focus point

The distinction between equity and non-equity interest could be tested as part of a published accounts question. You may also be required to analyse and explain.

Question 2

A company issues a convertible instrument which does not pay a coupon and is mandatorily convertible into shares of the issuer after 3 years. The holder is compensated through the conversion rights attached to the instrument. Although it is mandatorily convertible, the holders will rank as creditors in the event of insolvency of the issuer.

How should the instrument be classified?

Answer

Under FRS 4, this instrument should be classified in shareholders' funds as there is no 'obligation to transfer economic benefits'. Hence, this will be accounted for like a 'fully-paid' warrant. Its impact will be to dilute shareholders' interests in the future.

(Source: *Capital Instruments: A Guide to FRS 4, Ernst & Young*)

Accounting for debt instruments

5.13 **Debt should be recorded in the balance sheet at the fair value of the consideration received less costs incurred directly in connection with the issue of the instrument.** Such issue costs are narrowly defined and sometimes have to be written off immediately, but otherwise are spread over the life of the debt.

KEY TERM

Issues costs are those that are incurred directly, in connection with the issue of a capital instrument, that is, those costs that would not have been incurred had the specific instrument in question not been issued.

5.14 **The carrying amount of debt should be increased by the finance cost** in respect of the reporting period **and reduced by payments made in respect of the debt** in that period.

KEY TERM

The **finance cost** of debt is the difference between the total payments required to be made and the initial carrying value of the debt (that is the interest cost or the dividends plus any premium payable on redemption or other payments).

5.15 This **should be charged to the profit and loss account over the term of the instrument at a constant rate of interest on the outstanding amount of the debt**. The effective rate of interest implicit in the debt instrument will be required for that purpose.

5.16 Note that under s 130 CA 1985 discounts on the issue of debentures may be taken against the share premium account. This would be shown as a transfer in reserves.

Question 3

On 1 January 20X4, an entity issued a fixed rate debt instrument and received £900,000. Interest is payable annually in arrears at a rate of 5% on the stated principal amount of £1,000,000. The instrument has a 5 year term and the stated principal will be repaid at maturity. Issue costs of £50,000 were incurred.

State the disclosure of the instrument in the profit and loss account and the balance sheet for each year of the term.

Answer

The net proceeds of this issue are £850,000. The finance cost of this instrument is £400,000, being the difference between the total future payments (ie £1,250,000, see column (a) below) and the net proceeds from the issue.

The effective rate of interest implicit in this instrument is the discount rate which equates the present value of future cash flows to the net proceeds received. This is calculated as 8.84% by applying the NPV formula (use interpolation if not provided by the examiner).

The interest charge for the year (column (b) below) is calculated by applying this rate to the carrying value of the debt in the balance sheet during the year.

	(a)	*(b)*	*(c)*
	Cash flows	*Interest Charge at 8.84%*	*Carrying value in the balance sheet*
	£'000	£'000	£'000
At January 20X4	(850)		850.0
At 31 December 20X4	50	75.1	875.1
At 31 December 20X5	50	77.4	902.5
At 31 December 20X6	50	79.8	932.3
At 31 December 20X7	50	82.4	964.7
At 31 December 20X8	1,050	85.3	-
Total	400	400.0	

(Source: *Capital Instruments: A Guide to FRS 4*, Ernst & Young)

5.17 **If debt is repurchased or settled before its maturity, any gains or losses should be recognised immediately** in the profit and loss account.

Accounting for shares

5.18 **Share issues should be recorded at the fair value of the consideration received less issue costs.** Issue costs should be written off directly to reserves and should not be reported in the statement of total recognised gains and losses, ie those relating directly to the issue of the instrument should be accounted for as a reduction in the proceeds of a capital instrument.

Question 4

A company issues 100 £1 ordinary shares at par. Issue costs of £2 are incurred.

State how this transaction should be recorded and disclosed.

Answer

If there is a share premium account in existence, the share issue may be recorded by increasing share capital by £100 and setting off the issue costs against share premium account. In the analysis of total shareholders' funds, the equity interests will have increased by £98.

If there is no share premium account, share capital will be increased by £100 but the issue costs would be deducted from another reserve (usually profit and loss account reserve) subject to the provisions of the company's articles. Prior to FRS 4, companies in this situation had to charge the issue costs to the profit and loss account. The equity interest within shareholders' funds also increases by £98 in this case.

(Source: *Capital Instruments: A Guide to FRS 4*, Ernst & Young)

5.19 As stated above, under FRS 4 **the balance sheet should show the amount of shareholders' funds attributable to equity interests and the amount attributable to non-equity interests.**

5.20 The **finance cost of non-equity** shares should be **calculated on the same basis as for debt instruments. Dividends in respect of non-equity shares** have to be accounted for **on an accruals basis**. The only **exception** is where there are **insufficient distributable profits** and the **dividend rights** are **non-cumulative**. **Arrears of preference dividends** must therefore be **provided for rather than simply disclosed**.

> **Exam focus point**
>
> Be prepared in the exam to package up any bits of the foregoing material for a 5 to 10 mark question.
> You could be asked to compare one thing with another or perhaps to discuss one aspect such as voting rights or risk.

6 REVENUE RECOGNITION

ASB balance sheet driven approach

6.1 **Accruals accounting** is based on the requirement that the **non-cash impact** of transactions are recognised in the **period of occurrence** rather than in the period any cash is received or paid. It is crucially important under this convention that we can establish the **point** at which **revenue may be recognised** and **related costs** treated as an **asset**, being representative of a **right** to **future economic benefits**. For example, the costs of producing an item of finished goods should be carried as an asset in the balance sheet until such time as it is sold; they should then be derecognised as an asset and written off as a charge to the trading account. The treatment which should be applied cannot be decided upon until it is clear at what moment the sale of the item takes place; when one form of **right to economic benefits** is **replaced** by **another form** of **right to economic benefits**, ie **stock replace by a debtor**.

6.2 The decision has a direct impact on profit since under the prudence concept, where there is **uncertainty** regarding the **right to receive economic** benefits, **appropriate caution** must be **exercised in recognising revenue** and **profit** from a sale.

> **Exam focus point**
>
> Given the current USA controversies over the reporting of earnings by public companies there, consider how you might respond to a proposition by a director to accelerate revenue recognition.
>
> Remember that the ASB takes a balance sheet driven approach to defining revenue ie revenue arises from a recognisable increase in net assets. Any answer on revenue recognition must include wording that shows the examiner that you are up-to-date with the ASB approach.

Point of sale

6.3 **Revenue is generally recognised as earned at the point of sale, because at that point four criteria will generally have been met.**

(a) The product or service has been **provided** to the buyer.

(b) The buyer has **recognised** his **liability** to **pay** for the goods or services provided. The converse of this is that the seller has **recognised** that **ownership** of **goods** has **passed** from himself to the buyer.

(c) The buyer has indicated his **willingness** to **hand over cash** or other assets in **settlement** of his liability.

(d) The **monetary value** of the goods or services has been **established**.

6.4 At **earlier points** in the **business cycle** there will not in general be firm evidence that the above criteria will be met. **Until work** on a product is **complete**, there is a **risk** that some flaw in the manufacturing process will necessitate its **writing off**; even when the product is complete there is no guarantee that it will find a buyer, ie there is **uncertainty** whether the **stock** will **yield future economic benefits**, and the stock might need to be derecognised from the balance sheet.

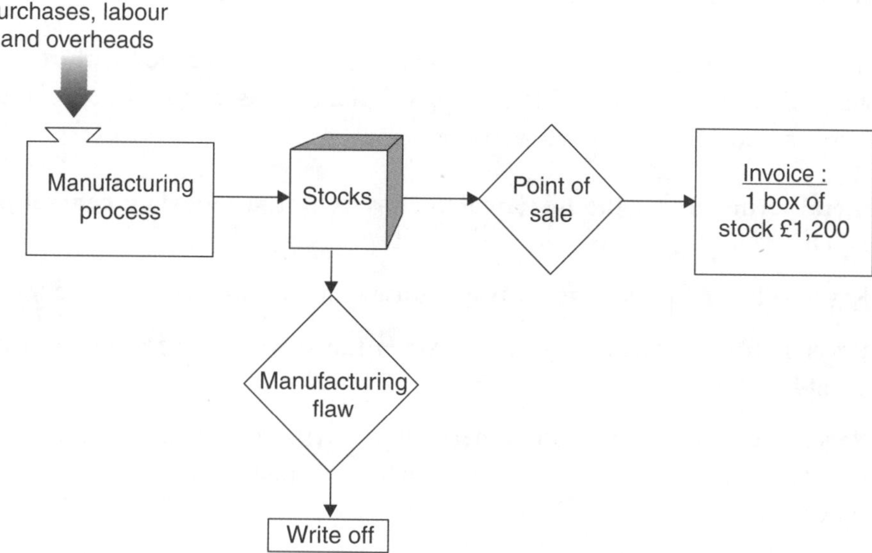

6.5 **At later points** in the **business cycle**, for example when cash is received for the sale, the recognition of revenue may occur in a period later than that in which the related costs were charged. Revenue recognition would then depend on **fortuitous circumstances**, such as the **cash flow** of a company's **debtors**, and might **fluctuate** misleadingly from one period to another. Again if collection of payment from any debtors is uncertain, they may need to be derecognised from the balance sheet.

Times other than point of sale

6.6 However, **occasionally revenue is recognised at other times** than at the completion of a sale.

(a) **Recognition of profit on long-term contract work in progress**. Under SSAP 9 *Stocks and long-term contracts*, credit is taken in the profit and loss account for 'that part of the total profit currently estimated to arise over the duration of the contract which fairly reflects the **profit attributable** to that part of the work performed at the accounting date'.

  (i) Owing to the length of time taken to complete such contracts, to defer taking profit into account until completion may result in the profit and loss account reflecting not so much a **fair view of the activity** of the company during the year but rather the results relating to contracts which have been completed by the year end.

  (ii) Revenue in this case is **recognised** when production on, say, a **section** of the **total contract** is **complete**, even though no sale can be made until the whole is complete. Remember, as suggested earlier in the text, the **presence of a contract is important**, This provides the **certainty** that allows **prudence** to be **avoided**.

(b) **Sale on hire purchase. Title** to goods provided on hire purchase terms does not pass until the **last payment** is made, at which point the sale is complete.

  (i) To **defer** the **recognition of revenue** until that point, however, would be to **distort** the **nature** of the **revenue earned**.

  (ii) The profits of an HP retailer in effect represent the **interest charged** on **finance provided** and such interest arises over the course of the HP agreement rather than at its completion. Revenue in this case is **recognised** when **each instalment** of cash is **received**.

6.7 **The determination of whether revenue should be recognised is primarily driven by accruals concept, but it is also desirable that prudence should be borne in mind, especially where uncertainty exists. Prudence also requires careful consideration of an appropriate level of confirmation that:**

- A suitable past event has indeed occurred
- A right to future economic benefits exists.

6.8 The question of revenue recognition is obviously closely associated with the definition of realised profits and the **reasonable certainty** that a **new asset** has been **created** and that it can be **measured** with **reasonable certainty**.

6.9 **In general terms, under the historical cost system, the following general practice has developed.**

(a) Revenue from the sale of goods is recognised on the **date of delivery** to the customer.

(b) Revenue from services is recognised when the **services** have been **performed** and are **billable**.

(c) Revenue derived from **letting** others use the resources of the businesses (for example royalty income, rent and interest) is recognised either as the **resources** are **used** or on a time basis.

(d) Revenue from the **sale of assets** (other than products of the business) is recognised at the **date of the sale**.

Exam focus point

Remember to link recognition to the principles set out in the *ASB Statement of Principles* and FRS 18. Recognition is divorced from realisation. **Recognition depends on the reasonable certainty that a new asset or liability exists and can be measured with reasonable reliability.**

Problem areas

6.10 The problems with revenue recognition, for businesses and their auditors, is that there are some areas where accounting standards have not (yet) been issued which deal with all types of transaction. We will not go into too much detail here about these situations, but you should be aware of them, and a list is given below (the list is not comprehensive).

(a) **Receipt of initial fees**, at the beginning of a service, may not have been 'earned' and it is often difficult to determine what they represent.

(b) **Franchise fees** can be incurred in complex franchise agreements and no **standard form of agreement** has allowed an accepted accounting practice to develop. **Each agreement** must be dealt with on its **own merits**.

(c) **Advance royalty or licence receipts** would normally be dealt with as deferred income and released to the profit and loss account when earned under the agreement. In some businesses, however, such advances consist of a number of **different components** which require **different accounting treatments**, for example in the record industry.

(d) **Loan arrangement fees** could be recognised in the year the loan is arranged or spread over the life of the loan.

(e) **Credit card fees** charged by credit card companies on their cardholders might be **recognised on receipt or spread over the period** that the fee allows the cardholder to use the card.

7 DISTRIBUTABLE PROFITS

Exam focus point

Beware of the various approaches the examiner could take, He might link the legal and accounting aspects governing dividend payments with other aspects of the syllabus such as cash flow management, dividend cover, financial adaptability, accounting ratios etc.

7.1 Companies legislation cannot prevent a company's *'permanent capital'* or *'creditors buffer'* being eroded through losses. However, it can rule against reduction as a result of distributions.

7.2 A **distribution** is defined by s 263(2) CA 1985 as every description of distribution of a company's assets to members (shareholders) of the company, whether in cash or otherwise, **with the exceptions of**:

(a) An issue of bonus shares.

(b) The redemption or purchase of the company's own shares out of capital (including the proceeds of a new issue) or out of unrealised profits.

(c) The reduction of share capital by:

- Reducing the liability on shares in respect of share capital not fully paid up
- Paying off paid-up share capital

(d) A distribution of assets to shareholders in a winding up of the company.

KEY TERM

Companies must not make a distribution except out of profits available for the purpose. These available profits are:

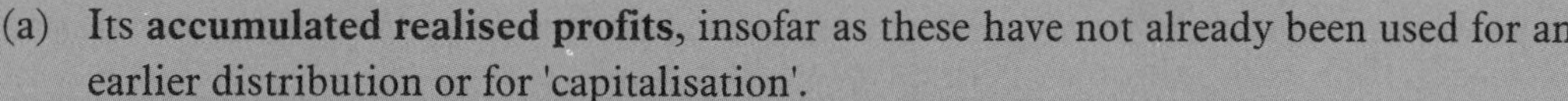

(a) Its **accumulated realised profits,** insofar as these have not already been used for an earlier distribution or for 'capitalisation'.

(b) **Minus its accumulated realised losses,** insofar as these have not already been written off in a reduction or reconstruction scheme.

7.3 Capital profits and revenue profits (if realised) are taken together and capital losses and revenue losses (if realised) are similarly grouped together. *Unrealised profits* cannot be distributed (for example profit on the revaluation of fixed assets); nor must a company apply unrealised profits to pay up debentures or any unpaid amounts on issued shares.

KEY TERM

Capitalisation of realised profits is the use of profits:

- To issue bonus shares
- As a transfer to the capital redemption reserve

7.4 Section 264 imposes **further restrictions on the distributions of public companies.**

BASIC REQUIREMENT

A public company cannot make a distribution if at the time:

(a) The amount of its net assets is less than the combined total of its called-up share capital plus its undistributable reserves.

(b) The distribution will reduce the amount of its net assets to below the combined total of its called-up share capital plus its undistributable reserves.

7.5 For the above purposes, '**undistributable reserves**' are:

(a) The share premium account.

(b) The capital redemption reserve.

(c) Any accumulated surplus of unrealised profits over unrealised losses.

(d) Any other reserve which cannot be distributed, whether by statute, or the company's memorandum or articles of association.

7.6 The above can be summarised as follows.

Private companies

Maximum dividend ≤ Accumulated realised profits – Accumulated realised losses

Public companies

Maximum dividend ≤ Accumulated realised profits – Accumulated realised losses – Accumulated unrealised losses.

7.7 EXAMPLE: PRIVATE COMPANY V PUBLIC COMPANY DISTRIBUTIONS

Henan Ltd is a private company and Jinlin plc is a public limited company. Both companies have a financial year ending on 31 December. On 31 December 20X5, the balance sheets of the companies, by a remarkable coincidence, were identical, as follows.

	Henan Ltd		*Jinlin plc*	
	£'000	£'000	£'000	£'000
Net assets		730		730
Share capital		600		600
Share premium account		120		120
Unrealised losses on asset revaluations		(50)		(50)
Realised profits	100		100	
Realised losses	(40)		(40)	
		60		60
		730		730

What is the maximum distribution that each company can make?

7.8 SOLUTION

(a) S 263 restricts the distributable profits of Henan Ltd to £60,000.

(b) S 264 further restricts the distributable profits of Jinlin plc to £60,000 – £50,000 = £10,000 (or alternatively, £730,000 – £600,000 – £120,000 = £10,000. This is the surplus of net assets over share capital plus undistributable reserves, which in this example are represented by the share premium account).

Realised profits

7.9 Legislation does not define realised profits very clearly. As a '**rule of thumb**', according to the Consultative Committee of Accounting Bodies, **profits in the profit and loss account are realised, while unrealised profits are credited directly to reserves.**

7.10 FRS 18 *Accounting policies* provides a framework for recognising realised profits. If FRS 18 is followed, profit and loss account profits will be realisable.

Exceptions

7.11 In the case of **sale of revalued fixed assets**, the **unrealised profit on revaluation previously credited to the revaluation reserve** does not pass through the profit and loss account. It is nevertheless to be **regarded as distributable.**

7.12 Where an asset has been revalued, the **increase in depreciation charge** can be treated as a realised profit. For example, an asset with book value of £2 million is revalued to £3 million. Depreciation is 20% reducing balance. Difference arising treated as realised profit = (£3m – £2m) × 20% = £200,000.

7.13 **Development expenditure** is a realised loss in the year in which it is incurred, except when the costs are capitalised within SSAP 13 guidelines, in which case the costs are amortised as realised losses over a number of years.

7.14 **Provisions** are generally treated as realised losses.

The relevant accounts

7.15 S 270 defines the 'relevant accounts' which should be used to determine the distributable profits. These are the most recent audited annual accounts of the company, prepared in compliance with the Companies Acts. If the accounts are qualified by the auditors, the auditors must state in their report whether they consider that the proposed distribution would contravene the Act.

7.16 **Companies may also base a distribution on interim accounts,** which need not be audited. However, in the case of a public company, such interim accounts must be properly prepared and comply with:

(a) s 228(2) (accounts to give a true and fair view).
(b) s 238 (directors to sign the company's balance sheet).

A copy of the interim accounts should be delivered to the Registrar.

Investment and insurance companies

7.17 S 265 makes a **special provision for investment companies which are public companies.** Investment companies may make a distribution out of realised revenue profits (insofar as they have not already been utilised or capitalised) less its realised and unrealised revenue losses (insofar as these have not already been written off in a capital reduction or reconstruction) provided that its assets equal at least one and a half times the aggregate amount of its liabilities.

7.18 S 268 refers to insurance companies which have long-term business. Any surplus of assets over liabilities on long-term business which has been properly transferred to the company's profit and loss account should be regarded as a *realised* profit. (This section makes a specific point of clarification, and is therefore relatively minor in importance.)

The duties of directors

4.19 S 309 CA 1985 states that the directors of a company must have regard to the interests of the company's employees in general, as well as to the interests of shareholders. This is a duty which is owed by directors to the company alone.

Question 5

Explain the implications of the following items to profits available for distribution in a public company.

(a) Research and development activities.
(b) Net deficit on revaluation reserve arising from an overall deficit on the revaluation of fixed assets.
(c) Excess depreciation.
(d) Goodwill.

Answer

(a) S 263 of the Companies Act 1985 provides that, for the purposes of calculating realised profits, development expenditure carried forward in the balance sheet should be treated as a realised loss. This means that development expenditure may not be regarded as part of net assets.

If, however, there are special circumstances which, in the opinion of the directors, justify the treatment of development expenditure as an asset and not as a loss, then this requirement need not apply. It is generally considered that, if the development expenditure qualifies for treatment as an asset under the provisions of SSAP 13, then it may be treated as an asset and not a loss for the purposes of calculating distributable profits.

(b) A revaluation reserve is a non-distributable reserve because it reflects unrealised profits and losses. A public company cannot make a distribution which reduces its net assets to below the total of called-up share capital and non-distributable reserves. Consequently, any reduction in a revaluation reserve (or an increase in a debit balance) reduces the profits available for distribution.

(c) Excess depreciation is the depreciation on revalued assets in excess of cost. Since excess depreciation is regarded as the realisation (through use) of part of the corresponding revaluation reserve, it is added back to profits available for distribution.

(d) Under FRS10, goodwill must be capitalised and amortised. The annual amount written off is considered a realised loss and reduces distributable profits.

8 PURCHASE OR REDEMPTION OF SHARES 5/01

Exam focus point

A question in the May 2001 exam involved 5 marks for the recalculation of the balance sheet after redemption, 10 marks for an explanation of the purpose of the capital redemption reserve and 5 marks for an explanation of why companies are permitted to buy back their own shares.

You could be asked to discuss the commercial benefits of being able to reduce, repurchase or redeem share capital.

Also be aware of how purchase or redemption might impact on accounting ratios.

Reduction of capital

8.1 **Any limited company is permitted without restriction to cancel unissued shares and in that way to reduce its authorised share capital.** That change does not alter its financial position, ie no ledger balance is affected.

Articles usually contain the necessary power. If not, the company in general meeting would first pass a special resolution to alter the articles appropriately.

8.2 Three factors need to be in place to give effect to a reduction of a company's issued share capital.

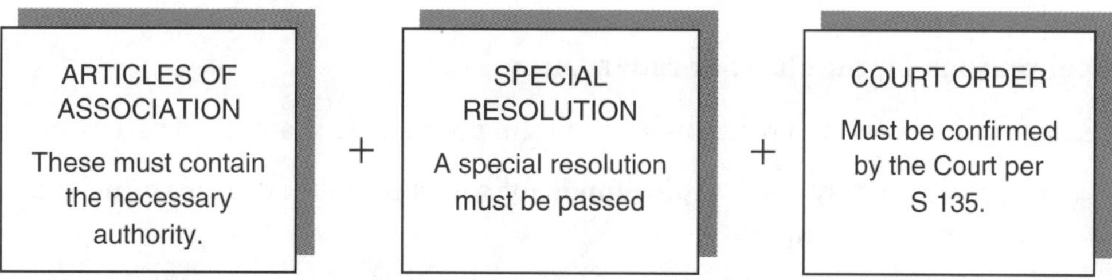

8.3 There are **three basic methods of reducing share capital** specified in s 35(2).

(a) **Extinguish or reduce liability on partly paid shares.** A company may have issued £1 (nominal) shares 75p paid up. The outstanding liability of 25p per share may be eliminated altogether by reducing each share to 75p (nominal) fully paid or some intermediate figure, eg 80p (nominal) 75p paid. **Nothing is returned** to the shareholders but the **company gives up a claim** against them for money which it could **call up** whenever needed.

(b) **Cancel paid up share capital which has been lost or which is no longer represented by available assets.** Suppose that the issued shares are £1 (nominal) fully paid but the net assets now represent a value of only 50p per share. The difference is probably matched by a debit balance on profit and loss account (or provision for fall in value of assets). The company could reduce the nominal value of its £1 shares to 50p (or some intermediate figure) and apply the amount to write off the debit balance or provision wholly or in part. It would then be able to resume payment of **dividends** out of **future profits without** being obliged to **make good past losses.** The resources of the company are not reduced by this procedure of part cancellation of nominal value of shares but it avoids having to rebuild lost capital by retaining profits.

(c) **Pay off part of the paid up share capital out of surplus assets.** The company might repay to shareholders, say, 30p in cash per £1 share by reducing the nominal value of the share to 70p. This **reduces the assets of the company** by 30p per share.

Share premium account

8.4 Whenever a company obtains for its shares a consideration in excess of their nominal value, it must transfer the excess to a share premium account. The general rule is that the **share premium account is subject to the same restriction as share capital. However, a bonus issue can be made using the share premium account** (reducing share premium in order to increase issued share capital).

The share premium account may be repaid to members (or otherwise eliminated) under a reduction of share capital authorised by the court, but may not distributed as a dividend because it is a non-distributable reserve.

8.5 Following the decision in *Shearer v Bercain 1980,* there is an exemption from the general rules on setting up a share premium account, in certain circumstances where new shares are issued as consideration for the acquisition of shares in another company.

8.6 The **share premium account may be utilised for other limited purposes.**

(a) Writing off capital expenses such as **preliminary expenses** of forming the company.
(b) Writing off **share** or **debenture** issue expenses, including commissions and discounts.
(c) **Premium** (if any) paid on **redemption** of **debentures**: s 130(2).

Private companies (but not public companies) may also use a share premium account in **purchasing** or **redeeming** their **own shares** out of capital.

Practical reasons for purchase or redemption

8.7 Companies may wish to repurchase or redeem their issued shares for a variety of reasons.

(a) The company may have **surplus funds** for which it cannot identify sufficiently attractive business opportunities.

(b) A reduction in the number of issued shares helps to **improve earnings per share** (EPS) and **return on capital employed** (ROCE).

(c) Dividend payments may be reduced, allowing the **cash** to be **used for other purposes**.

- Funding operation activities
- Capital expenditure
- Repayments of debts

(d) The **remaining shareholders** holdings will increase. Hence, even if the overall total dividends might not increase, **shareholders** could receive **more cash individually**.

(e) Problem or **dissident shareholders** in private companies can be **paid off** and leave the company without spreading the membership of the company beyond the existing shareholders.

(f) It provides a **potential exit route** for **venture capitalists** who intend to in be involved in the business for a limited period.

(g) It provides an **escape route** for **entrepreneurs** who have taken their companies to market to **take them back into private ownership** eg Virgin, Amstrad and Harvey Nicholls.

Redemption or purchase by a company of its own shares

Exam focus point

You obviously need to be able to do the basic number crunching and accounting gentries. However do not ignore the likelihood of discursive questions.

- Benefits of being able to purchase/redeem
- Impact on accounting ratios, cash management and financial adaptability.

8.8 There is a **general prohibition** (s 143) against any voluntary acquisition by a company of its own shares, but that prohibition is subject to **exceptions**.

8.9 A company may:

(a) Purchase its own shares in compliance with an **order of the court**.
(b) Issue **redeemable shares** and then redeem them.
(c) Purchase its own shares under certain **specified procedures**.
(d) **Forfeit** or accept the surrender of its shares.

These restrictions relate to the **purchase** of shares: there is no objection to accepting a gift.

8.10 The **conditions for the issue and redemption of redeemable shares** are set out in ss 159 to 161.

(a) The **articles** must give **authority** for the issue of redeemable shares. Articles do usually provide for it, but if they do not, the articles must be altered before the shares are issued: s 159.

(b) Redeemable shares may only be issued if at the time of issue the company also has issued shares which are not redeemable: a company's **capital** may **not consist entirely of redeemable shares**: s 159.

(c) Redeemable shares may **only** be **redeemed** if they are **fully paid**: s 159.

(d) The **terms** of redemption must provide for **payment on redemption**: s 159.

(e) The shares may be redeemed out of **distributable profits**, or the proceeds of a **new issue** of shares, or capital (if it is a private company) in accordance with the relevant rules: s 160.

(f) Any **premium payable** on redemption must be provided out of **distributable profits** subject to an **exception** described below: s 160.

8.11 The 1948 Act provided regulations which prevented companies from redeeming shares except by transferring a sum equal to the nominal value of shares redeemed from distributable profit reserves to a non-distributable '**capital redemption reserve**'. This reduction in distributable reserves is an example of the **capitalisation of profits, where previously distributable profits become undistributable.**

8.12 **The purpose of these regulations was to prevent companies from reducing their share capital investment so as to put creditors of the company at risk.**

8.13 EXAMPLE: CAPITALISATION OF PROFITS

Suppose, for example, that Muffin Ltd had £100,000 of preference shares, redeemable in the very near future at par. A balance sheet of the company is currently as follows.

	£	£
Assets		
Cash	100,000	
Other assets	300,000	
		400,000
Liabilities		
Trade creditors		120,000
Net assets		280,000
Capital and reserves		
Ordinary shares	30,000	
Redeemable preference shares	100,000	
		130,000
Profit and loss account		150,000
		280,000

8.14 Now if Muffin Ltd were able to redeem the preference shares without making any transfer from the profit and loss account to a capital redemption reserve, the effect of the share redemption on the balance sheet would be as follows.

	£
Net assets	
Non-cash assets	300,000
Less trade creditors	120,000
	180,000
Capital and reserves	
Ordinary shares	30,000
Profit and loss account	150,000
	180,000

In this example, the company would still be able to pay dividends out of profits of up to £150,000. If it did, the creditors of the company would be highly vulnerable, financing £120,000 out of a total of £150,000 assets of the company.

8.15 The regulations in the 1948 Act were intended to prevent such extreme situations arising. On redemption of the preference shares, Muffin Ltd would have been required to transfer £100,000 from its profit and loss account to a non-distributable reserve, called at that time a capital redemption reserve fund. The effect of the redemption of shares on the balance sheet would have been:

	£	£
Net assets		
Non-cash assets		300,000
Less trade creditors		120,000
		180,000
Capital and reserves		
Ordinary shares		30,000
Reserves		
Distributable (profit and loss account)	50,000	
Non-distributable (capital redemption reserve fund)	100,000	
		150,000
		180,000

The maximum distributable profits are now £50,000. If Muffin Ltd paid all these as a dividend, there would still be £250,000 of assets left in the company, just over half of which would be financed by non-distributable equity capital.

8.16 When a company redeems some shares, or purchases some of its own shares, they **should be redeemed**:

(a) **Out of distributable profits.**

(b) **Or out of the proceeds of a new issue of shares.**

KEY TERM

If there is any premium on redemption, **the premium must be paid out of distributable profits**, except that if the shares were issued at a premium, then any premium payable on their redemption may be paid out of the proceeds of a new share issue made for the purpose, up to an amount equal to the lesser of:

(a) The aggregate premiums received on issue of the redeemable shares.

(b) The balance on the share premium account (including premium on issue of the new shares).

8.17 EXAMPLE: REDEMPTION OF SHARES

A numerical example might help to clarify this point. Suppose that Pillary Ltd intends to redeem 10,000 shares of £1 each at a premium of 5 pence per share. The redemption must be financed out of:

(a) Distributable profits (10,000 × £1.05 = £10,500).

(b) The proceeds of a new share issue (say, by issuing 10,000 new £1 shares at par). The premium of £500 must be paid out of distributable profits.

(c) Combination of a new share issue and distributable profits.

(d) Out of the proceeds of a new share issue where the redeemable shares were issued at a premium. For example, if the redeemable shares had been issued at a premium of 3p per share, then (assuming that the balance on the share premium account after the new share issue was at least £300) £300 of the premium on redemption could be debited to the share premium account and only £200 need be debited to distributable profits.

8.18 (a) Where a company redeems shares or purchases its own shares wholly out of distributable profits, it must transfer to the capital redemption reserve an amount equal to the nominal value of the shares redeemed (s 170 (1)).

In example (a) above the accounting entries would be:

		£	£
DEBIT	Share capital account	10,000	
	Profit and loss account (premium on redemption)	500	
CREDIT	Cash		10,500
DEBIT	Profit and loss account	10,000	
CREDIT	Capital redemption reserve		10,000

(b) Where a company redeems shares or purchases its shares wholly or partly out of the proceeds of a new share issue, it must transfer to the capital redemption reserve an amount by which the nominal value of the shares redeemed exceeds the *aggregate* proceeds from the new issue (ie nominal value of new shares issued plus share premium) (s 170 (2)).

(i) In example (b) the accounting entries would be:

		£	£
DEBIT	Share capital account (redeemed shares)	10,000	
	Profit and loss account (premium)	500	
CREDIT	Cash (redemption of shares)		10,500
DEBIT	Cash (from new issue)	10,000	
CREDIT	Share capital account		10,000

No credit to the capital redemption reserve is necessary because there is no decrease in the creditors' buffer.

(ii) If the redemption in the same example were made by issuing 5,000 new £1 shares at par, and paying £5,500 out of distributable profits:

		£	£
DEBIT	Share capital account (redeemed shares)	10,000	
	Profit and loss account (premium)	500	
CREDIT	Cash (redemption of shares)		10,500
DEBIT	Cash (from new issue)	5,000	
CREDIT	Share capital account		5,000
DEBIT	Profit and loss account	5,000	
CREDIT	Capital redemption reserve		5,000

(iii) In the example (d) above (assuming a new issue of 10,000 £1 shares at a premium of 8p per share) the accounting entries would be:

		£	£
DEBIT	Cash (from new issue)	10,800	
CREDIT	Share capital account		10,000
	Share premium account		800
DEBIT	Share capital account (redeemed shares)	10,000	
	Share premium account	300	
	Profit and loss account	200	
CREDIT	Cash (redemption of shares)		10,500

No capital redemption reserve is required, as in (i) above. The redemption is financed entirely by a new issue of shares.

Redemption of shares out of capital

8.19 There is one further rule, which is a significant departure from the principle that shares must not be purchased or redeemed in a way which reduces non-distributable equity reserves. This rule applies to **private companies only** (provided that their articles of association authorise them to do so).

KEY TERM

A private company may redeem or purchase its own shares out of **capital** (ie non-redeemable share capital, capital redemption reserve, share premium account or revaluation reserve) but only on condition that the nominal value of shares redeemed (or purchased) both:

(a) Exceeds the proceeds of any new share issue to finance the redemption (or purchases).

(b) First exhausts the distributable profits of the company entirely.

8.20 In such a situation, a transfer must be made to the capital redemption reserve of the amount by which distributable profits exceed the premium on redemption or purchase. (If the premium on redemption or purchase exceeds the total of distributable profits, the difference must be deducted from non-redeemable share capital, and there will be no capital redemption reserve.)

8.21 EXAMPLE: REDEMPTION OF SHARES OUT OF CAPITAL

Suppose, for example, that Madigan Ltd has the following capital and reserves.

	£
Fully paid non-redeemable share capital	100,000
Fully paid redeemable share capital	40,000
	140,000
Distributable profits	18,000
	158,000

The redeemable shares are now to be redeemed at a cost of £46,000 (creating a premium of £6,000 on redemption). To partly cover the costs of redemption, a new issue of 25,000 ordinary £1 shares will be made at par.

The **permissible capital payment** under the Companies Act 1985 is:

	£	£
Cost of redemption		46,000
Less: proceeds of new issue	25,000	
distributable profits	18,000	
		43,000
Permissible capital payment		3,000

The distributable profits exceed the premium on redemption by £(18,000 – 6,000) = £12,000. A transfer of £12,000 will be made to the capital redemption reserve, leaving the company's capital and reserves as:

	£
Non-redeemable share capital	100,000
New shares issued	25,000
Capital redemption reserve	12,000
	137,000

The total capital is now £137,000 which is £3,000 less (the capital repayment) than the non-distributable reserves of the company before redemption (£140,000).

8.22 The rules explained above may seem lengthy and difficult to follow. However, you should bear in mind that **the purpose of the regulations is to protect creditors.** If a company pays out money to its shareholders, there may be insufficient 'liquid' funds left within the

business to pay its debts. The Companies Act 1985 tries to prevent creditors being 'cheated' out of repayments of the debts owing to them by 'underhand' prior payments to shareholders. (However, a private company is allowed to reduce its non-distributable reserves if it has first of all eliminated all its distributable reserves. This restricts the 'defence' for creditors provided by the Act.)

Commercial reasons for altering capital structure

8.23 These include the following.

- Greater security of finance
- Better image for third parties
- A 'neater' balance sheet
- Borrowing repaid sooner
- Cost of borrowing reduced

Question 6

Set out below are the summarised balance sheets of Argy plc and Bargy Ltd at 30 June 20X5.

	Argy £'000	*Bargy* £'000
Capital and reserves		
Called up share capital £1 ordinary shares	300	300
Share premium account	60	60
Profit and loss account	160	20
	520	380
Net assets	520	380

On 1 July 20X5 Argy plc and Bargy Ltd each purchased 50,000 of their own ordinary shares as follows.

Argy plc purchased its own shares at 150p each. The shares were originally issued at a premium of 20p. The redemption was partly financed by the issue at par of 5,000 10% redeemable preference shares of £1 each.

Bargy Ltd purchased its own shares out of capital at a price of 80p each.

Required

Prepare the summarised balance sheets of Argy plc and Bargy Ltd at 1 July 20X5 immediately after the above transactions have been effected.

Answer

Workings for Argy

	£	£
Cost of redemption (50,000 × £1.50)		75,000
Premium on redemption (50,000 × 50p)		25,000

No premium arises on the new issue.

Distributable profits

	£	£
Profit and loss account before redemption		160,000
Premium on redemption (must come out of distributable profits, no premium on new issue)		(25,000)
		135,000
Remainder of redemption costs	50,000	
Proceeds of new issue 5,000 × £1	(5,000)	
Remainder out of distributable profits		(45,000)
Balance on profit and loss account		90,000

Transfer to capital redemption reserve

	£
Nominal value of shares redeemed	50,000
Proceeds of new issue	(5,000)
Balance on CRR	45,000

BALANCE SHEET OF ARGY PLC AS AT 1 JULY 20X5

	£'000
Capital and reserves	
Preference shares	5
Ordinary shares	250
Share premium	60
Capital redemption reserve	45
	360
Profit and loss account	90
	450
Net assets	450

Workings for Bargy

	£
Cost of redemption (50,000 × 80p)	40,000
Discount on redemption (50,000 × 20p)	10,000
Cost of redemption	40,000
Distributable profits	(20,000)
Permissible capital payment (PCP)	20,000

Transfer to capital redemption reserve

	£
Nominal value of shares redeemed	50,000
PCP	20,000
Balance on capital redemption reserve	30,000

BALANCE SHEET OF BARGY LIMITED AS AT 1 JULY 20X5

	£'000
Capital and reserves	
Ordinary shares	250
Share premium	60
Capital redemption reserve	30
	340
Net assets	340

Chapter roundup

- Accounting for the **issue of shares and debentures** is a comparatively simple topic. The main complication is the use of application, allotment and call accounts, particularly when the issue price is to be paid in several instalments. Remember that the balances on these accounts must eventually be transferred to share capital or share premium accounts.
- **Revenue recognition** is straightforward in most business transactions, but some situations are more complicated. It is necessary to determine the **substance of each transaction, rather than the legal form**.
- You should be able to calculate **maximum distributions available to private and public companies** and to discuss the meaning of distributable and realisable profits.
- You must be able to carry out **simple calculations** showing the amounts to be transferred to the **capital redemption reserve** on purchase or redemption of own shares, how the amount of any **premium** on redemption would be treated, and how much the **permissible capital payment** would be for a private company.

Quick quiz

1 Define modified historical cost accounting.

2 Capital maintaince is concerned with sustaining the equity as business and is subject to two issues.

(i)

(ii)

3 List the limitations of HCA.

4 A rights issue involves a company issuing shares for no consideration to its members.

True ☐

False ☐

5 To which purposes can a share premium account be applied?

(i) Writing off share/debenture issue expenses
(ii) Paying a premium on redemption
(iii) Issuing fully paid bonus shares to members

Which is correct?

A (i) and (ii)
B (i) and (iii)
C (ii) and (iii)
D All the above

6 In general terms under HCA

- Revenue from the sale of goods is recognised on the ………………. ….. …………….. to the customer
- Revenue from services is recognised when the services have been …………….. and are ……………..

7 What are the profits statutorily available for distribution?

8 A company cannot make a distribution if this will reduce its net assets to below the value of its called up share capital plus undistributable reserves.

True ☐

False ☐

9 If a company has not got the power to reduce its issued share capital, per the articles of association, then it cannot do so.

True ☐

False ☐

10 A company can redeem shares out of which sources of funds?

(i) Distributable profits
(ii) Proceeds of new shares
(iii) The share premium account

A All three
B (i) and (ii)
C (ii) and (iii)
D (i) and (iii)

Answers to quick quiz

1 This involves recording transactions at their historical cost but some items such as fixed assets are revalued to a current value. (see para 1.18)

2 (i) The impact of inflation
(ii) What profits can be withdrawn (1.2)

3 Refer to para 1.6 to 1.15

4 False, that is a bonus issue. A rights issue involves offering new shares to existing shareholders.

5 D (8.4 to 8.6)

6 Date of delivery/performed/billable. (6.9)

7 See paragraph 7.2

8 True (7.4 Basic rule)

9 False, it can pass a special resolution to change the articles. (8.1)

10 B (8.16). Only a private company can redeem shares out of capital (share premium account) (8.19)

Now try the question below from the Exam Question Bank

Question to try	Level	Marks	Time
15	Exam level	20	36 mins

Part D
Performance

Chapter 12

INTERPRETATION OF ACCOUNTS

	Topic list	Syllabus reference	Ability required
1	The broad categories of ratios	(iv)	Application/Analysis
2	Profitability and return on capital	(iv)	Application/Analysis
3	Long-term solvency and stability	(iv)	Application/Analysis
4	Short-term solvency and liquidity	(iv)	Application/Analysis
5	Efficiencies	(iv)	Application/Analysis
6	Shareholders' investment ratios	(iv)	Application/Analysis
7	Accounting policies and the limitations of ratio analysis	(iv)	Comprehension
8	Reports on financial performance	(iv)	Comprehension

Introduction

You may remember some of the basic interpretation of accounts you studied at Stage 1. This chapter recaps and develops the calculation of ratios and covers more complex accounting relationships. More importantly this chapter looks at how ratios can be analysed, interpreted and how the results should be presented to management.

This is a key area which is likely to be examined at each sitting. It is not enough for you to master the calculation of the various ratios. You must consider the validity of the ratios you are calculating. You must look at the information on which the ratios are based, both financial and non-financial, and the information that they themselves provide. The most important element of any answer you will be required to give is your **use** of the ratios.

Wide reading is encouraged in this area. You should read professional journals and the business press It will give you in-sights which could be used in discussing performance.

You should be aware of the contents of the ASB's operating and financial review (OFR), which is discussed in Section 6, but you do not need a detailed knowledge of its contents.

If you want to look at real sets of accounts you could try the *Financial Times* Free Annual Reports Service - look in the FT at the London Share Service page.

Learning outcomes covered in this chapter

- **Calculate** a full range of accounting ratios
- **Analyse** financial statements to comment on the performance and position
- **Explain** the limitations of accounting ratio analysis

Syllabus content covered in this chapter

- The analysis of financial statements to interpret the position and performance of the business
- The application of ratio analysis to financial statements and its limitations

1 THE BROAD CATEGORIES OF RATIOS — Pilot paper

Focus on user needs

1.1 An underlying purpose of preparing financial statements is to provide **meaningful information** for **potential users** regarding **financial performance, financial position** and **financial adaptability**. As identified earlier, they fall into a few key categories.

- Shareholders and potential investors
- Management
- Creditors
- Bankers and other providers of finance.

1.2 In general, these users may calculate a range of ratios and performance indicators. However, they are likely to **interpret** them from their **own perspective**, based on their own particular **commercial needs and interests.** In practice, there may well be conflicts of interest between users. For example, **management** will focus on **profitability** whereas a **bank manager** might be more concerned about **solvency**. **Shareholders** are likely to be interested in how **value** is **generated** and sustained as well as **returns**.

Exam focus point

Your syllabus requires you to be able to interpret a set of accounts, in particular by the use of ratio analysis, and to present your analysis in the form of a report. This is a highly examinable subject area. You must be able not only to calculate the ratios, but also to discuss the meaning of your results.

A common thread is for you to discuss the impact of transactions during the year on the ratios calculated.

The May 2002 paper examined the business practices of three companies, whilst the November 2002 exam looked at the quality of management teams. In both cases, there was some detail provided in the profit and loss account to enable you to look at some non-standard ratios relating to the operations of the business.

The May 2003 paper asked candidates to review two takeover targets, one of which is a current supplier. Candidates were also asked to identify 'non-financial factors' which should be considered when deciding whether to acquire a company.

1.3 At its most basic, ratio analysis involves **comparing one figure against another** to produce a ratio, and then trying to interpret the meaning of the figure produced.

The broad categories of ratios

1.4 Broadly speaking, basic ratios can be grouped into five categories.

- **Profitability and return**
- **Long-term solvency and stability**
- **Short-term solvency and liquidity**
- **Efficiency (turnover ratios)**
- **Shareholders' investment ratios.**

1.5 Within each heading there are a number of standard measures or ratios that are traditionally calculated and generally accepted as meaningful indicators. However, **each individual business** must be **considered separately**, and a ratio that is meaningful for a manufacturing company may be completely meaningless for a financial institution. Avoid being **too mechanical when working out ratios.** Always be aware of the importance of **user focus.**

1.6 Further **useful insights** might also be gleaned from **companies' financial reports.**

(a) Comments in the **Chairman's report** and **directors' report**.

(b) A review of the **age and nature of the company's assets.**

(c) **Current and future developments** in the company's markets, at home and overseas, recent acquisitions or disposals of a subsidiary by the company.

(d) **Additional statements** and notes such as STRGL, note of historical profits and losses and reconciliation of movements in shareholders funds.

(e) **Exceptional items** in the P&L account.

(f) **Any other noticeable features** of the report and accounts, such as post balance sheet events, contingent liabilities, discontinued activities, qualified auditors' report, the company's taxation position, and so on.

(g) **Notes** dealing with **fixed assets.**

(h) **Notes** dealing with **employee details** and directors' remuneration.

1.7 Remember, the nature and scope of the analysis and the amount and quality of information available will depend on the circumstances and the brief provided. A shareholder may only have access to **published information,** whereas a **bank manager** is likely to be in a position to ask to see not only **financial statements**, but also documents such as **business plans,** periodic **management accounts** and **cash flow projections.**

1.8 In practice, you may be able to actually speak to management to obtain additional information. However, in an exam situation, you may have to identify what additional information might be useful and **explain tactfully** to the examiner how it might impact on your analysis and interpretation.

Industry specific performance indicators

1.9 In practice, businesses may also use a range of **industry and company specific ratios** to help them **manage the business** on a **day to day basis.**

Industry	Performance indicator
Hotels	Room occupancy
Accountants	Chargeable hours utilisation
Farms	Yields per acre
Hospitals	Patient waiting times
Pubs and restaurants	Till overs and unders
Motor manufacturer	Cars produced per worker
Training provider	Exam success rates
Airlines	Daily hours in air per plane

1.10 In practice, accounting firm and banks are developing **benchmarking services** for their clients whereby an individual client's **performance indicators** are shown (anonymously) alongside those of other subscribers to the **benchmarking survey.**

Holistic approach

1.11 Accounting ratios are only one part of the accountants diagnostic kit for analysing and interpreting financial statements. Other useful tools or sources of information, if available may comprise:

(a) The company's business plan
(b) Annual budgets
(c) Cash flow projections
(d) Management accounts
(e) Historic accounts figures (past trends)
(f) SWOT analysis
(g) Industry benchmark surveys
(h) Any other strategy or planning documents
(i) On line company and text search services
(j) Press releases and comments

1.12 The following diagram reinforces the importance of taking a **holistic approach** when reviewing a set of financial statements.

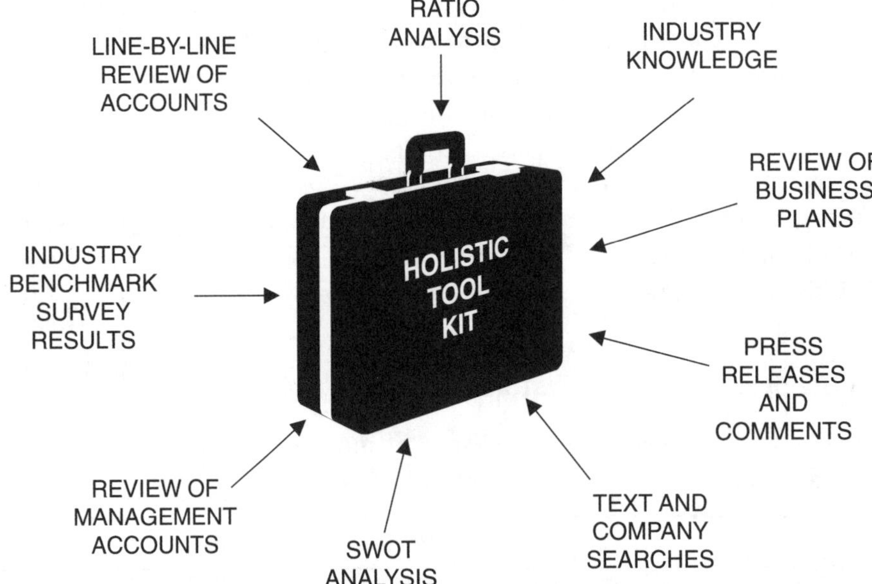

Basic ratios

1.13 The following are the **main accounting ratios** which would **traditionally** be **calculated.** However, in any question that requires you to interpret the financial statements of a company, you should **assess and select** the **most appropriate ratios** to use. Where necessary, you should also **be prepared to apply non-standard industry specific ratios** to support your interpretation.

	Accounting ratio	**Formula**
Profitability and return		
(a)	Gross margin	$\frac{\text{Gross profit}}{\text{Turnover}} \times 100$
(b)	Net margin	$\frac{\text{Profit on ordinary activities before interest and taxation (PBIT)}}{\text{Turnover}} \times 100$
(c)	Return on capital employed (ROCE)	$\frac{\text{Profit on ordinary activities before interest and taxation (PBIT)}}{\text{Capital employed}}$ where capital employed = total assets less current liabilities.
(d)	Asset turnover	$\frac{\text{Turnover}}{\text{Capital employed}}$
Long term solvency and stability		
(a)	Debt ratio	$\frac{\text{Total debt}}{\text{Total assets}}$
(b)	Capital gearing	$\frac{\text{Prior charge capital}}{\text{Total capital}}$
(c)	Debt/equity ratio	$\frac{\text{Prior charge capital}}{\text{Ordinary share capital and reserves}}$
(d)	Interest cover	$\frac{\text{Profit before interest and tax (PBIT)}}{\text{Interest charges}}$
(e)	Cash flow ratio	$\frac{\text{Net cash inflow}}{\text{Total debts}}$
Short term solvency and liquidity		
(a)	Current ratio	$\frac{\text{Current assets}}{\text{Current liabilities}}$
(b)	Quick ratio	$\frac{\text{Current assets less stocks}}{\text{Current liabilities}}$
(c)	Creditors turnover	$\frac{\text{Purchases}}{\text{Trade creditors}}$ or $\frac{\text{Trade creditors}}{\text{Purchases}} \times 365$
Efficiency		
(d)	Stock turnover	$\frac{\text{Cost of sales}}{\text{Stock}}$ or $\frac{\text{Stock}}{\text{Cost of sales}} \times 365$
(e)	Debtors turnover	$\frac{\text{Credit sales}}{\text{Trade debtors}}$ or $\frac{\text{Trade debtors}}{\text{Credit sales}} \times 365$
Shareholders' investment ratios		
(a)	Dividend cover	$\frac{\text{Earnings per share}}{\text{Net dividend per (ordinary) share}}$
(b)	Price earnings (P/E) ratio	$\frac{\text{Share price}}{\text{Earnings per share}}$
(c)	Dividend yield	$\frac{\text{Dividend on the share for the year}}{\text{Current market value of the share (ex div)}} \times 100$

Exam focus point

Be careful - read the exam question thoroughly. Statements providing monthly rather than the usual annual information have caught out candidates in the past. Do not automatically apply a formula using a 365-day year; a 30 or 31 day month may be appropriate instead.

1.14 EXAMPLE: CALCULATING RATIOS

The balance sheet and profit and loss account figures of Earwigo plc are provided to illustrate the calculation of ratios.

EARWIGO PLC PROFIT AND LOSS ACCOUNT
FOR THE YEAR ENDED 31 DECEMBER 20X8

	Notes	*20X8*	*20X7*
		£	£
Turnover	1	3,095,576	1,909,051
Operating profit	1	359,501	244,229
Interest	2	17,371	19,127
Profit on ordinary activities before taxation		342,130	225,102
Taxation on ordinary activities		74,200	31,272
Profit on ordinary activities after taxation		267,930	193,830
Dividend		41,000	16,800
Retained profit for the year		226,930	177,030
Earnings per share		12.8p	9.3p

EARWIGO PLC BALANCE SHEET
AS AT 31 DECEMBER 20X8

	Notes	*20X8*	*20X7*
		£	£
Fixed assets			
Tangible fixed assets		802,180	656,071
Current assets			
Stocks and work in progress		64,422	86,550
Debtors	3	1,002,701	853,441
Cash at bank and in hand		1,327	68,363
		1,068,450	1,008,354
Creditors: amounts falling due within one year	4	881,731	912,456
Net current assets		186,719	95,898
Total assets less current liabilities		988,899	751,969
Creditors: amounts falling due after more than one year			
10% first mortgage debenture stock 20Y4/20Y9		(100,000)	(100,000)
Provision for liabilities and charges			
Deferred taxation		(20,000)	(10,000)
		868,899	641,969
Capital and reserves			
Called up share capital	5	210,000	210,000
Share premium account		48,178	48,178
Profit and loss account		610,721	383,791
		868,899	641,969

NOTES TO THE ACCOUNTS

		20X8	20X7
1	*Turnover and profit*	£	£
	(i) Turnover	3,095,576	1,909,051
	Cost of sales	2,402,609	1,441,950
	Gross profit	692,967	467,101
	Administration expenses	333,466	222,872
	Operating profit	359,501	244,229
	(ii) Operating profit is stated after charging:		
	Depreciation	151,107	120,147
	Auditors' remuneration	6,500	5,000
	Leasing charges	47,636	46,336
	Directors' emoluments	94,945	66,675
2	*Interest*		
	Payable on bank overdrafts and other loans	8,115	11,909
	Payable on debenture stock	10,000	10,000
		18,115	21,909
	Receivable on short-term deposits	744	2,782
	Net payable	17,371	19,127
3	*Debtors*		
	Amounts falling due within one year		
	Trade debtors	884,559	760,252
	Prepayments and accrued income	97,022	45,729
		981,581	805,981
	Amounts falling due after more than one year		
	Trade debtors	21,120	47,460
	Total debtors	1,002,701	853,441

		20X8	20X7
		£	£
4	*Creditors: amounts falling due within one year*		
	Trade creditors	627,018	545,340
	Accruals and deferred income	81,279	280,464
	Corporation tax	108,000	37,200
	Other taxes and social security costs	44,434	32,652
	Dividend	21,000	16,800
		881,731	912,456
5	*Called up share capital*		
	Authorised ordinary shares of 10p each	1,000,000	1,000,000
	Issued and fully paid ordinary shares of 10p each	210,000	210,000

EARWIGO PLC

1.15 Review of year on year movements between 31 December 20X7 and 31 December 20X8

	Increase/(Decrease)
Turnover	62.2%
Operating profit	47.2%
Administration expenses	49.6%
Directors emoluments	42.4%
Net interest payable	(9.1%)
Profit on ordinary activities	52.0%
Taxation	137.3%
Profit on ordinary activities after tax	38.2%
PBIT	45.8%
Dividends	244.1%

1.16 Accounting ratios

	20X8	20X7
Profitability and return		
Gross margin	$\frac{692,967}{3,095,576} \times 100 = 22.4\%$	$\frac{467,101}{1,909,051} \times 100 = 24.5\%$
Net margin	$\frac{360,245}{3,095,576} \times 100 = 11.6\%$	$\frac{247,011}{1,909,051} \times 100 = 12.9\%$
ROCE	$\frac{360,245}{988,899} \times 100 = 36.4\%$	$\frac{247,011}{751,969} \times 100 = 32.8\%$
Asset turnover	$\frac{3,095,576}{988,899} = 3.1$ times	$\frac{1.909,051}{751,969} = 2.5$ times
Long term stability		
Debt ratio	$\frac{981,731}{1,870,630} \times 100 = 52.5\%$	$\frac{1,012,456}{1,664,425} \times 100 = 60.8\%$
Capital gearing	$\frac{100,000}{988,899} \times 100 = 10.1\%$	$\frac{100,000}{751,969} \times 100 = 13.3\%$
Long term solvency		
Debt/equity ratio	$\frac{100,000}{868,899} \times 100 = 11.5\%$	$\frac{100,000}{641,969} \times 100 = 15.6\%$
Interest cover	$\frac{360,245}{18,115} = 19.9$ times	$\frac{247,011}{21,909} = 11.3$ times
Cash flow ratio	$\frac{510,608}{981,731} \times 100 = 52.0\%$	$\frac{364,376}{1,012,456} \times 100 = 36.0\%$
Short term solvency/liquidity		
Current ratio	$\frac{1,068,450}{881,731} \times 100 = 121.2\%$	$\frac{1,008,354}{912,456} \times 100 = 110.5\%$
Quick ratio	$\frac{1,004,028}{881,731} \times 100 = 113.9\%$	$\frac{921,804}{912,456} \times 100 = 101.0\%$
Creditors turnover	$\frac{627,018}{2,402,609} \times 365 = 95.3$ days	$\frac{545,340}{1,441,950} \times 365 = 138.0$ days
Efficiency		
Stock turnover	$\frac{64,422}{2,402,609} \times 365 = 9.8$ days	$\frac{86,550}{1,441,950} \times 365 = 21.9$ days
Debtors turnover	$\frac{1,002,701}{3,095,576} \times 365 = 118.2$ days	$\frac{853,441}{1,909,051} \times 365 = 163.2$ days
Shareholder investment ratios		
Dividend cover	$\frac{267,930}{41,000} = 6.5$ times	$\frac{193,830}{16,800} = 11.5$ times

Workings

1 *Profit before interest and tax*

	20X8	20X7
	£	£
Profit on ordinary activities before tax	342,130	225,102
Interest payable	18,115	21,909
PBIT	360,245	247,011

2 *Capital employed*

Shareholders funds	868,899	641,969
Creditors: amounts falling due after more than one year	100,000	100,000
Long term provision for liabilities and charges	20,000	10,000
	988,899	751,969

3 *Total debts*

Creditors: amounts falling due within one year	881,731	912,456
Creditors: amounts falling due after more than one year	100,000	100,000
	981,731	1,012,456

4 *Total assets*

Tangible fixed assets	802,180	656,071
Current assets	1,068,450	1,008,354
	1,870,630	1,664,425

5 *Net cash inflow*

Operating profit	359,501	244,229
Depreciation	151,107	120,147
Increase in stocks	* -	-
Increase in debtors	* -	-
Increase in creditors	* -	-
	510,608	364,376

* Ignored for this purpose, because figures for 20X7 cannot be calculated as 20X6 accounts are not available.

6 *Quick assets*

Current assets	1,068,450	1,008,354
Less Stock and works-in-progress	(64,422)	(86,550)
	1,004,028	921,804

2 PROFITABILITY AND RETURN ON CAPITAL

Exam focus point

The November 2001 paper required a comparison of profitability and efficiency for two companies and an assessment of the quality of their management teams.

The impact of investments made on profitability ratios was tested in May 2002.

Gross margin

2.1 Earwigo's plc has increased its turnover significantly from 20X7 to 20X8 by 62.2%. Over this period, the gross margin has fallen from 24.5% to 22.4%.

2.2 Intuitively, there is a relationship between the level of sales and the gross margin. However, it is important to also consider the potential and **independent causes of fluctuations** in both sales levels and gross margins.

Sales levels	Gross profit margin
• Level of marketing effort and expenditure	• Pricing policy, discounts etc
• Product design and quality	• Sales mix
• Relocation of distribution outlets	• Production efficiency
• Service skills training	• Impact of inflation on costs
• Changes in consumer taste or product usage	• Control of waste and spillage
• General economic factors	• Sourcing of supplies, discounts etc
• Impact of legislation	• Stock valuation issues (obsolescence, overhead absorption, NRV etc)
• Competition	

2.3 Generally, the gross margin is an indicator of trading performance. Remember that **achievable margins** will **differ between industries**. In practice, you are likely to try to obtain additional information, such as **relevant industry benchmarking data**.

Net margin

2.4 Earwigo's net margin has fallen from 12.9% in 20X7 to 11.6% in 20X8. PBIT has increased from 20X7 to 20X8 by 45.8%. This is in line with the increase in operating profit for the year by 47.2%. Other items moving along similar lines are administration expenses and directors remuneration with increases of 49.6% and 42.4%, respectively.

2.5 **Net margin** is **not considered** to be **very meaningful** because of its **susceptibility** to **many factors**. In practice, it is difficult to carry out meaningful comparisons of net margins between companies. For example, one company may have purchased its buildings whereas another company prefer to rent its premises.

2.6 Trends in the net margin might provide pointers to the effectiveness of controls over the level of overheads. However, this would seem to be a **blunt tool** because there are **more direct ways** of **financially controlling overheads** for example by monitoring specific overhead accounts.

2.7 In practice, net profit is **more usefully compared** to factors such as **number of employees** or **square footage**.

ROCE

2.8 Earwigo's ROCE has improved from 32.8% in 20X7 to 36.4% in 20X8.

2.9 To assess the acceptability of these ratios **further information** is necessary.

(a) **Benchmark** against the ROCEs of other companies in the **same industry.**

(b) **Cost of servicing finance**. The level of return should be assessed against the returns available from **alternative investments** and should also reflect the level of **business risk** involved.

(c) **Target ROCE**. A comparison with **budgeted ROCE** may reveal whether management is **achieving expected returns**.

2.10 ROCE is probably the **key profitability ratio** in **measuring business performance**. It measures the **return generated** for investors against the **amount invested**. Because of its importance, ROCE is often referred to as the **primary ratio**.

2.11 There are certain **factors** which may **obscure** the **assessment** of ROCE.

(a) **Undervalued fixed assets**, such as property, may depress the capital employed figure and show a **rosier ROCE**.

(b) **Capitalised interest**, will increase capital employee and give a **more conservative ROCE**.

(c) **Aging fixed assets** mean lower capital employed and hence higher ROCE. However, this may indicate a variety of potential operational problems.

- Impending obsolescence/impairment
- Inefficiency owing to breakdowns
- Higher maintenance costs
- Probable labour intensive operation
- Competitive inefficiency

Review current carrying values and accumulated depreciation levels for clues of age of fixed assets. Learn to glean meaningful insights about the business from looking at the fixed assets note to the accounts.

(d) **Capitalised development costs**. Like capitalised interest above, will **depress ROCE**. Nevertheless the costs will hit reported profits, but only over a number of years, by way of depreciation or impairment.

(e) **Idle cash balances**. There is a school of thought that advocates these should be removed from capital employed. However, this is likely to give a **misleadingly better** ROCE. The ratio should effectively **measure all aspects of capital employed**.

Asset turnover

2.12 Earwigo plc has improved on its asset utilisation. This went up from 2.5 times in 20X7 to 3.1 times in 20X8.

2.13 Again, it is important to asses this ratio against available industry averages. **Manufacturing industries** are likely to be **capital intensive** and therefore have **low asset turnover**. On the other hand, **service industries** tend to be **human resource intensive** and hence likely to have relatively **high asset turnover**.

2.14 It might be tempting to think that a high profit margin is good, and a low asset turnover means sluggish trading. In broad terms, this is so. But **there is a trade-off between profit margin and asset turnover, and you cannot look at one without allowing for the other.**

(a) A high profit margin means a high profit per £1 of sales, but if this also means that sales prices are high, there is a strong possibility that sales turnover will be depressed, and so asset turnover lower.

(b) A high asset turnover means that the company is generating a lot of sales, but to do this it might have to keep its prices down and so accept a low profit margin per £1 of sales.

2.15 Remember that companies may well arrive at the same ROCE via different routes.

	Company A	*Company B*
Profit margin	20%	5%
Asset turnover	× 1	× 4
ROCE	20%	20%

3 LONG TERM SOLVENCE AND STABILITY

Debt ratio

3.1 Earwigo's debt ratio has shown an improvement from being 60.8% at the end 20X7 to being 52.5% at the end of 20X8.

3.2 There is no absolute guide to the maximum safe debt ratio, but as a **very general guide**, 50% is commonly regarded as a safe limit. In practice, many companies operate successfully with a higher debt ratio than this, but 50% is nonetheless a **helpful benchmark**. In addition, if the debt ratio is over 50% and getting worse, the company's debt position will be worth looking at more carefully.

3.3 In Earwigo's case, the debt ratio is quite high, mainly because of the large amount of current liabilities. However, the debt ratio has fallen from 60.8% to 52.5% between 20X7 and 20X8, and so the company appears to be improving its debt position.

Capital gearing

3.4 Earwigo plc's capital gearing ratio has fallen from 13.3% for 20X7 to 10.1% for 20X8.

3.5 Gearing **measures** the **relationship** between the **prior charge capital** of a company **and** its **total capital**. It is an indicator of the extent to which a company is reliant on prior charge capital as compared to equity capital.

Preference share capital is normally considered to be **prior charge capital**. Preference dividends must be paid out of profits before ordinary shareholders are entitled to an ordinary dividend. **Debentures** would usually **also** be classified as **prior change capital**.

3.6 **Total capital is ordinary share capital and reserves plus charge capital plus any long-term liabilities or provisions**. In **group accounts** we would also include **minority interests**. Do note that it is easier to identify the same figure for total capital as **total assets less current liabilities**, which you will find given to you in the balance sheet.

3.7 The level of gearing maintained by a company is likely to be part of its **corporate** and **financial strategy**. As with the debt ratio, there is **no absolute limit** to what a gearing ratio ought to be. A company with a gearing ratio of more than 50% is said to be high-geared, whereas low gearing means a gearing ratio of less than 50%.

3.8 In practice, **many companies** are **highly geared**. However, there are **risks** and **potential problems** associated with **high gearing**.

- **Prior changes** can **consume available profits**, leaving **little earnings for equity shareholders**.
- If **earnings** are **volatile**, this will have a consequential **impact** on the company **share price** (**given** a certain **price/earnings ratio**).
- As the company's **borrowing capacity decreases**, lenders will perceive a **greater risk** and hence the company's **marginal cost** of **borrowing** is **likely to rise**.
- If a **loss situation** prevails, the **financial viability** of the company may become **seriously challenged**.

3.9 Here is a little diagram that might help to reinforce your understanding of the implications of different financial structures.

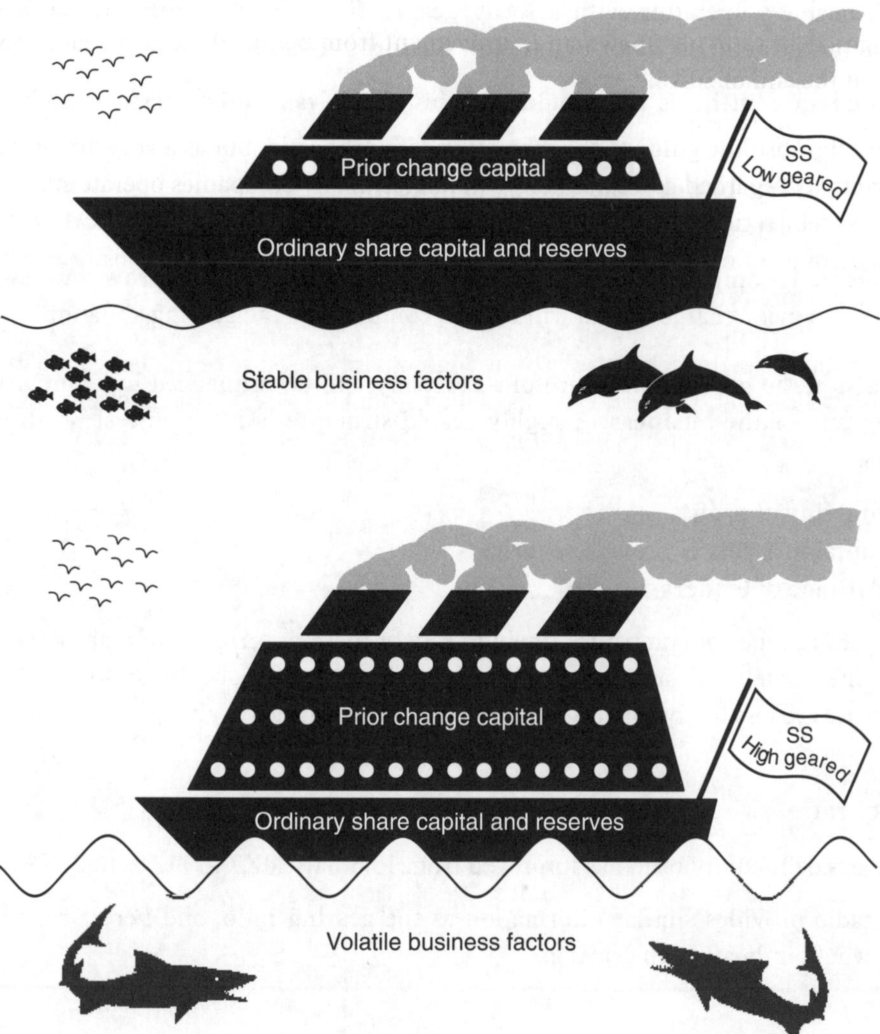

3.10 The two above scenarios can be seen within the context of four theoretical scenarios depicted in the two by two matrix below. This provides another tool which you might find useful in looking at a business.

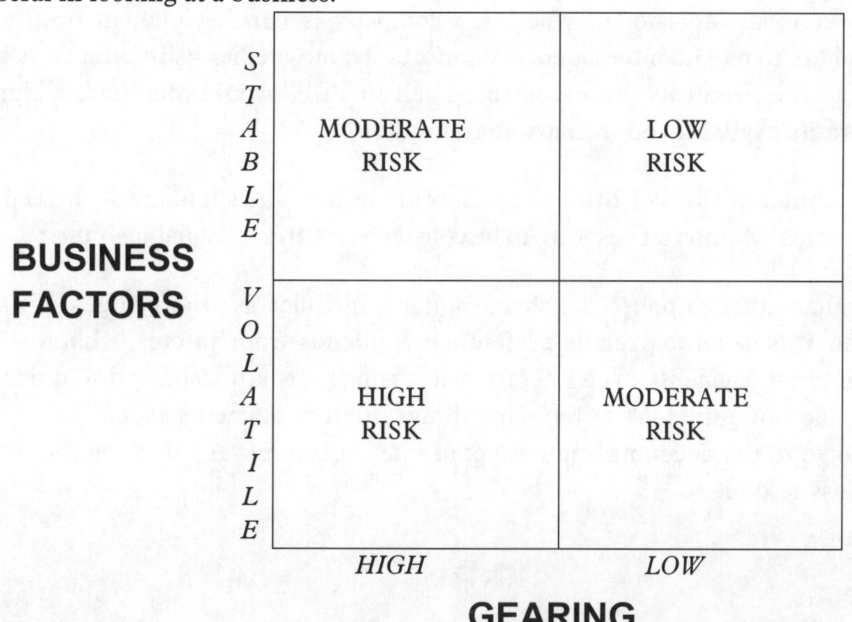

- A business operating with a **highly geared financial structure** and **volatile business factors** is likely to face **high business risk.**
- A business operating with a **lowly geared financial structure** and **stable business factors** structure is likely to have **low business risks.**
- **Moderate business risk** would probably be relevant to businesses with combinations of either:
  - **stable business factors** and **high gearing.**
  - **volatile business** factors and **low gearing.**

3.11 **Low geared companies** obviously have **more capacity** to **borrow money**. However increases in prior charge capital will in turn compromise the gearing situation!

3.12 In practice, the **gearing structure** of a company will be influenced by **company policy** as well **nature of the business**. A highly geared structure is likely to rest on three business factors.

- **Stability** of **profits**
- **Suitable assets** to provide **security**
- **Attitude** of **lenders**

3.13 Examples of types of companies likely to satisfy these criteria include property investment companies, hotels and supermarket chains. In general terms, companies in high technology industries are less likely to meet the criteria for sustaining a highly geared structure.

Debt/equity ratio

3.14 Earwigo's debt/equity ratio has improved from 15.6% in 20X7 to 11.5% in 20X8.

This radio provides similar information as the gearing ratio, and here a ratio of 100% or more would indicate high gearing.

Interest cover

3.15 Earwigo's interest cover has improved significantly from 11.3 times in 20X7 to 19.9 times in 20X8.

3.16 Interest cover is an indicator of whether a company is **earning enough profits before interest and tax to pay its interest costs comfortably,** or whether its interest costs are high in relation to the size of its profits, so that a fall in PBIT would then have a **significant effect on profits available for ordinary shareholders.**

3.17 Generally, an interest cover of 2 times or less would be low, and should really exceed 3 times before the company's interest costs are to be considered within acceptable limits.

3.18 Remember that although preference share capital is included as prior charge capital for the gearing ratio, **it is usual to exclude preference dividends from 'interest' charges.** We also look at all interest payments, even interest charges on short-term debt, and so interest cover and gearing do not quite look at the same thing. Interest payments should be taken gross from the **notes to the accounts** and not net of interest receipts as shown on the face of the profit and loss account.

3.19 **Low interest** cover suggests:

(a) Shareholders **dividends may be at risk**, because most profits are required to meet interest charges

(b) **Interest charges themselves** could be at **risk** if **profits decline further**.

3.20 Earwigo plc has more than sufficient interest cover. In view of the company's low gearing, this is not too surprising and so we finally obtain a picture of Earwigo plc as a company that does not seem to have a debt problem, in spite of its high (although declining) debt ratio.

Cash flow ratio

3.21 Earwigo's cash flow ratio has improved from 35.0% in 20X7 to 52.0% in 20X8.

3.22 The cash flow ratio is **the ratio of a company's net cash inflow to its total debts**.

(a) Net cash inflow is the amount of cash which the company has coming into the business from its operations. A suitable figure for net cash inflow can be obtained from the cash flow statement or profit and loss account, with depreciation being added back.

(b) Total debts are short-term and long-term creditors, together with provisions for liabilities and charges. A distinction can be made between debts payable within one year and other debts and provisions.

3.23 Obviously, a company needs to be earning enough cash from operations to be able to meet its foreseeable debts and future commitments, and the cash flow ratio, and changes in the cash flow ratio from one year to the next, provide a useful indicator of a company's cash position.

4 SHORT TERM SOLVENCY/LIQUIDITY

Current ratio

4.1 Earwigo's current ratio has improved from 1.1:1 in 20X7 to 1.2:1 in 20X8.

4.2 The current ratio is the **perennial 'standard' test of liquidity**. It can be obtained from the balance sheet.

4.3 Various books quote a range of acceptable current ratios from 1.0 to 2.0. Obviously 1.0 is a **baseline level** which ensures that the company has sufficient current assets to cover its current liabilities.

4.4 Current ratios are likely to **vary between industries** and may even **vary from company to company** within the same industry.

Exam focus point

If asked to calculate and comment on liquidity ratios, do not make the common mistake of limiting the discussion to comments about the ideal ratios and the change since last year. To score well on such a question you also need to comment on the change in the component parts of working capital and on any outflow on fixed assets.

4.5 In practice, various factors might influence the level of the current rates.

(a) **Seasonal factors**. Many companies have year ends after their busy period to minimise stock counting. The timing of the year end may well impact on the level of a company's current ratio.

Example

Santa Specials Limited is a company which specialises in buying and selling a special brand of Xmas Trees made out of genuine high grade Norwegian plastic.

The trees cost £10 each and are sold for £14 each. Details of its current assets and current liabilities per its monthly management accounts are as follows.

The company stocks up with trees in November. In December it sells the trees and in January it pays off the majority of its suppliers.

	31.11.X6	*31.12.X7*	*31.1.X8*
Current assets	£'000	£'000	£'000
Stock	100	-	-
Cash	50	190	91
	150	190	91
Current liabilities			
Trade creditors	100	100	1
Current ratio	1.5:1	1.9:1	91:1

This example illustrates how the **positioning of a company's year end** might **influence** the **level of its current ratio**. You could explore for yourself how the current ratio would change if the company were to pay a dividend in February!

The example also demonstrates the **potential for window dressing** by **processing creditors payments** though the accounting system but **not actually mailing the cheque**!

(b) **Timing of payment of long term liabilities**. This is an extension of the principle demonstrated in the Santa Specials example above. For example, consider the impact on the current ratio, if in March the company had to pay a long term liability.

The message here is that you need to **develop a good understanding** of the **business** and the **relevant industry** to help you make high quality comments in your examination.

Quick ratio

4.6 Earwigo's quick ratio has improved from 101.0% in 20X7 to 113.9% in 20X8.

4.7 Otherwise known as the acid test ratio, this indicator **focuses** on only those **current assets** that are **available** to **pay current liabilities when they fall due.**

4.8 Again a quick ratio of 1.0 is desirable but in practice companies might operate effectively at a lower level, depending on the particular business and industry.

4.9 Remembering the **holistic kit approach** suggested earlier. In practice, management is likely to use **cash flow projections** to enable a **proactive approach** to the **management** of its **liquidity**.

4.10 The quick ratio is as susceptible to window dressing as the current ratio, as described above.

Creditor's payment period

4.11 In 20X7, Earwigo took 138.0 days to settle its creditors, but this has accelerated to 95.3 days in 20X8.

4.12 This ratio measure the **average number of days taken to pay creditors.** Published financial statements are unlikely to disclose purchases so you may have to resort the using cost of sales in your calculation.

4.13 Factors to be considered in setting a supplier payment policy may pull in opposite directions.

(a) Delaying payments to creditors represents a source of interest free finance (However, an obvious question is whether suppliers will build this into their prices!)

(b) Slow payments may give an impression, rightly or wrongly, of liquidity problems. Any potential adverse impacts on the company's credit rating should be considered.

4.14 Public companies and members of groups where the parent is a public company, and the company does not qualify as a small or medium sized company under CA 1985, Section 247, must disclose 'creditor days' in respect of amounts due at the year end. This may influence a company's behaviour in relation to how quickly it pays its suppliers.

4.15 In addition, public sector bodies such as local authorities are likely to have publicly responsible credit payment targets. Of course, there may be private sector companies that have ethically driven policies for paying their suppliers quickly. It might be worth considering the converse impact on companies that have debtors who like to pay their creditors quickly.

4.16 In **certain circumstances,** businesses may be required by their **bankers** to **demonstrate their ability to clear their overdraft** on **specific dates** during the year. This will impact on the creditors payment period as well as the current ratio and quick ratio.

4.17 Again, the **creditors payment** period is **susceptible** to being **massaged** by **management.**

5 EFFICIENCY

Exam focus point

There was a full 20 mark question in the May 2001 exam on the working capital cycle. There were as many marks for the discussion of working capital issues as there were for the calculations.

Stock turnover

5.1 Earwigo has significantly improved its stock turnover rate from once every 21.9 days in 20X7 to once every 9.8 days in 20X8.

5.2 Stock turnover is an indicator of the **average number of days** a business takes to **sell an item of stock.** This can be calculated using the **figures** contained in **published accounts.**

5.3 Generally, there is **no universally acceptable level** at which stock should be turned over. A high stock turnover is considered to be better than a low turnover figure. However, in practice several aspects of **stock management policy** have to be balanced in setting a **target stock turnover** for the year.

- Lead times
- Seasonal fluctuations in orders
- Alternative uses of warehouse space
- Bulk buying discounts
- Likelihood of stock perishing or becoming obsolete.
- Minimising of stock holding costs

5.4 The **nature of the product traded** will impact on the stock turnover rate. For example, a **fruit and vegetable shop** is likely turnover its stock more frequently than say a **furniture retailer.**

5.5 A lengthening stock turnover period from one period to the next could indicate a slowdown in trading or build up in stock levels. **Consideration should be given to both business trading factors as well as stock management issues**, when seeking explanations for movements in stock turnover from one period to the next.

5.6 Also remember that:

(a) Excessively long stock turnover periods tend to increase the **risk of obsolesce**

(b) The computed turnover rate can be affected by the **timing of orders received or dispatched**, especially where these involve relatively **high values.**

5.7 **In practice**, many companies now use a '**just in time**' approach to stock control. This method seeks to **minimise stock holding costs**. Again, its suitability to a company will depend on the nature of the business including such as **alternative sources** and **level of customer loyalty.**

Debtor's turnover

5.8 Earwigo plc took an average of 118.2 days to collect its debtors in 20X8 as compared to 163.2 days in 20X7.

5.9 Debtors turnover is a **rough measure** of the **average length of time for a company's debtors to pay** what they owe the company.

5.10 The figure for sales should be taken as the turnover figure in the P & L account. The trade debtors are not the total figure for debtors in the balance sheet, which includes prepayments and non-trade debtors. The trade debtors figure will be itemised in an analysis of the debtors total, in a note to the accounts.

5.11 The estimate of debtor days is **only approximate**.

(a) The balance sheet value of debtors might be abnormally high or low compared with the 'normal' level the company usually has.

(b) Turnover in the P & L account is exclusive of VAT, but debtors in the balance sheet are inclusive of VAT. We are not strictly comparing like with like. (Some companies show turnover inclusive of VAT as well as turnover exclusive of VAT, and the 'inclusive' figure should therefore be used in these cases.)

5.12 Sales are usually made on 'normal credit terms' of payment within 30 days. Debtor days significantly in excess of this might be representative of poor management of funds of a business. However, some companies must allow generous credit terms to win customers.

Exporting companies in particular may have to carry large amounts of debtors, and so their average collection period might be well in excess of 30 days.

5.13 The **trend of the collection period (debtor days) over time is probably the best guide.** If debtor days are increasing year on year, this is indicative of a poorly managed credit control function (and potentially therefore a poorly managed company).

5.14 Stock turnover added to debtors turnover indicates how soon stock is converted into cash.

5.15 This is an area where an understanding of the business is important. For example, if you are analysing debtors turnover for a hotel you need to understand and the type of hotel it operates and hence the composition of its sales and debtors mix.

(a) Accommodation – non corporate guests paying cash for short stays.
(b) Accommodation – corporate guests staying on credit terms
(c) Catering – non-corporate guests paying each
(d) Catering – corporate guests with debtors accounts
(e) Conference facilities – corporate usage on debtors accounts.

5.16 It may be important to be able to **disaggregate the sale and debtors figures** to enable **meaningful debtors turnover figures** to be calculated. If your calculation can only be done on combined cash and credit sales figures, you should comment accordingly on its limitations and also suggest, in a positive way, what additional information might be useful.

5.17 Be careful over **cash oriented businesses** such as supermarket chains where any **debtors turnover** figure you might be able to calculate **is not likely to be very meaningful**.

5.18 Again when attempting to explain movements in debtors turnover rates between one year to the next, be aware of both **business trading factors** as well as **credit control factors**.

Business trading factors	Credit control factors
• Trying to attract more custom by allowing easier payment terms • Selling to higher collection risk debtors • Debtors themselves experiencing financial problems eg because of recession • Acquisition/loss of customers with quick settlement policies eg public sector organisations • General change in customer base • Debt factoring	• Efficiency of credit control department • Change in credit terms • Changes in policies on legal action to recover debts • Level of balances already written off

The cash cycle

5.19 The cash cycle describes the flow of **cash out** of a business and **back into it again** as a result of **normal trading operations**.

5.20 Cash goes out to pay for supplies, wages and salaries and other expenses, although payments can be delayed by taking some credit. A business might hold stock for a while and then sell it. Cash will come back into the business from the sales, although customers might delay payment by themselves taking some credit.

5.21 The main points about the cash cycle are as follows.

(a) The timing of cash flows in and out of a business does not coincide with the time when sales and costs of sales occur. **Cash flows out can be postponed by taking credit. Cash flows in can be delayed by having debtors.**

(b) The **time between making a purchase and making a sale also affects cash flows.** If stocks are held for a long time, the delay between the cash payment for stocks and cash receipts from selling them will also be a long one.

(c) **Holding stocks and having debtors** can therefore be seen as **two reasons why cash receipts are delayed**. Another way of saying this is that if a company invests in working capital, its cash position will show a corresponding decrease.

(d) Similarly, **taking credit** from creditors can be seen as a reason why **cash payments are delayed.** The company's liquidity position will worsen when it has to pay the creditors, unless it can get more cash in from sales and debtors in the meantime.

5.22 The liquidity ratios and working capital turnover ratios are used to test a company's liquidity, length of cash cycle, and investment in working capital.

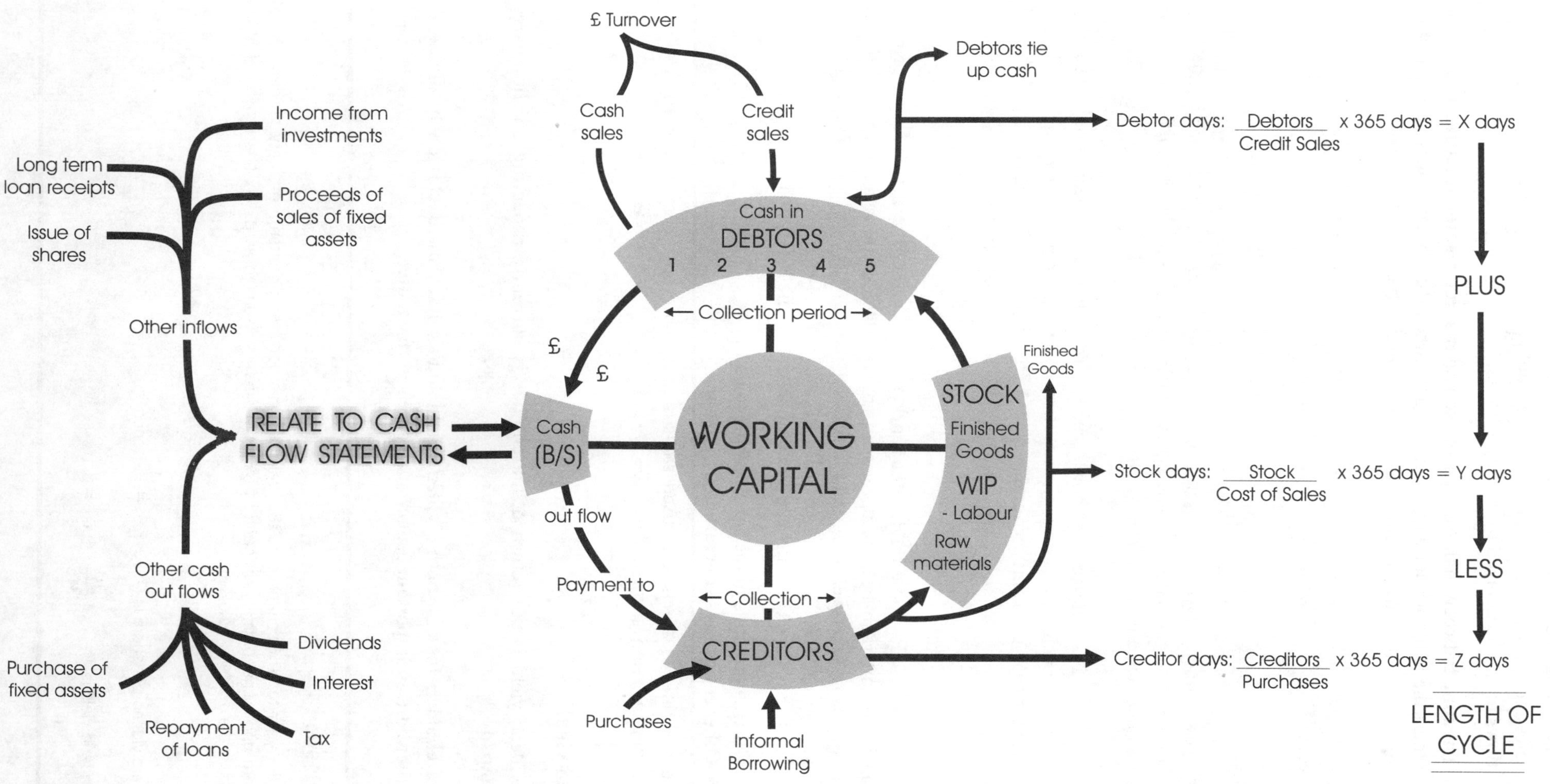
Long term loan receipts
Issue of shares
Income from investments
Proceeds of sales of fixed assets
Other inflows
RELATE TO CASH FLOW STATEMENTS
Other cash out flows
Purchase of fixed assets
Repayment of loans
Dividends
Interest
Tax
£ Turnover
Cash sales
Credit sales
Cash in DEBTORS
1 2 3 4 5
← Collection period →
£
£
Cash (B/S)
out flow
Payment to
WORKING CAPITAL
← Collection →
CREDITORS
Purchases
Informal Borrowing
STOCK
Finished Goods
WIP
- Labour
Raw materials
Finished Goods
Debtors tie up cash
Debtor days: Debtors / Credit Sales x 365 days = X days
PLUS
Stock days: Stock / Cost of Sales x 365 days = Y days
LESS
Creditor days: Creditors / Purchases x 365 days = Z days
LENGTH OF CYCLE

6 SHAREHOLDERS' INVESTMENT RATIOS

6.1 These are the ratios which **help equity shareholders and other investors to assess the value and quality of an investment in the ordinary shares of a company.** The value of an investment in ordinary shares in a listed company is its **market value**, and so investment ratios must have regard not only to information in the company's published accounts, but also to the current price, and **some of these ratios involve using the share price.**

6.2 Earnings per share is a valuable indicator of an ordinary share's performance and is the subject of FRS 14. This was dealt with in Chapter 9.

Dividend cover

6.3 Earwigo's dividend cover has fallen from 11.5 times in 20X7 to 6.5 times in 20X8. This is because the dividend paid has gone up by 244.1% over this period when the net profit after tax has only increased by 38.2%.

6.4 Divided cover is an indicator of how secure shareholders can expect to be in terms of their dividend being paid. It measures the number of times the current dividend could have been paid from available current earnings.

P/E ratio

6.5 The value of the P/E ratio reflects the **markets' appraisal** of the share's **future prospects.** It is an important ratio because it relates two key considerations for investors, the **market price** of a share and its **earnings capacity.**

6.6 The P/E ratio of one company can be **compared** with the P/E ratios of:

(a) Other **companies** in the **same business sector.**
(b) Other **companies generally.**

The P/E ratio is a generally used stock market ratio and is an important yardstick for assessing the relative worth of a share.

Dividend yield

6.7 Dividend yield is **the return a shareholder is currently expecting on the shares of a company.**

6.8 **Shareholders look for both dividend yield and capital growth. Obviously, dividend yield is therefore an important aspect of a share's performance.**

Question 1

In the year to 30 September 20X8, Wat-u-like plc declared an interim ordinary dividend of 7.4p per share and a final ordinary dividend of 8.6p per share. Assuming an ex div share price of 315 pence, what is the dividend yield?

Answer

The dividend per share is (7.4 + 8.6) = 16 pence

Dividend yield is $\frac{16}{315} \times 100 = 5.1\%$

Exam focus point

In the exam it is quite likely that you will have to make adjustments for a number of transactions before you can calculate ratios.

Earnings yield

6.9 Earnings yield is **a performance indicator** that is not given the same publicity as EPS, P/E ratio, dividend cover and dividend yield. It is **measured as earnings per share, grossed up, as a percentage of the current share price**. It therefore, indicates what the dividend yield could be if:

(a) The company paid out all its profits as dividend and retained nothing in the business.
(b) There were no extraordinary items in the P & L account.

6.10 Some companies retain a bigger proportion of their profits than others, and so the dividend yield between companies can vary for this reason. **Earnings yield overcomes the problem of comparison by assuming that all earnings are paid out as dividends.** *Note.* The earnings yield is equal to the dividend yield multiplied by the dividend cover.

7 ACCOUNTING POLICIES AND THE LIMITATIONS OF RATIO ANALYSIS

7.1 We discussed the disclosure of accounting policies in our examination of FRS 18. The choice of accounting policy and the effect of its implementation are almost as important as its disclosure. This is because the results of a company can be altered significantly by the choice of accounting policy.

Exam focus point

The November 2001 exam included an 8 mark question on the impact of the revaluation of fixed assets on key accounting ratios.

The impact of choice of accounting policies

7.2 Where accounting standards allow alternative treatment of items in the accounts, then the accounting policy note should declare which policy has been chosen. It should then be applied consistently.

7.3 The problem of comparability arises where companies with similar business adopt different policies. In recent years, financial reporting standard have restricted the selection of accounting treatments. However, there are a few areas where preparers are allowed significant choice.

Development expenditure

7.4 Although the criteria for capitalising development expenditure are very strict, the **choice** of whether to **capitalise and amortise or write off such costs** can have a significant impact on profit.

7.5 The **capitalisation** of development costs has **various impacts** on the figures used for analysing accounts.

(a) The capitalised development cost will be **amortised annually** and will **hit earnings,** including EPS, **until fully written off.**

(b) The capitalised development costs are included as part of **capital employed** and hence **ROCE will fall.**

(c) The **gearing ratio** will be **reduced** whilst any of the **capitalised development costs** are still **carried in the balance sheet.**

Capitalisation of finance costs

7.6 FRS 15 allows the capitalisation of finance costs that are **directly attributable** to the **construction** of tangible fixed assets. An entity **need not capitalise** finance costs. However, if an entity adopts a **policy of capitalisation** of finance costs, then it should be **applied consistently** to all tangible fixed assets where finance cost fall to be capitalised.

7.7 The impacts of capitalising finance costs in relation to tangible fixed assets on the calculation of accounting ratios is **similar** to those outlined above for **capitalised development costs.**

7.8 Remember that capitalisation of interest does not impact on interest cover because an appropriate adjustment must be made to include capitalised interest in the interest cover calculation.

Leases and the ninety per cent test

7.9 Companies might use the 90% test in such a way that ensures that leases are classified as **operating leases** and thereby kept **off the balance sheet**. This would entail **various impacts** on the accounting ratios.

(a) The **profit and loss account** would show a **lease charge instead of finance charges and depreciation.**

(b) The **balance sheet** would **not reflect the asset nor the corresponding liability. Capital employed** and **ROCE** would remain **roughly the same.**

(c) **Long term debt** will be **less** under an **operating lease scenario** with little impact on equity interests. Hence, the **gearing ratio** is **likely** to **fall significantly.**

Tangible fixed asset revaluation

7.10 Revaluation of fixed affects various figures shown in the accounts.

(a) The total amount of **depreciation written off** through the profit and loss account over the life of the asset **will increase. Reported profits** will therefore be **lower.**

(b) **Distributable profits** are however **not affected.** A **portion of revaluation reserves** may be **transferred to profit and loss reserves** as they become realised as result of additional depreciation of disposal.

(c) **Shareholder** funds, **capital employed** and **total net assets** will **increase.**

(d) **Debt** will be **unaffected.**

7.11 These changes in accounts balances will have consequential impacts on accounting ratios.

- The **gearing ratio** will **decrease**
- **ROCE** will **fall**
- **EPS** will also **fall**

Areas of judgment and estimation

7.12 The accounting standards specify detailed requirements in many areas of accounting and financial reporting. However, there still remains **significant scope** for the area of **professional judgement** in preparing accounts.

Accounts area	Scope for professional judgement on:
Tangible fixed assets	Depreciation rates and methods
Stocks	Overhead cost inclusion Net realisable value estimate
Long-term contracts	Turnover and profit recognition Decision to treat as long-term contract
General provisions	Existence of obligation Likelihood of transfer of economic benefit Measurement of liability

Limitations of ratio analysis

7.13 The consideration of how accounting policies may be used to massage company results leads us to some of the other limitations of ratio analysis. These can be summarised as follows.

(a) **Availability of comparable information.**
(b) **Use of historical/out of date information.**
(c) **Ratios are not definitive - they are only a guide.**
(d) **Interpretation needs careful analysis and should not be considered in isolation.**
(e) **It is a subjective exercise.**
(f) **It can be subject to manipulation and window dressing.**
(g) **Ratios are not defined in standard form.**
(h) **They are a type of tool in a more holistic approach (see section 1.11)**

Exam focus point

In the exam, always bear these points in mind; you may even be asked to discuss such limitations, but in any case they should have an impact on your analysis of a set of results.
The May 2002 paper required discussion of the limitations of using the annual report in reviewing business practices.

Question 2

The following are a selection of accounting ratios for a range of UK listed public companies in various industries ie

- Furniture
- Recruitment and business services
- Supermarket
- Cruise liner holidays
- Bakery shops

Review the table provided, then have a go at trying to identify which ratios relate to which industry. Write your response into the space provided at the foot of the table.

Standard ratios	*Company A*	*Company B*	*Company C*	*Company D*	*Company E*
Gross margin	8.0%	61.3%	49.6%	24.0%	-
ROCE	17.4%	26.3%	11.6%	10.1%	29.2%
Asset turnover	2.9 times	3.4 times	2.5 times	0.7 times	2.7 times
Current ratio	0.8:1	0.7:1	1.4:1	0.7:1	1.1:1
Stock turnover	20.4 days	15.7 days	102.2 days	12.0 days	N/A
Debtors turnover	1.1 days	0.5 days	15.0 days	5.8 days	56.2 days
Creditors turnover	40.0 days	54.7 days	53.7 days	30.2 days	-
Non-standard ratio					
Staff costs per employee	£17,566	£9,211	£22,279	£9,672	£24,646
Report date	1999	2000	2001	2000	2001
Industry involved					

Answer

Company	*Industry*
A	Supermarket chain
B	Bakery shop chain
C	Furniture retailer
D	Cruise holiday operator
E	Recruitment and business services

Operating and Financial Review (OFR)

7.14 The ASB document *Operating and Financial Review* is mentioned in the examinable documents for Paper 2.5. It introduces a statement which is **voluntary rather than mandatory**. It applies mainly to listed companies, but also those large corporations where there is a legitimate public interest. Such companies would be called on to produce an Operating and Financial Review (OFR) in their financial statements.

7.15 The purpose of the OFR is to provide:

> 'a framework for the directors to discuss and analyse the business's performance and the factors underlying its results and financial position, in order to assist users to assess for themselves the future potential of the business.'

7.16 The OFR should be developed in format and content to suit each organisation, but there would be some **essential features** of an OFR. It should:

(a) **Be written in a clear style and as succinctly as possible,** to be readily understandable by the general reader of annual reports, and should include only matters that are likely to be significant to investors.

(b) **Be balanced and objective,** dealing even-handedly with both good and bad aspects.

(c) **Refer to comments** made **in previous statements** where these have **not** been **borne out by events.**

(d) **Contain analytical discussion** rather than merely numerical analysis.

(e) **Follow a 'top-down' structure,** discussing individual aspects of the business in the context of a discussion of the business as a whole.

(f) Explain the reason for, and effect of any **changes in accounting policies**.

(g) **Make it clear how any ratios or other numerical information given relate to the financial statements.**

(h) **Include discussion of:**

(i) **Trends and factors** underlying the business that have affected the results but are not expected to continue in the future.

(ii) **Known events, trends and uncertainties** that are expected to have an impact on the business in the future.

7.17 The OFR is in two sections.

(a) **Operating review**

(i) Operating results for the period
(ii) Dynamics of the business
(iii) Investments for the future
(iv) Profit for the year, recognised gains/losses etc
(v) Dividends, EPS
(vi) Accounting policies

(b) **Financial review**

(i) Capital structure and treasury policy
(ii) Funds
(iii) Current liquidity
(iv) Going concern
(v) Balance sheet values

7.18 A statement of compliance with the OFR statement is not required, although it might be helpful to the users of the accounts. You can see that the OFR should be of great benefit to less sophisticated users of accounts as it should carry out the analysis of a company's performance on the user's behalf. It should thus highlight the important items in the current year annual report, as well as drawing out 'those aspects of the year under review that are relevant to an assessment of future prospects'.

8 REPORTS ON FINANCIAL PERFORMANCE

8.1 You may have experience already in writing reports within your organisation. Accountants are called upon to write reports for many different purposes. These range from very formal reports, such as those addressed to the board of directors or the audit committee, to one-off reports of a more informal nature.

8.2 The following chart is provided as an aid memoire to help you tackle accounts analysis questions in exams. You, of course, **may have an equally valid approach**, based on your **own practical experience**.

Identify:
- The purpose of you analysis and interpretation.
- The audience to which your comments are to be addressed.

↓

Review the accounts to develop an overall familiarity with the nature of the company, the industry in which it operates, company size, key account balances, significant changes between years etc.

↓

Do a quick brainstorm of the general business issues behind the accounts; market conditions, policies, consumer behaviour, management skills, competition, stability, volatility, risks, etc.

↓

Identify any additional information you might, in practice, have looked at. Recognised any limitations of your ratio analysis (in a positive way in an exam).

↓

Select and calculate an appropriate set of ratios, including any helpful non-standard or industry specific ratios.

↓

Perform comparisons and suggest explanation. Remember the importance of keeping comments constructive.

↓

Ensure your answer or report is relevant and helpful to the needs of the users.

Checklist for report writing

8.3 The following checklist for report writing is provided to help you identify factors that should be considered.

(a) **Purpose or terms of reference**

(i) Who are the **users** of the report and what are their **interests**?

(ii) What is the **purpose** of the report? What type of **focus** should it have?

(iii) What is wanted, **definite recommendations or less specific advice**?

(iv) What **outcomes** might the report have if its findings or **recommendations** are **implemented**?

(v) What **previous reviews or reports** have there been on the subject, what did they find or recommend, and what action was taken on these findings, or recommendations?

(b) **Information in the report**

(i) What is the **source** of each item of information in the report?

(ii) What is the **age** of the information? Is it **up-to-date**?

(iii) What **period** does the report **cover** - a month, a year?

(iv) How can the **accuracy** of the information be checked and **verified**? To what extent might it be subject to error?

(v) What **other information** might be useful.

(c) **Preparing the report**

(i) Decide on **structure** of report; headings, sub headings, summary, appendices and other aspects.

(ii) Decide on balance between **analysis** and **solution orientation**.

(iii) Consider **style** and **tone**.

(iv) For exam purposes, use an **easy** to follow **numbering system**.

(v) Be aware of putting content over in bite-size (**mark oriented**) chunks!

(vi) Beware of tact and diplomacy. Be **constructive**, not **critical**.

(d) **User-friendliness of the report**

(i) What **use** will the report be in its present form? What **action** is it intended to **trigger**?

(ii) Does the report meet the requirements of the **terms of reference**?

(iii) Will the users who asked for the report be **delighted**?

Format of reports in the examination

Exam focus point

In an examination your time is limited and you are under pressure. To make life a little easier, we suggest that you adopt the following format for any report you are requested to write.
Remember that report writing involves skill – you need to practice it till you can write clearly, positively and quickly under exam conditions.

REPORT (OR MEMORANDUM)

To:	Board of Directors (or Chief Accountant, etc)	
From:	Financial Controller	**Date:**
Subject:	Report format	

Body of report

Signed: Accountant

8.4 If you adopt this style in your practice questions, you should end up producing it automatically. This should ensure that you **do not lose any presentation marks**. Remember if the **question asks specifically for a report**, your **answer must look like a report**.

8.5 Now you have considered the knowledge and skills you will need to produce a report for the examiner. You might like to have a go at doing the following question.

Question 3

The following information has been extracted from the recently published accounts of Seymour Marx plc.

SEYMOUR MARX PLC
EXTRACTS FROM THE PROFIT AND LOSS ACCOUNT

	20X9	*20X8*
	£'000	£'000
Sales	11,200	9,750
Cost of sales	8,460	6,825
Net profit before tax	465	320
This is after charging:		
Depreciation	360	280
Debenture interest	80	60
Interest on bank overdraft	15	9
Audit fees	12	10

SEYMOUR MARX PLC
BALANCE SHEET AS AT 30 APRIL

	20X9	*20X8*
	£'000	£'000
Fixed assets	1,850	1,430
Current assets		
Stock	640	490
Debtors	1,230	1,080
Cash	80	120
	1,950	1,690
Current liabilities		
Bank overdraft	110	80
Creditors	750	690
Taxation	30	20
Dividends	65	55
	955	845
Total assets less current liabilities	2,845	2,275
Long-term capital and reserves		
Ordinary share capital	800	800
Reserves	1,245	875
	2,045	1,675
10% debentures	800	600
	2,845	2,275

The following ratios are those calculated for Seymour Marx plc, based on its published accounts for the previous year, and also the latest industry average ratios:

	Seymour Marx plc 30 April 20X8	*Industry average*
ROCE (capital employed = equity and debentures)	16.70%	18.50%
Profit/sales	3.90%	4.73%
Asset turnover	4.29	3.91
Current ratio	2.00	1.90
Quick ratio	1.42	1.27
Gross profit margin	30.00%	35.23%
Debtors control	40 days	52 days
Creditors control	37 days	49 days
Stock turnover	13.90	18.30
Gearing	26.37%	32.71%

Required

(a) Calculate comparable ratios (to two decimal places where appropriate) for Seymour Marx plc for the year ended 30 April 20X9. All calculations must be clearly shown.

(b) Write a report to your board of directors analysing the performance of Seymour Marx plc, comparing the results against the previous year and against the industry average.

Answer

(a)

	20X8	20X9	Industry average
ROCE	$\frac{320+60}{2,275}$ = 16.70%	$\frac{465+80}{2,845}$ = 19.16%	18.50%
Profit/sales	$\frac{320+60}{9,750}$ = 3.90%	$\frac{465+80}{11,200}$ = 4.87%	4.73%
Asset turnover	$\frac{9,750}{2,275}$ = 4.29x	$\frac{11,200}{2,845}$ = 3.94x	3.91x
Current ratio	$\frac{1,690}{845}$ = 2.00	$\frac{1,950}{955}$ = 2.04	1.90
Quick ratio	$\frac{1,080+120}{845}$ = 1.42	$\frac{1,230+80}{955}$ = 1.37	1.27
Gross profit margin	$\frac{9,750-6,825}{9,750}$ = 30.00%	$\frac{11,200-8,460}{11,200}$ = 24.46%	35.23%

	20X8	20X9	Industry average
Debtors turnover	$\frac{1,080}{9,750}$ × 365 = 40 days	$\frac{1,230}{11,200}$ × 365 = 40 days	52 days
Creditors turnover	$\frac{690}{6,825}$ × 365 = 37days	$\frac{750}{8,460}$ × 365 = 32days	49 days
Stock turnover	$\frac{6,825}{490}$ = 13.9x	$\frac{8,460}{640}$ = 13.2x	18.30x
Gearing	$\frac{600}{2,275}$ = 26.37%	$\frac{800}{2,845}$ = 28.12%	32.71%

(b) (i)

REPORT

To: *Board of Directors*
From: *Management accountant* Date: *xx/xx/xx*
Subject: *Analysis of performance of Seymour Marx plc*

This report should be read in conjunction with the appendix attached which shows the relevant ratios (from part (a)).

1 **Trading and profitability**

1.1 Return on capital employed has improved considerably between 20X8 and 20X9 and is now higher than the industry average.

1.2 Net income as a proportion of sales has also improved noticeably between the years and is also now marginally ahead of the industry average. Gross margin, however, is considerably lower than in the previous year and is only some 70% of the industry average.

1.3 The above suggests either that there has been a change in the cost structure of Seymour Marx plc or that there has been a change in the method of cost allocation between the periods. Either way, this is a marked change that requires further investigation.

1.4 The company appears to be in a period of transition as sales have increased by nearly 15% over the year and it would also appear that new fixed assets have been purchased.

1.5 Asset turnover has declined between the periods although the 20X9 figure is in line with the industry average. This reduction might indicate that the efficiency with which assets are used has deteriorated,

(a) The assets acquired in 20X9 have not yet fully contributed to the business.
(b) A longer term trend would clarify the picture.

2 **Liquidity and working capital management**

2.1 The current ratio has improved slightly over the year and is marginally higher than the industry average. It is also in line with what is generally regarded as satisfactory (2:1).

2.2 The quick ratio has declined marginally but is still better than the industry average. This suggests that Seymour Marx plc has no short term liquidity problems and should have no difficulty in paying its debts as they become due.

2.3 Debtors as a proportion of sales is unchanged from 20X8 and are considerably lower than the industry average. Consequently, there is probably little scope to reduce this further.

2.4 Consideration should be given to the likelihood that there may be pressure in the future from customers to increase the period of credit given.

2.5 The period of credit taken from suppliers has fallen from 37 days' purchases to 32 days' and is much lower than the industry average.

2.6 The above trends suggest that it may be possible to finance any additional debtors by negotiating better credit terms from suppliers.

2.7 Stock turnover has fallen slightly and is much slower than the industry average and this may partly reflect stocking up ahead of a significant increase in sales.

2.8 The above suggests that there may be some danger that the stock could contain certain obsolete items that may require writing off.

2.9 The relative increase in the level of stock has been financed by an increased overdraft which may reduce if the stock levels can be brought down.

2.10 The high levels of stock, overdraft and debtors compared to that of creditors suggests a labour intensive company or one where considerable value is added to bought-in products.

3 **Gearing**

3.1 The level of gearing has increased only slightly over the year and is below the industry average.

3.2 The return on capital employed is nearly twice the rate of interest on the debentures, hence profitability is likely to be increased by a modest increase in the level of gearing.

Signed: Accountant

Exam focus point

The above is quite a brief and focused answer but clearly includes 17 points (5+10+2). Marks would also be allocated for the heading and the sign off.

You may well find the above numbering system provides a marks-orientated approach for discursive questions generally.

Commercial awareness

8.6 Your interpretation should always demonstrate a **'real world' commercial awareness** sought by examiners. To develop this business acumen may involve a **variety of activities** on your part in addition to your formal academic studies.

(a) **Reading publications** such as the Financial Times, Economist etc.

(b) Watching the **business coverage** on **television** channels

(c) Taking on an **interest** in business of your **employer** or your **clients**, including discussing their **real concerns**

(d) Obtaining **published financial reports** for a range of companies in **different industry** sectors and developing an understanding of their financial structures and the **business factors** they face.

Exam focus point

Part of any question on interpretation of accounts is likely to test your ability to identify non-financial factors. Try to keep these in mind as you beaver away through the number crunching.

8.7 A useful address in this regard is the free FT annual reports service. Do have a look at the advert on the advert on the FT '*London share service*' page.

Chapter roundup

- This chapter has taken you through basic ratio analysis in a fairly comprehensive fashion. The ratios you should be able to calculate and/or comment on are as follows.
  - **Profitability and return**
    - Gross margin on sales
    - Return on capital employed
    - Net profit as a percentage of sales
    - Asset turnover ratio
  - **Long term solvency and stability**
    - Debt ratio
    - Gearing ratio
    - Debt/equity ratio
    - Interest cover
    - Cash flow ratio
  - **Short term solvency and liquidity**
    - Current ratio
    - Quick ratio (acid test ratio)
    - Creditors turnover
  - **Efficiency**
    - Stock turnvover
    - Debtors turnover
  - **Shareholders' investment ratios**
    - Earnings per share
    - Dividend cover
    - P/E ratio
    - Dividend yield
    - Earnings yield
- With the exception of the last three ratios, where the share's market price is required, all of these ratios **can be calculated from information in a company's published accounts.**
- Ratios provide **information through comparison**:
  - **trends** in a company's ratios from **one year to the next**, indicating an improving or worsening position
  - in some cases, **against a 'norm', or 'standard'**;
  - in some cases, **against the ratios of other companies** or **benchmarks**, although differences between one company and another should be taken into consideration.
- You must realise that, however many ratios you can find to calculate, **numbers alone will not answer a question**. You *must* interpret all the information available to you and support your interpretation with ratio calculations.
- Remember that the financial ratios must be viewed in conjunction with the **commercial** and **business issues** that might impact on a business. It is vital that your reports demonstrate **commercial awareness** and not just number crunching ability.

Quick quiz

1 Brainstorm a list of sources of information which would be useful in interpreting a company's accounts.

2 ROCE is $\frac{\text{Profit on ordinary activities before interest and tax}}{\text{Capital employed}}$.

True ☐

False ☐

3 Company Q has a profit margin of 7%. Briefly comment on this.

4 The debt ratio is a company's long term debt over its net assets.

True ☐

False ☐

5 Cash flow ratio is the ratio of:

A Gross cash inflow to total debt
B Gross cash inflow to net debt
C Net cash inflow to total debt
D Net cash inflow to net debt

6 List the formulae for:

(a) Current ratio
(b) Quick ratio
(c) Debtor days
(d) Stock turnover

7 List six limitations to ratio analysis.

Answers to quick quiz

1 There are a number of sources (see para 1.6 and para 1.11). Information on competitors and the economic climate are obvious items of information.

2 True (1.13)

3 You should be careful here. You have very little information. This is a low margin but you need to know what industry the company operates in. 7% may be good for a major retailer.

4 False. It is the ratio of total debt to total assets (1.13)

5 C (.1.13)

7 Compare your list to that in paragraph 7.13

Now try the questions below from the Exam Question Bank

Number	Level	Marks	Time
16	Exam level	20	36 mins
17	Exam level	20	36 mins
18	Exam level	20	36 mins

Part E
External audit

Chapter 13

EXTERNAL AUDIT

	Topic list	Syllabus reference	Ability required
1	External audit	(i)	Comprehension
2	The powers and duties of the external auditor	(i)	Comprehension
3	The audit report	(i)	Comprehension

Introduction

You have been introduced to external audit at foundation level in your paper 1 studies. Here we look further at the **role of the external auditors**. If you work for an organisation which is audited (internally or externally), you should try to talk to the auditors about the audit and gather as much information as possible. Because it is the audit of an organisation you know well, you should gain some insight into the role of the auditor.

The external auditors are employed to check the good **stewardship** of the directors of the company and the truth and fairness of the financial statements. To enable them to do this they have certain **rights and duties**. When the audit is completed and the auditors are satisfied with the information and explanations provided, an **audit report** is issued. The audit report is the instrument by which the auditors express an **opinion** on the truth and fairness of the financial statements. In section 3 we look at the standard audit report and its **qualification** when the auditors are not completely satisfied with the results of the audit. Although we refer to SASs, you are **not** required to learn them for the exam.

Learning outcomes covered in this chapter

- **Explain** the role of the auditor
- **Explain** the elements of the audit report and the qualifications of that report

Syllabus content covered in this chapter

- The powers and duties of the external auditors: the audit report and its qualification for accounting statements not in accordance with best practise.

1 EXTERNAL AUDIT **Pilot paper, 5/01**

Exam focus point

External audit came up in the pilot paper. A total of sixteen marks was available for describing the external auditors responsibilities and the differences between qualified and unqualified audit reports. 10 marks in the compulsory section of the May 2001 exam were available for a description of the auditors duties and how the audit report is affected by disagreement.

1.1 In the modern commercial environment, businesses which are operated as companies with limited liability need to produce accounts to indicate how successfully they are performing. However the owners of a business require something more than accounts because the managers responsible for preparing them may, either unintentionally or by deliberate manipulation, produce accounts which are misleading. An independent examination of the accounts is needed so that the owners of the business can assess how well management have discharged their *stewardship*.

Definition of an audit

1.2 The Auditing Practices Board (APB) is the main standard setting body for external auditors in the United Kingdom.

KEY TERM

An **audit** is an exercise whose objective is to enable auditors to express an opinion whether the financial statements give a true and fair view (or equivalent) of the entity's affairs at the period end and of its profit and loss (or income and expenditure) for the period then ended and have been properly prepared in accordance with the applicable reporting framework (for example relevant legislation and applicable accounting standards) or, where statutory or other specific requirements prescribe the term, whether the financial statements "resent fairly".

1.3 This wording follows very closely that of the auditors' report on financial statements, which we will look at later.

1.4 First of all, though, we need to look at what an audit is really about. This is the subject matter of the APB's Statement of Auditing Standards SAS 100 *Objective and general principles governing an audit of financial statements*. The first 'Statement of Auditing Standards' in SAS 100 is as follows.

SAS 100.1

In undertaking an audit of financial statements auditors should do the following.

(a) Carry out procedures designed to obtain sufficient appropriate audit evidence, in accordance with Auditing Standards contained in SASs, to determine with reasonable confidence whether the financial statements are free of material misstatement.

(b) Evaluate the overall presentation of the financial statements, in order to ascertain whether they have been prepared in accordance with relevant legislation and accounting standards.

(c) Issue a report containing a clear expression of their opinion on the financial statements.

1.5 The SAS's explanatory material highlights the credibility given to financial statements by the auditors' opinion; it provides '**reasonable assurance** from an **independent** source that they present a true and fair view'. That is to say the audit report reassures readers of the accounts that the accounts have been examined by a **knowledgeable, impartial** professional. SAS 100 goes on to stress further the importance of auditors acting **independently** and **ethically**.

Limitations of audit

1.6 There are provisos, of course. First of all, the auditors' opinion is *not:*

- A guarantee of the future viability of the entity
- An assurance of the management's effectiveness and efficiency

The auditors are reporting on past events and can in no way guarantee the future financial success of the company. The opinion is based on financial matters and does not cover many other aspects of an entity.

Responsibility of directors

1.7 Most importantly, the standard makes clear that the auditors do not bear any responsibility for the preparation and presentation of the financial statements.

SAS 100

The responsibility for the preparation and presentation of the financial statements is that of the directors of the entity. Auditors are responsible for forming and expressing an opinion on the financial statements. The audit of the financial statements does not relieve the directors of any of their responsibilities. (SAS 100, Para 6)

Forming an opinion

1.8 The assurance auditors give is governed by the fact that auditors use **judgement** in deciding what audit procedures to use and what conclusions to draw, and also because:

- **Auditors do not check every item** in the accounting records
- Accounting and control systems have inherent limitations
- **Client staff** might **not tell the truth**, or may collude in fraud
- **Audit evidence indicates** what is **probable** rather than what is certain

Auditors can only express an opinion; they cannot certify whether accounts are completely correct.

1.9 Material misstatements may exist in financial statements and auditors will plan their work on this basis, with **professional scepticism**. SAS 100 makes it clear that, even where auditors assess the risk of litigation or adverse publicity as very low, they must still perform sufficient procedures according to auditing standards. There can never be a reason for carrying out an audit of a lower quality than that demanded by the auditing standards.

SAS 100.2

In the conduct of any audit of financial statements auditors should comply with the ethical guidance issued by their relevant professional bodies.

The expectations gap

1.10 There are some common misconceptions in relation to the role of the auditors, even among 'financially aware' people, including the following examples.

- Many people think that the auditors report to the directors of a company, rather than the members.

- Some think that a qualified audit report is more favourable than an unqualified audit report, whereas the converse is true.
- There is a perception that it is the auditors' duty to detect fraud, when in fact the detection of fraud is the responsibility of the directors.

1.11 These findings highlight the 'expectations gap' between what auditors do and what people in general think that they do. Add the fact that many 'financially aware' people do not look at the report and accounts of a company they are considering investing in, and you have some sobering facts for the auditors to contemplate!

1.12 Some of the recent large company collapses have emphasised the need to reduce the expectation gap. For this reason, reports such as those of the Cadbury and Hampel Committee reports on corporate governance have been published. They aim to reduce the expectations gap by laying out a code of conduct for directors, as well as making suggestions for the content of company reports.

THE SCOPE OF EXTERNAL AUDIT

Statutory and non-statutory audits

1.13 Audits are required under statute in the case of a large number of undertakings, including the following.

Undertaking	*Principal Act*
Limited companies	Companies Act 1985
Building societies	Building Societies Act 1965
Trade unions and employer associations	Trade Union and Labour Relations Act 1974
Housing Associations	Various acts depending on the legal constitution of the housing association, including: Industrial and Provident Societies Act 1965; Friendly and Industrial and Provident Societies Act 1968; Housing Act 1980; Companies Act 1985; Housing Association Act 1985.
Certain charities	Various acts depending on the status of the charity, including special Acts of Parliament.
Unincorporated investment businesses	Regulations made under the Financial Services Act 1986.

1.14 **Non-statutory audits** are performed by independent auditors because the owners, proprietors, members, trustees, professional and governing bodies or other interested parties want them, rather than because the law requires them. In consequence, auditing may extend to every type of undertaking which produces accounts.

- Clubs
- Charities (assuming that an audit is not statutory)
- Sole traders
- Partnerships

1.15 Auditors may also give an audit opinion on statements other than annual accounts.

- Summaries of sales in support of a statement of royalties
- Statements of expenditure in support of applications for regional development grants

- The circulation figures of a newspaper or magazine

1.16 In all such audits the auditors must take into account any **regulations** contained in the internal rules or constitution of the undertaking such as:

- The rules of clubs, societies and charities
- Partnership agreements

Advantages of the non-statutory audit

1.17 In addition to the advantages common to all forms of audit, including the verification of accounts, recommendations on accounting and control systems and the possible detection of errors and fraud, the audit of the accounts of a **partnership** may be seen to have the following advantages.

(a) It can provide a means of **settling accounts** between the partners.

(b) Where audited accounts are available this may make the **accounts more acceptable** to the **Inland Revenue** when it comes to agreeing an individual partner's liability to tax. The partners may well wish to take advantage of the auditors' services in the additional role of tax advisers.

(c) The **sale of** the business or the **negotiation of loan** or overdraft facilities may be facilitated if the firm is able to produce audited accounts.

(d) An audit on behalf of a '**sleeping partner**' is useful since generally such a person will have little other means of checking the accounts of the business, or confirming the share of profits due to him or her.

Question 1

Some of the advantages above will also apply in the audit of the accounts of a sole trader, club or charity. Which ones? And can you think of others? Have a go and jot down your thoughts.

External and internal audit

1.18 We have discussed auditing in particular in the context of the APB definition quoted at the start of this section. The definition relates to the work of *external* auditors, independent persons brought in from outside an organisation to review the accounts prepared by management. **Internal auditors** perform a different role, which we covered briefly at Paper 1, and will in more depth with Paper 10.

1.19 The management of an organisation will wish to establish systems to ensure that business activities are carried out efficiently. They will institute clerical, administrative and financial controls.

1.20 Larger organisations may appoint full-time staff whose function is to monitor and report on the running of the company's operations. **Internal** audit staff members are one type of control. Although some of the work carried out by internal auditors is similar to that performed by external auditors, there are important distinctions between the nature of the two functions.

DIFFERENCES BETWEEN EXTERNAL AND INTERNAL AUDITS		
	External	*Internal*
Independence	Independent of organisation	Appointed by management
Responsibilities	Fixed by statute	Decided by management
Report to	Members	Management
Scope of work	Express an opinion on truth and fairness of accounts	Consider whatever financial and operational areas management determines

The chronology of an audit

1.21 The chart on the next page outlines the normal main stages of an audit.

1.22 Before examining each stage in detail it is worth stating the more important duties of the auditors of a limited company. They must satisfy themselves that:

- Proper **accounting records** have been **kept**
- The **accounts** are in **agreement** with the **accounting records**
- The **accounts** have been **prepared** in accordance with the **Companies Act**, and relevant **accounting standards**
- The **balance sheet** shows a **true and fair view** of the **state** of the **company's affairs** and the **profit** and **loss account** shows a **true and fair view** of the results for the period

The objects of most other audits will be broadly similar.

1.23 Thus a major part of the auditors' work will involve:

(a) **Making such tests** and enquiries as they consider necessary to form an opinion as to the reliability of the accounting records as a basis for the preparation of accounts.

(b) **Checking the accounts** against the underlying records.

(c) **Reviewing the accounts** for compliance with the Companies Act and accounting standards.

1.24 We will now look at the various stages identified in the diagram shown on the next page.

Determine audit approach

Stage 1

1.25 The first stage in any audit should be to determine its scope and the auditors' general approach. For statutory audits the scope is clearly laid down in the Companies Act as expanded by the SASs.

1.26 Auditors should prepare an **audit plan** to be placed on the audit file. The purpose of this memorandum is to provide a record of the major areas to which the auditors attach special significance and to highlight any particular difficulties or points of concern peculiar to the audit client.

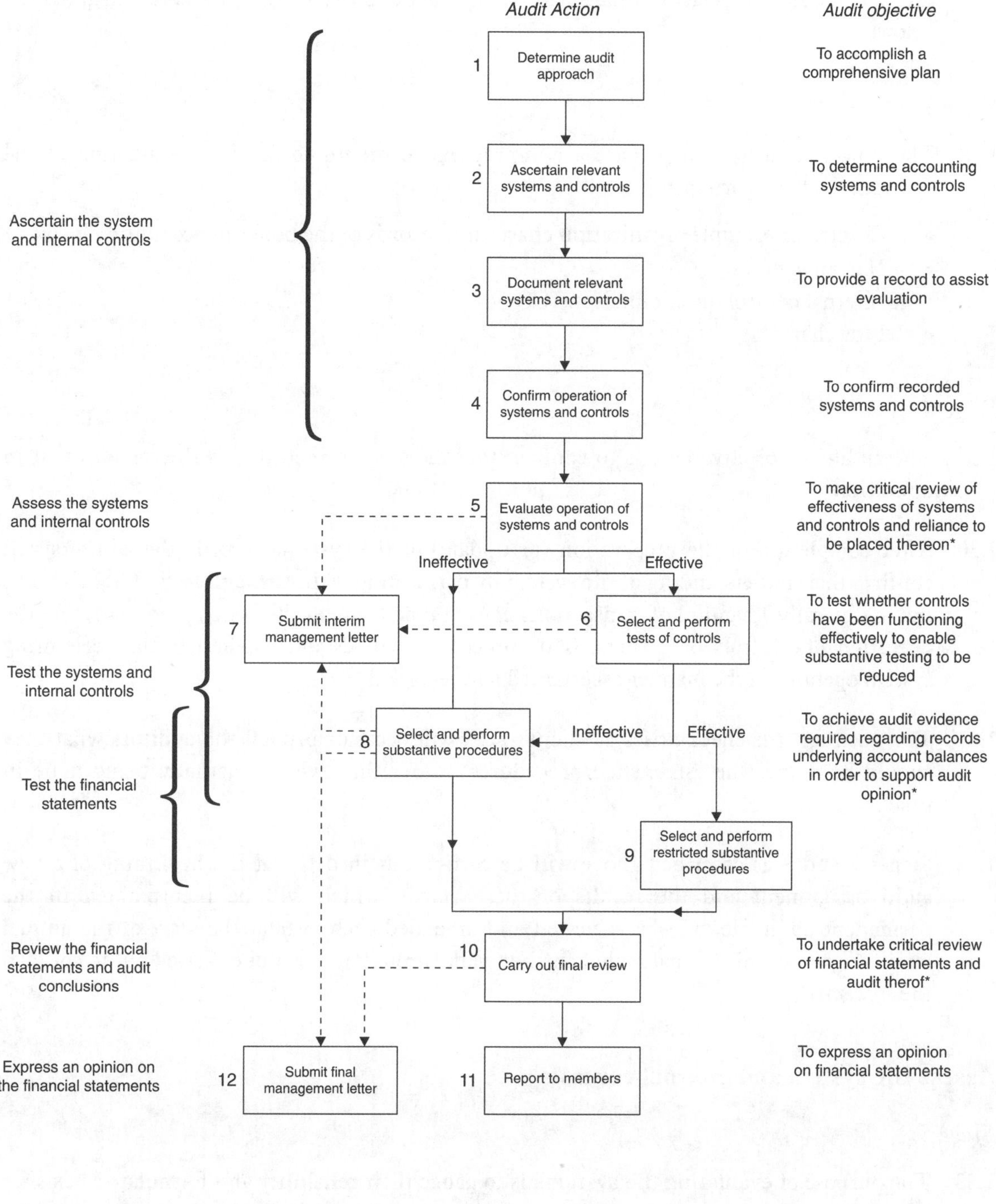

Ascertain the system and internal controls

Stage 2

1.27 The objective at this stage is to determine the **flow of documents** and **extent of controls** in existence. This is very much a fact-finding exercise, achieved by discussing the accounting system and document flow with all the relevant departments, including typically, sales, purchases, cash, stock and accounts personnel. It is good practice to make a rough record of the system during this fact finding stage, which will be converted to a formal record at Stage 3 below.

Stage 3

1.28 The objective here is to prepare a **comprehensive record** to facilitate evaluation of the systems. Such a record may include

- Charts, for example organisation charts and records of the books of account
- Narrative notes
- Internal control questionnaires (ICQs)
- Flowcharts

Stage 4

1.29 The auditors' objective here is to confirm that the **system recorded** is the same as that in **operation**.

1.30 After completion of the preparation (or update) of the systems records the auditors will confirm their understanding of the system by performing **walk-through** tests. These involve tracing literally a handful of transactions of each type through the system and observing the operation of controls over them. This procedure will establish whether the accounting system operates in the manner ascertained and recorded.

1.31 The need for this check arises as client's staff will occasionally tell the auditors what they should be doing (the established procedures) rather than what is actually being done in practice.

1.32 Stages 2 and 3 as described above will be carried out in detail at the beginning of a new audit assignment and the results of these stages, which will be incorporated in the permanent audit file, will be reviewed and amended each year at the start of the annual audit. As part of this annual review further walk-through tests will be carried out to confirm the system.

Assess the system and internal controls

Stage 5

1.33 The purpose of **evaluating the systems** is to gauge their reliability and formulate a basis for testing their effectiveness in practice. Following the evaluation, the auditors will be able to recommend improvements to the system and determine the extent of the further tests to be carried out at Stages 6 and 8 below.

Test the system and internal controls

Stage 6

1.34 Given effective controls, the objective is to select and perform tests designed to establish compliance with the system. One of the most important points underlying modern auditing is that, if the controls are strong, the records should be reliable and consequently the amount of detailed testing can be reduced.

1.35 Auditors should however check that the controls are as effective in practice as they are on paper. They will therefore carry out **tests of controls**. These are like walk-through checks in so far as they are concerned with the workings of the system. They differ in that they:

- Are concerned only with those areas subject to effective control
- Cover a representative sample of transactions throughout the period
- Are likely to cover a larger number of items than walk-through tests

1.36 The conclusion drawn from the results of a test of controls may be either:

(a) That the **controls are effective**, in which case the auditors will only need to carry out restricted substantive procedures.

(b) That the **controls are ineffective** in practice, although they had appeared strong on paper, in which case the auditors will need to carry out more extensive substantive procedures.

1.37 Stage 6 should only be carried out if the controls are evaluated at Stage 5 as being effective. If the auditors know that the controls are ineffective then there is no point in carrying out tests of controls which will merely confirm what is already known. Instead the auditors should go straight on to carry out full substantive procedures.

Stage 7

1.38 After evaluating the systems and carrying out tests of controls, auditors normally send management an **interim management letter** identifying weaknesses and recommending improvements.

Test the financial statements

Stages 8 and 9

1.39 These tests are not concerned with the workings of the system, but with substantiating the figures in the books of account, and eventually, in the final accounts themselves.

1.40 Substantive tests also serve to assess the effect of errors, should errors exist. Before designing a substantive procedure it is essential to consider whether any errors produced could be significant. If the answer is 'NO' there is no point in performing a test.

Review the financial statements

Stage 10

1.41 'The aim of the overall review is to determine the overall reliability of the accounts by making a critical analysis of content and presentation.

Express an opinion

Stage 11

1.42 The report to the members is the end product of the audit in which the auditors express their opinion of the accounts.

Stage 12

1.43 The final letter to management is an important non-statutory end product of the audit. Its purpose is to make further suggestions for improvements in the systems and to place on record specific points in connection with the audit and accounts.

Risk-based audits

1.44 In recent years there has been a shift towards risk-based auditing. This refers to the development of auditing techniques which are responsive to **risk factors** in an audit. Auditors apply judgement to determine what level of risk pertains to different areas of a client's system and devise appropriate audit tests. This approach should ensure that the greatest audit effort is directed at the riskiest areas, so that the chance of detecting errors is improved and excessive time is not spent on 'safe' areas.

1.45 The increased use of risk-based auditing reflects two factors.

(a) The growing **complexity** of the business environment increases the danger of fraud or misstatement; factors such as the developing use of computerised systems and the growing internationalisation of business are relevant here.

(b) Pressures are increasingly exerted by audit clients for the auditors to keep **fee levels down** while providing an improved level of service.

Risk-based auditing is responsive to both factors. The stages of the audit shown in the diagram will still be followed in a risk-based audit.

2 THE POWERS AND DUTIES OF THE EXTERNAL AUDITOR

Duties

2.1 The audit of a limited company is governed by **statute**. The auditor has certain powers and duties which are in place to ensure the audit is conducted **without any restrictions** to its **scope and accuracy**. The auditors must report on **every** balance sheet and profit and loss account laid before the company in a general meeting.

Rights

2.2 The Companies Act allows auditors certain **statutory rights** which enable them to carry out their duties.

Access to records	The right of access to the books, accounts and vouchers of the company at all times.
Information and **explanations**	The right to expect from the company's officers the information and explanations they think are necessary for the performance of their duties as auditors.
Attendance at, and notice of, **general meetings**	The right to attend all general meetings of the company and to receive all notices of, and communications relating to, such meetings which any member of the company is entitled to receive.
Right to speak at general meetings	The right to be heard at any general meetings which they attend on any part of the business which concerns them as auditors.
Right to **receive written resolutions**	The right to receive a copy of any written resolution proposed.
Right to require the **laying of the accounts**	The right to give written notice of a general meeting for the purpose of laying the accounts and reports before the company (if elective resolution dispensing with the laying of the accounts is in force).

Rights to information

2.3 The auditor has a right to all information and explanations they consider necessary. If they do not receive them they should say so in their audit report.

2.4 It is an offence for a company's officer to knowingly or recklessly make a statement in any form to the auditor which is materially misleading, false or deceptive.

3 THE AUDIT REPORT

Statutory requirements

Requirements of the 1985 Act

3.1 The Companies Act requires the auditors to state *explicitly* (s 235) whether in their opinion the annual accounts have been properly prepared in accordance with the Act and in particular whether a **true and fair view** is given.

(a) The balance sheet should reflect the **state of the company's affairs** at the end of the financial year.

(b) The profit and loss account should give the **company's profit or loss** for the financial year.

3.2 In addition certain requirements are reported on by **exception**; the auditor only has to report if they have not been met. The following are matters with which the auditors *imply* satisfaction in an unqualified report under s 237 of the Companies Act 1985.

(a) **Proper accounting records** have been kept and proper returns adequate for the audit received from branches not visited.

(b) The **accounts** are in **agreement** with the **accounting records** and returns.

(c) **All information** and **explanations** have been **received** as the auditors think necessary and they have had access at all times to the company's books, accounts and vouchers.

(d) **Details** of **directors' emoluments** and other benefits have been correctly **disclosed** in the financial statements.

(e) **Particulars of loans** and other **transactions** in favour of **directors** and others have been correctly **disclosed** in the financial statements.

(f) The information given in the **directors' report** is **consistent** with the **accounts**.

Directors' emoluments

3.3 The auditors should include in their report the required disclosure particulars of directors' emoluments and transactions with directors, if these requirements have not been complied with in the accounts (s 237). This means that the auditors will carry out various procedures to ensure that they are aware of all such emoluments and transactions by reference to directors' service contracts, board minutes, cash book payments and so on. Benefits received in kind may be particularly hard to identify.

SAS 600 Auditors' Reports on financial statements

SAS 600.1

Auditors' reports on financial statements should contain a clear expression of opinion, based on review and assessment of the conclusions drawn from evidence obtained in the course of the audit.

3.4 The auditors' report should be placed before the financial statements. The directors' responsibilities statement should be placed before the auditors' report.

Basic elements of the auditors' report

SAS 600.2

Auditors' reports on financial statements should include.

(a) A title identifying the person or persons to whom the report is addressed.

(b) An introductory paragraph identifying the financial statements audited.

(c) Separate sections, appropriately headed, dealing with:

 (i) Respective responsibilities of directors (or equivalent persons) and auditors
 (ii) The basis of the auditors' opinion
 (iii) The auditors' opinion on the financial statements

(d) The manuscript or printed signature of the auditors.

(e) The date of the auditors' report.

3.5 The following is given as an example of an unqualified audit report in an appendix to the SAS. You will *not* need to reproduce an audit report in the examination.

Example 1. Unqualified opinion: company incorporated in Great Britain

AUDITORS' REPORT TO THE SHAREHOLDERS OF XYZ PLC

We have audited the financial statements on pages ... to ... which have been prepared under the historical cost convention (as modified by the revaluation of certain fixed assets) and the accounting policies set out on page ....

Respective responsibilities of directors and auditors

As described on page ... the company's directors are responsible for the preparation of financial statements. It is our responsibility to form an independent opinion, based on our audit, on those statements and to report our opinion to you.

Basis of opinion

We conducted our audit in accordance with Auditing Standards issued by the Auditing Practices Board. An audit includes examination, on a test basis, of evidence relevant to the amounts and disclosures in the financial statements. It also includes an assessment of the significant estimates and judgements made by the directors in the preparation of the financial statements, and of whether the accounting policies are appropriate to the company's circumstances, consistently applied and adequately disclosed.

We planned and performed our audit so as to obtain all the information and explanations which we considered necessary in order to provide us with sufficient evidence to give reasonable assurance that the financial statements are free from material misstatement, whether caused by fraud or other irregularity or error. In forming our opinion we also evaluated the overall adequacy of the presentation of information in the financial statements.

Opinion

In our opinion the financial statements give a true and fair view of the state of the company's affairs as at 31 December 20.. and of its profit (loss) for the year then ended and have been properly prepared in accordance with the Companies Act 1985.

Registered auditors

Address

Date

3.6 The report recommends the use of standard format as an aid to the reader, including headings for each section, for example 'Qualified opinion'. The title and addressee and the introductory paragraph are fairly self explanatory.

Statements of responsibility and basic opinion

SAS 600.3

(a) Auditors should distinguish between their responsibilities and those of the directors. Their report should include:

(i) A statement that the financial statements are the responsibility of the reporting entity's directors.

(ii) A reference to a description of those responsibilities when set out elsewhere in the financial statements or accompanying information.

(iii) A statement that the auditors' responsibility is to express an opinion on the financial statements.

(b) Where the financial statements or accompanying information (for example the directors' report) do not include an adequate description of directors' relevant responsibilities the auditors' report should include a description of those responsibilities.

Example wording of a description of the directors' responsibilities for inclusion in a company's financial statements

3.7

Company law requires the directors to prepare financial statements for each financial year which give a true and fair view of the state of affairs of the company and of the profit or loss of the company for that period. In preparing those financial statements, the directors are required to:

(a) Select suitable accounting policies and then apply them consistently.

(b) Make judgements and estimates that are reasonable and prudent.

(c) State whether applicable accounting standards have been followed, subject to any material departures disclosed and explained in the financial statements (large companies only).

(d) Prepare the financial statements on the going concern basis unless it is inappropriate to presume that the company will continue in business (if no separate statement on going concern is made by the directors).

The directors are responsible for keeping proper accounting records which disclose with reasonable accuracy at any time the financial position of the company and to enable them to ensure that the financial statements comply with the Companies Act 1985. They are also responsible for safeguarding the assets of the company and hence for taking reasonable steps for the prevention and detection of fraud and other irregularities.

This wording can be adapted to suit the specific situation.

Explanation of auditors' opinion

SAS 600.4

Auditors should explain the basis of their opinion by including in their report:.

(a) A statement as to their compliance or otherwise with Auditing Standards, together with the reasons for any departure therefrom.

(b) A statement that the audit process includes

(i) Examining, on a test basis, evidence relevant to the amounts and disclosures in the financial statements.

(ii) Assessing the significant estimates and judgements made by the reporting entity's directors in preparing the financial statements.

(iii) Considering whether the accounting policies are appropriate to the reporting entity's circumstances, consistently applied and adequately disclosed.

(c) A statement that they planned and performed the audit so as to obtain reasonable assurance that the financial statements are free from material misstatement, whether caused by fraud or other irregularity or error, and that they have evaluated the overall presentation of the financial statements. (SAS 600.4)

3.8 Other than in exceptional circumstances, a departure from an auditing standard is a limitation on the scope of work undertaken by the auditors.

Expression of opinion

> **SAS 600.5**
>
> An auditors' report should contain a clear expression of opinion on the financial statements and on any further matters required by statute or other requirements applicable to the particular engagement.

3.9 An unqualified opinion on financial statements is expressed when in the auditors' judgement they give a true and fair view (where relevant) and have been prepared in accordance with relevant accounting or other requirements. This judgement entails concluding whether:

(a) The financial statements have been prepared using **appropriate, consistently applied accounting policies.**

(b) The financial statements have been **prepared** in accordance with **relevant legislation, regulations** or **applicable accounting standards** (and that any departures are justified and adequately explained in the financial statements).

(c) There is **adequate disclosure** of all information relevant to the proper understanding of the financial statements.

Date and signature of the auditors' report

> **SAS 600.9**
>
> (a) Auditors should not express an opinion on financial statements until those statements and all other financial information contained in a report of which the audited financial statements form a part have been approved by the directors, and the auditors have considered all necessary available evidence.
>
> (b) The date of an auditors' report on a reporting entity's financial statements is the date on which the auditors sign their report expressing an opinion on those statements.

Forming an opinion on financial statements

3.10 Appendix 1 of the SAS considers the process of forming an audit opinion using the flowchart shown on the next page. The flowchart is drawn up on the basis that the directors make no further amendments to the financial statements following the audit.

3.11 The principal matters which auditors consider in forming an opinion may be expressed in three questions.

(a) Have they **completed all procedures necessary** to meet auditing standards and to obtain all the information and explanations necessary for their audit?

(b) Have the financial statements been **prepared in accordance** with the **applicable accounting requirements**?

(c) Do the financial statements, as prepared by the directors, give **a true and fair view**?

Question 2

The following is a series of extracts from an unqualified audit report which has been signed by the auditors of Kiln Ltd.

AUDITORS' REPORT TO THE SHAREHOLDERS OF KILN LIMITED

We have audited *the financial statements on pages .... to ....* which have been prepared under the historical cost convention.

We have conducted our audit *in accordance with Auditing Standards* issued by the Auditing Practices Board. An audit includes examination on a test basis of evidence relevant to the amounts and disclosures in the financial statements.

In our opinion the financial statements give a true and fair view of the state of the company's affairs as at 31 December 20... and of its profit for the year then ended and have been properly prepared in accordance with the Companies Act 1985.

Required

Explain the purpose and meaning of the following phrases taken from the above extracts of an unqualified audit report.

(a) '... the financial statements on pages .... to ....'
(b) '... in accordance with Auditing Standards.'
(c) 'In our opinion ...'

Answer

(a) '...the financial statements on pages ... to ...'

Purpose

The purpose of this phrase is to make it clear to the reader of an audit report the part of a company's annual report upon which the auditors are reporting their opinion.

Meaning

An annual report may include documents such as a chairman's report, employee report, five year summary and other voluntary information. However, under the Companies Act, only the profit and loss account, balance sheet and associated notes are required to be audited in true and fair terms. FRS 1 requires a cash flow statement and FRS 3 requires a statement of total recognised gains and losses which, under auditing standards, are audited in true and fair terms. Thus the page references (for instance, 8 to 20) cover only the profit and loss account, balance sheet, notes to the accounts, cash flow statement and statement of total recognised gains and losses. The directors' report, although examined and reported on by exception if it contains inconsistencies, is not included in these page references.

(b) '...in accordance with Auditing Standards...'

Purpose

This phrase is included in order to confirm to the reader that best practice, as laid down in Auditing Standards, has been adopted by the auditors in both carrying out their audit and in drafting their audit opinion. This means that the reader can be assured that the audit has been properly conducted, and that should he or she wish to discover what such standards are, or what certain key phrases mean, he or she can have recourse to Auditing Standards to explain such matters.

Meaning

Auditing Standards are those auditing standards prepared by the Auditing Practices Board.

These prescribe the principles and practices to be followed by auditors in the planning, designing and carrying out of various aspects of their audit work, the content of audit reports, both qualified and unqualified and so on. Members are expected to follow all of these standards.

(c) 'In our opinion ...'

Purpose

Under the Companies Act, auditors are required to report on every balance sheet, profit and loss account or group accounts laid before members. In reporting, they are required to state their opinion on those accounts. Thus, the purpose of this phrase is to comply with the statutory requirement to report an opinion.

FORMING AN OPINION ON FINANCIAL STATEMENTS

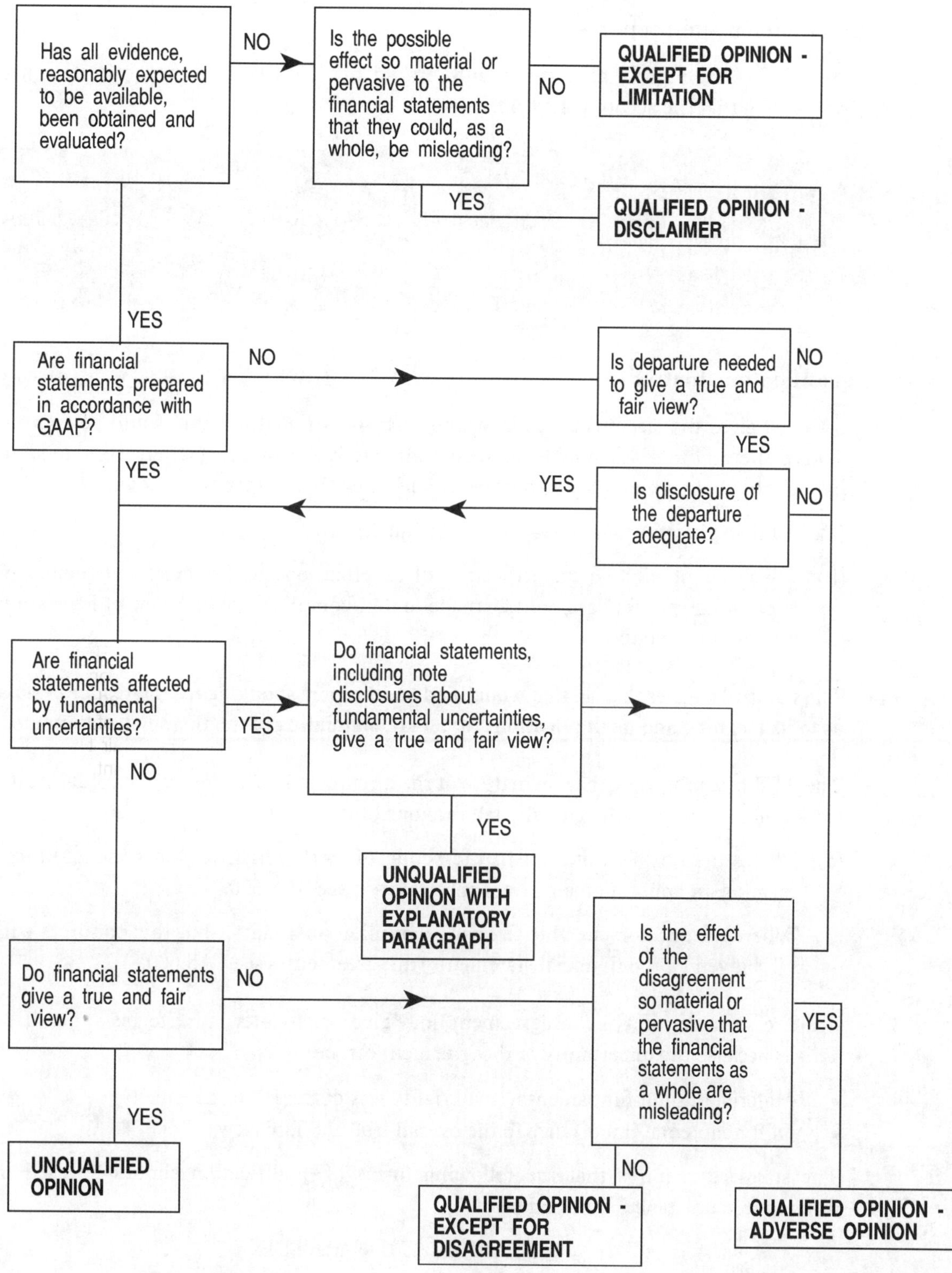

Meaning

An audit report is an expression of opinion by suitably qualified auditors as to whether the financial statements give a true and fair view, and have been properly prepared in accordance with the Companies Act. It is not a certificate; rather it is a statement of whether or not, in the professional judgement of the auditors, the financial statements give a true and fair view.

Qualifications in audit reports

3.12 Qualified audit reports arise when auditors do not believe that they can state without reservation that the accounts give a true and fair view.

Exam focus point

The November 2002 paper asked candidates to explain how material disagreements are reflected in an auditors report.

Do be prepared for another aspect of the qualification matrix coming up in a future paper.

The qualification 'matrix'

3.13 SAS 600 gives the circumstances in which each sort of qualification would be appropriate. Where the auditors are unable to report affirmatively on the matters contained in the paragraphs about which they have reservations, they should give the following.

(a) A full explanation of the reasons for the qualification.

(b) Whenever possible, a quantification of its effect on the financial statements. Where appropriate, reference should be made to non-compliance with relevant legislation and other requirements.

3.14 The standard stresses the fact that **a qualified audit report should leave the reader in no doubt as to its meaning and its implications for an understanding of the financial statements.**

3.15 The APB takes the view that the nature of the circumstances giving rise to a qualification of the auditor's opinion will generally fall into one of two categories.

(a) Where there is a **limitation in the scope of work** which prevents the auditors from forming an opinion on a matter (uncertainty – see SAS 600.7).

(b) Where the auditors are able to form an opinion on a matter but this **conflicts** with the view given by the financial statements (disagreement – see SAS 600.8).

3.16 Either case, uncertainty or disagreement, may give rise to alternative forms of qualification. This is because the uncertainty or disagreement can be:

- Material but not fundamental (materiality was discussed in chapter 1)
- Of fundamental importance to the overall true and fair view

The standard requires that the following forms of qualification should be used in the different circumstances outlined below.

QUALIFICATION MATRIX

Nature of circumstances	*Material but not fundamental*	*Fundamental*
Limitation in scope	Except for .. might	Disclaimer of opinion
Disagreement	Except for ...	Adverse opinion

Except for . . . might	Auditors disclaim an opinion on a particular aspect of the accounts which is not considered fundamental.
Disclaimer of opinion	Auditors state they are unable to form an opinion on truth and fairness.
Except for	Auditors express an adverse opinion on a particular aspect of the accounts which is not considered fundamental.
Adverse opinion	Auditors state the accounts do not give a true and fair view.

Limitations on the scope of an audit

3.17 One source of uncertainties is **limitations in the scope of the audit**. Scope limitations will arise where the auditors are unable for any reason to obtain all the information and explanations which they consider necessary for the purpose of their audit, arising from:

(a) Absence of proper accounting records

(b) An inability to carry out audit procedures considered necessary where for example, the auditors are unable to obtain satisfactory evidence of the existence or ownership of material assets

SAS 600.7

When there has been a limitation on the scope of the auditors' work that prevents them from obtaining sufficient evidence to express an unqualified opinion:

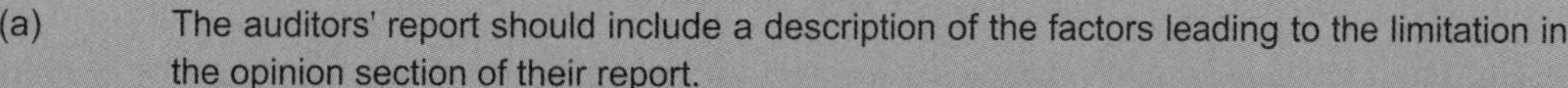

(a) The auditors' report should include a description of the factors leading to the limitation in the opinion section of their report.

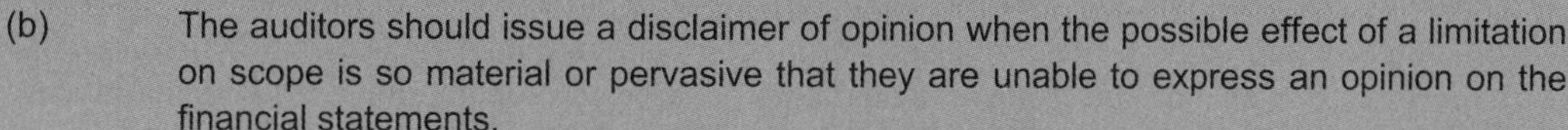

(b) The auditors should issue a disclaimer of opinion when the possible effect of a limitation on scope is so material or pervasive that they are unable to express an opinion on the financial statements.

(c) A qualified opinion should be issued when the effect of the limitation is not as material or pervasive as to require a disclaimer, and the wording of the opinion should indicate that it is qualified as to the possible adjustments to the financial statements that might have been determined to be necessary had the limitation not existed.

3.18 When giving this type of qualified opinion, auditors should assess:

- The **quantity and type of evidence** which may reasonably be expected to be available to support the figure or disclosure in the financial statements
- The **possible effect** on the financial statements of the matter for which insufficient evidence is available

3.19 SAS 600 gives the following examples.

Example 8. Qualified opinion: limitation on the auditors' work

(Basis of opinion: excerpt)

.... or error. However, the evidence available to us was limited because £... of the company's recorded turnover comprises cash sales, over which there was no system of control on which we could rely for the purposes of our audit. There were no other satisfactory audit procedures that we could adopt to confirm that cash sales were properly recorded.

In forming our opinion we also evaluated the overall adequacy of the presentation of information in the financial statements.

Qualified opinion arising from limitation in audit scope

Except for any adjustments that might have been found to be necessary had we been able to obtain sufficient evidence concerning cash sales, in our opinion the financial statements give a true and fair view of the state of the company's affairs as at 31 December 20.. and of its profit (loss) for the year then ended and have been properly prepared in accordance with the Companies Act 1985.

In respect alone of the limitation on our work relating to cash sales.

(a) We have not obtained all the information and explanations that we considered necessary for the purpose of our audit.

(b) We were unable to determine whether proper accounting records had been maintained.

Example 9. Disclaimer of opinion

(Basis of opinion: excerpt)

.... or error. However, the evidence available to us was limited because we were appointed auditors on (date) and in consequence we were unable to carry out auditing procedures necessary to obtain adequate assurance regarding the quantities and condition of stock and work in progress, appearing in the balance sheet at £... . Any adjustment to this figure would have a consequential significant effect on the profit for the year.

In forming our opinion we also evaluated the overall adequacy of the presentation of information in the financial statements.

Opinion: disclaimer on view given by financial statements

Because of the possible effect of the limitation in evidence available to us, we are unable to form an opinion as to whether the financial statements give a true and fair view of the state of the company's affairs as at 31 December 20.. or of its profit (loss) for the year then ended. In all other respects, in our opinion the financial statements have been properly prepared in accordance with the Companies Act 1985.

In respect of the limitation on our work relating to stock and work-in-progress:

(a) We have not obtained all the information and explanations that we considered necessary for the purpose of our audit.

(b) We were unable to determine whether proper accounting records had been maintained.

Note. Because of the length of the audit report, we have only shown those parts of each qualified report which differ from the unqualified report shown in paragraph 3.5

3.20 In March 1999 the APB published SAS 601 *Imposed limitation of audit scope* which provides guidance for auditors when the directors or those who appoint the auditors place limitations upon the scope of the audit

SAS 601.1

If the auditors are aware, before accepting an audit engagement, that the directors of the entity, or those who appoint its auditors, will impose a limitation on the scope of the audit work which they consider likely to result in the need to issue a disclaimer of opinion on the financial statements, they should not accept that engagement, unless required to do so by statute.

3.21 The SAS points out that agreeing to such a limitation would **threaten** the **independence** of auditors and make it impossible for them to meet the requirements of auditing standards. The APB also believes that in accepting such a limited engagement, the auditors are complicit in the client evading the spirit of the legal requirement to be audited. The SAS points out that even if there is a requirement for an entity to appoint auditors, this does not automatically mean that there is a requirement on the auditors to accept appointment.

SAS 601.2

If the auditors become aware, after accepting an audit engagement, that the directors of the entity, or those who appointed them as auditors, have imposed a limitation on the scope of their work which they consider likely to result in the need to issue a disclaimer on the financial statements, they should request the removal of the limitation. If the limitation is not removed, they should consider resigning from the audit engagement.

3.22 If the auditors do not consider it necessary to resign but do issue a disclaimer, the audit report should give full details of why the disclaimer was given.

Circumstances giving rise to disagreements

3.23 The explanatory notes suggest that circumstances giving rise to disagreement include the following.

(a) Inappropriate accounting policies.

(b) **Disagreement** as to the **facts or amounts** included in the financial statements.

(c) **Disagreement** as to the **manner or extent of disclosure** of facts or amounts in the financial statements.

(d) Failure to comply with relevant legislation or other requirements.

SAS 600.8

Where the auditors disagree with the accounting treatment or disclosure of a matter in the financial statements, and in the auditors' opinion the effect of that disagreement is material to the financial statements:

(a) The auditors should include in the opinion section of their report:

- A description of all substantive factors giving rise to the disagreement
- Their implications for the financial statements
- Whenever practicable, a quantification of the effect on the financial statements

(b) When the auditors conclude that the effect of the matter giving rise to disagreement is so material or pervasive that the financial statements are seriously misleading, they should issue an adverse opinion.

(c) In the case of other material disagreements, the auditors should issue a qualified opinion indicating that it is expressed except for the effects of the matter giving rise to the disagreement.

Example 7. Qualified opinion: disagreement

Qualified opinion arising from disagreement about accounting treatment

Included in the debtors shown on the balance sheet is an amount of £Y due from a company which has ceased trading. XYZ plc has no security for this debt. In our opinion the company is unlikely to receive any payment and full provision of £Y should have been made, reducing profit before tax and net assets by that amount.

Except for the absence of this provision, in our opinion the financial statements give a true and fair view of the state of the company's affairs as at 31 December 20.. and of its profit (loss) for the year then ended and have been properly prepared in accordance with the Companies Act 1985.

Example 10. Adverse opinion

Adverse opinion

As more fully explained in note ... no provision has been made for losses expected to arise on certain long-term contracts currently in progress, as the directors consider that such losses should be off-set against amounts recoverable on other long-term contracts. In our opinion, provision should be made for foreseeable losses on individual contracts as required by Statement of Standard Accounting Practice 9. If losses had been so recognised the effect would have been to reduce the profit before and after tax for the year and the contract work in progress at 31 December 20.. by £.. .

In view of the effect of the failure to provide for the losses referred to above, in our opinion the financial statements do not give a true and fair view of the state of the company's affairs as at 31 December 20.. and of its profit (loss) for the year then ended. In all other respects, in our opinion the financial statements have been properly prepared in accordance with the Companies Act 1985.

REPORTING INHERENT UNCERTAINTY

Inherent and fundamental uncertainty

KEY TERMS

An **inherent uncertainty** is an uncertainty whose resolution is dependent upon uncertain future events outside the control of the reporting entity's directors at the date the financial statements are approved.

A **fundamental uncertainty** is an inherent uncertainty where the magnitude of its potential impact is so great that, without clear disclosure of the nature and implications of the uncertainty, the view given by the financial statements would be seriously misleading.

SAS 600.6

(a) In forming their opinion on financial statements, auditors should consider whether the view given by the financial statements could be affected by inherent uncertainties which, in their opinion, are fundamental.

(b) When an inherent uncertainty exists which:

- In the auditors' opinion is fundamental
- And is adequately accounted for and disclosed in the financial statements

The auditors should include an explanatory paragraph referring to the fundamental uncertainty in the section of their report setting out the basis of their opinion.

(c) When adding an explanatory paragraph, auditors should use words which clearly indicate that their opinion on the financial statements is not qualified in respect of its concepts.

3.24 The following points are relevant.

(a) Inherent uncertainties about the outcome of future events frequently affect, to some degree, a wide range of components of the financial statements at the date they are approved.

(b) In forming an opinion, auditors take into account.

- The appropriateness of the accounting policies
- The adequacy of the accounting treatment
- **Estimates and disclosures of inherent uncertainties** in the light of evidence available at the date they express their opinion

Inherent uncertainties are regarded as **fundamental** when they involve a **significant level of doubt** about whether the organisation can continue as a **going concern** or other matters whose potential effect on the fundamental statements is unusually great. A common example of a fundamental uncertainty is the outcome of major litigation.

3.25 The auditors will need to consider:

- The possibility that the **estimate** included in the accounts may be **subject to change**
- The possible range of values it may take
- The **consequences** of that range of potential values on the view shown in the financial statements

Example 4. Unqualified opinion with explanatory paragraph describing a fundamental uncertainty.

Fundamental uncertainty (insert just before opinion paragraph)

In forming our opinion, we have considered the adequacy of the disclosures made in the financial statements concerning the possible outcome of litigation against B Limited, a subsidiary undertaking of the company, for an alleged breach of environmental regulations. The future settlement of this litigation could result in additional liabilities and the closure of B Limited's business, whose net assets included in the consolidated balance sheet total £... and whose profit before tax for the year is £.... . Details of the circumstances relating to this fundamental uncertainty are described in note .... . Our opinion is not qualified in this respect.

Question 3

During the course of the audit of the fixed assets of Eddy Engineering plc at 31 March 20.. two problems have arisen.

(i) The calculations of the cost of direct labour incurred on assets in course of construction by the company's employees have been accidentally destroyed for the early part of the year. The direct labour cost involved is £10,000.

(ii) The company has received a government grant of £25,000 towards the cost of plant and equipment acquired during the year and expected to last for ten years. The grant has been credited in full to the profit and loss account as exceptional income.

(iii) Other relevant financial information is as follows.

	£
Profit before tax	100,000
Fixed asset additions	133,000
Assets constructed by company	34,000
Fixed assets at net book value	666,667

Required

(a) List the general forms of qualification available to auditors in drafting their report and state the circumstances in which each is appropriate.

(b) State whether you feel that a qualified audit report would be necessary for each of the two circumstances outlined above, giving reasons in each case.

(c) On the assumption that you decide that a qualified audit report is necessary with respect to the treatment of the government grant, draft the section of the report describing the matter (the whole report is not required).

(d) Outline the auditors' general responsibility with regard to the statement in the directors' report concerning the valuation of land and buildings.

Answer

(a) SAS 600 *Auditors' report on financial statements* suggests that the auditors may need to qualify their audit opinion under one of two main circumstances:

- Limitation in scope of the auditors' examination
- Disagreement with the treatment or disclosure of a matter in the financial statements (including inherent uncertainties)

For both circumstances there can be two 'levels' of qualified opinion.

(i) *Material but not fundamental,* where the circumstances prompting the uncertainty or disagreement is material but confined to one particular aspect of the financial statements, so that it does not affect their overall value to any potential user.

(ii) The more serious qualification where the extent of the uncertainty or disagreement is such that it will be *fundamental* to the overall view shown by the financial statements, ie the financial statements are or could be misleading.

The general form of qualification appropriate to each potential situation may be seen by the following table.

Circumstance	*Material but not fundamental*	*Fundamental*
Limitation of scope	Except for ... might	Disclaimer of opinion
Disagreement	Except for ...	Adverse opinion

(b) Whether a qualification of the audit opinion would be required in relation to either of the two circumstances described in the question would depend on whether or not the auditors considered either of them to be material. An item is likely to be considered as material in the context of a company's financial statements if its omission, misstatement or non-disclosure would prevent a proper understanding of those statements on the part of a potential user. Whilst for some audit purposes materiality will be considered in absolute terms, more often than not it will be considered as a relative term.

(i) Loss of records relating to direct labour costs for assets in the course of construction

The loss of records supporting one of the asset figures in the balance sheet would cause a limitation in scope of the auditors' work. The £10,000, which is the value covered by the lost records, represents 29.4% of the expenditure incurred during the year on assets in course of construction but only 6% of total additions to fixed assets during the year and 1.5% of the year end net book value for fixed assets. The total amount of £10,000 represents 10% of pre-tax profit but, as in relation to asset values, the real consideration by the auditors should be the materiality of any over- or under-statement of assets resulting from error in arriving at the £10,000 rather than the total figure itself.

Provided there are no suspicious circumstances surrounding the loss of these records and the total figure for additions to assets in the course of construction seems reasonable in the light of other audit evidence obtained, then it is unlikely that this matter would be seen as sufficiently material to merit any qualification of the audit opinion. If other records have been lost as well, however, it may be necessary for the auditors to comment on the directors' failure to maintain proper books and records.

(ii) Government grant credited in total to profit and loss account

The situation here is one of disagreement, since best accounting practice, as laid down by SSAP 4, requires that capital-based grants should be credited to the profit and loss account over the useful life of the asset to which they relate.

This departure from SSAP 4 does not seem to be justifiable and would be material to the reported pre-tax profits for the year, representing as it does 22.5% of that figure.

Whilst this overstatement of profit (and corresponding understatement of undistributable reserves) would be material to the financial statements, it is not likely to be seen as fundamental and therefore an 'except for' qualified opinion would be appropriate.

(c) Qualified audit report extract

'As explained in note ... government grants in respect of new plant and equipment have been credited in full to profits instead of being spread over the lives of the relevant assets as required by Statement of Standard Accounting Practice 4; the effect of so doing has been to increase profits before and after tax for the year by £22,500.

Except for ...'

(d) The auditors' general responsibility with regard to the statement in the directors' report concerning the valuation of land and buildings is to satisfy themselves that this is consistent with the treatment and disclosure of this item in the audited financial statements. If the auditors are not satisfied on the question of consistency then an appropriate opinion will be required following their audit report.

The audit report as a means of communication

3.26 Unqualified audit reports may not appear to give a great deal of information. The report says a lot, however, by implication.

3.27 The real problem here is that, unfortunately, most users do not know that this is what an unqualified audit report tells them.

3.28 The APB made it clear that the audit report in SAS 600 was to be seen as a step towards closing the 'expectation gap'. The Board has addressed specific issues that relate to the expectation gap in other SASs.

3.29 The Cadbury Report *The Financial Aspects of Corporate Governance* also recommends many of the suggestions made in SAS 600, particularly the statement of both directors' and auditors' responsibilities.

Exam focus point

There was a total of 16 marks available for external audit in the pilot paper. Eight marks were for describing the external auditor's responsibilities and a further eight required you to describe unqualified and qualified audit reports.

Chapter roundup

- An audit is essentially an independent review.
- External auditors are regulated by statute, professional bodies and the **Auditing Practises Board** (APB).
- The APB defines the key stages of an audit as being:
  - Carry out procedures to obtain **sufficient appropriate audit evidence**
  - **Evaluate** the **presentation** of accounts
  - Issue a report containing a **clear expression** of **opinion**
- The auditors' report on company accounts is in terms of **truth** and **fairness.**
- The APB also points out that audits at best give **reasonable assurance** that the accounts are free from material misstatement.
- The **expectations gap** is the difference between the work auditors actually carry out and the work non-auditors think they carry out.
- As well as audits of accounts, there are various other types of audit, **statutory** and **non-statutory**.
- Auditors' **duties** include the duties to report explicitly on the **truth** and **fairness** of the accounts audited and their **compliance** with legislation.
- Auditors have a duty to **report** on other matters, such as whether proper accounting records have been kept, by **exception.**
- Auditors' rights include the rights of **access** to **records** and to receive **information** and **explanations**, also rights relating to **attendance** and **speaking** at **general meetings**.
- The Companies Act requires certain matters to be reported on by **exception**:
  - Proper accounting records kept and proper returns received
  - Accounts in agreement with the accounting records and returns
  - All information and explanations received
  - Details of directors' emoluments correctly disclosed
  - Details of loans and other transactions in favour of directors and related parties correctly disclosed
  - Information given in the directors' report consistent with the accounts
- The main elements of an **unqualified audit report** under SAS 600 are:
  - A **title** identifying the addressee
  - An introductory paragraph identifying the financial statements audited
  - Sections dealing with: **responsibilities** of **directors** and **auditors, basis** of the **auditors**' opinion, a **clear statement of opinion.**
- Auditors may qualify their audit opinion on the grounds of **uncertainty or limitation of scope**; these may be **material** or **fundamental.**
- Auditors are principally concerned with the correct **treatment** and **disclosure** of **inherent** and **fundamental uncertainties**, which relate to uncertain future events.
- Auditors should include an **explanatory paragraph** in their audit report if **fundamental uncertainties** exist.

Quick quiz

1 Define an audit of financial statements.

2 What work should auditors do when undertaking an audit?

3 What is the main reason why an audit is considered to be necessary?

4 What advantages is a partnership likely to gain from an audit?

5 What are the main statutory duties of the auditors?

6 What are the statutory rights of the auditors?

7 What are the express references in an audit report required by CA 1985?

8 What are the basic elements of the auditors' report?

9 When will a qualified opinion be issued?

Answers to quick quiz

1 An audit is the work required to enable the auditor to express an opinion as to whether the financial statements give a true and fair view of the profit or loss of the company for the financial year and its state of affairs at the year end. (see para 1.2)

2
- Carry out procedures designed to obtain significant appropriate evidence
- Evaluate the overall presentation of the financial statements
- Issue an audit report (1.4)

3 The audit gives the financial statements credibility

4
- It can settle accounts between partners
- The Inland Revenue are more likely to accept the accounts
- The negotiation of finance will be easier
- Sleeping partners will find the audit useful in giving them a confirmation of their profit share (1.17)

5 The auditor must report on the truth and fairness of every balance sheet and profit and loss account laid before the company in general meeting. They must also report on compliance with relevant legislation. (2.1)

6
- Access to records
- Attendance at general meetings
- Receipt of written resolutions
- Information and explanations
- Right to speak at general meetings
- Right to require the laying of the accounts

(2.2)

7 That the accounts have been prepared in accordance with the Companies Act and that they give a true and fair view. The balance sheet should reflect the company's affairs at the financial year end. The profit and loss account should give the company's profit for the year. (3.1, 3.2)

8
- The report should be addressed to its recipients
- It should identify the financial statements audited
- Separate sections should deal with the responsibilities of the directors, basis of the auditors' opinion, and the auditors' opinion
- Signature of the auditors
- Date of the audit report (3.4)

9 When there is limitation of scope preventing the auditors from forming an opinion or where there is disagreement. (3.15)

Now try the question below from the Exam Question Bank

Number	Level	Marks	Time
Scenario B: Q 2b	Exam	16	29 mins

Objective testing question and answer bank

1 The bodies involved in the current UK standard setting process are:

A Accounting Standards Council, Urgent Issues Task Force, Financial Reporting Council, Review Panel

B Accounting Standards Board, Urgent Issues Task Force, Financial Reporting Council, Review Panel

C Accounting Standards Board, Accounting Standard Council, Financial Reporting Council, Review Panel

D Accounting Standards Board, Accounting Standard Council, Urgent Issues Task Force, Review Panel

2 Fill in the four missing words.

The accruals basis of accounting requires that the non-cash impact of transactions should be reflected in the financial statements for the period in which they ...., and not, in the period any .... involved is .... or ....

3 When carrying out an audit an external auditor must satisfy himself of a number of matters. Which of the following are not one of those matters?

A The accounts have been prepared by a qualified accountant
B Proper accounting records have been kept
C The accounts have been prepared in accordance with the Companies Act
D The accounts are in agreement with accounting records

4 According to FRS 18, the two pervasive accounting concepts are

A Prudence and matching
B Accruals and consistency
C Accruals and going concern
D Prudence and consistency

5 Retention requirements for accounting records

(a) Private companies ______ years

(b) Public companies ______ years

6 The purpose of the Financial Reporting Review Panel is to:

A Review comments on Financial Reporting Exposure Drafts

B Examine departures from CA 1985 and accounting standards by large public and private companies

C Examine departures from CA 1985 and accounting standards by large companies, as well as by small companies

D Examine departures from CA 1985 and accounting standards by public companies and large private companies

7 Tina Ltd purchases production machinery costing £200,000 and having an estimated useful life of 20 years with a residual value of £4,000. After being in use for 6 years the remaining useful life of the machinery is revised and estimated to be 25 years, with an unchanged residual value. The annual depreciation charge after these events is £ ______

8 Fill in the two missing words.

Assets are .... to future economic .... controlled by the entity as a result of past transactions or events.

9 FRS 12 *Provisions, contingent assets and contingent liabilities* requires that material contingencies, other than those where the probability of the outcome is remote, existing at the balance sheet date should be treated as follows.

A Contingent assets and contingent liabilities must always be either accrued or disclosed in the financial statements

B Contingent liabilities must always be accrued and contingent assets must always be disclosed in the financial statements

C Contingent liabilities must always be either accrued or disclosed and contingent assets must always be disclosed in the financial statements

D Contingent liabilities must always be either accrued or disclosed and contingent assets must sometimes be disclosed in the financial statements

10 A company purchases a new major machine and the costs involved in this are given below.

	£
Purchase price	680,000
Delivery costs	30,000
Installation costs	80,000
Cleaning costs after first production run	4,000

At what figure would the machine initially be included in the balance sheet? £

11 An auditor's walk-through test is designed to:

A Establish any physical security in premises
B Establish how the accounting system works
C Confirm the workings of the accounting system
D Determine the number of errors in an accounting process

12 Heskey Ltd has prepared its financial statements for the year ending 30 June 20X8. On 15 July a major fraud was uncovered by the auditors which had taken place during the year to 30 June. On 31 July the company made a large debenture issue which has significantly increased the company's gearing level.

In accordance with SSAP 17 *Accounting for post balance sheet events*, how should the two events be treated in the financial statements?

	Fraud	*Debenture issue*
A	Accrued in accounts	Disclosed in notes
B	Accrued in accounts	Accrued in accounts
C	Disclosed in notes	Disclosed in notes
D	Disclosed in notes	Accrued in accounts

13 Identify which if the following statements is untrue.

A Prudence relates to the uncertainty that may be associated with recognition and measurement of assets and liabilities

B The existence of an asset requires stronger confirmatory evidence than that required to acknowledge the existence of a liability

C Where there is tension between neutrality and prudence, prudence should always prevail

D Prudence should not be seen as a means for smoothing of results.

14 Tammy Ltd had a profit before dividends of £80,000 for the year ended 31 December 20X4 and £110,000 for the year ended 31 December 20X5. On 1 January 20X5 there were £100,000 of 25 pence ordinary shares in issue. On 1 April 20X5 there was a 1 for 4 bonus issue.

What are the EPS figures that would be shown in the financial statements for the year ending 31 December 20X2 for both 20X5 and 20X4?

	20X5	*20X4*
A	22 pence	16 pence
B	22 pence	20 pence
C	88 pence	64 pence
D	88 pence	80 pence

15 The primary financial statements as identified by the *Statement of Principles* are:

A Balance sheet, profit and loss account, cash flow statement and directors' report

B Balance sheet, profit and loss account, notes to the accounts and directors' report

C Balance sheet, profit and loss account statement of total recognised gains and losses and notes to the accounts

D Balance sheet, profit and loss account, statement of total recognised gains and losses and cash flow statement

16 Define accounting polices in not more than thirty words.

17 According to FRS 11 *Impairment of fixed assets and goodwill* what is the recoverable amount of a fixed asset?

A Net realisable value
B Value in use
C The higher of net realisable value and value in use
D The lower of net realisable value and value in use

18 Which of the following types of research and development expenditure must be written off in the year it is incurred?

A Market research costs confirming the ultimate commercial viability of a product
B Legal costs in connection with registration of a patent
C Costs of searching for possible alternative products
D Costs of research work which are to be reimbursed by a customer

19 If an auditor finds that his audit has been limited in scope as regards a fundamental matter what type of audit report would be issued?

A Unqualified report
B Qualified report with 'except for' paragraph
C Disclaimer of opinion
D Adverse opinion

20 Fill in the missing word.

Similar asset which are grouped together because there is no reason to view them separately in economic terms are called .... assets.

21 Fill in the missing words.

Cash is cash in hand and .... repayable on demand with any qualifying .... institution, less .... from any qualifying .... institution repayable on demand. Deposits are repayable on demand if they can be withdrawn at any time without .... and without .... of if a .... or period of .... of not more than .... hours or one working day has been agreed. Cash includes cash in hand and deposits denominated in .... currencies.

22 At 31 December 20X8 Jiang Ltd has trade debtors of £14,000, trade creditors of 75% of this figure, stocks of finished goods of £7,000 and stocks of raw materials of £5,000. The business also has a bank overdraft of £2,500 and £25,000 6% debentures. There were also accruals of £1,000, prepayments of £500 and petty cash of £100.

What is the current ratio at 31 December 20X8?

A 0.68
B 0.69
C 1.90
D 2.00

23 Define in no more than twenty words what is meant by a dilutive potential ordinary share.

24 A provision for the costs of removing pollution arising from a company's operations should be recognised if?

A The accounts would reveal an understated net profit figure without the provision

B The directors recognise there is a legal or constructive obligation to remove the pollution by spending money in the future

C Other companies in the same industry have recognised similar provisions

D The company auditors instruct the directors to set up a provision.

25 Insert the two missing words.

In terms of FRS 18, prudence relates to the .... that may be associated with the .... and measurement of assets and liabilities.

26 Which of the following is not a feature identified by FRS 5 *Reporting the substance of transactions*, as potentially requiring its requirements to be applied?

A The legal owner of an asset is not the person benefiting from it

B The transaction is part of a series and the substance of the transaction can only be determined by viewing the whole series

C Sale and leaseback transactions

D The inclusion of options and conditions which are likely to be exercised

27 According to FRS 11 *Impairment of fixed assets and goodwill*, how often should fixed assets be tested for impairment?

A Every year
B Every 3 years
C Every time fixed assets are revalued
D When there is an indication that impairment has occurred

28 Goran Ltd has revalued one of its buildings to £1,200,000 at 31 December 20X8. The building was purchased 8 years ago at a cost of £840,000 and is being depreciated over a period of 40 years.

The depreciation charge for the year ending 31 December 20X9 will be £

29 Henman plc changes the depreciation method for its motor vehicles from the straight line method to the reducing balance method. How would this be treated in the financial statements?

A Changing the current year figures but not previous year's figures
B Putting through a prior period adjustment
C No alteration of any figures but disclosure in the notes
D No alteration of any figures nor disclosure in the notes

30 A company has a profit before tax of £390,000 and a tax charge for the year of £115,000. The business is funded by 200,000 £1 5% preference shares and 1,000,000 25 pence ordinary shares. At the start of the year the company's share price was £3.40 but had fallen to £2.90 by the end of the year.

What is the price earnings ratio for the company?

A 10.5
B 10.9
C 11.5
D 11.9

31 FRS 18 requires that where the going concern concept is not met, the directors must prepare the account using break-up values which are more informative to users of the accounts.

True 

False 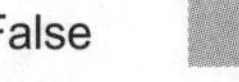

32 Shah plc has a year end of 31 March 20X8. During that year the decision was made to shut down two divisions, A and B. The results of the divisions for the year were:

	Division A	Division B
Turnover	£490,000	£188,000
Operating costs	£450,000	£164,000

The final closure of Division A occurred on 5 July 20X8 and Division B on 28 February 20X8.

What figures would appear in the discontinued operations column of the profit and loss account for the year ended 31 March 20X8?

	Turnover	*Operating profit*
	£	£
A	188,000	24,000
B	490,000	40,000
C	188,000	40,000
D	678,000	64,000

33 The numbers of people employed by Azrina plc under contracts of service as follows.

Full time:	UK	56
	overseas	10
Part time		12

Which is the average number of employees that must be disclosed in the accounts in accordance with the Companies Act 1985?

A 56
B 66
C 68
D 78

34 Given below are details of one of a Sandra Ltd's long term contracts.

	£
Costs incurred to date	140,000
Estimated costs to completion	280,000
Progress payments invoiced	280,000
Total contract price	680,000

The contract is estimated to be 45% complete.

What figure would appear on the balance sheet for work in progress? £

35 Fill in the eight missing words.

FRS 3 defines prior year adjustments as .... adjustments applicable to prior periods arising from .... in accounting .... or from the .... of .... errors. They do not include normal .... adjustment or .... of accounting .... made in prior periods.

36 According to FRS 8 *Related party disclosures,* which of the following would not be a related party of Chen plc?

A An associated undertaking of Chen plc
B The Managing director of Chen plc's parent company
C A company in which Chen plc holds a 10% investment
D Chen plc's pension fund for its employees

37 State the definition of a non-adjusting event is no more than twenty-five words.

38 On 1 January 20X8 Kudles plc purchased a fixed asset for £700,000 and received a 20% government grant. The asset has an expected life of ten years at the end off which it is expected to have a nil scrap value. The company has treated the amount of the grant as a deferred credit. What is the correct accounting treatment to be adopted in Kudles plc's profit and loss account for the year ended 31 December 20X8?

	Depreciation	*Related government grant*
A	£70,000 debit	£14,000 credit
B	£70,000 debit	Nil
C	£56,000 debit	£14,000 credit
D	£56,000 debit	Nil

39 Which of the following statements are true and in accordance with FRS 17 *Retirement benefits*?

(i) The assets of a defined benefit scheme are valued at their fair value at the balance sheet date

(ii) Companies have a choice as to whether or not to discount defined benefit scheme liabilities

(iii) Actuarial gains and losses should be recognised in the statement of total recognised gains and losses

A (i) and (ii)
B (i) and (iii)
C (ii) and (iii)
D all three

40 Two unconnected private companies, in their draft accounts for the year ended 31 December 20X7, show the following figures.

	Turnover	*Gross assets*	*Employees (monthly average)*
	£	£	
Waugh Ltd	3.74 million	1,367,000	49
Pearce Ltd	2.72 million	1,498,000	55

Which, if either, of the two companies is a small company within the meaning of the Companies Act 1985?

A Waugh Ltd only
B Pearce Ltd only
C Both Waugh Ltd and Pearce Ltd
D Neither Waugh Ltd nor Pearce Ltd

41 Where there is a tension between the concept of prudence and accruals, prudence always prevails.

True 

False

42 Define a provision in no more than ten words.

43 Harpal Ltd owns three properties held for investment potential as follows.

1 Fully completed, but not currently let
2 Fully completed, let on the open market
3 Fully completed, let to and occupied by an associated company at the open market rate

Which are investment properties as defined in SSAP 19?

A 2 only
B 1 and 2
C 2 and 3
D 1, 2 and 3

44 Which of the following does not accurately describe '*true and fair view*'?

A It is a dynamic concept that evolves in response to changes in accounting and business practice

B Even reasonable businessmen and accountants may not share a consensus as to the degree of accuracy and completeness required

C Courts are likely to examine the meanings of the word 'true' and the word 'fair' in interpreting the meaning of 'true and fair'

D Courts are likely to look to the ordinary practices of professional accountants

45 FRS 18 suggests that comparability is achieved through:

(a) (one word)

(b) (one word)

1 B The current standard setting body is the Accounting Standards Board. In 1990 this body took over from the disbanded Accounting Standards Council.

2 The accruals basis of accounting requires that the **non-cash impact of transactions** should be reflected in the financial statements for the **period** in which they **occur**, and not, in the period any **cash** involved is **received** or **paid**.

3 A In order to state that the financial statements show a true and fair view the auditor must satisfy himself that the other three matters are valid.

4 C FRS 18 does not mention matching. Consistency is a desirable feature and supports comparability.

5 Retention requirements for accounting records

(a) Private companies | 3 | years

(b) Public companies | 6 | years

6 D

7 D

			£
Cost			200,000
Depreciation	$6\times\left(\frac{200,000-4,000}{20}\right)$		58,800
NBV end year 6			141,200
Depreciation year 7	$\frac{141,200-4,000}{25}$	=	£5,488

8 Assets are **rights** to future economic **benefits** controlled by the entity as a result of past transactions or events.

9 D Probable liabilities should be accrued
Probable liabilities should be disclosed
Contingent assets are only disclosed if they are probable

10 £790,000. The cost to appear initially in the balance sheet is the cost of getting the machine ready for production. This will include the delivery and installation costs but not the cleaning costs after the first production run.

11 C After preparing or up-dating the systems records the auditor would confirm his understanding of those systems by tracing a handful of transactions through the system.

12 A The fraud is an adjusting post balance sheet event as it took place during the year to 30 June although was not discovered until after the year end. The debenture issue is a non-adjusting event but due to its materiality should be disclosed in the notes.

13 C It is not true that where there is tension between neutrality and prudence, prudence should always prevail. FRS 18 recommends an approach that is driven by the true and fair criteria.

14 A

Number of shares in issue 1 Jan 20X5	=	£100,000 ÷ 25 pence
	=	400,000
1 for 4 bonus issue		100,000
Number of shares after bonus issue		500,000
EPS 20X2	=	$\frac{£110,000}{500,000}$
	=	22 pence
EPS 20X1	=	$\frac{£80,000}{500,000}$
	=	16 pence

15 D The directors' report is not a financial statement. The notes 'amplify and explore' the financial statements.

16 Accounting policies are the principles, conventions, rules and practices applied by an entity that prescribes how transactions and other events are to be reflected in its financial statements.

17 C

18 C Items A and B are costs incurred in the *development* of a product. Note that while SSAP 13 (revised) says that market research costs are not normally development costs, they *may be* treated as such when confirming ultimate commercial viability.

C is research and therefore must be written off.

D is work in progress (stock) which you are being paid to do.

19 C

20 Similar assets which are grouped together because there is no reason to view them separately in economic terms are called **fungible** assets.

21 Cash is cash in hand and **deposits** repayable on demand with any qualifying **financial** institution, less **overdrafts** from any qualifying **financial** institution repayable on demand. Deposits are repayable on demand if they can be withdrawn at any time without **notice** and without **penalty** of if a **maturity** or period of **notice** of not more than **24** hours or one working day has been agreed. Cash includes cash in hand and deposits denominated in **foreign** currencies.

22 C Current ratio = $\frac{\text{Current assets}}{\text{Current liabilities}}$

	£
Current assets	
Debtors	14,000
Finished goods stocks	7,000
Raw materials stocks	5,000
Prepayments	500
Petty cash	100
	26,600
Current liabilities	
Creditors (£14,000 × 75%)	10,500
Bank overdraft	2,500
Accruals	1,000
	14,000

Current assets = $\frac{£26,600}{£14,000}$ = 1.9

23 A dilutive potential ordinary share is one which decreases the share of net profit or increases the loss shared.

24 B Correct. It is the existence of an obligation which creates the need of a provision.

25 In terms of FRS 18, prudence relates to the **uncertainty** that may be associated with the **recognition** and measurement of assets and liabilities.

26 B

27 D

28 Depreciation charge $= \frac{£1,200,000}{32 \text{ years}}$

$= \underline{\underline{£37,500}}$

29 A Changing the method of depreciation is a change of estimation technique not a change of accounting policy and therefore it is not treated as a prior period adjustment. However the current year figures must be changed to reflect the change in estimation technique and the change must be disclosed.

30 B Price/earnings ratio $= \frac{\text{Current marke price of share}}{\text{Earnings per share}}$

Earnings per share $= \frac{£390,000 - 115,000 - (£200,000 \times 5\%)}{1000,000}$

$=$ 26.5 pence

P/E ratio $= \frac{£2.90}{£0.265}$

$= \underline{\underline{10.9}}$

31 False. FRS 18 suggests that financial statement prepared on a **break-up values basis** might **not provide** users with much **useful information**, on matters such as:

- **Financial adaptability**
- **Cash generation ability.**

32 A Only Division B falls within the definition from FRS 3 of discontinued operations as Division A was not actually closed down within three months of the year end.

33 **D** The number of employees includes all those employed under a contract of services, regardless of where they work or number of hours.

34 £6,000

	Total	*45% completed*
	£	£
Costs to date	240,000	
Estimated costs to date	280,000	
	520,000	234,000
Contract price	680,000	306,000
Total attributable profit	160,000	72,000

CONTRACT ACCOUNT

	£		£
Costs incurred	240,000	Cost of sales	234,000
		Work in progress c/d	6,000
	240,000		240,000

35 FRS 3 defines prior year adjustments as **material** adjustments applicable to prior periods arising from **changes** in accounting **policies** or from the **correction** of **fundamental** errors. They do not include normal **recurring** adjustments or **correction** of accounting **estimates** made in prior periods.

36 C The general requirements of FRS 8 for related party status are that two or more parties are related if:

- one party has control of the other
- the parties are subject to common control
- one party has influence over the financial and operating policies of another party
- the parties are subject to influence from the same source.

An 10% investment in another company does not fall into any of these categories.

37 Non-adjusting events **arise after the balance sheet date** and concern **conditions** which did **not exist** at that time.

38 A Where the grant has been treated as a deferred credit the depreciation will be based on the original cost of the asset and the grant should be credited to the profit and loss account over the useful economic life of the asset.

Depreciation $\frac{£700,000}{10 \text{ years}} = £70,000\text{DR}$

Grant $\frac{£140,000}{10 \text{ years}} = £14,000 \text{ CR}$

39 B (ii) is not true as FRS 17 requires that the liabilities should be discounted.

40 A

	Turnover	*Assets*	*Employees*	*Overall*
Waugh	M	S	S	S
Pearce	S	M	M	M

41 False. FRS 18 suggests the use of an approach driven by the need to reflect a true and fair view.

42 A provision is a **liability** of **uncertain timing** or **amount.**

Note. Although the amount is uncertain, it should be susceptible to **measurement** with **sufficient reliability**. Where no reliable estimate can be made, a liability exist which cannot be recognised. Such liability should be disclosed as a contingent liability.

43 D An investment property need not be let but if it is, it cannot be to a group company, however an associated company is not a group company.

44 C Courts are **not likely** to examine the individual meanings of the word 'true' and the word 'fair' in interpreting the meaning of 'true and fair' The courts are likely to use an approach that applies the **concepts implied** by the **expression** '*true and fair*'.

45 FRS 18 suggests that comparability is achieved through:

(a) Consistency

(b) Disclosure

Consistency is no longer a fundamental accounting concept in its own right and is subsumed under the objective of comparability.

1 B The current standard setting body is the Accounting Standards Board. In 1990 this body took over from the disbanded Accounting Standards Council.

2 The accruals basis of accounting requires that the **non-cash impact of transactions** should be reflected in the financial statements for the **period** in which they **occur**, and not, in the period any **cash** involved is **received** or **paid**.

3 A In order to state that the financial statements show a true and fair view the auditor must satisfy himself that the other three matters are valid.

4 C FRS 18 does not mention matching. Consistency is a desirable feature and supports comparability.

5 Retention requirements for accounting records

(a)	Private companies	3	years
(b)	Public companies	6	years

6 D

7 D

			£
Cost			200,000
Depreciation	$6 \times \left(\frac{200{,}000 - 4{,}000}{20}\right)$		58,800
NBV end year 6			141,200
Depreciation year 7	$\frac{141{,}200 - 4{,}000}{25}$	=	£5,488

8 Assets are **rights** to future economic **benefits** controlled by the entity as a result of past transactions or events.

9 D Probable liabilities should be accrued
Probable liabilities should be disclosed
Contingent assets are only disclosed if they are probable

10 £790,000. The cost to appear initially in the balance sheet is the cost of getting the machine ready for production. This will include the delivery and installation costs but not the cleaning costs after the first production run.

11 C After preparing or up-dating the systems records the auditor would confirm his understanding of those systems by tracing a handful of transactions through the system.

12 A The fraud is an adjusting post balance sheet event as it took place during the year to 30 June although was not discovered until after the year end. The debenture issue is a non-adjusting event but due to its materiality should be disclosed in the notes.

13 C It is not true that where there is tension between neutrality and prudence, prudence should always prevail. FRS 18 recommends an approach that is driven by the true and fair criteria.

24 B Correct. It is the existence of an obligation which creates the need of a provision.

25 In terms of FRS 18, prudence relates to the **uncertainty** that may be associated with the **recognition** and measurement of assets and liabilities.

26 B

27 D

28 Depreciation charge $= \dfrac{£1{,}200{,}000}{32 \text{ years}}$

$= \underline{\underline{£37{,}500}}$

29 A Changing the method of depreciation is a change of estimation technique not a change of accounting policy and therefore it is not treated as a prior period adjustment. However the current year figures must be changed to reflect the change in estimation technique and the change must be disclosed.

30 B Price/earnings ratio $= \dfrac{\text{Current marke price of share}}{\text{Earnings per share}}$

Earnings per share $= \dfrac{£390{,}000 - 115{,}000 - (£200{,}000 \times 5\%)}{1000{,}000}$

$= 26.5$ pence

P/E ratio $= \dfrac{£2.90}{£0.265}$

$= \underline{\underline{10.9}}$

31 False. FRS 18 suggests that financial statement prepared on a **break-up values basis** might **not provide** users with much **useful information**, on matters such as:

- **Financial adaptability**
- **Cash generation ability.**

32 A Only Division B falls within the definition from FRS 3 of discontinued operations as Division A was not actually closed down within three months of the year end.

33 **D** The number of employees includes all those employed under a contract of services, regardless of where they work or number of hours.

34 £6,000

	Total	*45% completed*
	£	£
Costs to date	240,000	
Estimated costs to date	280,000	
	520,000	234,000
Contract price	680,000	306,000
Total attributable profit	160,000	72,000

Exam question and answer bank

Examination standard questions are indicated by mark allocations and time limits.

1 REGULATORS

State three different regulatory influences on the preparation of the published accounts of quoted companies and briefly explain the role of each one. Comment briefly on the effectiveness of this regulatory system.

2 FRS 3 STATEMENTS

Using the information below prepare the statement of recognised gains and losses, the reconciliation of shareholders' funds and the reconciliation of profit to historical cost profit for Linda Ltd for the year ended 31 December 20X9.

(a) *Linda Ltd profit and loss account extract*

	£'000
Operating profit	792
Interest receivable	24
Interest payable	(10)
Profit before tax	806
Taxation	(240)
Profit after tax	566
Dividend	(200)
Retained profit	366

(b) *Note.* The following items have (where appropriate) already passed through the profit and loss account.

Fixed assets

(i) Assets held at cost were written down by £25,000, the reduction in value was deemed to be permanent.

(ii) Freehold land and buildings were revalued to £500,000 (book value £375,000). The remaining life of the assets is 25 years.

(iii) A previously revalued asset was sold for £60,000.

Details of the revaluation and subsequent depreciation are as follows.

	£
Book value at revaluation	30,000
Revaluation	50,000
	80,000
Depreciation ((80,000/10) $\times$ 3)	24,000
	56,000

(iv) Details of investment properties are as follows.

	£
Cost	120,000
Investment revaluation reserve	40,000
Value at 1.1.20X9	160,000

The properties had a valuation on 31 December 20X9 of £100,000. This fall in value is expected to be temporary.

(c) *Share capital*

During the year the company had the following changes to its capital structure.

(i) An issue of £200,000 £1 ordinary bonus shares.
(ii) An issue of 400,000 £1 ordinary shares (issue price £1.50 per share)

(d) *Shareholders' funds*

The book value of shareholders' funds at the start of the year amounted to £6,820,000.

3 CEE EFF *45 mins*

The balance sheet of CF plc for the year ended 31 December 20X4, together with comparative figures for the previous year, is shown below (all figures £'000).

	20X4		20X3	
	£'000	£'000	£'000	£'000
Fixed assets		270		180
Less depreciation		(90)		(56)
		180		124
Current assets				
Stock	50		42	
Debtors	40		33	
Cash	-		11	
	90		86	
Current liabilities				
Trade and operating creditors	33		24	
Taxation	19		17	
Dividend	28		26	
Bank overdraft	10		-	
	90		67	
Net current assets		-		19
Net assets		180		143
Represented by				
Ordinary share capital £1 shares		25		20
Share premium		10		8
Profit and loss account		65		55
Shareholders' funds		100		83
15% debentures, repayable 20X8		80		60
Capital employed		180		143

You are informed that:

(a) There were no sales of fixed assets during 20X4
(b) The company does not pay interim dividends
(c) New debentures and shares issued in 20X4 were issued on 1 January

REQUIREMENT:

(a) Show your calculation of the operating profit of CF plc for the year ended 31 December 20X4. **4 Marks**

(b) Prepare a cash flow statement for the year, in accordance with FRS 1 (revised) *Cash flow statements* including the reconciliation of operating profit to net cash inflow from operating activities and Note 1 as required by the standard, ie the 'gross cash flows'. **10 Marks**

(c) State the headings of the other reconciliation and note which you would be required to include in practice under FRS 1 (revised). **2 Marks**

(d) Comment on the implications of the information given in the question plus the statements you have prepared, regarding the financial position of the company. **6 Marks**

(e) FRS 1 supports the use of the indirect method of arriving at the net cash inflow from operating activities, which is the method you have used to prepare 'Note 1' required in part (b) of this question.

What is the direct method of arriving at the net cash inflow from operations?

State, with reasons, whether you agree with the FRS 1 acceptance of the indirect method.

3 Marks

Total Marks = 25

4 FURROW

27 mins

The Furrow Manufacturing Company has recently purchased a machine for £256,000 and expects to use it for three years at the end of which period it will be sold as scrap for £4,000. The following estimates have been agreed concerning its operations.

	'000 Hours
Year 1	10
Year 2	18
Year 3	14

REQUIREMENTS:

(a) Calculate in respect of each of the three years the annual depreciation charge using each of the following methods:

(i) Straight line.

(ii) Machine hour.

(iii) Reducing balance (at 75% per annum). **6 Marks**

(b) Suppose that the Furrow Manufacturing Company adopted the reducing balance method and depreciated the machine for one year; then at the end of the following year the company decided to change from the reducing balance method to the straight line method. Indicate how the machine should appear in the balance sheet at the end of its second year (including any notes relating thereto) assuming that all the original estimates had proved accurate, and bearing in mind the requirements of FRS 15. **9 Marks**

Total Marks = 15

5 SSAP 19

In relation to SSAP 19 *Accounting for investment properties* you are required:

(a) To define the term 'investment property'.

(b) To explain the accounting treatment of investment properties in the annual financial statements.

(c) To state the arguments in favour of the treatment specified in SSAP 19.

6 FRS 10 (May 2003)

(a) FRS 10 *Goodwill and intangible assets* makes the following provisions:

(i) Only purchased goodwill may be shown as a fixed asset.

(ii) Goodwill must be capitalised and amortised systematically over a period not exceeding its useful economic life.

Explain and comment on these provisions.

(b) What is negative goodwill? What is the accounting treatment prescribed by FRS 10 in respect of negative goodwill?

7 SSAP 9

36 mins

(a) Name five groups into which business stocks can be categorised. State the general rule for the accounting treatment of stock and relate that rule to the concepts or conventions on which accounting is based. **8 Marks**

(b) Explain how best accounting practice, embodied in SSAP 9, follows the general rule. **4 Marks**

(c) Baggaley Leather Goods operate a shop selling ladies shoes and handbags. Until recently they had always purchased goods for resale, but have decided to make all the handbags they sell, from 1 January 20X1.

The trading account for the year to 31 December 20X1 shows the following figures for handbags sales through the shop.

	£
Opening stock at cost (500 × £3)	1,500
Received from workshop at transfer price (10,000 × £4)	40,000
	41,500
Less closing stock (1,000 × £4)	4,000
Cost of sales	37,500
Gross profit	22,500
Sales	60,000

Mr Baggaley comments that buying the bags from his own workshop at £4 each was a mistake, since he could have bought them through the trade at £3.80. However, he says the workshop did well to produce them at £3.50 each and show a profit of 50p on each one.

Show how the stock of handbags would appear in the balance sheet as at 31 December 20X1.

8 Marks

Total Marks = 20

8 BEAVERS *36 mins*

During its financial year ended 30 June 20X7, Beavers Ltd, an engineering company, has worked on several contracts. Information relating to one of them is given below.

CONTRACT X201	
Date commenced	1 July 20X6
Original estimate of completion date	30 September 20X7
Contract price	£240,000
Proportion of work certified as satisfactorily completed and invoiced) up to 30 June 20X7	£180,000
Amount received from contractee	£150,000
Costs up to 30 June 20X7	
Wages	£91,000
Materials sent to site	£36,000
Other contract costs	£18,000
Proportion of head office costs	£6,000
Plant and equipment transferred to the site (at book value on 1 July 20X6)	£9,000

The plant and equipment is expected to have a book value of about £1,000 when the contract is completed. Depreciation for the year to 30 June 20X7 is £6,400.

Stock of materials at site 30 June 20X7	£3,000
Expected additional costs to complete the contract	
Wages	£10,000
Materials (including stock at 30 June 20X7)	£12,000
Other (including head office costs)	£8,000

At 30 June 20X7 it is estimated that work to a cost value of £19,000 has been completed, but not included in the certifications.

If the contract is completed one month earlier than originally scheduled, an extra £10,000 will be paid to the contractors. At the end of June 20X7 there seemed to be a good chance that this would happen.

REQUIREMENTS:

(a) Show the account for the contract in the books of Beavers Ltd up to 30 June 20X7 (including any transfer to the profit and loss account which you think is appropriate) and the personal account of the contractee. **10 Marks**

(b) Show how the work in progress would be displayed on the balance sheet. **5 Marks**

(c) Briefly justify your calculation of the profit (or loss) to be recognised in the 20X6/X7 accounts. **5 Marks**

Total Marks = 20

9 EXE PLC

36 mins

Exe plc is a company in the building industry, which also operates several factories which make preformed and prestressed concrete products.

How would you deal with the following transactions in the accounts of Exe plc as at 31 December 20X2 according to best accounting practice?

(a) During the year Exe plc revalued its headquarters building, of which it owns the freehold. The only entry in the books concerning this property records the cost when built as £500,000, but the valuer now suggests a value of £1,250,000 with the land contributing £400,000 of that amount. **4 Marks**

(b) Exe plc has opened a research department to develop new techniques which the company intends to exploit in the future. The department has cost £47,000 to operate in the year, and the board suggests that this expenditure should be carried forward to set off against revenue at a future date under the matching convention (accruals concept). **4 Marks**

(c) On 5 February 20X3 the net realisable value of raw material stock as at 31 December 20X2 was found to be £40,000 lower than their historical cost. On 25 January 20X3 the board decided to close a factory situated at Exeter. **4 Marks**

(d) During the year an abnormal provision of £50,000 was made for losses on a long-term contract. On another contract a mistake was discovered in the calculation of stocks of work in progress, as at 31 December 20X0. The amount had been overstated by £36,000. **4 Marks**

(e) During the year Exe plc received a capital grant from the Government, in the sum of £30,000, against the purchase by the company of plant in the sum of £120,000. **4 Marks**

Total Marks = 20

10 C PLC (Pilot paper)

36 mins

C plc is a civil engineering company. It started work on two long-term projects during the year ended 31 December 20X0. The following figures relate to those projects at the balance sheet date.

	Maryhill bypass	*Rottenrow Centre*
	£'000	£'000
Contract price	9,000	8,000
Costs incurred to date	1,400	2,900
Estimated costs to completion	5,600	5,200
Value of work certified to date	2,800	3,000
Cash received from contractee	2,600	3,400

An old mineshaft has been discovered under the site for the Rottenrow Centre and the costs of dealing with this have been taken into account in the calculation of estimated costs to completion. C plc's lawyers are reasonably confident that the customer will have to bear the additional costs which will be incurred in stabilising the land. If negotiations are successful then the contract price will increase to £10m.

C plc recognises turnover and profits on long-term contracts on the basis of work certified to date.

REQUIREMENTS:

(a) Calculate the figures which would appear in C plc's financial statements in respect of these two projects. **14 marks**

(b) It has been suggested that profit on long-term contracts should not be recognised until the contract is completed. Briefly explain whether you believe that this suggestion would improve the quality of financial reporting for long-term contracts. **6 marks**

Total marks = 20

11 EASY *36 mins*

Extracts from the draft accounts of Easy Ltd show the following.

	£'000	
Balances brought forward 1.1.X8		
20X7 proposed final dividend	20	
Taxation payable		
Estimated tax charge for 20X7	102	
Deferred tax	5	(Dr)
20X7 dividend paid	20	
Dividends received	25	
Debenture interest received (net)	28	
Debenture interest paid (gross)	20	
20X8 interim dividend paid	24	
Full settlement of 20X7 tax charge	102	

The proposed final dividend for 20X8 is £8,000, and the estimated tax charge for 20X8 is £112,000.

The applicable rate of income tax is 20%.

REQUIREMENT:

Prepare calculations to show the figures which would be included in the profit and loss account and balance sheet for 20X8. **20 Marks**

12 BULWELL *36 mins*

Bulwell Aggregates Ltd wish to expand their transport fleet and have purchased three heavy lorries with a list price of £18,000 each. Robert Bulwell has negotiated hire purchase finance to fund this expansion, and the company has entered into a hire purchase agreement with Granby Garages plc on 1 January 20X1. The agreement states that Bulwell Aggregates will pay a deposit of £9,000 on 1 January 20X1, and two annual instalments of £24,000 on 31 December 20X1, 20X2 and a final instalment of £20,391 on 31 December 20X3.

Interest is to be calculated at 25% on the balance outstanding on 1 January each year and paid on 31 December each year.

The depreciation policy of Bulwell Aggregates Ltd is to write off the vehicles over a four year period using the straight line method and assuming a scrap value of £1,333 for each vehicle at the end of its useful life.

The cost of the vehicles to Granby Garages is £14,400 each.

REQUIREMENTS:

(a) Account for the above transactions in the books of Bulwell Aggregates Ltd showing the entries in the profit and loss account and balance sheet for the years 20X1, 20X2, 20X3 and 20X4. **10 Marks**

(b) Account for the above transactions in the books of Granby Garages plc, showing the entries in the hire purchase trading account for the years 20X1, 20X2 and 20X3. This is the only hire purchase transaction undertaken by this company **10 Marks**

Calculations to the nearest £.

Total Marks = 20

13 STATEMENT OF PRINCIPLES (Pilot paper) *36 mins*

The following definitions have been taken from the Accounting Standards Board's *Draft Statement of Principles*.

- 'Assets are rights or other access to future economic benefits controlled by an entity as a result of past transactions or events.'
- 'Liabilities are obligations of an entity to transfer economic benefits as a result of past transactions or events.'

SSAP 21 *Leases and hire purchase contracts* requires lessees to capitalise finance leases in their financial statements.

REQUIREMENTS:

(a) Explain how SSAP 21's treatment of finance leases applies the definitions of assets and liabilities. **10 Marks**

(b) Explain how the finalised *Statement of Principles* will assist in the standard-setting process. **10 Marks**

Total Marks = 20

14 FABRICATORS *36 mins*

Fabricators Ltd, an engineering company, makes up its financial statements to 31 March in each year. The financial statements for the year ended 31 March 20X1 showed a turnover of £3m and trading profit of £400,000.

Before approval of the financial statements by the board of directors on 30 June 20X1 the following events took place.

(a) The financial statements of Patchup Ltd for the year ended 28 February 20X1 were received which indicated a permanent decline in that company's financial position. Fabricators Ltd had bought shares in Patchup Ltd some years ago and this purchase was included in unquoted investments at its cost of £100,000. The financial statements received indicated that this investment was now worth only £50,000.

(b) There was a fire at the company's warehouse on 30 April 20X1 when stock to the value of £500,000 was destroyed. It transpired that the stock in the warehouse was under-insured by some 50%.

(c) It was announced on 1 June 20X1 that the company's design for tank cleaning equipment had been approved by the major oil companies and this could result in an increase in the annual turnover of some £1m with a relative effect on profits.

The following points have also to be taken into consideration.

(d) Bills receivable of £150,000 were discounted on 15 March 20X1 and are due for maturity on 15 September 20X1.

(e) The company is expecting to receive orders worth up to £2 million for a new item of equipment which is at present on field trials. The equipment is being imported by the company at selling price less a trade discount of 25%. A quantity of this new equipment was held in stock on 31 March 20X1.

REQUIREMENT:

Explain how, if at all, items (a) to (e) above should be reflected in the accounts of Fabricators Ltd for the year ended 31 March 20X1. **20 Marks**

15 WISTERIA *36 mins*

Wisteria plc made an issue of 500,000 ordinary shares of £1 each at a premium of 15p a share. Under the terms of issue cash payments were due:

20X7		per share
1 January	On application (inclusive of 15p premium on issue)	40p
1 February	On allotment	60p
1 March	Balance	15p

The response to the issue is summarised below.

Number of applicants in categories	*Number of shares*	
	Applied for by each applicant	*Allotted to each applicant*
40	10,000	5,000
20	100,000	10,000
1	400,000	100,000

It was a condition of the issue that amounts overpaid were to be retained by the company and used in reduction of further sums due on shares allotted. All surplus contributions were returned on 15 February 20X7.

Schwein, who had subscribed £4,000 on an application for 10,000 shares, was unable to meet the balance due on the allotment of 5,000 shares. On 1 April 20X7, the directors forfeited the 5,000 shares. All other shareholders paid the sums requested on the due dates.

On 1 May 20X7 the directors reissued the 5,000 shares as fully paid to Goody and received his cheque for £5,250 in full settlement on the day of allotment.

REQUIREMENTS:

(a) Prepare a statement as on 1 February 20X7, showing the overpayments or underpayments in respect of each category of applicants. **10 Marks**

(b) Show how the above transactions would appear in the books of the company. **10 Marks**

Total Marks = 20

16 RATIO ANALYSIS *36 mins*

(a) Explain the uses and limitations of ratio analysis when used to interpret the published financial accounts of a company. **8 Marks**

(b) State and express *two* ratios which can be used to analyse *each* of the following:

- Profitability
- Liquidity
- Management control **3 Marks**

(c) Explain briefly points which are important when using ratios to interpret accounts under each of the headings in (b) above. **9 Marks**

Total Marks = 20

17 CONGLOMERATE *36 mins*

Conglomerate plc is a diversified trading group with over 50 subsidiary companies. Two of its subsidiaries AB Ltd and CD Ltd are manufacturers in the same industry. A summary of the latest accounts of both companies is set out below.

	Historical cost accounts	
	Year ended 31 March 20X1	
	AB	*CD*
	£'000	£'000
Turnover	3,505	6,147
Manufacturing expenses		
Direct labour	481	624
Materials consumed	1,380	2,601
Depreciation	272	450
Plant hire	42	127
Factory overhead	244	380
Selling and administrative expenses	360	525
Interest	60	280
	2,839	4,987
Profit before taxation	666	1,160
Taxation	305	410
Retained profit	361	750
Fixed assets (book value)	2,635	3,969
Current assets	3,195	2,350
Current liabilities	2,018	1,682
Equity capital	3,312	2,637
Loan capital	500	2,000
Average number of employees	95	119

The Board of Conglomerate plc wishes to review the performance and position of the two companies and requires a comparison of their results with those that can be expected in the industry.

A recent report published by the trade association for the industry includes the following average ratios achieved by companies in the industry (based on historical cost accounts).

Pre-tax return on capital employed	19%
Pre-tax profit to sales	21%
Asset turnover	0.9
Current ratio	1.7
Capital gearing (fixed interest capital/total capital)	28%

REQUIREMENT:

Prepare a report for the board of Conglomerate plc comparing the performance and position of the two subsidiaries with each other and with the information produced by the trade association. Include in your report comment on the limitations of using ratios for such interpretation particularly mentioning the effects of inflation. **20 Marks**

18 INHERITANCE (Pilot paper) *36 mins*

Your friend inherited a small manufacturing company during 19X9. At the beginning of 20X0 he appointed a full-time managing director to run the company on his behalf. The new managing director has made a number of changes to the company's business strategy. Your friend has very little business experience, and is concerned that the new director's changes have not been particularly beneficial.

The profit and loss accounts for the years ended 31 December 19X9 and 20X0 are shown below, along with the balance sheets at those dates.

Profit and loss accounts for the year ended 31 December

	19X9	*20X0*
	£'000	£'000
Sales	2,700	8,400
Cost of sales	(1,080)	(5,040)
Gross profit	1,620	3,360
Selling expenses	(450)	(810)
Bad debts	(54)	(420)
Depreciation	(174)	(624)
Interest	(36)	(576)
Net profit	906	930
Balance brought forward	981	1,887
	1,887	2,817

Balance sheets as at 31 December

	19X9		*20X0*	
	£'000	£'000	£'000	£'000
Fixed assets				
Factory		1,350		1,323
machinery		1,470		5,289
		2,820		6,612
Current assets				
Stock	90		714	
Debtors	249		1,749	
Bank	36		-	
	375		2,463	
Current liabilities				
Creditors	(108)		(525)	
Bank	-		(33)	
	(108)		(558)	
Working capital		267		1,905
		3,087		8,517
Borrowings		(300)		(4,800)
		2,787		3,717
Share capital		900		900
Profit and loss		1,887		2,817
		2,787		3,717

REQUIREMENTS:

(a) List and explain three major changes which the new managing director has made to the running of the company and explain whether each has been beneficial. You should support your answer with appropriate ratios. **15 Marks**

(b) Explain why it might be misleading to evaluate the effects of the changes after just one year. **5 Marks**

Total Marks = 20

SCENARIO A

Midas plc is a conglomerate that produces its accounts at 31 December. John Poor is the head office accountant. He has been reviewing the accounts of Fencing Ltd, a recently acquired group company that carries on business as a fencing company, and considered the rate of stock and debtor turnover to be unexpectedly high.

In response to his enquiry, Fencing Ltd produced the following information concerning stock and debtors.

Stocks

Stocks were made up of raw materials at cost of £86,000 and finished goods at a cost of £27,000.

The raw materials consisted of 8,600 metres of teak fencing at £10 per metre. The finished goods consisted of 10 security gates the company had manufactured in its own foundry in Scotland at a cost of £1,500 each and 1,000 metres of metal fencing manufactured in the foundry at a cost of £12 per metre.

Debtors

Debtors were made up of trade debtors at £55,000 and amounts recoverable on contracts at £24,000.

The trade debtors consists of £25,000 for completed work that had been invoiced in the latter half of December 20X1 and £30,000 that had been sold back by Factors plc. The amounts recoverable on contracts consisted of £19,000 due on a contract with Broad Rail plc and £5,000 due on a contract with Adsa plc.

John Poor made some further enquiries and obtained the following additional information.

Raw materials

Cheap supplies of teak had started coming into the country in January 20X2 from Indonesia at a list price of £5 per metre. The trade press had described these imports as dumping and had been making representations to government for the imports to be restricted.

Finished goods

Security gates could from mid January 20X2 be imported from Germany at £750 per gate. The German supplier had invested in the last decade in advanced technology and the company could not match its costs at its own foundry in Scotland.

Trade debtors

Fencing Ltd had a factoring arrangement whereby it sold all of its trade debts to Factors plc. The procedure was for Fencing Ltd to send invoices to Factors plc at two weekly intervals. Factors plc administered the sales ledger and handled all aspects of collection of the debt in return for an administration charge at a rate of 1.5% payable monthly. Factors plc pays the full amount of the debts to Fencing Ltd and charges interest at 4% above base rate. Any debts unrecovered by Factors plc after three months are sold back to Fencing Ltd. As mentioned above there is £30,000 included in the balance sheet that has arisen from such a sale-back. Factors plc confirmed that as at 31 December 20X1 they held unpaid invoices for which they had paid Fencing Ltd amounting to £102,000.

Amounts recoverable on contracts: Broad Rail plc contract

The contract with Broad Rail plc had been entered into on 1 July 20X0 and is due for completion on 30 June 20X2. The contract price was £120,000 and costs were estimated at £80,000 and were expected to accrue evenly over the period of the contract.

In the 20X0 accounts the amount due on the contract was calculated as follows.

	£	£
Cost to 31.12.X0		20,000
Total profit on contract	40,000	
Attribute 25% for six months		10,000
Turnover		30,000
Progress payments		25,000
Amount recoverable on contract		5,000

During 20X1 Fencing Ltd received progress payments of £50,000. The company had experienced difficulties in controlling the scheduling of the work and due to their inefficiency had incurred additional costs of £16,000 during the year.

It was normal industry practice for the customer to hold a 5% retention. The company explained that the high rate of retention had been stipulated by the customer because in 20X0 Fencing Ltd had only just been listed as an approved supplier and had little experience of managing large contracts. It was expected that the management problems that had arisen in 20X1 had been overcome and that the costs of 20X2 would be in line with the original estimate.

Applying Paragraph 23 of SSAP 9, the amount recoverable on contracts had been calculated at 31 December 20X1 as follows.

	£	£	£
Cost in 20X1			56,000
Total profit on contract	40,000		
Less cost escalation	16,000		
Revised profit	24,000		
Attribute 75% for 18 months		18,000	
Less profit taken in 20X0		10,000	
			8,000
Turnover			64,000
Progress payments			50,000
Amount recoverable on contract			14,000
Amount recoverable 20X0			5,000
			19,000

Amounts recoverable on contracts: Adsa plc contract

The contract with Adsa plc had been entered into on 1 October 20X1 and was due for completion on 31 March 20X2.

The contract price was £10,000 and costs were estimated at £7,500 and were expected to accrue evenly over the period of the contract.

The amount due on contract was calculated as follows.

	£	£
Cost to 31.12.X1		3,750
Total profit on contract	2,500	
Attribute 50% for three months		1,250
Turnover		5,000
Progress payments		-
Amount recoverable on contract		5,000

Note. You should answer both questions. Each is worth 15 marks and should take 27 minutes.

1 (a) Discuss whether you consider that the figure of £19,000 that had been calculated as the amount due on contract from the Broad Rail plc contract gave a true and fair view. **7 Marks**

(b) State with clear reasons, the amounts at which you consider the stock figures should appear in the accounts. **8 Marks**

2 State, with clear reasons, the amounts at which you consider the following items should appear in the accounts of Fencing Ltd as at 31 December 20X1 together with any notes to the accounts.

(a) Debtors **10 Marks**
(b) Factors plc **5 Marks**

SCENARIO B (Pilot paper) *47 mins*

T plc is a quoted company which owns a large number of hotels throughout the UK. The company's latest trial balance at 31 December 20X0 is as follows.

	£'000	£'000
Administrative expenses	3,000	
Bank	300	
Creditors		1,700
Distribution costs	4,000	
Food purchases	2,100	
Heating and lighting	3,000	
Hotel buildings: cost	490,000	
depreciation to date		46,200
Hotel fixtures and fittings: cost	18,000	
depreciation to date		9,400
Interest	4,950	
Interim dividend paid	1,000	
Loans, repayable 20X8		110,000
Profit and loss		86,000
Sales of accommodation and food		68,500
Share capital: £1 shares, fully paid		220,000
Stock as at 31 December 19X9	400	
Taxation	50	
Wages: administrative staff	6,000	
housekeeping and restaurant staff	9,000	
	541,800	541,800

Additional information

(i) During the year the company spent a total of £12m on a new hotel and purchased new fixtures for £7m. These acquisitions have been included in the relevant trial balance totals.

You will need the breakdown for the fixed asset note

(ii) Hotels are to be depreciated by 2 per cent of cost, and fixtures and fittings by 25 per cent of the reducing balance, with a full year's depreciation to be charged in the year of acquisition or revaluation.

(iii) Closing stocks of foodstuffs and other consumables were valued at £470,000 on 31 December 20X0.

(iv) The balance on the taxation account is the amount remaining after the settlement of the corporation tax liability for the year ended 31 December 19X9. The directors have estimated the corporation tax liability for the year ended 31 December 20X0 at £10.2m.

The £50,000 is therefore an underprovision

(v) The directors have proposed a final dividend of £6m.

The following information relates to question 2 only

(vi) During the year the company's external auditors expressed some concern that a large proportion of the hotels were several years old and yet none had ever been professionally valued. The directors were unsure whether there was a material difference between market valuations and net book values, and commissioned a valuation on three of the company's oldest hotels in order to see whether a more detailed valuation might prove useful.

	Original cost	*Depreciation to 31.12.20X0*	*Market value at 31.12.20X0*	*Estimated useful life at 31.12.20X0*
	£'000	£'000	£'000	Years
Hotel A	800	180	1,300	50
Hotel B	700	120	850	30
Hotel C	1,000	140	650	40

During the year ended 31 December 2001 the directors are planning to start a major programme of repairs and refurbishment on the company's hotels. Over a five-year period the buildings will be checked to ensure that they are structurally sound, and they will be repaired wherever necessary. Preliminary investigations suggest that some of the hotels will not achieve their expected useful lives if the company does not invest in this preventative maintenance. The company will also redecorate the hotels and replace most of the furniture in the bedrooms and restaurants. The redecoration will create a new corporate image for all of T plc's hotels that will improve the company's marketing and promotion.

An indication that they are **business assets**

Required

1 Prepare T plc's profit and loss account for the year ended 31 December 20X0 and its balance sheet at that date. These should be in a form suitable for publication and should be accompanied by notes as far as you are able to prepare these from the information provided.

You are *not* required to prepare a statement of accounting policies, nor a statement of total recognised gains and losses, nor a reconciliation of movements in shareholders' funds. **26 Marks**

2 *61 mins*

(a) The directors are keen to evaluate the effects of the revaluation of the hotels. They have asked for some further analyses and reports.

Required

(i) Calculate the effects of the revaluation on the depreciation charge on the three hotels for the year ended 31 December 20X1, assuming that a full year's depreciation is charged on the revalued amounts. **3 Marks**

(ii) Calculate the balance which would appear on the revaluation reserve in respect of the revalued hotels. **3 Marks**

The directors regard the company's hotels as assets which generate both income and capital gains. Two of the hotels which were valued are appreciating in value. The company has sold hotels in the past in order to realise such gains.

(iii) Explain whether it would be feasible for the directors to justify charging no depreciation, on the grounds that their hotels tend to increase in value or are held as investment properties. Your answer should refer to accounting concepts and to relevant accounting standards. **7 Marks**

The inference, usually, for exams, is that the directors need putting straight!!

(iv) The directors are keen to capitalise the costs of the programme of repairs and refurbishment. Describe the factors which will have to be considered in deciding whether this will be acceptable from an accounting point of view. Your answer should refer to accounting concepts and to the relevant accounting standards as appropriate. **5 Marks**

(b) One of T plc's directors believes that the company should not have revalued the hotels just because of the external auditors' concerns. He has suggested that the finance director should withhold the results of the valuation from the auditor until the board has had an opportunity to consider its implications. The information should be released only if the directors decide to incorporate the results in the financial statements. The finance director is unhappy with this suggestion because he is concerned that it might lead to a qualified audit report.

Required

(i) Describe the external auditors' responsibilities with respect to the financial statements. **8 Marks**

Tests of your knowledge

(ii) Explain what is meant by a 'qualified' audit report and describe the differences between a 'qualified' and an 'unqualified' report. **8 Marks**

Total marks = 34

1 REGULATORS

Stock Exchange Listing Rules

A listed company is a public limited company whose shares are bought and sold on The Stock Exchange. This involves the signing of a listing agreement which requires compliance with the 'Listing Rules' (formerly known as the Yellow Book). This contains amongst other things The Stock Exchange's detailed rules on the information to be disclosed in listed companies' accounts. This, then, is one regulatory influence on a listed company's accounts. The Stock Exchange enforces compliance by monitoring accounts and reserving the right to withdraw a company's shares from The Stock Exchange List: ie the company's shares would no longer be traded through The Stock Exchange. There is, however, no statutory requirement to obey these rules.

Companies Acts

All companies in the UK have to comply with the Companies Acts, which lay down detailed requirements on the preparation of accounts. Company law is becoming more and more detailed, partly because of EC Directives. Another reason to increase statutory regulation is that listed companies are under great pressure to show profit growth and an obvious way to achieve this is to manipulate accounting policies. If this involves breaking the law, as opposed to ignoring professional guidance, company directors may think twice before bending the rules - or, at least, this is the government's hope.

Accounting Standards

Professional guidance is given by the Accounting Standards Board (ASB), overseen by the Financial Reporting Council. Prescriptive guidance is given in Statements of Standard Accounting Practice (SSAPs) and Financial Reporting Standards (FRSs) which must be applied in all accounts required to show a 'true and fair view' (ie all companies). SSAPs and FRSs are issued after extensive consultation and are revised as required to reflect economic or legal changes. Until fairly recently, companies have been able to disguise non-compliance if their auditors did not qualify the audit report. However, the Companies Act 1989 requires details of non-compliance to be disclosed in the accounts. The Review Panel examines such 'defective' accounts and they could be revised under court order if necessary and directors signing such accounts can be prosecuted and fined (or even imprisoned). This sanction applies to breach of both accounting standards and company law.

2 FRS 3 STATEMENTS

(a) *Statement of total recognised gains and losses*

	£'000
Profit for the financial year	566
Surplus on revaluation of freehold land and buildings (500 – 375-5 (see (c) below)	120
Deficit on revaluation of investment properties (160 – 100)	(60)
	626

(b) *Reconciliation of movements in shareholders' funds*

	£'000
Profit for the financial year	566
Dividend	(200)
	366
Other recognised gains and losses	
Temporary write down to IRR	(60)
Surplus on revaluation	120
New share capital subscribed	600
Net addition to shareholders' funds	1,026
Opening shareholders' funds	6,820
Closing shareholders' funds	7,846

(c) *Note of historical cost profits for the period*

	£'000
Reported profit before tax	806
Realisation of property revaluation gains of previous years	
$(50{,}000 - (\frac{50{,}000}{10} \times 3))$	* 35
Difference between an historical cost depreciation charge and the actual depreciation charge of the year calculated on the revalued amount ((500,000 – 375,000)/25)	5
	846
Historical cost retained profit for the year (366 + 35* + 5)	406

* Paper 6 examiner does not require you to put through the annual transfer from revaluation reserve to profit and loss reserve. The above answer includes such annual transfer for technical completeness.

3 CEE EFF

(a) *Calculation of operating profit*

PROFIT AND LOSS ACCOUNT

	£'000		£'000
Taxation*	19	Balance at 1.1.X4	55
Dividends	28	Profit for the year (bal fig)	69
Debenture interest (80 × 15%)	12		
Balance at 31.12.X4	65		
	124		124

* Last year's year end provision

(b) CF PLC
CASH FLOW STATEMENT
FOR THE YEAR ENDED 31 DECEMBER 20X4

Reconciliation of operating profit to net cash inflow from operating activities

	£'000
Operating profit (part (a))	69
Depreciation (90 – 56)	34
Increase in stocks	(8)
Increase in debtors	(7)
Increase in creditors	9
Net cash inflow from operating activities	97

CASH FLOW STATEMENT

	£'000
Net cash inflow from operating activities	97
Returns on investments and servicing of finance (note 1)	(12)
Taxation	(17)
Capital expenditure (note 1)	(90)
	(22)
Equity dividends paid	(26)
	(48)
Financing (note 1)	27
Decrease in cash	(21)

Note 1 - Gross cash flows

	£'000	£'000
Returns on investments and servicing of finance		
Interest paid		(12)
Capital expenditure		
Purchase of fixed assets (270 – 180)		(90)
Financing		
Issue of share capital	5	
Share premium	2	
Issue of debentures	20	
		27

(c) Attached to the cash flow statement is a reconciliation of net cash flow to movement in net debt. Note 2 to the cash flow statement is an analysis of changes in net debt.

(d) The cash flow statement shows a decrease in cash of £21,000. On the face of it, this is a matter of concern from the point of view of liquidity especially as the debentures are all repayable in 19X8.

However, it is clear that the decrease in cash has not come about because of unsuccessful operating activities, which have in fact been cash generating. Additionally, the company is spending cash in order to expand: capital expenditure amounts to £90,000. This should lead to better operating results in future years when the assets purchased are brought into use, assuming that the investment in fixed assets is now complete. A close eye must be kept on the cash situation, however, since many companies have gone under by trying to expand too quickly.

(e) The direct method of arriving at net cash inflow from operating activities looks at the actual cash flows, for example:

	£
Cash received from customers	X
Cash payments to suppliers	(X)
Cash paid to and on behalf of employees	(X)
Other cash payments	(X)
Net cash inflow from operating activities	X

The direct method is encouraged where the necessary information is not too costly to obtain, but FRS 1 (revised) does not require it, and favours the indirect method. In practice, therefore, the direct method is rarely used.

Marks and Spencer is an example of a company which has opted for the direct method, possibly because the nature of the business is such that its information systems collect the information in any event.

It is not obvious that FRS 1 (revised) is right in favouring the indirect method. It could be argued that companies ought to monitor their cash flows carefully enough on an ongoing basis to be able to use the direct method at minimal extra cost.

4 FURROW

(a) The depreciable amount of the machine is £(256,000 – 4,000) = £252,000

(i) The annual depreciation charge $\frac{£252{,}000}{3} = £84{,}000$

(ii) The annual depreciation charge is as follows.

	£'000
Year 1 £252,000 × 10/42	60
Year 2 £252,000 × 18/42	108
Year 3 £252,000 × 14/42	84
	252

(iii) The annual depreciation charge is as follows.

		NBV	Charge for year
		£'000	£'000
Year 1:	cost	256	
	depreciation (75%)	(192)	192
	net book value	64	
Year 2:	depreciation (75%)	(48)	48
	net book value	16	
Year 3:	depreciation (75%)	(12)	12
	net book value	4	
			252

(b) FRS 15 requires that if the depreciation method is changed it is unnecessary to adjust amounts charged in previous years. Instead, the new method is simply applied to the unamortised cost of the asset over its remaining useful life.

At the end of year 1, the machine's net book value (after one year's depreciation on the reducing balance method) is £64,000. At that stage it is decided to use the straight line method over the remaining two years of useful life. The charge for depreciation in year 2 will therefore be £30,000 and the asset's net book value at the end of year 2 will be £34,000.

FURROW MANUFACTURING COMPANY
BALANCE SHEET AT END OF YEAR 2 (EXTRACT)

		£
Fixed assets		
Tangible assets		
Plant and machinery:	cost	256,000
	depreciation	(222,000)
		34,000

Note. the directors have decided to change the method of depreciation of the plant and machinery from the reducing balance method to the straight line method in order to allocate the cost of the asset fairly. This has resulted in a depreciation charge for the year which is £18,000 less than under the previous method. (This note is only required if £18,000 is material.)

5 SSAP 19

(a) An investment property is an interest in land and/or buildings:

(i) In respect of which construction work and development have been completed.

(ii) Which is held for its investment potential, any rental income being negotiated at arm's length.

The following are exceptions from the definition.

(i) A property which is owned and occupied by a company for its own purposes is not an investment property.

(ii) A property let to and occupied by another group company is not an investment property for the purposes of its own accounts or the group accounts.

(b) Investment properties should not be subject to periodic charges for depreciation on the basis set out in FRS 15, except for properties held on leases which should be depreciated on the basis set out in FRS 15 at least over the period when the unexpired term is 20 years or less.

Investment properties should be included in the balance sheet at their open market value.

The names of the persons making the valuation, or particulars of their qualifications should be disclosed together with the bases of valuation used by them. If a person making a valuation is an employee or officer of the company or group which owns the property this fact should be disclosed.

Changes in the value of investment properties should not be taken to the profit and loss account but should be disclosed as a movement on an investment revaluation reserve (IRR), unless the total of the investment revaluation reserve is insufficient to cover a deficit, in which case the amount by which the deficit exceeds the amount in the investment revaluation reserve should be charged in the profit and loss account (permanent deficit). A temporary deficit on the IRR is permitted.

(c) Investment properties are not held by an enterprise to be consumed within the business; they are held for their investment potential. In such a situation it is the current value of these investments, and changes in that current value, that is of prime importance rather than a calculation of systematic annual depreciation. Consequently a proper appreciation of the financial position of the company is achieved by valuing these properties at their open market value, recognising rental income in the profit and loss account, rather than valuing them at net book value, establishing how much of the depreciable amount remains unconsumed at the balance sheet date.

6 FRS 10 (May 2003)

(a) (i) Goodwill may be *defined* as the excess of the value of a business as a whole over the fair value of its separately identifiable and accountable net assets (including intangible assets other than goodwill). There are many reasons why goodwill might occur, but positive goodwill arises from favourable circumstances such as an efficient management team, the weakness of competitors, a prime location or a substantial number of loyal customers.

Goodwill should exist in any successful business, created by the circumstances of the business and the people working for it. However, its value is constantly changing and fluctuates according to circumstances and the subjective opinion of the valuer. Any amount attributed to goodwill is unique to the valuer and to the specific point in time at which it is measured, and is only valid for that point in time, and in the circumstances then prevailing.

It should therefore follow that since the value of goodwill which is inherent to the business is continually changing, and is a subjective valuation anyway, it would be inappropriate to 'capitalise' this goodwill and attribute a money value to it in the balance sheet.

The only time that goodwill has an identifiable money value is when one business purchases another. The difference between the purchase price and the fair value of separable net assets is the agreed valuation of goodwill at that time, and the goodwill is paid for - ie 'purchased'. Because purchased goodwill has an objectively verifiable value, and because a business is willing to pay for goodwill in order to derive future benefits from it, perhaps over a period of several years, it is argued that purchased goodwill is an investment and should be capitalised. In order to apply the matching concept, purchased goodwill should then be amortised over the years when the benefits of its purchase are thought to be obtained.

(ii) *Purchased goodwill* need not be capitalised. It may be written off against reserves in the period when it is purchased. However, when purchased goodwill is capitalised it should be depreciated in a systematic way over a period not exceeding its useful economic life. The Companies Act 1985 does not define how the useful economic life should be chosen, but the Act states that the period should be chosen by the directors and their reasons for choosing that period should be disclosed in a note to the accounts. There is a rebuttable presumption in FRS 10 that the useful economic life will not exceed 20 years. The ASC suggested a reason why purchased goodwill ought to be depreciated: 'in the period following an acquisition the value of the purchased goodwill will diminish, and may be replaced, to a greater or lesser extent, by non-purchased goodwill generated by the subsequent activities and circumstances of the business'. Since goodwill fluctuates over time, the purchased goodwill will inevitably be outdated and overtaken by changing circumstances, and will eventually cease to exist entirely.

Non-purchased goodwill must not be shown as a fixed asset, so although this may replace purchased goodwill, it is nevertheless appropriate to depreciate the purchased goodwill entirely.

(b) *Negative goodwill* arises when the fair value of the separable net assets of a business exceeds the value of the business as a whole. Negative goodwill is only significant when it is 'purchased' - ie when one business acquires another. Negative goodwill may arise as the result of a bargain purchase, perhaps because the seller has been forced to make a quick sale. FRS 10 states that negative goodwill should be included in the balance sheet as a 'negative asset' and should be netted off against positive goodwill.

7 SSAP 9

(a) Five stock categories listed in SSAP 9 are:

- Goods purchased for resale
- Consumable goods
- Raw materials and components
- Work in progress
- Finished goods for resale

The general rule of stock valuation is that stock should be valued at the lower of cost and net realisable value.

Valuation at cost follows naturally from the accruals convention. Sales should be matched against costs incurred in generating those sales. Any stocks purchased in a period which remain unsold at the end of that period should be carried forward as an asset so that their cost can be charged against revenue of the period in which they are eventually sold.

In cases where net realisable value is less than cost, a loss should be recognised. This accords with the prudence concept which requires that losses should be recognised as soon as they are foreseen. The loss is recognised by writing down the stock valuation from cost to net realisable value.

(b) SSAP 9 specifies rules for establishing both cost and net realisable value.

Cost

Cost is defined as expenditure incurred in the normal course of business in bringing the stock to its present location and condition. It includes not only purchase price (established on a basis such as FIFO, unit cost or average cost) but also conversion costs including an appropriate proportion of production overheads.

Net realisable value

NRV is defined as the actual or estimated selling price of the stock net of trade discounts, but before settlement discounts, less any further costs to be incurred to put the stock into saleable condition and to market, sell and distribute it. Any relevant events occurring after the balance sheet date but before approval of the accounts should be taken into account in determining NRV.

SSAP 9 also specifies that as far as practicable the comparison of cost and NRV should be done for each stock item separately. Otherwise, foreseeable losses might unacceptably be offset against unrealised profits.

(c) The amount at which Baggaley could have bought the bags from external suppliers is irrelevant; so too is the internal transfer price charged by the workshop to the shop. The relevant amount is the cost of the goods. In this case, the relevant cost is the cost of production, £3.50 per bag. The balance sheet valuation is 1,000 × £3.50 = £3,500.

BAGGALEY LEATHER GOODS
BALANCE SHEET AS AT 31 DECEMBER 20X1 (EXTRACT)

	£
Current assets	
Stock of finished goods	3,500

8 BEAVERS

(a)

CONTRACT ACCOUNT X 201

	£		£
Wages	91,000	Stock c/d	3,000
Materials	36,000	Plant c/d £(9,000 – 6,400)	2,600
Other costs	18,000	Cost of sales transfer (W)	139,500
Head office costs	6,000	∴ Work in progress c/d	14,900
Plant and equipment	9,000		
	160,000		160,000
Stock b/d	3,000		
Plant b/d	2,600		
Work in progress b/d	14,900		

CONTRACTEE ACCOUNT

	£		£
		Bank	150,000
Turnover	180,000	Balance c/d	30,000
	180,000		180,000
Balance b/d	30,000		

Working

	£	£
Actual costs to date		
Wages	91,000	
Materials	33,000	
Other costs	18,000	
HO costs	6,000	
Plant	6,400	
		154,400
Expected future costs		
Wages	10,000	
Materials	12,000	
Other costs	8,000	
Plant	1,600	
		31,600
Estimated total costs		186,000

Proportion charged in the current year:

$\frac{180,000}{240,000} \times £186,000$ 139,500

(b) BALANCE SHEET (extract)

	£
Current assets	
Stocks	
Work in progress	14,900
Debtors	
Amounts recoverable on contracts	30,000

(c)

	£
Turnover (work certified)	180,000
Cost of sales (transferred from work in progress)	139,500
Attributable profit	40,500

It is justifiable to take credit for profit because the contract is nearing its end and results can be foreseen with reasonable certainty. However, the possible bonus has been ignored on the grounds of prudence. It is assumed that profit accrues evenly in proportion to the completed work and that no provisions have to be made for penalties or other contingencies.

9 EXE PLC

(a) *Revaluation*

Exe plc may (optionally) incorporate the revaluation in its books. The entries would be to debit the asset account and credit a revaluation reserve with the surplus of £750,000.

FRS 15 makes it obligatory to provide depreciation on freehold buildings, unless they are investment properties, but not on land. The company should therefore begin to depreciate the building valuation of £850,000 over its estimated useful life.

(b) *R&D*

Expenditure on research, whether pure or applied, must be written off as incurred. However, if any part of the £47,000 can be identified separately as development expenditure, it may (at the company's option) be carried forward as an intangible fixed asset, subject to the criteria in SSAP 13 being satisfied. These criteria relate principally to the technical feasibility and commercial viability of the development project.

(c) *Stocks*

Stock must be stated at the lower of cost and net realisable value. If 5 February 20X3 is earlier than the date on which the accounts were approved by the board, this would be an adjusting post balance sheet event. Cost of sales would be increased and the balance sheet value of stock would be decreased by £40,000.

Factory closure

The factory closure is a non-adjusting post balance sheet event (assuming that 25 January 20X3 is earlier than the date of Board approval of the accounts) because the decision was taken after the balance sheet date. Even so, the notes to the accounts should mention the event and explain its financial effect, if omission of this information would prevent a proper understanding of the accounts.

(d) *Long-term contract losses*

Abnormal provisions for losses on long-term contracts should be charged in arriving at profit on ordinary activities, with separate disclosure by way of note if material in accordance with FRS 3 *Reporting financial performance*, ie as an exceptional item.

Stocks

If the stock error in 20X0 is regarded as a fundamental error it should be treated as a prior period adjustment. The figure of retained profits brought forward at 1 January 20X2 (and also the comparative figure - ie the retained profits brought forward at 1 January 20X1) should be restated in the 20X2 accounts.

(e) *Grant*

Capital-based grants should be credited to revenue over the estimated useful lives of the related assets. This may be achieved in either of two ways (both permitted by SSAP 4):

(i) Net off the grant with the purchase cost of the plant and charge depreciation on the net cost of £90,000.

(ii) Charge depreciation on the gross cost of £120,000, while setting up the £30,000 as a deferred credit in the balance sheet. The deferred credit would then be released to income over the same period as that chosen for depreciating the plant.

10 C PLC

(a)

	Maryhill bypass	*Rottenrow centre*
	£'000	£'000
Turnover	2,800	3,000
Profit/(Loss) (1)	622	(100)
Cost of sales	2,178	3,100
Current assets		
Amount recoverable on contract (2,800 – 2,600)	200	-
Current liabilities		
Payment on account (3,400 – 3,000)	-	(400)
Accrued cost of sales (2,178 – 1,400)	(778)	-
Accrued future losses (3,100 – 2,900)	-	(200)

(1) Maryhill: $(9{,}000 - (1{,}400 + 5{,}600)) \times \frac{2{,}800}{9{,}000} = 622$

Rottenrow: 8,000 – (2,900 + 5,200) = 100

(b) Long-term contracts are recognised as such when they cover at least two accounting periods. If they were not to be treated as they are under SSAP 9 then the costs incurred during the early years of the contract would be recognised but with no corresponding turnover. This would lead to several years of losses then one year of high profits regardless of how profitable the contract really was. The advantage of this approach however would be that there would be no need to use estimates and forecasts.

The current treatment matches an element of the turnover to the costs incurred. There is an attempt to maintain prudence by ensuring that any foreseeable losses are accounted for immediately. This gives a fairer representation of the underlying financial substance of the transaction and makes it easier for the user of the accounts to assess the financial position of the company.

11 EASY

PROFIT AND LOSS ACCOUNT FOR THE YEAR
ENDED 31 DECEMBER 20X8 (EXTRACTS)

	£'000
Income from all fixed asset investments (28 × 5/4) + 25	60
Interest payable and similar charges	20
Tax on profit on ordinary activities	112
Dividends paid and proposed (24 + 8)	32

BALANCE SHEET AS AT 31 DECEMBER 20X8 (EXTRACTS)

	£'000	£'000
Deferred tax asset		5
Taxation payable (CT charge 20X8)	112	
Less: IT suffered (W1)	(3)	
		109
20X8 proposed final dividend		8

Workings

1 *Income tax*

	£'000
Debenture interest received (gross)	35
Debenture interest paid (gross)	20
	15

IT suffered 20% × 15 = 3

12 BULWELL

(a) *Books of Bulwell Aggregates Limited*

LORRIES ACCOUNT

		£
20X1		
1 Jan	Granby Garages	54,000

PROVISION FOR DEPRECIATION ON LORRIES

		£			£
20X1			*20X1*		
			31 Dec	P & L account: 1/4 ×	
31 Dec	Balance c/d	12,500		£(54,000 – (3 × 1,333))	12,500
20X2			*20X2*		
31 Dec	Balance c/d	25,000	1 Jan	Balance b/d	12,500
			31 Dec	P & L account	12,500
		25,000			25,000
20X3			*20X3*		
31 Dec	Balance c/d	37,500	1 Jan	Balance b/d	25,000
			31 Dec	P & L account	12,500
		37,500			37,500
20X4			*20X4*		
31 Dec	Balance c/d	50,000	1 Jan	Balance b/d	37,500
			31 Dec	P & L account	12,500
		50,000			50,000
			20X5		
			1 Jan	Balance b/d	50,000

HP INTEREST PAYABLE

		£			£
20X1			*20X1*		
31 Dec	Bank (W)	11,250	31 Dec	P & L account	11,250
20X2			*20X2*		
31 Dec	Bank (W)	8,063	31 Dec	P & L account	8,063
20X3			*20X3*		
31 Dec	Bank (W)	4,078	31 Dec	P & L account	4,078

GRANBY GARAGES PLC

		£			£
20X1			*20X1*		
1 Jan	Bank - deposit	9,000	1 Jan	Lorries a/c	54,000
31 Dec	Bank (W)	12,750			
	Balance c/d	32,250			
		54,000			54,000
20X2			*20X2*		
31 Dec	Bank (W)	15,937	1 Jan	Balance b/d	32,250
	Balance c/d	16,313			
		32,250			32,250
20X3			*20X3*		
31 Dec	Bank (W)	16,313	1 Jan	Balance b/d	16,313

PROFIT AND LOSS ACCOUNTS (EXTRACTS)

	20X1	*20X2*	*20X3*	*20X4*
	£	£	£	£
HP interest	11,250	8,063	4,078	
Depreciation on lorries	12,500	12,500	12,500	12,500

BALANCE SHEETS AT 31 DECEMBER (EXTRACTS)

		20X1	*20X2*	*20X3*	*20X4*
		£	£	£	£
Fixed assets					
Lorries:	at cost	54,000	54,000	54,000	54,000
	depreciation	12,500	25,000	37,500	50,000
	net book value	41,500	29,000	16,500	4,000
Current liabilities					
HP obligations		15,937	16,313	-	-
Long-term liabilities					
HP obligations		16,313	-	-	-

(b) *Books of Granby Garages plc*

BULWELL AGGREGATES LIMITED

		£			£
20X1			*20X1*		
1 Jan	Sales	54,000	1 Jan	Bank	9,000
			31 Dec	Bank	12,750
				Balance c/d	32,250
		54,000			54,000
20X2			*20X2*		
1 Jan	Balance b/d	32,250	31 Dec	Bank	15,937
				Balance c/d	16,313
		32,250			32,250
20X3			*20X3*		
1 Jan	Balance b/d	16,313	31 Dec	Bank	16,313

HP INTEREST RECEIVABLE

		£			£
20X1			*20X1*		
31 Dec	P & L account	11,250	31 Dec	Bank	11,250
20X2			*20X2*		
31 Dec	P & L account	8,063	31 Dec	Bank	8,063
20X3			*20X3*		
31 Dec	P & L account	4,078	31 Dec	Bank	4,078

TRADING AND PROFIT AND LOSS ACCOUNTS (EXTRACTS)

		20X1	20X2	20X3
	£	£	£	£
Sales	54,000		-	-
Cost of sales on HP	43,200	-	-	
Gross profit on HP sales		10,800	-	-
HP interest receivable		11,250	8,063	4,078

Working

Apportionment of HP instalments between interest and capital repayment.

	20X1	20X2	20X3
	£	£	£
Opening liability (after deposit)	45,000	32,250	16,313
Add interest at 25%	11,250	8,063	4,078
	56,250	40,313	20,391
Less instalment	24,000	24,000	20,391
Closing liability	32,250	16,313	Nil
Interest element as above	11,250	8,063	4,078
∴ Capital repayment	12,750	15,937	16,313
Total instalment	24,000	24,000	20,391

13 STATEMENT OF PRINCIPLES

(a) SSAP 21 is an example of substance triumphing over form where HP contracts or finance leases are concerned. In legal terms the lessor may be the owner of the asset, but the lessee enjoys all the risks and rewards which ownership of the asset would convey. This is the key element to SSAP 21. The lessee is deemed to have an asset as they must maintain and run the asset through its useful life.

The lessee enjoys the future economic benefits of the asset as a result of entering into the lease. There is a corresponding liability which is the obligation to pay the instalments on the lease until it expires. Assets and liabilities cannot be netted off. If finance leases were treated in a similar manner to the existing treatment of operating leases then no asset would be recognised and lease payments would be expensed through the profit and loss as they were incurred. This is off balance sheet finance. The company has assets in use and liabilities to lessors which are not recorded in the financial statements. This would be misleading to the users of the accounts and make it appear as though the assets which were recorded were more efficient in producing returns than was actually the case.

(b) The *Statement of Principles* provides a framework of principles for standard setters and those involved in the preparation of accounts. At one stage accounting standards were produced to address major flaws in the approach to preparing accounts. This was a fire fighting approach and lead to some inconsistencies.

The Statement helps guide the standard setters as they produce standards. It also means that the process should be more efficient and less controversial. Anyone involved in accountancy will be aware of the content of the Statement and therefore any objections to new standards should be based on how they compare with the guidelines in the Statement.

The enforcement of standards will be more straightforward as the underlying principles of financial reporting have been made more transparent by the Statement.

This transparency should enhance the standing of the accountancy profession and allow a platform for discussion and debate in the future.

14 FABRICATORS

The treatment of the events arising in the case of Fabricators Ltd would be as follows.

(a) *Investment*

The fall in value of the investment in Patchup Ltd has arisen over the previous year and that company's financial accounts for the year to 28 February 20X1 provide additional evidence of conditions that existed at the balance sheet date. The loss of £50,000 is material in terms of the

trading profit figure and, as an adjusting event, should be reflected in the financial statements of Fabricators Ltd as an exceptional item in accordance with FRS 3.

(b) *Stock fire*

The destruction of stock by fire on 30 April (one month after the balance sheet date) must be considered to be a non-adjusting event (ie this is 'a new condition which did not exist at the balance sheet date'). Since the loss is material, being £250,000, it should be disclosed by way of a note to the accounts. The note should describe the nature of the event and an estimate of its financial effect. Non-reporting of this event would prevent users of the financial statements from reaching a proper understanding of the financial position.

(c) *New equipment*

The approval on 1 June of the company's design for tank cleaning equipment creates a new condition which did not exist at the balance sheet date. This is, therefore, a non-adjusting event and if it is of such material significance that non-reporting would prevent a proper understanding of the financial position it should be disclosed by way of note. In this instance non-disclosure should not prevent a proper understanding of the financial position and disclosure by note may be unnecessary.

(d) *Bills of exchange*

The bills would have been discounted with recourse and hence there is a possibility of a liability arising if the bills are not honoured. Under FRS 12, the contingent liability of £150,000 in respect of bills discounted should be disclosed by way of note in the financial statements.

(e) *New orders*

In these circumstances, if the field trials are not successful, then there is a possibility that it will be difficult to sell the equipment. Therefore, consideration should be given as to whether the equipment should be written down in the accounts to net realisable value. If the loss is not probable, a write down would not be required but consideration should be given as to whether the contingent liability should be disclosed by way of note. In the circumstances given, it would appear that the possibility of loss is remote and therefore, under FRS 12, no disclosure would be required. The expected future sales which might arise should not be included in the financial statements.

15 WISTERIA

(a) APPLICATION AND ALLOTMENT CASH STATEMENT

APPLICATION				ALLOTMENT				
No. of applicants In catego-ries	*No. of shares per applicant*	*Total shares*	*Applica-tion monies*	*Issued to each*	*Total shares*	*Total due on appli-cation & allotment*	*Over-payments*	*Under-payments*
			£			£	£	£
40	10,000	400,000	160,000	5,000	200,000	200,000		40,000
20	100,000	2,000,000	800,000	10,000	200,000	200,000	600,000	
1	400,000	400,000	160,000	100,000	100,000	100,000	60,000	
		2,800,000	1,120,000		500,000	500,000	660,000	40,000

(b)

BANK ACCOUNT

	£		£
Application & allotment a/c	1,120,000	Application & allotment a/c	660,000
Application & allotment a/c	39,000		
Call a/c	74,250	Balance c/f	578,500
Forfeited shares a/c	5,250		
	1,238,500		1,238,500

APPLICATION AND ALLOTMENT ACCOUNT

20X7		£	*20X7*		£
Feb 1	Ordinary share a/c	425,000	Jan 1	Bank: application monies on 2,800,000 shares of 40p per share	1,120,000
	Share premium a/c	75,000	Feb 1	Bank	39,000
Feb 15	Bank: excess application monies returned	660,000	Apr 1	Forfeited shares a/c	1,000
		1,160,000			1,160,000

SHARE CAPITAL: £1 ORDINARY SHARES

20X7		£	*20X7*		£
Apr 1	Forfeited shares a/c	5,000	Feb 1	Application & allotment a/c	425,000
Mar 1	Balance c/f	500,000	Mar 1	Call a/c	75,000
				Forfeited shares a/c	5,000
		505,000			505,000

SHARE PREMIUM ACCOUNT

20X7		£	*20X7*		£
Mar 1	Balance c/f	78,500	Feb 1	Application & allotment a/c	75,000
			Mar 1	Forfeited shares a/c	3,500
		78,500			78,500

CALL ACCOUNT

20X7		£	*20X7*		£
Mar 1	Ordinary share capital a/c	75,000	Mar 1	Bank	74,250
			Apr 1	Forfeited shares a/c	750
		75,000			75,000

FORFEITED SHARES ACCOUNT

20X7		£	*20X7*		£
Apr 1	Application & allotment a/c	1,000	Apr 1	Ordinary share capital a/c	5,000
	Call a/c	750			
Mar 1	Ordinary share capital a/c	5,000	May 1	Bank (Goody)	5,250
	Share premium a/c	3,500			
		10,250			10,250

Note. A separate forfeited shares reissued account may be used to record the transactions for the reissue of shares.

16 RATIO ANALYSIS

(a) *Uses.* Ratio analysis can be used to assess the performance and financial condition of an enterprise over time and in comparison with other enterprises. Ratios are more useful than assessments based on the absolute values of financial or operational measurements because valid comparisons cannot be made using absolute measures. For example, a higher profit in absolute terms may represent a lower return on capital employed than a much smaller figure in absolute terms. Consequently, such values can best be assessed by measuring and comparing ratios.

For example, it is difficult to assess the relative profits of two enterprises or an enterprise in two different periods without reference to the asset base or the level of sales which have generated those profits.

Ratios are also useful in summarising the information in published accounts and in directing the user's attention to key areas, which may vary from company to company.

Limitations. The main limitations on the usefulness of ratio analysis are the implicit assumptions about the relationships between the elements of the ratio and the effect of accounting policies on

these calculations. Such ratios as return on capital employed assume that there is a relationship between the asset base of an enterprise and its profitability. This may not be a valid assumption particularly in the short term and particularly for fast growing companies. This relationship may also be invalidated by the accounting methods used; for example, a comparison of ROCE between two companies may not be valid if each has a different policy regarding the capitalisation of development costs, depreciation of fixed assets or the amortisation of goodwill. Again, small companies may not be readily comparable with large companies because of differences in, say, cost structure and distribution policy.

Calculation of ratios can become an end, not a means, and can obscure important features only apparent from scrutiny of the accounts themselves. Additionally, unusual features of a business or one-off factors (such as a strike) can make ratios meaningless, as can creative accounting.

(b) (i) Gross margin $= \dfrac{\text{Gross profit}}{\text{Turnover}}$

Return on capital employed $= \dfrac{\text{Profit before tax and interest}}{\text{Total capital employed}}$

(Alternatives: net profit margin, asset turnover)

(ii) Current ratio $= \dfrac{\text{Current assets}}{\text{Current liabilities}}$

Acid test (quick ratio) $= \dfrac{\text{Cash, current investments and debtors}}{\text{Current liabilities}}$

(iii) Stock turnover $= \dfrac{\text{Stock and WIP}}{\text{Cost of sales}} \times 365$

Fixed asset turnover $= \dfrac{\text{Fixed assets}}{\text{Turnover}}$

(Alternatives: debtors and creditors turnover periods)

(c) *Important points in using ratios*

(i) *Profitability* is assumed to be one of the chief aims of a business. The providers of capital must be recompensed with an adequate level of return or they will take their funds elsewhere. Additionally, profit must be earned for retention to allow for asset replacement and expansion. Looking at profit growth is one of the easiest ways of measuring directors' stewardship of a company and of assessing a company's true market value. However, profit is also very easily manipulated and vulnerable to factors outside the directors' control, such as recession

Gross margin. This ratio will vary within any one enterprise for different products or product groups, and will, therefore, need further analysis. Products with relatively high gross margins will often command a premium price in the market because they have some competitive advantage; they may enjoy patent protection or some other monopoly position. As competition increases and rival products are introduced, gross margins may fall. Additionally, in published accounts gross profit will vary depending on the constituents of cost of sales (not determined by statute).

ROCE depends considerably on accounting measurement. In particular, companies that have an ageing fixed asset base are likely to show an improving trend of ROCE. Also, in the short term, ROCE can be enhanced by reducing such expenses as research and advertising or by less conservative depreciation policies. In interpreting ROCE it is, therefore, important the effect of accounting policies are known and understood.

(ii) *Liquidity* is of paramount importance since a profitable company which cannot meet its short-term commitments may have to resort to expensive short-term borrowing to enable it to go on in business, thus eroding profitability and endangering its financial stability.

On the other hand, a company may not be using its working capital efficiently. It is not a good idea to maintain high stock debtor and cash balances since there is no return on these assets and in the case of stock and debtors there is a risk of loss of value over time from obsolescence, theft or damage of stock and bad debts.

Trends in liquidity ratios are therefore very important. Deterioration signals loss of management control whereas improvement signals either better management or stagnation. Ratios which appear odd in isolation can be put in context if compared with other years. If ratios are consistent and the company appears otherwise stable, then the ratios are probably satisfactory (although changes in the business or financial environment may necessitate changes in liquidity management).

Current ratio. A value of two is normally regarded as satisfactory, representing an appropriate degree of liquidity. However, the actual composition of the current assets is important, since if a large proportion consists of stocks which may take several months to liquidate, the company may have difficulty in meeting its short term liabilities. Additionally, each industry has a different norm. Retailers, for example, selling for cash and turning stock over very quickly, often have extremely low current ratios which do not signal liquidity problems.

The *acid test* is often a more useful measure of a company's short term liquidity. Even then, if debtors or a major portion of them are likely to be slow to pay even an acid test ratio of one may disguise some potential liquidity problems.

(iii) *Management control* is assessed by determining how efficiently each asset is being used and how well short-term credit is being used compared with short-term assets. Efficiency has to be balanced against other objectives, however, such as maintaining customer and supplier goodwill by allowing sufficient credit, minimising stock-outs and not exceeding credit terms granted. The policy adopted in each area will affect profitability.

Stock turnover is a means of assessing how successful the company is in turning stock into sales. This is normally expressed as a number of days sales currently in stock and will vary from industry to industry. If this ratio is too high or increasing it may mean that too much capital is tied up unproductively; if it is too low or decreasing, sales may be lost due to stock-outs.

Fixed asset turnover measures the effective use of fixed assets, how intensively they are used. Other things being equal, the higher this ratio, the more efficient is the use of fixed assets to create sales and the more profitable the company. However, this ratio will vary from industry to industry reflecting differing capital intensities.

17 CONGLOMERATE

To: The Board of Directors of Conglomerate plc
From: The Chief Accountant Date: xx/xx/xx

Performance and position of AB Ltd and CD Ltd

This report has been prepared following the board decision to review the performance and relative position of two subsidiary companies of Conglomerate plc, AB Ltd and CD Ltd.

A mere examination of accounting figures is normally insufficient to allow for any meaningful conclusions to be reached, and ratio analysis enables the available data to be placed on a more comparable basis. The information used to produce this report was extracted from the historical cost accounts for the year ended 31 March 20X1 of the two companies, and from average ratios for the industry published by the industry trade association. The calculation of relevant ratios is illustrated in the appendix attached to the report.

Performance

The primary ratio, the return on capital employed (ROCE), is perhaps the most important profitability ratio. That for AB Ltd (19%) is comparable with the industry average, but considerably less than the ROCE for CD Ltd (31%). An examination of *secondary ratios* reveals that the reasons for this are CD Ltd's better than industry average profit margin and asset turnover.

AB Ltd's profit margin is 2.7% less than that of CD Ltd and this is probably due to the higher relative costs of AB Ltd as revealed by the expenses to sales ratios. Action should be taken either to reduce these costs (in particular direct labour costs and selling and distribution costs) or possibly to raise selling prices (although market considerations may prevent this action).

Asset utilisation

The asset turnover reveals that CD Ltd is using its assets more effectively than either AB Ltd or the industry average. This efficiency can be further examined by looking at the fixed asset turnover and working capital ratios, which show that CD Ltd not only uses its fixed assets more efficiently, but has a lower level of working capital. Since working capital does not directly earn profit for a business, AB Ltd is unable to match CD Ltd's return on capital employed. However, if working capital is too low a company may be in danger of over-trading and becoming unable to meet its financial commitments.

The current ratio reveals that both companies are below the industry average and CD Ltd's position may be unacceptable. The quick ratio (details not available) would reveal whether immediate problems exist.

Capital structure

The permanent capital of a company may be divided into two categories, share capital and loan capital. A highly geared company (where fixed interest capital is almost as great or greater than equity capital including reserves) must earn sufficient profits to cover interest charges before any amount is available for the equity shareholders; and the higher the gearing the more difficult it may be to raise further long-term loans. The gearing of AB Ltd (13%) is below the industry average (28%) while that of CD Ltd (43%) is well above. In fact, CD Ltd is highly geared compared to the UK industry as a whole but may still be able to raise further long-term funds as the interest cover of 5 indicates that the risk is not too high. AB Ltd should be able to borrow long term and increase its gearing without too much difficulty.

Limitations of ratio analysis

Care should be taken in drawing conclusions from the ratios provided. The reasons for this include the following.

(a) Ratios on their own do not provide information to enable managers to gauge performance or make control decisions. It is necessary to provide budgeted or target ratios, ratios of previous accounting periods, or ratios of other companies or divisions, as a yardstick for comparison.

(b) There must be a careful definition of ratios used. For example, should return equal profit before interest and taxation, profit after taxation, profit before interest, taxation and investment income? Similarly, should capital employed include or exclude intangible assets, and should assets be valued at net book value, gross book value or net replacement cost?

(c) Ratios compared over a period of time at historical cost will not be properly comparable where inflation in prices has occurred during the period unless adjustment is made to the ratios to make allowance for price level differences (eg using current values of assets).

(d) The ratios of different companies cannot be properly compared where each company uses a different method to:

- Value closing stocks (eg FIFO, LIFO, etc or marginal cost/absorbed cost).
- Apportion overheads, in absorption costing.
- Value fixed assets (eg at net book value, revalued amount etc).
- Estimate the life of assets in order to calculate depreciation (ie should depreciation be spread over 5 years or 10 years etc?).
- Account for research and development costs.
- Account for goodwill.

It should also be remembered that ratios calculated on historical costs may not be a guide to the future. Care must be taken in the selection and interpretation of ratios for control.

Conclusion

Considering the limitations outlined above it is difficult to reach any definite conclusions as to the performance and position of the two subsidiary companies. However CD Ltd appears to be performing better than AB Ltd, utilising its assets and workforce more efficiently and taking greater advantage of its borrowing capacity. The main problem for CD Ltd appears to be in its level of solvency.

Appendix

The ratios used to support this report are as follows.

		AB Limited	*CD Limited*	*Industry average*
1	*ROCE*			
	$\frac{\text{Profit before interest \& tax}}{\text{Capital employed}}$	$\frac{726}{3,812} \times 100 = 19\%$	$\frac{1,440}{4,637} \times 100 = 31\%$	19%
2	*Profit margin*			
	$\frac{\text{Profit before interest \& tax}}{\text{Sales}}$	$\frac{726}{3,505} \times 100 = 20.7\%$	$\frac{1,440}{6,147} \times 100 = 23.4\%$	21%
3	*Asset turnover*			
	$\frac{\text{Sales}}{\text{Capital employed}}$	$\frac{3,505}{3,812} = 0.92$	$\frac{6,147}{4,637} = 1.33$	0.9
4	*Expenses to sales ratios*			
	(a) $\frac{\text{Total expenses}}{\text{Sales}}$	$\frac{2,779}{3,505} \times 100 = 79.3\%$	$\frac{4,707}{6,147} \times 100 = 76.6\%$	*N/A
	(b) $\frac{\text{Manufacturing expenses}}{\text{Sales}}$	$\frac{2,419}{3,505} \times 100 = 69\%$	$\frac{4,182}{6,147} \times 100 = 68\%$	*N/A
	(c) $\frac{\text{Direct labour expenses}}{\text{Sales}}$	$\frac{481}{3,505} \times 100 = 13.7\%$	$\frac{624}{6,147} \times 100 = 10.2\%$	*N/A
	(d) $\frac{\text{Selling \& admin expenses}}{\text{Sales}}$	$\frac{360}{3,505} \times 100 = 10.3\%$	$\frac{525}{6,147} \times 100 = 8.5\%$	*N/A
5	*Fixed asset turnover*			
	$\frac{\text{Sales}}{\text{Fixed assets}}$	$\frac{3,505}{2,635} = 1.33$	$\frac{6,147}{3,969} = 1.55$	*N/A
6	*Sales to working capital*			
	$\frac{\text{Sales}}{\text{Working capital}}$	$\frac{3,505}{1,177} = 2.98$	$\frac{6,147}{668} = 9.20$	*N/A
7	*Current ratio*			
	$\frac{\text{Current assets}}{\text{Current liabilities}}$	$\frac{3,195}{2,018} = 1.6$	$\frac{2,350}{1,682} = 1.4$	1.7
8	*Capital gearing*			
	$\frac{\text{Fixed interest capital}}{\text{Total capital}}$	$\frac{500}{3,812} \times 100 = 13.1\%$	$\frac{2,000}{4,637} \times 100 = 43.1\%$	28%
9	*Interest cover*			
	$\frac{\text{Profits before interest \& tax}}{\text{Interest}}$	$\frac{726}{60} = 12.1$	$\frac{1,440}{280} = 5.1$	*N/A

* N/A - Not available

Note. There are various other ratios which may also be used as an aid in the interpretation of these accounts.

18 INHERITANCE

(a) Three major changes to the running of the company are

- Increased turnover
- Investment in new machinery
- Significant increase in borrowings

Note that you could have included a discussion of the changes to working capital and in particular the rise in stocks, debtors and creditors and the adverse cash position at the year end. If you did then ensure that you calculated the appropriate ratios and that you included a comment on the high level of bad debts.

Turnovor

Turnover has increased threefold. The company has increased sales significantly. The gross margin has fallen from 60% to 40%. This decrease in pricing may have helped increase sales. It is not clear how this affects the company's market share or how the company's competitors are responding to this. The company may be filling a new niche or staging a price war to consolidate the market. One concern is that bad debts have risen. This may be due to poor credit control or the quality of the products sold may not be as high.

Net margin has fallen from 34% to 11%. This is due to the increases in bad debts, depreciation and interest. Selling expenses have not increased in proportion to the increase in turnover pointing to increased efficiency in this area, perhaps the company is selling more to existing customers.

Machinery

Investment in machinery has seen the balance sheet valuation increase by 3.6 times. There has been no revaluation as there is no corresponding revaluation reserve. The increase in machinery may go some way to explaining the increase in turnover. Capacity has been increased. The sales generated by the machinery are now 1.6 times (19X9: 1.8 times) the machinery's value. It is likely that the machinery has only been in use for part of the year and there would be a period where production would be hindered whilst the machinery was delivered, installed and "bedded in", so this rate of asset turnover would seem quite healthy in comparison with the previous year.

Borrowings

The loan is £4.5m higher than the previous year. Borrowings are therefore 16 times greater. The majority of the loan appears to have been used to buy the machinery (£4.4m). The gearing of the company has increased significantly (56%) which in turn increases the financial risk of the company. The cash position of the company has worsened with an overdraft of £33,000 replacing a cash balance of £36,000. The cash position may be a short term problem. There may be a delay between earning financial profits and seeing the beneficial cashflows and an improvement in managing working capital may help this situation.

(b) The changes discussed in part (a) are quite dramatic. We have assessed the impact they have had so far but not the impact they may have in the future. We do not know when the changes were made. There is always a lag between the decision making stage and the implementation of the decision. If the machinery was installed in June 20X0 and the sales relied upon increased production then we could expect sales to be as high as £14m in 20X1. The cash position should improve as the increased profits are translated into cashflows. The new director may be looking at a longer term strategy which involves undercutting competitors and gaining a dominant market position. It would be useful to gain more information as to the directors plans in order to make more sense of the position of the company to date.

Workings

1 *Sales* $\frac{8,400}{2,700}$ = 3.1 increase

Gross margin 19X9: $\frac{1,620}{2,700}$ = 60% 2,0X0: $\frac{3,360}{8,400}$ = 40%

Net margin 19X9: $\frac{906}{2,700}$ = 33.6% 2,0X0: $\frac{930}{8,400}$ = 11.1%

2 *Machinery* $\frac{5,289}{1,470}$ = 3.6 increase

Sales generated 19X9: $\frac{2,700}{1,470}$ = 1.8 times 20X0: $\frac{8,400}{5,289}$ = 1.6 times

3 *Loan* $\frac{4,800}{300}$ = 16 increase

Gearing 19X9: $\frac{300}{300+900+1,887}$ = 9.7% 20X0: $\frac{4,800}{4,800+900+2,817}$ = 56.4%

Debt equity 19X9: $\frac{300}{900+1887}$ = 10.8% 20X0: $\frac{4,800}{900+2,817}$ = 129.1%

Loan application: machinery 5,289 – 1,470 + 624 – (1,350 – 1,323) = £4,416

SCENARIO A

1 (a) The amounts relating to the contract with Broad Rail plc should be stated as follows.

	£
Turnover (£120,000 × 50%)	60,000
Costs to date (£80,000 × 50%) + £16,000	(56,000)
Profit	4,000

Debtors: amounts recoverable on contracts	£
Included as turnover	60,000
Less payments on account (50 – 5)	45,000
	15,000

(b) *Stock*

	Cost	*NRV*	*Final figure*
	£	£	£
Raw materials	86,000	43,000	43,000
Finished goods: gates	15,000	7,500	7,500
fencing	12,000	?	12,000
			62,500

The circumstances highlighted in the scenario lead to consideration of SSAP 17 *Accounting for post balance sheet events*. While the new competition appeared in January, it provides evidence of the NRV of the stocks held at the balance sheet date. The value of goods to Fencing is therefore affected and the value needs to be reduced to reflect the net book value.

2 (a) *Debtors*

(i) *Trade debtors*

The trade debtors figure of £25,000 for sales in December appears to be correctly included in trade debtors.

The £30,000 of invoices sold back by Factors plc should be subject to close scrutiny for bad debts which may be substantial due to the length of time the debts have been outstanding. The £30,000 should be included in trade debtors, subject to bad debt provisions.

Factors plc currently holds £102,000 of invoices belonging to Fencing Ltd which might be returned if payment is not received within four months. As such, the substance of the transaction is that (per FRS 5) the invoices remain debtors of Fencing Ltd and they should therefore be included in trade debtors. The amount advanced to Fencing Ltd by Factors plc should therefore be included in current liabilities as it may have to be repaid within three months.

(ii) *Adsa contract*

This contract is short term, lasting only six months. SSAP 9 *Stocks and long-term contracts* states that 'a duration exceeding one year is not an essential feature of a long-term contract'. The criteria for treating contracts lasting less than one year are materiality and consistency. This contract is not material to the results of the company, particularly in the context of the other contract examined. If not treated as a long-term contract then the work in progress figure of £3,750 should be included in stock.

There is a case, however, for allowing the contract to be treated as long-term if all such contracts are treated thus by the company and have been in the past. In this case, £5,000 will be included in debtors as amounts recoverable on contracts.

The total debtors figure would be made up as follows.

	£
Trade debtors (£25,000 + £30,000 + £102,000)	157,000
Amounts recoverable on contracts (£14,000 + £5,000)	19,000
	176,000

(b) *Factors plc*

The treatment of the invoices held by Factors plc was discussed in (i) above. The costs, in terms of charges and interest relating to the factoring arrangement, should be taken to the profit and loss account.

A note to the accounts should set out the relationship between Factors plc and Fencing Ltd and highlight the treatment of the relevant figures in the accounts.

SCENARIO B

1 (a) T PLC
PROFIT AND LOSS ACCOUNT
FOR THE YEAR ENDED 31 DECEMBER 20X0

	Note	£'000
Turnover		68,500
Cost of sales		(25,980)
Gross profit		42,520
Distribution costs		(4,000)
Administrative expenses		(9,000)
Operating profit	1	29,520
Interest		(4,950)
		24,570
Taxation	2	(10,250)
		14,320
Dividends	3	(7,000)
		7,320
Retained profit b/f		86,000
Retained profit c/f		93,320
Earnings per share		6.5p

T PLC
BALANCE SHEET AS AT 31 DECEMBER 20X0

	Note	£'000	£'000
Fixed assets			
Tangible fixed assets	4		440,450
Current assets			
Stock		470	
Cash at bank		300	
		770	
Creditors: amount due within one year			
Trade creditors		1,700	
Taxation		10,200	
Proposed dividend		6,000	
		17,900	
Net current liabilities			(17,130)
			423,320
Creditors: amount due after one year			
Loans			(110,000)
			313,320
Capital and reserves			
Share capital			220,000
Profit and loss reserve			93,320
			313,320

Notes to the accounts

1 *Operating profit*

The operating figure has been calculated after allowing for:

	£'000
Depreciation	11,950
Employment costs	15,000

2 *Taxation*

	£'000
Taxation charge for the year	10,200
Underprovision from the previous year	50
	10,250

3 *Dividends*

	£'000
Interim: paid	1,000
Final: proposed	6,000
	7,000

4 *Tangible fixed assets*

	Hotels	*Fixtures and fittings*	*Total*
	£'000	£'000	£'000
Cost or valuation			
As at 1 January 20X0	478,000	11,000	489,000
Additions	12,000	7,000	19,000
As at 31 December 20X0	490,000	18,000	508,000
Depreciation			
As at 1 January 20X0	46,200	9,400	55,600
Charge for the year (1)	9,800	2,150	11,950
As at 31 December 20X0	56,000	11,550	67,550
Net book value as at 31 December 20X0	434,000	6,450	440,450
Net book value as at 1 January 20X0	431,800	1,600	433,400

Workings

1 *Depreciation*

	£'000
Hotels 490,000 @ 2%	9,800
Fixtures and fittings (18,000 – 9,400) @ 25%	2,150

2 *Cost of sales*

	£'000
Food purchases	2,100
Heating and lighting	3,000
Housekeeping and restaurant staff	9,000
Opening stock	400
Closing stock	(470)
Depreciation	11,950
	25,980

3 *Administrative expenses*

	£'000
Administration	3,000
Staff wages	6,000
	9,000

4 *Earnings per share*

$$\frac{\text{PAIT}}{\text{Share capital}} = \frac{£14,320}{220,000} = 6.5 \text{ pence}$$

2 (a) (i) Original depreciation charge (800 + 700 + 1,000) @ 2% = £50,000

Hotel A $\frac{1,300,000}{50}$ = £26,000

Hotel B $\frac{850,000}{30}$ = £28,333

Hotel C $\frac{650,000}{40}$ £16,250

£70,583

There is therefore an increase in annual depreciation of £20,583 due to the revaluation.

(ii) NB. Hotel C has been revalued to an amount lower than NBV

	£'000
∴NBV (1,000 – 140) =	860,000
Revalued amount =	650,000
Amount written off to P&L	210,000

Revaluation reserve

	£'000
Hotel A (1,300 – (800 – 180)) =	680
Hotel B (850 – (700 – 120)) =	270
Increase in the revaluation reserve	950

(iii) The hotels are used on a continuous basis as business assets. This means that they are fixed assets as defined in FRS 15 and that they cannot be investment properties as defined by SSAP 19.

SSAP 19 defines an investment property as an interest in land or buildings in respect of which all construction work has been completed and which is held for its investment potential. Any rental income received must be at arms length. The hotels are primarily being used by T plc to generate income. Sale of a hotel diminishes the trading income of the company.

FRS 15 states that depreciation must be charged on fixed assets. Depreciation represents the use over time of an asset, it is therefore matching the use of the asset with the revenue it generates. In the case of the hotels, the directors have decided on a useful economic life of fifty years. The cost of the hotels is spread over this time. The fact that the hotels may appreciate in value is a separate matter. The NBV of an asset does not necessarily equate to its market value. The directors can revalue the properties on a regular basis if they wish the balance sheet values to mirror market value. They should not avoid charging depreciation.

If T plc did not charge depreciation they would be required to conduct an impairment review instead. This could end up having the same overall effect as charging depreciation except there may be large expenses in the profit and loss in one year and none the next.

(iv) The programme of repairs and refurbishment is unlikely to be eligible for capitalisation as it does not appear that the work will enhance the existing assets or prolong their useful lives.

Per FRS 15 repairs and maintenance are required for the upkeep of an asset. It is suggested that the repairs are required to prevent the properties falling in value and to allow them to achieve their expected useful lives. They should be expensed through the profit and loss account as they are incurred. This closely follows the rationale behind depreciation; the cost of the asset is matched to the revenue generated.

The refurbishment involves the replacement of existing furniture. This may be capitalised under fixtures and fittings as long as the existing furniture is written off. The decoration may not be capitalised as it is again part of the upkeep of the building.

(b) (i) The external auditors' responsibilities with respect to the financial statements are concerned with ensuring that the accounts show a true and fair view of the affairs of the company for the year. The auditors must express an opinion on the financial statements to this effect.

The auditors conduct an audit which examines the figures in the financial statements and agrees them back to the underlying accounting information. They are required to ensure that the directors have prepared the accounts correctly and that there is no materially misleading information within them. To this ends the auditors have a statutory right to all information and explanations deemed necessary to perform the audit. In the case of the valuations these could well fall within this definition.

(ii) If the auditors' work leads them to conclude that the financial statements are free from material error or misstatement and that they give a true and fair view of the financial affairs of the company then they will issue an unqualified opinion. This opinion covers the profit and loss account, the balance sheet, the statement of recognised gains and losses and the notes to the accounts. By convention the opinion usually covers the cashflow statement as well. They also review the directors report to ensure that this does not contain information which is materially misleading or which conflicts with elements of the financial statements. The auditors' report is the statement of their opinion on these elements of the financial statements. They state explicitly that the balance sheet reflects the state of the company's affairs at the year end and that the profit and loss account gives the company's profit or loss for the year. The report also covers a number of other elements, such as the fact that proper accounting records were kept, by exception.

A qualified report contains a qualified opinion because the auditors are concerned that the financial statements do not give a true and fair view. This may occur due to disagreement or uncertainty. Disagreement occurs when the auditors form an opinion which conflicts with the view given by the financial statements. Uncertainty arises when there is a limitation in scope and the auditors are unable to form an opinion.

The extent of the qualification is determined by whether the disagreement or uncertainty is material or fundamental.

When the auditors issue a qualified report it must contain a full explanation of the reasons for the qualification and, where possible, a quantification of the effects on the financial statements. This means that a qualified report will contain at least one more paragraph than an unqualified report.

The qualified report should leave the reader in no doubt as to its meaning and the implications it has on an understanding of the financial statements.

Appendix
Examination questions on published accounts

Introduction

(a) Before attempting these questions, you should be familiar with the requirements both of statute and of accounting standards (SSAPs and FRSs) in respect of the presentation and content of published accounts.

(b) Provided that you know the legal and accounting regulations, published accounts questions are not difficult to answer. They are, however, very time consuming and almost certainly you will not have time in the examination unless you adopt a clear and systematic approach. In this appendix we suggest an approach which should provide you with a useful guide. However, it is not the only approach, and you might develop your own method and means of answering such questions. Never be put off by the volume of detail given; it provides you with all the information necessary to produce a clear and detailed solution.

(c) Your aim in answering these questions should be to disclose the minimum information required by statute, SSAPs and FRSs. To disclose more than this might suggest to the examiner that you are unclear about what information is *required* to be disclosed and what information is sometimes *voluntarily* disclosed in practice.

(d) In the time available in the examination it is virtually impossible to provide the examiner with all the information normally given in an actual set of accounts, and indeed, the examiner does not expect you to do so. It is only necessary to comply with the statutory and quasi-statutory requirements so far as you are able from the information given. There is generally no need to embellish your solution with made-up information.

Suggested approach

(e) Read the question carefully to ensure you do not do more than the examiner wants. For example, questions often end with a statement that you may ignore the requirement to disclose accounting policies.

(f) It is likely that the examiner will ask you to prepare accounts for presentation to the members (ie the 'full' accounts rather than the modified versions for small and medium-sized companies) and it is suggested that you adopt the 'operational format' profit and loss account (unless otherwise requested) and the vertical balance sheet in your solutions. As far as possible, use the words given in the CA 1985 formats, but remember that certain alternative or additional headings are allowable and may be used in the examination.

(g) Head up a sheet of paper for the profit and loss account, a second sheet for the balance sheet and a third for the notes to the accounts. Keep a fourth sheet ready for your workings. Begin by writing a statement of accounting policies as note 1 to the accounts, unless the question has instructed you to ignore this requirement.

(h) Now, keeping in mind the 1985 Act pro-formas and the FRS 3 requirements, write out the profit and loss account, beginning with turnover and working line by line through the pro-forma. Search through the question for the information relevant to each line as you come to it and mark the question paper to indicate which bits of information have been used.

(i) While you are writing out the profit and loss account you should be building up the notes to the accounts, writing out each in conjunction with the profit and loss caption to which it refers and, of course, entering the cross reference on the face of the profit and loss account. The process of writing out the relevant note will often remove the need to prepare a working and thus save valuable time.

(j) Don't forget to disclose the EPS at the foot of the profit and loss account for a public company, if the figure is given. (You should assume that the company is listed unless told to the contrary.)

(k) Once the profit and loss account and related notes are complete, follow the same procedure to construct the balance sheet, again working line by line through the pro-forma and writing out the relevant notes at the same time as entering the figures on the balance sheet.

(l) Complete the notes to the accounts by considering whether any notes are necessary other than those arising directly from the profit and loss account and balance sheet. Common examples include:

- Post balance sheet events
- Contingent liabilities

(m) If you *are* asked to produce financial statements which comply with FRS 3, you may be asked to produce:

(i) A statement of total recognised gains and losses.

(ii) A profit and loss account which shows the turnover and operating profit from continuing activities, acquisitions and discontinued activities.

(iii) A note of historical cost profits and losses, reconciling P & L retained profit to historical cost profit.

(iv) A reconciliation of movements in shareholders' funds.

(v) A reserves note

We have ignored the requirements of FRS 3 in the two questions given here, partly because practice is given in those areas elsewhere in the text, but also to avoid distracting you from the main focus of the preparation of the standard CA 1985 pro formas. Any FRS 3 requirements will be an 'extra' to your questions. Refer back to Chapter 3 to refresh your memory of these formats and notes.

(n) Finally, do not forget that SSAP 17 requires that the balance sheet should be dated. Indicate at the foot of the balance sheet where the date and director's signature are to appear.

(o) You should now attempt to apply this approach to the illustrative questions which follow. Do not set yourself any time limit in answering these questions. Published accounts can only be mastered by absorbing the mass of detail required by statute and professional practice.

1 KITCHENTECH

The following list of balances was extracted from the books of Kitchentech Ltd on 31 December 20X1. The company is involved in the retailing of hardware through four shops which it owns in various parts of the country.

	£
Sales	1,875,893
Cost of sales	1,597,777
Administrative expenses	124,723
Directors' salaries	43,352
Debenture interest to 30.6.X1	3,000
Freehold premises at cost (land £100,000)	215,000
Motor vehicles, at cost	37,581
Accumulated depreciation on motor vehicles to 31.12.X0	16,581
Fixtures and fittings at cost	26,550
Accumulated depreciation on fixtures & fittings to 31.12.X0	8,200
Stock	88,452
Debtors	18,550
Creditors and accruals	47,609
Bank overdraft	11,433
Cash in hand	386
Provision for bad debts at 31.12.X0	1,200
Share capital	100,000
Profit and loss account at 31.12.X0	18,455
General reserve	16,000
10% debentures 20X8/X9 (secured on the freehold buildings)	60,000

The following adjustments are to be made.

(a) Directors' remuneration is divided amongst the three directors as follows.

	£
Mr Ames - Chairman	4,000
Mr Bird - Marketing director	20,000
Mr Crown - Finance director	19,352
	43,352

Fees of £2,000 each are to be provided for the directors.

A pension of £1,900 paid to Mr Jones, a former director, is included in the administration expenses.

The salary of Mr James, the company secretary, is £18,000 and is also included in the administrative expenses.

(b) Depreciation is to be provided in the accounts for the year as follows.

Buildings 2% on cost
Motor vehicles 25% on written down value
Fixtures and fittings 10% on cost

(c) Messrs Checkit and See, the company's auditors, rendered an account in early March 20X2 as follows.

	£
Assistance in preparation of taxation computation for the year ended 31.12.X0	500
Audit of accounts for the year ended 31.12.X0	1,000
	1,500

This bill was the subject of an accrual of £1,200 on 31 December 20X0. A similar bill for £1,500 is expected for the 20X1 accounts in due course.

(d) The debtors include a balance of £400 owing from Catering Supplies Ltd. This is to be written off as it has proved irrecoverable. The provision for bad debts is to be adjusted to 10% of debtors.

(e) Corporation tax based upon the profits for the year at the rate of 30% amounting to £40,000 is to be provided.

(f) A dividend of 14% is to be provided on the ordinary share capital. The authorised ordinary share capital is £200,000 divided into £1 shares. All issued shares are fully paid.

(g) £30,000 is to be transferred to general reserve.

Required

Within the limits of the information given, prepare a profit and loss account and balance sheet for the year ended 31 December 20X1 for submission to the members of the company in accordance with statutory requirements and best professional practice.

2 ALPINE

Alpine Athletic Training plc is a manufacturer of sports equipment. Set out below is a trial balance extracted from the books of the company as at 31 December 20X3.

	£	£
Sales		2,925,900
Cost of sales	1,785,897	
Selling expenses	120,000	
Administrative expenses	649,296	
Debtors/creditors	470,032	371,022
Provision for doubtful debts		22,500
Directors' remuneration	181,500	
Audit fee	3,000	
Debenture interest	7,500	
Half year preference dividend paid on 30.6.X3	2,100	
Premises at cost	600,000	
Plant and machinery at cost	135,000	
Provision for depreciation on plant and machinery at 1.1.X3		60,000
Motor vehicles at cost (salesmen's cars)	54,000	
Provision for depreciation on motor vehicles at 1.1.X3		24,000
Stock in trade and work in progress	282,728	
Trade investment at cost	72,000	
Bank overdraft		354,528
Profit and loss account balance at 1.1.X3		65,103
General reserve		30,000
Ordinary share capital		300,000
7% preference share capital		60,000
10% debentures 20X9 secured on premises		150,000
	4,363,053	4,363,053

The following information is also related to the accounts for the year to 31 December 20X3.

(a) The bad debt provision is to be increased to an amount which is equal to 1% of the turnover for the year.

(b) The directors' remuneration is divided amongst the four directors of the company as follows.

	£
Chairman	24,000
Managing director	60,000
Finance director	49,500
Sales director	48,000
	181,500

In addition provision must be made for directors' fees of £5,000 to each of the above directors.

(c) Depreciation is to be provided for the year as follows.

Buildings	2% on cost
Plant and machinery	10% on cost
Motor vehicles	25% on written down value

The only changes in fixed assets during the year were an addition to plant and machinery in early January 20X3 costing £30,000 and the purchase of premises for £600,000 comprising £150,000 for buildings and £450,000 for land.

(d) A provision of £60,000 is to be made for corporation tax at 30% based upon the profits for the year. This will be payable on 30 September 20X4.

(e) The half year preference dividend to 31 December 20X3 and a final dividend of 6.5 pence a share on the ordinary share capital, are to be provided in the accounts.

(f) The sum of £15,000 is to be transferred to general reserve.

(g) The authorised preference share capital is £60,000 in £1 shares.

(h) The authorised ordinary share capital is £600,000 in 50p shares. All shares in issue are fully paid.

(i) Administrative expenses include £5,244 interest on the overdraft.

(j) The directors consider the value of the trade investment to be £75,000. It consists of 10,000 20p ordinary shares in Crampon Ltd, a company with an issued share capital of 200,000 ordinary shares.

Required

Within the limits of the above information, prepare the final accounts of Alpine Athletic Training plc for the year ended 31 December 20X3 in a form suitable for presentation to the members and which complies with the requirements of the Companies Act 1985.

The required information should be shown as part of the accounting statements or by way of note, whichever is considered most appropriate.

1 KITCHENTECH

PROFIT AND LOSS ACCOUNT FOR THE YEAR ENDED 31 DECEMBER 20X1

	Notes	£	£
Turnover	1		1,875,893
Cost of sales			(1,597,777)
Gross profit			278,116
Distribution costs (W1)		30,920	
Administrative expenses (W1)		156,175	
			(187,095)
Operating profit	2		91,021
Interest payable	3		(6,000)
Profit on ordinary activities before taxation			85,021
Tax on profit on ordinary activities	4		(40,000)
Profit on ordinary activities after taxation			45,021
Dividend: proposed ordinary dividend		14,000	
Transfer to general reserve		30,000	
			44,000
Retained profit for the year			1,021
Earnings per share	5		45.0p

STATEMENT OF RETAINED PROFITS

	£
Retained profit for the year	1,021
Retained profits brought forward	18,455
Retained profits carried forward	19,476

BALANCE SHEET AS AT 31 DECEMBER 20X1

	Notes	£	£
Fixed assets			
Tangible assets	6		244,145
Current assets			
Stock		88,452	
Debtors £(18,550 – 400 – 1,815)		16,335	
Cash in hand		386	
		105,173	
Creditors: amounts falling due within one year			
Bank overdraft		11,433	
Creditors and accruals (W2)		58,409	
Other creditors including taxation	7	54,000	
		123,842	
Net current liabilities			(18,669)
Total assets less current liabilities			225,476
Creditors: amounts falling due after more than one year			
10% debentures 20X8/X9			(60,000)
			165,476
Capital and reserves			
Called up share capital			
£1 ordinary shares fully paid (authorised: £200,000)			100,000
Reserves			
General reserve		46,000	
Profit and loss account		19,476	
			65,476
			165,476

Approved by the Board of Directors on....................

...............................Director

NOTES TO THE ACCOUNTS

1 *Turnover*

Turnover is the value, net of VAT, of goods sold during the year in a single class of business in the UK.

2 *Operating profit*

	£	£
Operating profit is stated after charging:		
Directors' remuneration		
Salaries	43,352	
Fees	6,000	
Pension to former director	1,900	
		51,252
Depreciation		10,205
Auditors' remuneration		1,000

(*Tutorial note*. No further details are required of directors' remuneration, since in total it is less than £200,000. Note that Mr James is *not* a director and so his salary is not included in the above total.)

3 *Interest payable*

Interest on 10% debentures 20X8/X9 £6,000

4 *Tax on profit on ordinary activities*

UK corporation tax at 30% on the profit of the year £40,000

5 *Earnings per share*

Earnings per share is based on earnings of £45,021 and 100,000 ordinary shares in issue during the year

6 *Fixed assets*

	Land and buildings	*Motor vehicles*	*Fixtures & fittings*	*Total*
	£	£	£	£
Cost				
At 1 January and 31 December 20X1	215,000	37,581	26,550	279,131
Depreciation				
At 1 January 20X1	-	16,581	8,200	24,781
Charge for year	2,300	5,250	2,655	10,205
At 31 December 20X1	2,300	21,831	10,855	34,986
Net book value				
At 1 January 20X1	215,000	21,000	18,350	254,350
At 31 December 20X1	212,700	15,750	15,695	244,145

7 *Other creditors including taxation*

	£
Corporation tax	40,000
Proposed dividend	14,000
	54,000

Workings

1 *Allocation of costs*

	Distribution costs	*Administrative expenses*
	£	£
Per list of balances		124,723
Directors' salaries	20,000	23,352
Directors' fees	2,000	4,000
Depreciation:		
Buildings (2% × £115,000)		2,300
Motor vehicles 25% × £(37,581 – 16,581)	5,250	
Fixtures (10% × £26,550)	2,655	
Audit and tax advice		1,800
(includes £300 under-provided in previous year)		
Bad debt	400	
Provision for doubtful debts		
10% × £(18,550 – 400) – £1,200	615	
	30,920	156,175

(*Note.* The allocation above is somewhat arbitrary, especially as regards the depreciation costs. Other allocations would be acceptable.)

2 *Creditors and accruals*

	£
Per list of balances	47,609
Directors' fees	6,000
Half-year's debenture interest	3,000
20X1 audit and tax fee	1,500
Increase in accrual for 20X0 and audit tax fee	300
	58,409

2 ALPINE

PROFIT AND LOSS ACCOUNT FOR THE YEAR ENDED 31 DECEMBER 20X3

	Note	£	£
Turnover (continuing operations)	1		2,925,900
Cost of sales (W1)			(1,799,397)
Gross profit			1,126,503
Distribution costs (W2)		187,259	
Administrative expenses (W3)		798,552	
			(985,811)
Operating profit	2		140,692
Interest payable	3		(20,244)
Profit on ordinary activities before taxation			120,448
Tax on profit on ordinary activities	4		(60,000)
Profit on ordinary activities after taxation			60,448
Dividends	5	43,200	
Transfer to general reserve		15,000	
			(58,200)
Retained profit for the financial year			2,248
Earnings per share	6		9.37p

STATEMENT OF RETAINED PROFITS

	£
Retained profit for the financial year	2,248
Retained profits brought forward	65,103
Retained profits carried forward	67,351

BALANCE SHEET AS AT 31 DECEMBER 20X3

	Note	£	£
Fixed assets			
Tangible assets	7		681,000
Investments (directors' valuation: £75,000)			72,000
			753,000
Current assets			
Stocks and work in progress		282,728	
Debtors £(470,032 – 29,259)		440,773	
		723,501	
Creditors: amounts falling due within one year			
Bank overdraft		354,528	
Trade creditors		371,022	
Other creditors including taxation	8	101,100	
Accruals (£7,500 deb int + £20,000 dir rem)		27,500	
		854,150	
Net current liabilities			(130,649)
Total assets less current liabilities			622,351
Creditors: amounts falling due after more than one year			
10% debentures 20X9			(150,000)
			472,351
Capital and reserves			
Called up share capital			
50p ordinary shares fully paid (authorised: £600,000)		300,000	
£1 7% preference shares fully paid (authorised:£60,000)		60,000	
			360,000
Reserves			
General reserve		45,000	
Profit and loss account (£65,103 + £2,248)		67,351	
			112,351
			472,351

Approved by the Board of Directors on ....

....................Director

NOTES TO THE ACCOUNTS

1 *Turnover*

Turnover represents amounts invoiced, net of VAT, for goods and services supplied during the year in a single class of business in the UK.

2 *Operating profit*

Operating profit is stated after charging:

	£
Depreciation	24,000
Directors' emoluments	201,500
Auditors' remuneration	3,000

Directors' emoluments comprise fees of £20,000 and remuneration of £181,500.

The emoluments of the highest paid director were £65,000. (This information is required because the total of directors' emoluments is over £200,000.)

3 *Interest payable*

	£
On debentures repayable in more than five years	15,000
On bank overdraft	5,244
	20,244

4 *Taxation*

UK corporation tax at 35% on the profits for the year	£60,000

5 *Dividends*

		£
Preference:	interim paid	2,100
	final proposed	2,100
		4,200
Ordinary: final proposed (600,000 × 6.5p)		39,000
		43,200

6 *Earnings per share*

Earnings per share is based on earnings of £(60,448 - 4,200) = £56,248 and 600,000 ordinary shares in issue during the year.

7 *Fixed assets*

	Premises	*Plant and machinery*	*Motor vehicles*	*Total*
	£	£	£	£
Cost				
At 1 January 20X3	-	105,000	54,000	159,000
Additions in year	600,000	30,000	-	630,000
At 31 December 20X3	600,000	135,000	54,000	789,000
Depreciation				
At 1 January 20X3	-	60,000	24,000	84,000
Charge for the year	3,000	13,500	7,500	24,000
At 31 December 20X3	3,000	73,500	31,500	108,000
Net book value				
At 1 January 20X3	-	45,000	30,000	75,000
At 31 December 20X3	597,000	61,500	22,500	681,000

8 *Other creditors including taxation*

	£
Corporation tax	60,000
Dividends proposed	41,100
	101,100

Workings

1 *Cost of sales*

	£
Per TB	1,785,897
Add depreciation on plant (10% × £135,000)	13,500
	1,799,397

2 *Distribution costs*

	£	£
Selling expenses		120,000
Sales director's remuneration £(48,000 + 5,000)		53,000
Provision for doubtful debts:		
Provision required (1% × £2,925,900)	29,259	
Less existing provision	22,500	
Increase in provision		6,759
Depreciation on motor vehicles (25% × £30,000)		7,500
		187,259

3 *Administrative expenses*

	£
Per TB	649,296
Directors' remuneration £(24,000 + 60,000 + 49,500 + 15,000)	148,500
Audit fee	3,000
Depreciation on buildings (2% × £150,000)	3,000
	803,796
Less overdraft interest	5,244
	798,552

Index

Note: Key Terms and their references are given in **bold.**

BPP
PROFESSIONAL EDUCATION

REVIEW FORM & FREE PRIZE DRAW

All original review forms from the entire BPP range, completed with genuine comments, will be entered into one of two draws on 31 January 2004 and 31 July 2004. The names on the first four forms picked out on each occasion will be sent a cheque for £50.

Name: ______________________ **Address**: ______________________

____

How have you used this Text?
(Tick one box only)

☐ Home study (book only)

☐ On a course: college ______________________

☐ With 'correspondence' package

☐ Other ______________________

Why did you decide to purchase this Text?
(Tick one box only)

☐ Have used BPP Texts in the past

☐ Recommendation by friend/colleague

☐ Recommendation by a lecturer at college

☐ Saw advertising

☐ Other ______________________

During the past six months do you recall seeing/receiving any of the following?
(Tick as many boxes as are relevant)

☐ Our advertisement in CIMA *Insider*

☐ Our advertisement in *Financial Management*

☐ Our advertisement in *Pass*

☐ Our advertisement in *PQ*

☐ Our brochure with a letter through the post

☐ Our website www.bpp.com

Which (if any) aspects of our advertising do you find useful?
(Tick as many boxes as are relevant)

☐ Prices and publication dates of new editions

☐ Information on Text content

☐ Facility to order books off-the-page

☐ None of the above

Which BPP products have you used?

Text	☑	**MCQ cards**	☐	**i-Learn**	☐
Kit	☐	**Tape**	☐	**i-Pass**	☐
Passcard	☐	**CD**	☐	**Virtual Campus**	☐

Your ratings, comments and suggestions would be appreciated on the following areas.

	Very useful	*Useful*	*Not useful*
Introductory section (Key study steps, personal study)	☐	☐	☐
Chapter introductions	☐	☐	☐
Key terms	☐	☐	☐
Quality of explanations	☐	☐	☐
Case examples and other examples	☐	☐	☐
Questions and answers in each chapter	☐	☐	☐
Chapter roundups	☐	☐	☐
Quick quizzes	☐	☐	☐
Exam focus points	☐	☐	☐
Question bank	☐	☐	☐
MCQ bank	☐	☐	☐
Answer bank	☐	☐	☐
Index	☐	☐	☐
Icons	☐	☐	☐

Overall opinion of this Study Text *Excellent* ☐ *Good* ☐ *Adequate* ☐ *Poor* ☐

Do you intend to continue using BPP products? Yes ☐ No ☐

On the reverse of this page are noted particular areas of the text about which we would welcome your feedback.

Please note any further comments and suggestions/errors on the reverse of this page. The BPP author of this edition can be e-mailed at: philfontbin@bpp.com

Please return this form to: Nick Weller, CIMA Range Manager, BPP Professional Education, FREEPOST, London, W12 8BR

REVIEW FORM & FREE PRIZE DRAW (continued)

TELL US WHAT YOU THINK

Because the following specific areas of the text contain new material and cover highly examinable topics etc, your comments on their usefulness are particularly welcome.

- Regulatory framework

- Tangible fixed assets

- Share capital transactions

- Exam focus points

Please note any further comments and suggestions/errors below.

FREE PRIZE DRAW RULES

1 Closing date for 31 January 2004 draw is 31 December 2003. Closing date for 31 July 2004 draw is 30 June 2004.

2 No purchase necessary. Entry forms are available upon request from BPP Professional Education. No more than one entry per title, per person. Draw restricted to persons aged 16 and over.

3 Winners will be notified by post and receive their cheques not later than 6 weeks after the draw date.

4 The decision of the promoter in all matters is final and binding. No correspondence will be entered into.

See overleaf for information on other
BPP products and how to order

CIMA Order

To BPP Professional Education, Aldine Place, London W12 8AW
Tel: 020 8740 2211 Fax: 020 8740 1184
email: publishing@bpp.com website: www.bpp.com
Order online www.bpp.com

Mr/Mrs/Ms (Full name)

Daytime delivery address

Postcode

Daytime Tel Email Date of exam (month/year)

	7/03 Texts	1/03 Kits	1/03 Passcards	Success Tapes	Success CDs	Virtual Campus	7/03 i-Pass	7/03 i-Learn	5/03 MCQ cards
FOUNDATION									
1 Financial Accounting Fundamentals	£20.95 ☐	£10.95 ☐	£6.95 ☐	£12.95 ☐	£14.95 ☐	£50 ☐	£24.95 ☐		£5.95 ☐
2 Management Accounting Fundamentals	£20.95 ☐	£10.95 ☐	£6.95 ☐	£12.95 ☐	£14.95 ☐	£50 ☐	£24.95 ☐		£5.95 ☐
3A Economics for Business	£20.95 ☐	£10.95 ☐	£6.95 ☐	£12.95 ☐	£14.95 ☐	£50 ☐	£24.95 ☐		£5.95 ☐
3B Business Law	£20.95 ☐	£10.95 ☐	£6.95 ☐	£12.95 ☐	£14.95 ☐	£50 ☐	£24.95 ☐		£5.95 ☐
3C Business Mathematics	£20.95 ☐	£10.95 ☐	£6.95 ☐	£12.95 ☐	£14.95 ☐	£50 ☐	£24.95 ☐		£5.95 ☐
INTERMEDIATE									
4 Finance	£20.95 ☐	£10.95 ☐	£6.95 ☐	£12.95 ☐	£14.95 ☐	£90 ☐	£24.95 ☐	£34.95 ☐	£5.95 ☐
5 Business Tax (FA 2002) (10/02)	£20.95 ☐	£10.95 ☐	£6.95 ☐	£12.95 ☐	£14.95 ☐	£90 ☐	£24.95 ☐	£34.95 ☐	£5.95 ☐
6 Financial Accounting	£20.95 ☐	£10.95 ☐	£6.95 ☐	£12.95 ☐	£14.95 ☐	£90 ☐	£24.95 ☐	£34.95 ☐	£5.95 ☐
6i Financial Accounting International	£20.95 ☐	£10.95 ☐	£6.95 ☐ (7/03)						
7 Financial Reporting	£20.95 ☐	£10.95 ☐	£6.95 ☐	£12.95 ☐	£14.95 ☐	£90 ☐	£24.95 ☐	£34.95 ☐	£5.95 ☐
7i Financial Reporting International	£20.95 ☐	£10.95 ☐	£6.95 ☐ (7/03)						
8 Management Accounting - Performance Management	£20.95 ☐	£10.95 ☐	£6.95 ☐	£12.95 ☐	£14.95 ☐	£90 ☐	£24.95 ☐	£34.95 ☐	£5.95 ☐
9 Management Accounting - Decision Making	£20.95 ☐	£10.95 ☐	£6.95 ☐	£12.95 ☐	£14.95 ☐	£90 ☐	£24.95 ☐	£34.95 ☐	£5.95 ☐
10 Systems and Project Management	£20.95 ☐	£10.95 ☐	£6.95 ☐	£12.95 ☐	£14.95 ☐	£90 ☐	£24.95 ☐	£34.95 ☐	£5.95 ☐
11 Organisational Management	£20.95 ☐	£10.95 ☐	£6.95 ☐	£12.95 ☐	£14.95 ☐	£90 ☐	£24.95 ☐	£34.95 ☐	£5.95 ☐
FINAL									
12 Management Accounting - Business Strategy	£20.95 ☐	£10.95 ☐	£6.95 ☐	£12.95 ☐	£14.95 ☐		£24.95 ☐		
13 Management Accounting - Financial Strategy	£20.95 ☐	£10.95 ☐	£6.95 ☐	£12.95 ☐	£14.95 ☐		£24.95 ☐		
14 Management Accounting - Information Strategy	£20.95 ☐	£10.95 ☐	£6.95 ☐	£12.95 ☐	£14.95 ☐		£24.95 ☐		
15 Case Study				£12.95 ☐	£14.95 ☐				
(1) Workbook	£19.95 ☐								
(2) Toolkit		£19.95 ☐ (For 11/03: available 9/03. For 5/04: available 3/04)							
Learning to Learn Accountancy (7/02)	£9.95 ☐								

Total ☐

POSTAGE & PACKING

Study Texts

	First	Each extra	Online	
UK	£5.00	£2.00	£2.00	£
Europe*	£6.00	£4.00	£4.00	£
Rest of world	£20.00	£10.00	£10.00	£

Kits

	First	Each extra	Online	
UK	£5.00	£2.00	£2.00	£
Europe*	£6.00	£4.00	£4.00	£
Rest of world	£20.00	£10.00	£10.00	£

Passcards/Success Tapes/MCQ Cards/CDs

	First	Each extra	Online	
UK	£2.00	£1.00	£1.00	£
Europe*	£3.00	£2.00	£2.00	£
Rest of world	£8.00	£8.00	£8.00	£

Grand Total (incl. Postage)

I enclose a cheque for £
(Cheques to *BPP Professional Education*)

Or charge to Visa/Mastercard/Switch

Card Number

Expiry date Start Date

Issue Number (Switch Only)

Signature

We aim to deliver to all UK addresses inside 5 working days. A signature will be required. Orders to all EU addresses should be delivered within 6 working days. All other orders to overseas addresses should be delivered